H

THE LAST SIX MONTHS

The Last Six Months

RUSSIA'S FINAL BATTLES

WITH HITLER'S ARMIES

IN WORLD WAR II

General of the Soviet Army
S.M. Shtemenko

Translated by Guy Daniels

1977

DOUBLEDAY & COMPANY, INC.

GARDEN CITY, NEW YORK

ISBN: 0-385-00368-4
LIBRARY OF CONGRESS CATALOG CARD NUMBER 73–18779
TRANSLATION COPYRIGHT © 1977 BY DOUBLEDAY & COMPANY, INC.
ALL RIGHTS RESERVED
PRINTED IN THE UNITED STATES OF AMERICA
FIRST EDITION

CONTENTS

Contents

Contents

Contents

Before the assault. The shadow of Allen Dulles. Karl Renner's letter to the Kremlin. The beginning of peaceful coexistence. The Austrian burgomeister and the Soviet commandant.

What a secondary theater is. The Finns request and reject an armistice. K. A. Meretskov at the Karelian Front. Unofficial talks in Moscow. We prepare for an offensive. Defeat. Official talks. The liberation of the Soviet Arctic and the northern part of Norway. Bornholm Island.

Disorder in the enemy camp. Intrigues behind our back. A démarche by the Soviet Government. Forecasts by the General Staff. The talks in Reims. Should one sign? "We must cut through the spider web." The fall of Berlin. Where is Hitler? The rats leave the sinking ship. Onward to Prague! Events in the capital of Czechoslovakia. Unconditional surrender. Schörner "washes his hands." The traitors' end.

AUTHOR'S PREFACE

I will not conceal from the reader that I had no intention of writing another volume of memoirs.[1] Not only that, but I had given myself a solemn pledge to write no more books. It is a difficult job, especially for someone still on active duty. And besides, it seemed to me that I had already said the most important things.

But events developed otherwise. After the publication of my first book of memoirs about the General Staff, I received several thousand letters. My correspondents were people of various ages, occupations, nationalities, and degrees of education. Their letters contained not only criticisms and evaluations of the book but various kinds of suggestions, observations, and supplementary material. Some readers even sent their reminiscences about different events in the Great Patriotic War[2] and asked me to make use of them in the next edition of the book. But many of them simply asked that I go on with my memoirs. The same thing happened at many of those speaking engagements where the author can talk confidentially with his readers.

Also, those letters and talks with readers brought home to me very strongly how great was the interest of our people in the he-

[1] General Shtemenko's first volume of memoirs was published in the USSR in 1970 and had limited distribution in the West. That first book, entitled *The Soviet General Staff at War,* concentrated on Soviet military activities from 1941 to 1945. (Publisher's note.)
[2] I.e., the Russo-German War of 1941–45, which the Russians distinguish from World War II as a whole. (Translator's note.)

roic past. That interest does not grow old. Rather, it lives in us, helping us to build communism in the Soviet land and to strengthen friendship among peoples beyond its borders in the interests of peace and socialism.

Thus it is you readers who have compelled me to take up the pen once again. It is only thanks to you that this new book has appeared.

And there is another reason why I decided to write a second book rather than to get out a revised edition of the first one. To repeat what one has said before, expanding and supplementing it, is much easier than to write something new. What prompted me to take up my pen was the reflection that one must above all undertake what is really difficult.

This book, like the first one, contains no chronological account of military operations. Rather, it is concerned chiefly with the General Staff: the people composing it and what it did. There is great emphasis on the work of the Stavka[3] of the Supreme Command and on individual moments in the activity of the Supreme Commander. There are also some thoughts and opinions about military leaders and their staffs—something to which individual chapters are devoted.

Basically, this book gives an account of the Soviet Army's liberation mission in Europe. In those unforgettable days the soldiers of our country crushed the enemy and brought an end to the war in the center of the European continent, destroying Hitlerite fascism's military machine. It was a great feat for the cause of freedom and the happiness of peoples—one achieved through the military skill and selfless heroism of legendary Soviet warriors. But victory cost us a great deal. It cost us the lives of millions of people.

Owing to the nature of my official duties, I often have occasion to have a look at the armies of those states who are members of the Warsaw Pact: to see how the men of those armies live, and to

[3] Roughly, the GHQ, but "Stavka" is the preferred usage in most English-language writings on Soviet military affairs. The Supreme Command, set up in July 1941, consisted of Stalin, V. M. Molotov, K. E. Voroshilov, S. K. Timoshenko, S. M. Budenny, B. M. Shaposhnikov, and G. K. Zhukov. (Translator's note.)

meet not only with military people but with civilians. I can affirm that in all the socialist countries the people honor the feat of the Soviet soldiers and remember those who fell in battle—those who perished while liberating peoples from the fascist yoke. They remember that our friendship is sealed with the blood which, together, we shed on the fields of battle.

In these memoirs I would like once again to remind the reader of the invaluable contribution made by the Soviet Armed Forces in liberating the peoples of Europe from fascism, and tell how they were helped in that sacred mission by our friends in Poland, Czechoslovakia, Yugoslavia, Bulgaria, Rumania, and Hungary.

Finally—and this may well be the most important thing—I hope that my humble labors will serve as a symbol of my very great respect for the heroic soldier, and for his very great courage and self-sacrifice in the struggle against the Nazi aggressors.

And now I hand over my new book for your judgment.

S. M. Shtemenko

THE LAST SIX MONTHS

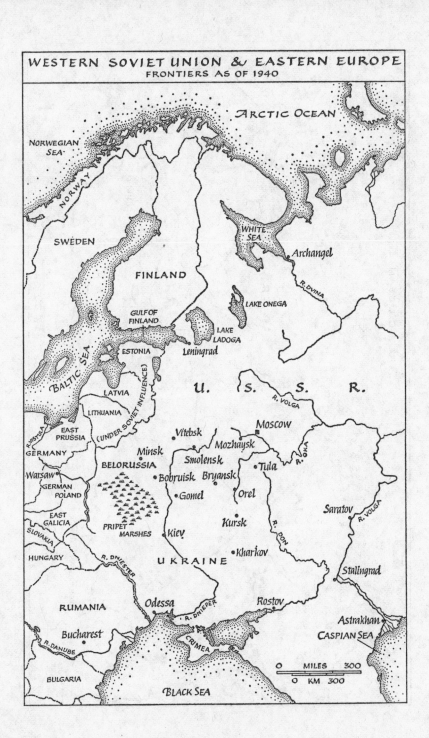

WESTERN SOVIET UNION & EASTERN EUROPE
FRONTIERS AS OF 1940

ARCTIC OCEAN

NORWEGIAN SEA

NORWAY

SWEDEN

WHITE SEA

Archangel

FINLAND

R. DVINA

LAKE ONEGA

GULF OF FINLAND

LAKE LADOGA

Leningrad

BALTIC SEA

ESTONIA

U.   S.   S.   R.

R. VOLGA

LATVIA

LITHUANIA

(UNDER SOVIET INFLUENCE)

Vitebsk

Moscow

R. VISTULA

EAST PRUSSIA

GERMANY

Minsk

BELORUSSIA

Smolensk

Mozhaysk

R. OKA

Warsaw

Bobruisk

Bryansk

Tula

GERMAN POLAND

Gomel

Orel

Saratov

EAST GALICIA

PRIPET MARSHES

Kursk

R. VOLGA

SLOVAKIA

Kiev

R. DON

HUNGARY

R. DNIESTER

UKRAINE

Kharkov

Stalingrad

RUMANIA

Odessa

Rostov

Astrakhan

Bucharest

R. DNIEPER

CASPIAN SEA

R. DANUBE

CRIMEA

BULGARIA

0   MILES   300

0   KM   300

BLACK SEA

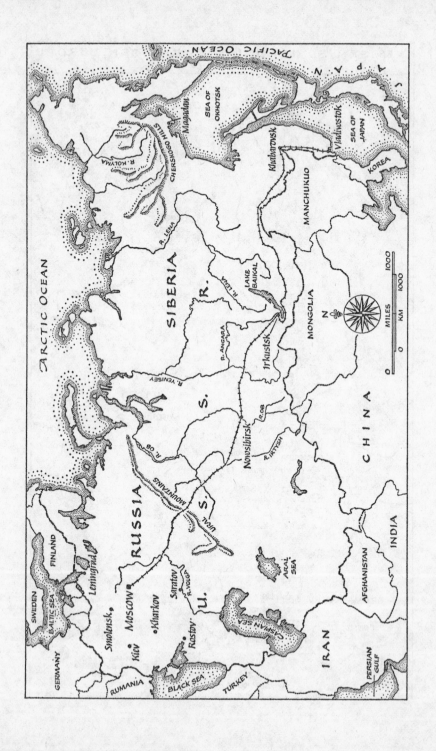

1

MORE ABOUT
THE GENERAL STAFF:
ITS PERSONNEL
AND ITS DOINGS

Experiments on organizational problems. The organization of forces is a job for the General Staff. From parallelism to centralization. The closest comrades of the operations officers. Combat experience must be studied. Combat troops in favor of drawing up regulations. On contacts with allies. Special missions. A few words on commanding troops. The Supreme Commander on Stavka representatives. A visit from Field Marshal Montgomery.

I must begin this book with some words about my friends and comrades-in-arms and their work on the General Staff.[1] It is difficult to cover everything and everybody: What was done bulks too large, and we are still too close, historically, to those events. In this chapter I want merely to supplement what I said earlier; to

---

[1] The late General of the Army Shtemenko was chief of the Operations Department and deputy chief of the General Staff during much of World War II. (Translator's note.)

express some thoughts on organizational, scientific, and other matters, and mention the comrades associated with them.

Owing to the nature of my duties on the General Staff during the war, I was in close contact with organizational matters and was very familiar with the generals and other officers who dealt with them. After the war I was for more than three years, as chief of the General Staff, directly in charge of building the Armed Forces, developing their organizational structure, and mobilizing effectives; and later I served as deputy chief of the General Staff for more than five years. All this enables me—and gives me the moral right—to dwell in greater detail on these matters, which at first glance are boring.

Structuring the Armed Forces and co-ordinating their organization with the tasks of defending the country are basic problems determining the might and—in the last analysis—the defensive capacity of the state. Hence they must constantly be the cynosure of the Party Central Committee and of the government. Among the military organs implementing the decisions of the party and the government, a prominent role is played by the General Staff, which plans and elaborates all matters bearing upon the Armed Forces.

Among the responsibilities of bureaus handling organizational matters is that of solving such important and complex problems as the composition, size, and structure of the Armed Forces, the ratios between the types and kinds of forces and their composition. Also, elaborating methods and ways of seeing that they always correspond to the character of the war, the operation, or the battle, depending upon the state of armaments and equipment and the demands of the war. They also elaborate the organizational structure of the forces, the tables of organization for formations and units, and solve many other problems having to do with the latter's life and activity. Everyone knows how important it is to find the right ratio between the different arms of the services, and among kinds of forces; to determine what weapons should be provided to forces, and in what quantity; and what organs are needed successfully to conduct military actions, operations, and battles. This is an ancient problem, but one that is always very relevant.

2

Whereas the operations officers, after determining the aim of the operations and the tasks of the forces, state what is to be done, where it is to be done, how it is to be done, and what effectives and equipment will be required for this, the organization officers[2] compute the number of effectives and amount of equipment, and state what their structure should be.

Under wartime conditions, operations officers and organization officers are very frequently faced with different specific demands. For example, it may be required that our division be stronger than an analogous enemy division. The operations officer must substantiate that requirement. It is the job of the organization officer to examine carefully the composition of both divisions, and to state what is necessary to increase firepower and striking force on offense, to strengthen stability on defense, etc. It is on a basis of this analysis that the numerical size of the division is determined, and that the quantity of tanks, artillery, and other armament and equipment is decided upon in terms of types and function.

In wartime, organization officers also elaborate plans for bringing formations up to strength, or placing them on reserve status, and deal with many other problems. No large staff—and especially not the General Staff—can do without a department that deals with matters of planning. Yet in neither peacetime nor wartime is any single staff given the right to make any organizational changes in its forces. This right is possessed only by the General Staff, which works constantly to improve the organization of forces.

Service with the General Staff during the war years taught me a lot. It was precisely then, during the war, that one could see fully displayed the importance of the work done by organization officers—a job that was in a way inconspicuous but was indispensable to victory over the enemy.

For many of us, the famous formula set forth by Friedrich Engels in *Anti-Dühring* was given tangible and visible form:

> Nothing is so dependent upon economic conditions as an army and a fleet. Their armament, composition, organization,

[2] I.e., staff officers of the "Organization Department," as Dept. 2 of the Soviet General Staff is called. (Translator's note.)

3

tactics, and strategy depend primarily upon the degree of production and the means of communication achieved at the given moment. In this case, it is not the "free mental creativity" of great commanders that has functioned in a revolutionary way but the invention of the best weapons and the change in the human raw material. At best, the influence of the great commanders is limited to their adapting the methods of fighting to the new weapons and the new soldiers.[3]

In those days and nights of the war, life itself confirmed the great profundity of that scientific principle. And for us officers of the General Staff it became the key to working out plans for the future.

At the outbreak of the war, the General Staff had its own sections concerned with organizing forces, mobilizing them, calling up conscripts for them, and bringing them up to strength. A month after the start of the war—on July 29, 1941, to be more exact—a decree of the People's Commissariat of Defense created Glavupraform (Main Administration for Forming and Bringing up to Strength the Forces of the Red Army); and all sections of the General Staff handling such problems were transferred to that administration. On August 8 Army Commissar First Class E. A. Shchadenke was appointed chief of Glavupraform, while at the same time remaining deputy people's commissar of defense. All that was left in the Operations Department of the General Staff was the Organizational Statistics Section, which for the most part kept statistics on the forces and their distribution.

To a great extent, that decision was governed by the very trying situation that had developed in the first months of the war: apparently it was taken with a view to lightening the work load of the General Staff and concentrating its attention on operational matters. But whereas in wartime questions of mobilizing forces and bringing them up to strength can in fact be removed—and should be removed—from the competence of the General Staff,

[3] F. Engels, *Izbrannye voyennye proizvedeniya* (Moscow: Voyenizdat, 1956), p. 11.

4

the same thing should not be done vis-à-vis organizational questions. Experience soon showed that the organization of the forces was the job of the General Staff, and made it necessary to correct the decision taken earlier.

In the first months of the war, we General Staff officers were faced with a severe shortage of tanks for our forces. Meantime the enemy, who had air superiority, was continuing to advance, using his armor in huge, wedge-shaped formations, and trying to rip up the Soviet forces' defense lines. This raised the problem of making the organizational structure of our forces correspond to the conditions that had developed.

In particular, we had to decide whether we should continue the policy, adopted before the war, of creating mechanized corps. Was that policy correct under the new circumstances? Theoretically, it was still correct; but it was ascertained that in those difficult times, our industry could not in a short time fully supply the equipment needed by such large formations. Hence it was more correct to do without such formations until such time as the national economy could provide the forces with the requisite quantities of armored vehicles.

But how to proceed under the immediate circumstances? We calculated roughly as follows. The Soviet infantry was a real force capable of resisting the Nazi tanks and motorized infantry. In order to be strengthened, it had to be supplied with antitank artillery and tanks. Substantial tank support could be provided by smaller formations, units, and subunits (i.e., tank brigades, regiments, and battalions) and not by corps, which acted independently. Such was our conclusion.

Subsequently, the situation with regard to tank production improved. At that point we began to think about coming back to the notion of corps, since combat experience had shown that without them it was impossible to develop operations in great depth requiring a combination of great firepower with great striking power, mobility, maneuverability, and the capacity to act independently of the infantry. Thus in the spring of 1942 we began to form tank armies, tank corps, and mechanized corps. At first the composition of the tank armies was mixed: three tank corps and two or three infantry divisions. This organization proved sufficiently modern for operations in which the tank corps did not have to become far separated from the infantry. But when the tank formations penetrated deeply into the enemy's rear, it hampered the army's maneuvering, since in such cases the infantry divisions inevitably lagged behind, and it became very difficult to control the army's forces. Also, the heterogeneous make-up of such an army created several other difficulties.

The nature of our operations in depth in 1943–45, beginning with the counterattack near Stalingrad, demanded that we abandon the mixed composition of such armies. By the time of the Battle of Kursk (July 5, 1943), their make-up was homogeneous: two tank corps, one mechanized corps, antitank, artillery, and other units, rear-area services. Along with the tank armies, individual tank and mechanized corps and brigades were retained. The organizational structure of the tank forces became very flexible. It assured the action of tanks together with infantry and the independent use of great tank formations working jointly with aircraft. This organization corresponded to the "maneuver warfare" then being waged by the Soviet forces on the field of battle.

The foregoing is one small example of the importance of making the organizational structure of forces correspond to the material basis and to the current situation. The changing and development of organizational forms were observed literally in all types and kinds of forces.

Naturally, such very important organizational measures could not be decided apart from the General Staff. Also, the General Staff was instructed to study them and make its own recommendations. Together with representatives of Glavupraform, officers from the General Staff went to the various fronts, where under combat conditions they could see how well the organizational forms of a particular organism corresponded to the demands of combat.

In late April 1942, wartime experience and the work of the General Staff made it necessary to revive our Organization Department, which was made responsible for drafting organizational and other directives, for follow-up on their implementation, and

6

for keeping track of the forces at the fronts. The Operations Department's Organizational Statistics Section was transferred to this new department. To some extent, problems of the organization of forces were removed from the jurisdiction of Glavupraform, although it retained the Organization and Personnel Department.

Owing to such halfway measures, there naturally arose a parallelism between the work of the General Staff and that of Glavupraform. Therefore, in June of that year Stalin issued a special directive defining the boundaries between the functions of the General Staff and those of Glavupraform. That directive, however, also proved to be a halfway measure.

In the spring of 1943, by way of preparation for the Battle of Kursk, the Stavka and the General Staff carried out sweeping organizational measures. Infantry, air, and artillery divisions were formed. The corps link of command had been restored earlier. The scope of the work is indicated by the fact that by April 1943 the Stavka's reserves included ten armies, a number of tank, mechanized, and artillery corps, and control of the Reserve (later the Steppe) Front.[4] The General Staff, lacking the appropriate bureau, could not cope with such a volume of work. Meantime, the parallelism with Glavupraform still obtained. This situation made it necessary to solve the organizational problem radically. The Staff Organization and Personnel Department of Glavupraform was closed down, and the General Staff was finally provided with a bureau handling the organization of forces. On May 4 Stalin signed a directive fixing the make-up and tasks of that bureau.

The operations officers did organizational work every day. It was an obligatory element of planning operations, since there was essentially no standard table of organization for the fronts, although it was assumed that a front would comprise several armies, including one air army and one or two tank armies. But in terms of specific magnitudes this TO was never uniform. For example, tank armies were never needed on the Karelian Front. On the other hand, we had light infantry corps there which were never used anywhere else. For each new operation, the make-up of the

[4] When used to designate a formation, the Russian "front" is roughly the equivalent of the English "army group." (Translator's note.)

fronts was revised: They were given extra forces (or deprived of forces), but always in that combination that the circumstances dictated as regards types of forces and the nature of the formations.

Our organization officers always worked hand in glove with the operations officers. They studied combat experience and promptly restructured combat organisms so that they could cope successfully with tasks that arose in the course of the war. Without such comrades and their labors, not even a single major operation at the front would have been thinkable. They could always answer one's questions as to the size of any division on any sector of the front, its losses, and the time it would take to get new troops. And they could provide similar data on my corps, army, or front, or for the Armed Forces as a whole. About reserves, they knew exactly where, how, and in what strength they were being formed, their degree of combat-readiness, their location en route to the front, etc. The hard-working organization officers were the right hand of the operations officers.

From April 1942 to October 1946 the bureaus handling organizational matters were headed by Lt. Gen. A. G. Karponosov. He was a regular General Staff officer: intelligent, very hard-working and efficient, and polite—but gentle and a bit shy. He had a very good knowledge of the kind of work entrusted to him; he did his work skillfully and thoroughly; and he always spoke the truth. But for some reason he didn't have good luck in his career. There are people in the world called "losers": Every mistake they make is noticed; they are blamed for the mistakes of others when they are not themselves at fault; and they are never able to defend themselves. If reserves did not reach the front in time, it was Karponosov's fault, although the communications people were actually responsible. If Glavupraform had failed to provide a division with replacements promptly, Karponosov would be blamed on the grounds that he had not put in the requisition for the replacements on time. And so on. More than once, A. I. Antonov[5] and I heard

[5] Lt. Gen. (later General, the Army) Aleksei Innokentyevich Antonov, appointed deputy chief of the General Staff and chief of the Operations Department on December 11, 1942. (Translator's note.)

Stalin make unflattering remarks about Karponosov, although he (the Supreme Commander) knew that Karponosov knew his job well and did it well. And on more than one occasion, Antonov defended him when Stalin proposed replacing him with another general.

Shortly after the end of the war in the Far East, Stalin again raised the question of Karponosov. "The experience acquired in the General Staff should be passed on to the military districts," he said, impatiently pacing around the table as usual. "We must now reduce the General Staff, and send all those relieved of their duties off to military districts. Your favorite Karponosov, for example," he continued. "He too should be sent off to pass along experience. Where do you intend to send him?"

Antonov's words stuck in his throat. He had been making ready to defend Karponosov. But with his question, Stalin deprived him of the opportunity. (This was something he did quite often when he didn't want to listen to explanations.)

"Let me think it over," Antonov replied.

"All right. Give him a post as deputy chief of staff in one of the districts."

On October 20, 1946, A. G. Karponosov was named deputy chief of staff of the Volga Military District, where he served until his death.

Beginning in May 1943, Karponosov's deputy was Lt. Gen. Nikolai Ivanovich Chetverikov, who headed up the Organization Department. Chetverikov was a veteran General Staff officer. He had served on the General Staff for more than twenty-five years in various capacities, and for more than half that time had headed up bureaus handling organizational matters. He was retired in the early sixties with the rank of colonel general.

Chetverikov was a demanding man whose few words were rather sharp. He loved precision to the point of pedantry. His closest colleague was Maj. Gen. A. I. Efremov, who later became military adviser to the First Deputy Minister of Defense.

Experienced officers who knew their job well were chosen as section chiefs dealing with various kinds of forces and carrying out special tasks. Thus at various times Col. A. N. Nyrkov and

Col. F. F. Trishin were concerned with infantry and airborne divisions. Cavalry and armored forces were the job of Maj. Gen. S. V. Sretensky, while Maj. Gen. P. I. Kanyukov handled artillery and mortar units. Technical forces (engineers, communications, etc.) were the responsibility of Col. V. V. Vishnyakov and, later, of Col. P. A. Polityko. (The latter at one time handled problems of troop dispositions.) The air forces were the responsibility of Col. I. S. Alekseyev (and, beginning in 1944, of Col. N. K. Ermakov); the organs of administration were handled by Col. F. M. Arkhipov (and toward the end of the war, by Maj. Gen. A. I. Suchev).

The very special problem of military training institutions was handled by Col. I. O. Skvortsov (and, beginning in 1944, by Col. A. V. Goldenkov). Rear-area units and institutions were the job of Col. I. M. Eshchenko.

Cols. I. A. Kiselev, S. N. Ryabokobylko, P. V. Dudoladov, I. I. Ilchenko, A. A. Bochkov, and M. N. Kostin were experts in organized planning. Col. (later Maj. Gen.) S. M. Podolsky kept strict account of the size of the forces. Col. I. V. Smirnov was in custody of banners, and in charge of awarding them. Col. I. I. Zotkin (later, Col. P. V. Dudoladov) was responsible for follow-up on bringing units up to strength.

The vigorous and "penetrating" Col. I. K. Tkachenko was the permanent chief of the Operational Transport Section. Without him, the operations officers could not have drawn a single breath, as the saying goes. He always knew what was being delivered to any front, and where the trains were.

Col. A. K. Nemchinov handled questions involving the disposition of forces. The inspection group was headed by Col. A. N. Shumilov. Maj. V. N. Khrustalev and Capt. I. I. Zubkov were trouble shooters for the organizational bureaus.

I have named only those officers who handled organizational problems and did follow-up on the solutions elaborated. Naturally, I am quite simply unable to give a complete description of each of them. But I can say that all of the above generals and other officers had a thorough knowledge of their jobs and that each of them contributed his mite to the general cause of victory over the enemy. Each of them was assisted by dozens of other officers. And on the whole it was a well-knit and skilled team which handled the most important problems of building and organizing the Red Army.

During the war each commander was given broad latitude, both in tactics generally and in the tactics of using kinds of forces. He even had rights with respect to the "operational art."[6] But in the matter of organizational structure the field commanders could only point out the merits and defects of the organization of forces and report on them to the General Staff—making their own suggestions for improvement, naturally. This procedure was not a mistake: Any other was out of the question. The organization of the military formations of regiments, divisions, armies, and fronts —including their size, and the quality and quantity of armament, as derivatives from one kind of organization or another—must be stable and unshakable over a certain period of time: a period that is not brief but considerable. Only in this case can organization of forces correspond to the tactics and the operational art, and have an effect on the process of improving the art of war, since the relationship between the latter and the organizational forms of forces is dialectical. The organization of forces, if it is correct, must change only when new weapons and technology make their appearance, or when it is demanded by the specific conditions of the theater of operations.

As was said above, suggestions came into the General Staff from commanders and staffs at all levels, who had submitted various kinds of troop organisms to practical testing. The General Staff relied primarily on these very well founded considerations when improving the organization of forces.

Whenever substantial organizational changes were being made in wartime, we never failed to call in the commanding officers of divisions, regiments, and even battalions from the Field Forces. Their opinions on the organization of forces were attentively heard as a matter of course. And it goes without saying that when the Stavka considered such changes, it called in commanding officers from the fronts.

Both the Stavka and the General Staff laid especially great em-

[6] I.e., on the level between tactics and strategy. (Translator's note.)

phasis on studying the latest combat experience and putting it into practice. At the General Staff we set up a Section for the Utilization of Combat Experience based on the Operational Training Division. This section was headed up by Maj. Gen. P. P. Vechny. It was made responsible for studying combat experience and conveying to the broad masses of commanders those conclusions useful in connection with the actions of forces. This same section was also made responsible for elaborating a wide variety of Army-wide instructions, orders, and regulations.

The young section soon carved out a place for itself, and by the autumn of 1942 was already publishing *A Miscellany of Materials for Studying Combat Experience,* No. 1, which dealt with the events of July and August of that year.

In the brief introduction to the publication it was stated that its aim was

> . . . to impart to forces of the Field Army, to reserve formations, to military academies, and the officers in charge of the main and central administrations of the People's Commissariat of Defense the experience of military actions in the Great Patriotic War.[7]

The publication was sent to all commanders down to the regimental level in all types of forces. It included materials dealing with both the experience of Soviet forces and that of the enemy's forces. Although the times were very trying (July–August 1942!), the General Staff looked far ahead and considered it possible to print, in that publication, materials on destroying surrounded enemy formations, although up to that time we ourselves had been getting into that kind of dangerous situation. The next article presented certain conclusions about amphibious operations in 1941. Next came a brief survey of combat experience in using means of antitank defense, and materials on using the resources of troops in fighting off enemy aircraft.

Foreseeing the preparation and effectuation of large-scale offensive operations, the editors of the publication also included an article titled "An Experiment in Carrying Out Operational War

[7] *Sbornik materialov po izucheniyu opyta voiny,* No. 1 (Moscow: Voyenizdat, 1942), p. 3.

Games at the Front." Several items were devoted to defense in the field, and to the use of AA guns against the Nazi forces, training them on surface (ground) targets. The final article in the miscellany was a brief one titled "Problems of Studying Combat Experience." It dealt with the necessity of generalizing that experience, of making the forces familiar with the best methods of conducting combat operations, the necessity of rapidly and thoroughly disseminating information on new methods of warfare.

The Supreme Commander looked over the first miscellany carefully and found it to his liking. And it soon became feasible to elaborate, on the basis of combat experience, an important order from the Commissar of Defense: No. 325, which played a significant role with regard to the employment of tanks during the war years. The order was signed by Stalin on October 16, 1942, a month before the counterattack at Stalingrad in which tank forces performed brilliantly.

By this time it had become clear that the Section for the Utilization of Combat Experience was functioning correctly, and we awaited the second number of the publication with impatience. It came out in November, and carried a lead article titled "Operational and Tactical Lessons from the Winter Campaign of 1941–42." In general, this number of the publication was more impressive. It included several articles on winter operations and on the struggle for air superiority, which was very apropos. But the most significant thing was that the publication had clearly shown the importance of its work in utilizing combat experience. As if in confirmation of that, it printed the above-mentioned order (No. 325) of the Commissar of Defense. It also printed a directive from the General Staff on the study and utilization of combat experience, and instructions on that head from the staffs of fronts and armies.

P. P. Vechny edited the publication himself; and it must be said that he did it so well that, to some extent, he rehabilitated himself in the eyes of Stalin, who had not forgotten that Vechny had been involved in the failure of the Crimean Front in May 1942.

All in all, twenty-six issues of the miscellany were published up until the time it was discontinued in 1948.

The volume of work continued to expand. In March 1944 the section was expanded into a Department for the Study of Combat Experience, with the same chief. But now, in addition to the miscellany, the department published an *Information Bulletin* and a *Tactical Methods Miscellany*. The bulletins contained information on the forces' combat experience at the tactical level, for the most part: on reconnaissance, order of battle, methods of command control, of forcing rivers, etc. The *Tactical Methods Miscellany* published descriptions of interesting battles (basically at the company and battalion level), including battles fought under special conditions. By the time it ceased publication in 1946, twenty-three issues had appeared.

The Department for the Utilization of Combat Experience (abbreviated UPIOV) had a small but select staff of officers. In the past, our Armed Forces had never dealt with such a problem on such a scale. The officers of the department studied the art of summarizing combat experience and sought out the most rapid and correct ways of formulating the information in the course of daily work. They had to maintain very close contact with the Operations Department so as to meet the demands placed upon them. From us they got the necessary information on the operations of the forces—in particular, the reports from the General Staff's representatives at the fronts. In their turn, many of our section chiefs, who often visited the fronts, took part in preparing articles for the various publications. Thus among the names of the authors one often finds those of V. A. Bolyatko, K. F. Vasilchenko, Ya. A. Kutsev, V. F. Mernov, V. I. Sumin, and other operations officers.

The officers from that department often went themselves to the front lines, where they studied combat experience (not always positive experience, of course). We helped them to organize the collection of information directly from the troops, and hence they were often hot on the scent of the war. Teachers from military academies and members of the Military History Section were also involved in this.

That department played an important role in other matters besides studying combat experience. It stimulated the thinking of our staff. And from it came many outstanding historians of the Great Patriotic War, together with scientific workers.

The Supreme Commander kept track of the work done by the General Staff in studying combat experience, and took an interest in the material published for the forces. Each new issue of a publication was sent to him without fail.

In 1942, when the department had found its footing and acquired a certain amount of experience, a draft service field manual for the infantry was prepared on instructions from Stalin. It was prepared in a unique way—likewise on his instructions. The first drafts were drawn up in Moscow; then several groups of officers went to the front. The final draft of the manual was drawn up there, with the participation of the most capable and experienced commanding officers of companies, battalions, and regiments who had been specially designated for that purpose. In Moscow a special commission was set up to look over the draft manual and make the final corrections. Then the manual was examined at a two-day session of the Stavka to which commanding officers at various levels—from the regimental to the divisional—had been invited. Only after all this was the manual approved (on November 9, 1942) and promulgated by the Commissariat of Defense.

Stalin realized how important it was to develop the initiative of commanding officers and their skill in making decisions under any circumstances, including the most complex—something that no manual could provide for. Hence the order he wrote by way of putting the manual into effect included a paragraph (para. 4) that afforded an opportunity for commanding officers to show creativity and to use broad initiative. It stated: "The instructions in this manual must be followed strictly in accordance with the circumstances."

This method of preparing a field manual, with the participation of experienced commanding officers from the field army, plus specialists, who provided very valuable recommendations, became well established and is still being used. Although not all of the regulations were reviewed by the Stavka, it was *de rigueur* to report on them.

15

In this connection I shall take the liberty of recounting an instructive anecdote. Early in December 1944, during a situation report, the Supreme Commander asked how the new Department for the Study of Combat Experience was coming along. A. I. Antonov replied that it was functioning normally. "The officers are working hard," he said. "They often go to the front, and we submit copies of the publications to you."

"But in my opinion it is functioning badly," Stalin said. "Do the General Staff and the department know that this year two artillery manuals were published—both of them with serious violations of the established rules and procedures?"

Antonov and I exchanged glances. I knew nothing, and decided to keep still. Antonov did likewise. Then the Supreme Commander, without waiting for an answer, demanded that we look into the matter thoroughly and report to him in two days' time.

It turned out that, unknown to the Stavka, Chief Marshal of Artillery N. N. Voronov, artillery commander of the Red Army, had worked up and submitted for approval two manuals: an Antiaircraft Manual, submitted on May 29, 1944, and a Red Army Artillery Manual, submitted on October 18 of the same year. Both had been approved by Marshal of the Soviet Union G. K. Zhukov.

On the appointed day, our report on the situation at the front and on the "case of the manuals" began immediately after a session of the Politburo. For a long time Stalin paced around the room. Then he turned to the members of the Politburo and said, "We'll have to issue an order in this case. No doubt it would be awkward for the General Staff to write about two important leaders, so we'll have to write it ourselves."

"On May 29, 1944," Stalin began to dictate, "Comrade Voronov, Chief Marshal of Artillery, submitted a Red Army Antiaircraft Manual (two parts) for approval by Marshal Zhukov, Deputy Commissar of Defense, without prior approval by the Stavka of the Supreme Commander."

Then, leafing through the manuals lying on his desk, he went on, "On October 18, 1944, Comrade Voronov, again without any presentation or report to the Stavka of the Supreme Commander, submitted for the approval of Marshal Zhukov a Red Army Artillery Manual. Without adequately checking it, without calling in people from the front, and without reporting to the Stavka, Marshal Zhukov approved the manual and put it into effect."

Stalin paused for a little while, then continued, "A check has shown that owing to the haste with which they were approved, these manuals have serious lacks. They do not take into account several new weapons systems, and they are not co-ordinated with the plan for the use of manuals by the Red Army Artillery."

It should be noted that the Supreme Commander usually gave the reason why it was necessary to issue any particular order. And that is what he did in this case.

"The People's Commissariat of Defense proceeds on the assumption that a manual is not an order effective only for a brief period. A manual of regulations is a code of laws governing the Red Army for years. Therefore, before a manual is issued it should be carefully checked, and comrades from the front should be called in to assist. It was in this way that the Infantry Field Manual was issued. And the same procedure should have been used in submitting these manuals for approval so as not to make mistakes and so that, later on, military personnel would not be groundlessly punished for violating defective regulations. Comrade Voronov disregarded this method of elaborating manuals and submitting them for approval, and Marshal Zhukov forgot it. . . ."

Then came the concluding part of the order. Everyone present listened closely, as Stalin said in an even voice: "Therefore . . ." Then, slowing down a bit as though to emphasize his thought, he dictated: *"First.* I here abrogate"—again he looked in the manuals where the numbers of the orders were given—"Order No. 76 of May 29, 1944, and Order No. 209 of October 18, 1944, from Marshal Zhukov, Deputy Commissar of Defense, approving and promulgating the Antiaircraft Manual and the Red Army Artillery Manual. *Second,* I call the attention of Comrade Voronov, Marshal of Artillery, to his negligent attitude toward artillery manuals. *Third,* I require of Marshal Zhukov that henceforth he not be hasty in dealing with serious problems.

"I order:

"That commissions be formed for checking the above-mentioned manuals:

"(a) a commission for reviewing and checking the Antiaircraft Manual;

"(b) a commission for reviewing and checking the Artillery Manual.

"That Comrade Bulganin, Deputy Commissar of Defense, name the members of the commissions, and submit the names to me for approval.

"The present order is to be disseminated to all COs of fronts (districts), armies, to chiefs of main and central administrations (or departments), and to C. in C.'s of branches of the Armed Forces of the USSR Commissariat of Defense. . . ."

Like everyone else affected by it, I remembered that lesson always.

Maintaining liaison with allies posed several new problems before the General Staff. The operations officers simply could not manage at one and the same time to handle such liaison, do their own work, and analyze the military consequences of each specific move by the allies. It soon became apparent that even the Liaison Section was groaning under the weight of its responsibilities. The section was first expanded. Then it was used as a basis for creating a new department handling special tasks associated with our allies and all problems of the General Staff's foreign policy activity. It was headed up by Gen. N. V. Slavin, who had long worked in that sphere. Oversight of the Soviet military missions in the countries of our Allies was also effected through that department.

It should be noted that at first contacts with our allies were very limited and were basically confined to exchange of information on the progress of military operations, exchange of combat experience, of certain intelligence data, and new technical information. Trips to the front by Allied military delegations were organized, and protocol and other work were done.

Prior to 1944, co-operation between the armed forces of the anti-Hitler coalition was relative. After all, with the exception of

18

local operations in Italy, the Allies were not carrying on large-scale operations on the territory of Europe. Even at that time, however, military missions from the Allied countries were accredited to the General Staff: from the United States (headed by Gen. John R. Deane), from Great Britain (Gen. Montagu Burrows), and the Government of the Fighting French (Gen. Jean de Lattre de Tassigny). Also, there was a military mission from Norway headed by Col. Arne D. Dahl, and one from the Czechoslovak Republic headed by Brig. Gen. Heliodor Pika. The mission from the Yugoslav National Committee of Liberation was headed by Lt. Gen. Volimir Terzić.

It should be noted that the foreign missions were especially interested in the trips to the front, where our allies learned a lot.

Likewise, Soviet military missions were accredited to the general staffs of our allies. They were subordinated directly to the Stavka through the General Staff, and did not come under the authority of ambassadors. This was done after a close examination of the functional responsibilities and working conditions of the missions, which were essentially performing operational tasks. The same thing was true, in Moscow, of our allies.

The first Soviet military mission to be established was the one to Great Britain. On July 8, 1941, after a dangerous and exhausting flight from Arkhangelsk to Glasgow, it arrived in London. It was headed by Lt. Gen. F. I. Golikov, who returned to the Soviet Union a few days later, and was replaced by Rear Adm. N. M. Kharlamov, a thirty-five-year-old line officer of the Soviet Navy. He was distinguished by his intelligence and high principles, and as a specialist in military planning. Also, by his detailed knowledge of naval technics and tactics. Other salient aspects of Admiral Kharlamov's character were manifested in London, as we shall see later.

At first the Soviet mission was very small: only six persons, not counting the chief. Later it grew considerably in accordance with the volume of work to be done.

In view of their particular importance, the tasks of the chief of mission in England were set by V. M. Molotov, the Commissar of Foreign Affairs. They consisted first of all in securing the opening of a second front in Europe, "in one month, if possible." The next task was to organize military deliveries to the Soviet Union from Great Britain and the United States, and the sailing of convoys from Britain to our maritime ports. The question of stimulating Allied air raids on military objectives in fascist Germany assumed great importance later on. Also, among the problems dealt with were those typical of the practical co-operation of the armed forces of the anti-Hitler coalition: exchanging information on the enemy, exchanging combat experience, and co-ordinating the timetables, procedures, and scope of military operations.

The reception accorded our mission at the London station showed that the English people were warmly sympathetic toward the land of the Soviets, which had been attacked by our common enemy. The entire staff of the mission felt this sympathy later on as well, in the course of its work. The common people of England then realized that with its struggle the Soviet Union was also saving their own homeland. So the broad laboring masses of the country began to exert pressure on the Conservatives in the government (who had not always had an unprejudiced attitude toward us), and tried to compel them to carry out their obligation as Allies in an honest manner.

I shall not describe the work of the mission in detail at this point. Let me say only that there were some tense moments when Admiral Kharlamov was face to face with some people of very high rank in the British Government and its military hierarchy, and that he always manifested unusual will power and an enviable skill at defending the interests of the Soviet state.

The well-publicized story of the enemy's destruction of Convoy P.Q. 17 is typical in this connection. As we know, on June 27, 1942, P.Q. 17, the largest convoy of the war up to that time sailed from Iceland for Arkhangelsk and Murmansk. It consisted of thirty-four merchant ships (two Soviet, one Panamanian, and the rest British and American) and twenty-one escort vessels. Also, there were two covering forces from the British fleet. One comprised four cruisers and three destroyers, and the other two battleships, an aircraft carrier, two cruisers, and eight destroyers. On July 4 the convoy reached an area where individual German submarines and aircraft operating from the Norwegian coast made scattered attacks on the merchant ships and escort vessels. Adm. Dudley Pound, the Navy chief of staff, interpreted these attacks (which could have been warded off by the powerful British force) as a sure sign of an overwhelming onslaught by the main forces of the German surface fleet headed by the *Tirpitz*. Although the British admiral had completely accurate information that the enemy's battleships had not yet put out to sea, Pound personally gave the order: "Cruiser force withdraw to the westward at high speed." And a few minutes later he radioed: "Owing to threat from surface ships, convoy is to disperse and proceed to Russian ports."[8]

As was learned later, during this time the heavy German ships were at anchor in the harbor of Alta Fjord and had no intention of approaching the convoy. Not only that, but the German High Command was afraid of losing the heavy ships of its fleet and would not risk keeping them in the open sea. Meantime, noticing the unusual measures taken by the British, the enemy threw his submarines and aircraft against the slow merchant ships, which had been left without any protection. Since they were defenseless, they were an easy prey to the fascist vultures.

On the next day, July 5, 1942, feeling completely safe, the battleship *Tirpitz* put out to sea. Accompanied by two submarines, it hurried to intercept the merchant ships of the dispersed convoy. The only thing in the way of the Hitlerites was the Soviet submarine *K-21*, commanded by Hero of the Soviet Union, Commander N. A. Lunin. He fearlessly sailed into the middle of the enemy formation, damaged the *Tirpitz* with a torpedo hit, and made a getaway thanks to the consternation of the enemy.

All that remained of Convoy P.Q. 17 after that naval slaughter was eleven merchant ships. The ships that had been sunk were carrying 3,350 trucks, 430 tanks, 210 bombers, and 100,000 tons of other cargo. How that equipment could have been used at Stalingrad!

Apart from everything else, the loss of Convoy P.Q. 17 was a

---

[8] Winston Churchill, *Vtoraya mirovaya voina* [*The Second World War*] (Moscow: Voyenizdat, 1955), Vol. IV, p. 267 [pp. 263–64 in the English-language edition—translator's note].

great political lesson. Indeed, representatives of British Conservatism (and in particular, Admiral Pound) tried to interpret the catastrophe as proof positive of the unfeasibility of sending any more convoys to the USSR via the northern route. The cost was just too great, they said. Let us remember that on July 17 the Hitlerites started the battle for Stalingrad, that on July 25 they launched their attack on the Northern Caucasus, and that our defensive operations were in a very bad way.

Through its ambassador in England, I. M. Maisky, the Soviet Government asked the British Government about the sailing dates for the next convoys carrying matériel. Anthony Eden replied that P.Q. 17 was too costly an enterprise; and Pound averred that if he were on the German side, not a single convoy would reach its destination. The Admiralty did not consider it feasible to send any convoys—not before autumn, at any rate.

At this critical moment, N. M. Kharlamov had his say. He reported to Moscow his opinion (the opinion of a specialist in naval affairs) that the actions of the British Admiralty were alarming and completely untenable. N. G. Kuznetsov, commissar of the Navy, supported him. The Soviet Government called the attention of the British to the fact that our naval officers disagreed with their naval leaders. In view of this situation, Churchill asked Anthony Eden to arrange a meeting between the Admiralty officials and representatives of the Soviet Union to investigate the reasons for the loss of Convoy P.Q. 17. It was held in Anthony Eden's office at the House of Commons on July 28, 1942.

The meeting was chaired by Eden. In addition to him, the British were represented by Albert Alexander, the First Lord of the Admiralty, and Admiral Pound. The Soviet Union was represented by Ambassador I. M. Maisky, Rear Admiral Kharlamov, and the latter's deputy.

A tense atmosphere developed in the course of the account given by Pound, who was unable to offer convincing proofs of the correctness of his actions, as a result of which the enemy had destroyed the convoy with impunity. To the amazement of those present, in giving his account Pound used an ordinary students' geography map—one on which many elements in the circumstances of the convoy's loss could not possibly be reflected.

The Soviet admiral had brought a detailed naval chart with him to the meeting. It made many things clear. Admiral Kharlamov showed that by reason of the depths of the water the *Tirpitz* could not have posed a threat to either the merchant ships or the covering force. Thus it followed that the withdrawal of the cruiser force and the dispersal of the convoy was a great mistake on the part of the British chief of naval staff. Admiral Kharlamov destroyed Pound's arguments one after another.

Driven into a corner by the deadly logic of the chief of the Soviet Military Mission, Pound could not carry on a reasonable dialogue and resorted to sharp language. In an attempt to smooth things over, Alexander got into the conversation, apologizing for Pound and for the mistake of the British Admiralty. The tactful I. M. Maisky noted, with typically penetrating sarcasm, that "even British admirals make mistakes." When he heard that, Pound flew into a completely unpardonable rage. Kharlamov remained outwardly calm, but he was ruthless in his further criticism of all Pound's behavior at the time Convoy P.Q. 17 was destroyed.

The meeting was going very badly for the British. It was becoming completely clear that the chief reason for the tragedy in the Barents Sea was not military circumstances but politics and the hostility of the British ruling circles toward the USSR. Since a political scandal was not consonant with the calculations of Churchill and the British Government, Eden made haste to terminate the meeting "in view of the strained relations between the parties."

Such were our people abroad. They, too, fought battles. But, strange as it may seem, they fought them with our allies, in order to get them to fulfill their obligations honorably.

I do not intend to overrate Admiral Kharlamov's contributions. But the mite he contributed to the general cause proved to be weighty at that time. After his remarks, the British leaders began to pay heed to our military mission, and convoys with arms and equipment for the USSR continued to sail.

Kharlamov's job was not an easy one. The United Kingdom was a complex ally whose military and governmental leaders varied in their attitudes toward the Soviet Union. Some of them were outright hostile; e.g., Pound and Margesson,[9] the Secretary of State for War. The latter secretary hampered military deliveries; and Churchill, under pressure from public opinion, had to remove him from his post. But others, while not expressing any special liking for the USSR, were not hostile toward us. This facilitated the mission's work, and made it possible to solve many practical problems satisfactorily. Those Kharlamov assigned to this category included Lord Beaverbrook, Albert Alexander (mentioned above), the First Lord of the Admiralty; John G. Dill, the RAF chief of staff; and a few more. Still others liked us and openly helped the mission. Rear Admiral Phillips, in charge of military deliveries, understood the real meaning of relations among the Allies and promoted them in every way. We had many friends among the workers in the Admiralty and Army headquarters without whose help not a single big job would have been accomplished.

The mission also had a lot of work to do in connection with the opening of a second front in Europe. At that time, the American command was devoting great attention to it. Kharlamov and his subordinates never had enough time in one day: They had to attend training exercises for forces preparing to land in France, check on the readiness and departure of convoys, etc. When the second front was opened, the chief of the Soviet Military Mission was on the cruiser *Mauritius* in the zone of operations. He landed in Normandy, from where he was soon recalled to the USSR. From November 1944 until the end of the war the Soviet Military Mission in Britain was headed by Gen. A. F. Vasilyev, who had come there from the Italian sector of the Allied front.

Maj. Gen. I. A. Susloparov was the Soviet military representative attached to the headquarters of the Fighting French and to SHAEF, the headquarters of Gen. Dwight D. Eisenhower, Supreme Commander of the Allied Expeditionary Force. A former peasant, a participant in World War I and in the October Armed Uprising, Ivan Susloparov became our military attaché in

[9] Strictly transliterated, the Russian reads "Markinson," but the individual mentioned was Capt. David Margesson. (Translator's note.)

Paris in 1939. He carried out his duties worthily and skillfully. The tragedy of the defeat and capitulation of France, betrayed by her miserable leaders, took place before the eyes of the Soviet military attaché. At the outbreak of the Great Patriotic War, Susloparov returned to the Soviet Union. He served on the staff of the Red Army Artillery, and from 1942 through the middle of 1944 successfully commanded the artillery of the 10th Army of the Western Front.

But in the summer of 1944 he was again selected for military-diplomatic work, and was soon assigned as chief of the Soviet Military Mission in France. There he had the heavy responsibility of maintaining liaison with our allies, who had opened a second front in Europe. Things became especially difficult when the henchmen of the Nazi state, faced with a catastrophe on the Russo-German front, began in secret to seek out ways of salvation by surrendering to the Anglo-American forces in the West. The situation was complicated by the fact that the chief of the Soviet Military Mission was posted to Paris, whereas the headquarters of Eisenhower, to whom the Nazis were making advances, was located in Reims, 125 kilometers east of the French capital.

The Stavka and the General Staff had foreseen the possibility that the enemy might try to make an agreement with the Allies behind our back. In the event of a surrender, Susloparov was empowered to represent our country, and the Allies were informed of this. It soon became necessary to exercise that authority and, in that connection, to manifest not only a readiness to take on great responsibilities but skill in defending the interests of the USSR. I refer to the signing of the German surrender in Reims on May 7, 1945, which will be recounted in Chapter Eleven. Here I shall say only that at that time the circumstances were very trying, and that Susloparov emerged with honor from a very ticklish situation.

The Soviet Military Mission in Yugoslavia occupied a very noticeable place in the General Staff's work on special problems. As is known, the Communists and peoples of that country had risen up against the Nazi occupiers. With the outbreak of the Great Patriotic War, the brotherly relations between the Communists and peoples of the USSR and of Yugoslavia were strengthened even further.

The Yugoslav soldiers and partisans had to wage war under very difficult conditions. Of necessity, they were based in inaccessible mountainous regions that lacked foodstuffs; and they experienced a great shortage of literally all kinds of supplies—above all, of weapons and ammunition. Moreover, the enemy was trying to stir up discord between the peoples of that multinational state, and thereby to complicate the situation. But these difficulties were overcome; and by the end of 1943, with our aid, much had been accomplished. The flames of the people's struggle encompassed the whole country. Yugoslavia was proclaimed a democratic federative republic, and the King was forbidden to return. In the course of the armed struggle against the occupying troops, the resistance forces had grown stronger; and the time had come to switch over from partisan actions to planned operations—from scattered detachments to regular military formations. The National Liberation Army was well organized, and the systems for supplying and training troops were well set up. Staffs on all levels were organized and began to function well.

Following the Teheran Conference (November 28–December 1, 1943), the General Staff received instructions to send a Soviet Military Mission to Comrade Tito (Josip Broz) in Yugoslavia. In view of the fact that what was involved was not only an armed struggle but the restructuring of armed forces on regular bases, the chief of mission had to be someone with a broad knowledge in the field of military science and military building.

The choice fell on Gen. Nikolai Vasilyevich Korneyev, a former instructor at the General Staff Academy. I had studied with him, and I must say the choice was excellent. Korneyev was forty-two years old. He had a good knowledge of military affairs, and, along with everything else, he combined boldness with caution—a trait by no means superfluous in the Yugoslavia of that time. The person named deputy chief was Col. S. V. Sokolov, an experienced man of forty who had a good understanding of air operations in mountainous country.

On January 17, 1944, in two planes—one piloted by A. S.

Shornikov and the other by Lebedev—the small staff of the mission flew from Moscow via Astrakhan, Teheran, Habbaniya, Cairo, and Tunis to the Italian town of Bari. Here, in the very "heel" of the Italian boot, a British air base was located. From this point the mission was to fly to the mountainous region of Bosnia, where the Supreme Headquarters of the National Liberation Army of Yugoslavia (AVNOJ) was located.

In Bari the Soviet general and the other officers were accorded an appropriate welcome by all British allies. Bari had a good airfield and the necessary warehouses and communications facilities. Later all this was transferred to the Soviet Armed Forces at the request of our government, since Soviet aid to the forces of the AVNOJ was being delivered on a very broad scale. Prior to the creation of a Soviet front in Yugoslavia, all deliveries went by air across the Adriatic. Our allies, who had other and better air bases, also took part in these operations.

But getting into Yugoslavia was no easy matter. The British military authorities, personified by Air Vice-marshal William Elliot, kept putting off the departure of our aircraft, citing the fog over the Adriatic, the deep snows, and the impossibility of landing in the region where we were supposed to set down. Day after day passed. . . .

The temperamental commanders of our aircraft proposed to fly nonetheless, but the risk was very great. Korneyev ordered the entire staff of his military mission to train every day in methods of making glider landings—or in parachuting, if glider landings were not feasible. There was, of course, a risk in this case, but it was not all that great; and Moscow decided to permit it. On Red Army Day (February 23, 1944) the glider landing of our military mission was successfully accomplished. From that day on, General Korneyev and the officers of his mission were constantly with the Supreme Staff of the AVNOJ. They shared with their Yugoslav comrades all the hardships of the war and the joy of victory over the Nazi occupying forces.

S. V. Sokolov remained in Bari at the base which (as said earlier) was soon transferred to us. He had at his disposal transport and fighter squadrons of twelve planes each. They were supposed to transport cargo (weapons, ammunition, and medical supplies) to the AVNOJ, to fly in officers and medical personnel, and to bring out wounded. They had their hands full. It suffices to say that the Soviet pilots flew more than five thousand Yugoslav officers and soldiers across the front line to various zones of operations. Also, many other unforeseen problems arose; for example, rescuing the AVNOJ Supreme Staff and Tito himself from a critical situation. The pilots had to fly over the sea, through the mountains, and in the most varied parts of the country. Cargoes were flown into Chernogoria, Serbia, Bosnia, Dalmatia, Macedonia, Slovenia, and Croatia. It was also necessary to fly into Albania and Greece.

Like Korneyev, Sokolov had to take important decisions on his own more than once; in June 1944, for example, when the enemy tried to do away with the leadership of the AVNOJ in Drvar— something we shall recount later. Over and over again the CO of the base (Sokolov) flew to areas where Soviet planes were supposed to land and checked on the conditions for landing. It was only after having done this that he would issue his orders. The entire staff of the Soviet base in Bari was closely knit in relations of comradeship and friendship. Far from their homeland, the pilots, ground crews, and supporting personnel felt that they represented the great world of socialism, and worthily carried out their difficult military duties until the end of the war.

A Soviet Military Mission headed by Maj. Gen. A. A. Kislenko was attached to the staff of the commander of the Allied Mediterranean Expeditionary Forces. And in the last stage of World War II, when the destruction of imperialist Japan was being completed, a group of Soviet liaison officers, headed by Rear Admiral Ivanovsky, was attached to the U. S. Pacific Fleet.

After the Teheran Conference, there was a greater development of co-operation among the Soviet Armed Forces and their allies. As we know, the very important question of opening a second front in Europe was finally settled. I have already written how it came about that I was with the Supreme Commander at Teheran and had to maintain his daily contact with the General Staff and the fronts.

The Soviet delegation was very impressive. The talks were held in the Soviet Embassy; and one could see how great and authoritative was the significance of the victories of our Armed Forces. The results of the turn of the tide in the war—a turn that took place at Stalingrad and Kursk, Kharkov and Kiev, on the Dnieper and on the Sozh—were tangible and visible. They were the chief reason why our allies sat down at that round table and agreed to open a second front. One possibility was becoming all too plain: that the Soviet soldier would defeat the Nazis all on his own, while our allies were left in the background of victory.

The Soviet delegation was able at that time to defeat Churchill's reactionary scheme of a "Balkan variant" of the attack by the Western Allies, and insisted on the incomparably more effective and politically important landing of Anglo-American forces in France. The Teheran Conference was a kind of brilliant summing-up of the glorious victories of Soviet arms in 1943; and at the same time it served as a governing principle for the crushing blows (united by a single design) of the Allied coalition on the fronts of Europe in the next year.

In the second half of 1944, when the Soviet Armed Forces were developing their great liberation campaign beyond the borders of the USSR and the second front had been opened, the question of co-operation among the coalition forces began to be solved practically and on a large scale. In this connection the General Staff had to take on much more work. Every day, we had to inform our allies as to the situation on the front of our forces, to specify targets and delineations for bombings by Soviet and Allied aircraft, and to co-ordinate timetables for operations and departures of forces and fleets. We lent several airfields in the Poltava region to Anglo-American air units that had come from England and Italy to bomb enemy targets.

Meetings between A. I. Antonov, N. V. Slavin, and other General Staff officers and the chiefs and representatives of missions, various kinds of delegations, and individuals from Allied countries became a standard component of our working day. The matters agreed upon at such meetings were later discussed and decided upon by the Stavka.

29

The supreme organ of the coalition of anti-Nazi powers was the Big Three, at whose conferences were taken the basic decisions determining the character, time, and size of impending operations by armed forces and the direction of the main blows of the Allied armies. I have already mentioned Teheran. But there were also the Crimean (Yalta) and Potsdam conferences, which were held in 1945 on February 4–11 and July 17–August 2, respectively.

The co-ordination of strategic plans—which were carefully executed subsequently—was arranged at the first conference. A. I. Antonov delivered a briefing on the military situation, with a prognosis for the future. The same thing was done by the chiefs of staff of the two other nations of the Big Three. The Soviet General Staff expressed the hope that the Allied armies would take into account the weakening of the Nazi forces in the west due to the Red Army's advance to the Oder, and would go over to the attack in the first half of February 1945. And it was at Yalta that the timetable and conditions were fixed for the USSR's entry into the war against Japan.

Finally, at the Potsdam Conference the joint policy of the members of the anti-Nazi coalition toward Germany was worked out. This was the main subject of the talks. Also, at Potsdam the Soviet Government confirmed its commitment to enter the war against Japan. The defeat of that militaristic aggressor liberated peoples enslaved by the Japanese occupying forces and brought World War II to an end.

In addition to conferences, urgent correspondence often helped to solve pressing problems of the war—in particular, those concerning operations of the Armed Forces. Such was the case, for example, in the winter of 1945, when the Allies were in a critical position in the Ardennes. It was on the basis of a message from Churchill, ending with the phrase "I regard the matter as urgent," that it was decided to move up the date for launching our Vistula-Oder operation. Our forces attacked on January 12.

Prior to all three conferences, the General Staff prepared material on military questions for the head of the Soviet Government.

By solving many important problems, the General Staff assured that the Supreme Command would have control over the forces at all fronts of the war. This began with the preparation of proposals for the solution, and ended with follow-up on its execution. Along with the big, important, and laborious job of gathering and processing data on the situation, the General Staff organized and maintained constant contact with the forces.

The security aspect of controlling the forces was also very important. Codes, ciphers, and security procedures—all these were handled by one special bureau. I shall always gratefully remember Sr. Lt. Peter Stepanovich Baklykov, who used to go to the front with me. Also, it was he who handled the military cipher communications during the Teheran Conference. In 1970 I chanced across Peter Stepanovich, now a colonel, and we exchanged reminiscences with great pleasure.

Beginning in late 1944 the General Staff's control function became somewhat more complicated, since the practice of having Stavka representatives at the front was being sharply restricted. As the reader will recall, the necessity for this practice was determined in the first year of the Great Patriotic War; and since then the work of the representatives had been an important, if temporary, element in strategic decision-making. But on the eve of the war's end the question was posed: Should this link in strategic decision-making be retained? Things were going well on the front, and the commanders had learned from experience. But at this point there arose a doubt as to whether the Stavka could, from Moscow, oversee the huge military operations on the front and at sea. Might it not, with an unexpected change in the course of the war, lose command control of the Armed Forces?

It should be noted that Stalin first posed this question when he was hearing a briefing on the General Staff's first drafts of operational plans for the concluding campaign of the war. General Antonov asked for time to think it over. The Supreme Commander took an understanding attitude toward Antonov's request, but asked the same question of G. K. Zhukov. The latter said he felt that at this stage of the war the Stavka could get along without representatives: The number of fronts had diminished, the length of the fronts was shorter, control of the fronts by the Center was functioning well, and the commanders had acquired greater skill in their métier. In his opinion, these things made it possible to exercise reliable control over the fronts without the aid of Stavka representatives.

As always in such situations, Antonov immediately got in touch with A. M. Vasilevsky, chief of the General Staff, who at the time was in the Baltic area. They conferred. The General Staff, it turned out, did not agree that the institution of Stavka representatives should be immediately and completely eliminated. There were many reasons. Although the length of the front was shorter, the line still extended for more than two thousand kilometers, and the winter campaign was to be launched all along that front. The headquarters of fronts and armies were far away. The situation on various sectors of the front differed greatly, and sometimes changed radically (near Balaton, for example). Therefore the General Staff felt that the Stavka could do without representatives only in certain cases when the stability and effectiveness of control from the Center had been fully guaranteed.

The Supreme Commander took the side of the General Staff. He did eliminate the practice of having Stavka representatives at the fronts in the main sector, the west,[10] and took over control of the fronts personally. But Marshal of the Soviet Union S. K. Timoshenko remained the Stavka representative with the 2nd and 3rd Ukrainian fronts (Stavka Directive No. 11012, dated January 21, 1945). At the time, Vasilevsky was Stavka representative with the 1st and 2nd Baltic fronts. (Incidentally, his reports to the Stavka on the situation at the fronts and his proposals for operations were distinguished by exhaustive thoroughness and clarity.) After Vasilevsky returned (briefly) to Moscow, the position of Stavka representative with these fronts was taken (as a second job) by Marshal of the Soviet Union L. A. Govorov, who continued to command the Leningrad Front (Stavka Directive No. 11018, dated February 2, 1945).

Subsequent events confirmed the correctness of that decision.

Many other bureaus—e.g., the military transport service—played a very great role in the work of the General Staff. The

---

[10] I.e., the center of the Soviet-German front, as opposed to its northern and southern flanks. (Translator's note.)

regrouping and forward movement of forces, the delivery of materials and supplies, and evacuation—these things would have been unthinkable without an efficient military transport service. The movement of troops via railroad and waterways, through the air and along the ground—all this is handled by the staff. The staff plans what is to be moved, where, by what kind of transport, and when; and the special bureaus handling these services are the executors of the plan. It is they who organize traffic control for all ways and means of communication.

In addition to the military transport service, all large staffs, from the General Staff on down, have bureaus handling the planning of supplying troops with arms, ammunition, equipment, fuel and lubricants, clothing, foodstuffs, and other supplies required by the troops. But these are not quartermaster officers. They have no warehouses, no bases, no means of transportation. They have only documents: plans, lists, summaries (and today, computers). The most valuable possession of such bureaus is the skill of the personnel, who are experts at their job. They keep track of all kinds of materials being supplied. They know what is in the warehouses and what the output of industry is. They draw up long-range plans on whose basis requisitions are made out; they submit, for approval, lists showing the distribution of material resources. In a word, these supply bureaus control the basis on which the combat-readiness of an army is built. An operations officer may plan a very promising operation; but if he does it without taking material possibilities into account, the operation remains merely red arrows on a map and will never be put into effect.

We operations officers realized the importance of correct relations with all these services and endeavored to help them. In their turn, they did everything they could to fulfill the operations officers' requisitions promptly and as well as possible. Therefore there has always existed between us not only a feeling of solidarity on the job but human warmth and strong friendship.

The most important jobs are inevitably accompanied by irksome tasks that are often completely unforeseen. We had an especially large number of the latter right after the war. The following is an example. Shortly after the war it was decided to extend an official invitation to Field Marshal Bernard Montgomery to visit our country. He was the most prominent British field commander, and besides he had by this time received the title Viscount of Alamein. As usual, there was considerable discussion as to the time of the visit. Finally, January 1947 was settled upon.

On the very day of his arrival, the marshal was to pay a visit to the chief of the General Staff, Marshal of the Soviet Union A. M. Vasilevsky. It was decided that on this occasion Montgomery would be given a Russian souvenir. We thought long and hard about what we should give our eminent guest, but none of the usual Russian souvenirs seemed to be right. And at that time no special souvenirs were yet being manufactured. Finally someone suggested giving Russian military togs: a squirrel-skin *bekesha* (winter coat) and a general's *papakha* (Caucasian fur cap) made of gray Astrakhan. The suggestion was approved, and the bekesha and papakha were ordered. By the time of his arrival they were ready and were being kept in the office of Gen. M. M. Potapov.

Finally the field marshal arrived and came into the office, where he was met by A. M. Vasilevsky, A. I. Antonov, N. V. Slavin, and the present writer, who was to accompany Montgomery on his visit to the General Staff Academy. After an exchange of greetings, we had a brief talk. Then final adjustments were made in the program for the visit. Montgomery, either because he wanted to be considered eccentric or from some other motive, announced that he would start his working day at 6 A.M. and go to bed at 9 P.M. He told us that he had followed this schedule throughout the war, even during its most critical moments. We promised to maintain that schedule, although to ourselves we thought he was lucky to have been able to keep such a schedule while fighting a war. As we understood things, in wartime one could sleep only when the situation permitted it. And that, by the way, is what all of us had done.

At this point Marshal Vasilevsky, with a few words appropriate to the occasion, presented the bekesha and the papakha. Montgomery was very pleased with the gifts. He looked them over at length and asked whether the squirrel skin was genuine and how much the fur had cost. No one could tell him the price, so I had to go to the telephone and try to find out. Then Montgomery decided to try on the bekesha and the papakha. When he put them on, it turned out that while the papakha was a perfect fit the bekesha was too long. The "reliable data" (as they are called) that we had got for the tailor were sharply at odds with reality. The British field marshal, not being distinguished for his mighty hero's frame, simply swam in the bekesha.

Vasilevsky said soothingly, "We can fix that. By tomorrow morning the bekesha will be delivered to you, properly tailored."

But this wasn't enough for the field marshal. He wanted the bekesha shortened right then and there, while he waited. The rest of us exchanged puzzled glances.

"Sergei Matveyevich," Vasilevsky said to me, "handle the business of the tailor."

I went out. Some forty minutes later I came back, bringing a tailor with a sewing machine. Measurements were taken, and in the reception room of the chief of the General Staff, the tailor sat down to work.

Meanwhile, the time allotted for the official part of the visit had elapsed. We got into an unconstrained conversation, recalling deeds of the past. Freely and in great detail, Montgomery recounted the battle of El Alamein (well known to us) in which he had beat Rommel. The coffee cups went the rounds for the third time. Finally the tailor finished his work. The bekesha was tried on once more, and this time it fitted. Satisfied, and without taking it off, Montgomery left the General Staff offices.

The next day I accompanied him to the General Staff Academy. After visiting the auditoriums and the laboratories Montgomery gave a lecture on that same battle of El Alamein. A few minutes after he started talking, two British officers began, quite unexpectedly, to distribute leaflets among the audience. That went beyond the scope of the program, and I began to worry: Why these leaflets? What was in them? Taking one, I asked the interpreter sitting next to me to read it. It turned out that the leaflet, too, was about El Alamein—a brief account. . . . I wondered how many leaflets and titles such as "viscount" would be suitable for our field commanders, like Zhukov or Konev, under whose leadership we had won a whole series of brilliant victories that were several times as important as El Alamein, in both their results and their scope.

On the eve of the field marshal's departure, Stalin gave a dinner in Montgomery's honor. Some twenty persons were invited. At the appointed time we military men and the representatives of the Ministry of Foreign Affairs gathered in the Great Kremlin Palace. Five minutes remained before the dinner was to begin, and Montgomery had still not arrived. We phoned the residence, and were told he had already left. Just then the door opened, and Montgomery entered the reception room, wearing his bekesha and papakha.

"What's the matter?" we asked, rushing to meet the Soviet officers who were escorting him. "Why didn't you take off his hat and coat at the cloakroom?"

"He categorically refused," was the answer.

Montgomery, noticing our interference and the puzzlement on the faces of all present, said, "I want Generalissimo Stalin to see me in a Russian uniform."

At that moment, Stalin and the members of his Cabinet entered. Montgomery explained to him what was going on. Stalin laughed, and had himself photographed with Montgomery. Then Monty (as the English call him) took off his coat and hat, and the dinner began.

The next day we went to the Central Airport to see Montgomery off. He showed up in the same bekesha and papakha, received the report from the officer commanding the guard of honor, and then flew off, never parting from our gifts. . . .

During the war years, our duties at the General Staff completely absorbed us. They left us neither time nor energy for any other activity. The few hours set aside for rest could only be used for that purpose. We treasured every minute, and learned to fall asleep instantly. Even when the enemy's fate was sealed, we General Staff officers continued to live in the General Staff building. Every day we would move in the same fixed pattern: from the work area to the cafeteria, then back to work, then to one's cot, then back to the work area again. There was no time off, except to go for a haircut. In the barbershop the mirrors gleamed, one heard the swishing of the white towels, and one rested one's eyes, while the master barber's hands touched one's hair so softly and gently that we often fell asleep. Then, having had our rest, freshly shaven and with a haircut, and having smoked a cigarette after getting out of the barber's chair, we would go back to the work area again.

Even after the war the schedule for the General Staff remained very trying. The times demanded it. The nation and the Armed Forces had switched to a peacetime footing, but the state of readiness and alarm was maintained: The United States was already brandishing the atomic bomb.

As had been his practice during the war years, Stalin almost never left himself any free time. He lived to work, and did not alter his habit of working up until three or four in the morning (and sometimes later), then getting back to work at ten. And he made everyone else having working relations with him—including the General Staff—follow the same schedule.

We often had to go to the Kremlin or to "Near House" (the nearby *dacha*) with reports on various problems of national defense. One may say that Stalin's hours of rest during the war were very few. Nor did he have many hours of rest after the war.

Stalin never went anywhere, except for holiday concerts and the entertainment that was usually given after ceremonial gatherings. His domestic "theater" consisted of music from the radio and phonograph records. Of the new phonograph records delivered to him, he tried out the greater part himself, and immediately rated them. Each record was labeled in his own hand as "good," "tolerable," "bad," or "trash." Only records bearing the first two labels were left on his night table and on the table in the living room near the awkward, console-type automatic record player given him by the Americans in 1945. The other records were taken away. In addition to the automatic record player, he had a Russian-made phonograph with a crank. The boss himself carried it to where he wanted it.

Also, we knew about his fondness for *gorodki* (a kind of skittles). For a game of gorodki, we split into teams of four or five persons each. (Naturally, the teams were formed of those who wanted to play. The others loudly proclaimed they were "sick.") As a rule, ten persons played. We began with the "cannon." Those who failed were taunted, sometimes rather roughly—something that Stalin himself did not escape. He played rather unskillfully but with much excitement. After each strike he was very satisfied and invariably said, "That's what we do to them!" But when he missed he would begin to search his pockets for matches and then light his pipe, or suck at it hard.

At this villa there was no park or orchard, no "nicely" trimmed hedges or trees. Stalin loved nature in its natural state, untouched by the hand of man. Around the house was a wild growth of conifers and leaf-bearing trees, everywhere thick, which had never known the ax.

Not far from the house stood several hollow trees without branches where birds had nested and squirrels had made their homes. This was a real kingdom of birds. Before this city of hollow trees stood tables for feeding the birds. Almost every day Stalin came there and fed his feathered foster children.

In concluding this chapter I should like to emphasize that my account of the people in the departments of the General Staff with whom I, as an operations officer, had close dealings during the war years is of course far from complete. They did a very big, complex, and responsible job making it possible for the Stavka and the Supreme Commander to oversee military operations. The General Staff officers' patriotism, their clear minds and their skill, plus their tireless and self-sacrificing work, served the common cause of victory over the enemy.

2

THE BEGINNINGS OF
CO-OPERATION IN WAR

**Spring joys. A wounded beast is even more danger-
ous. The tortuous route of Anders's army. The intrigues of the Polish bourgeois government. Creating the Army of People's Poland. The baptism of
fire of the Polish adopted brothers. A letter from
the Supreme Commander to Churchill. Look before
you leap. On Polish soil. The offensive must be
secured. A conference at the Stavka. The mysterious
carafe.**

March 26, 1944: the 1,009th day of the war. Under conditions of
the spring *rasputitsa,* or time of the muddy roads, the unprecedented offensive of the Ukrainian fronts had led to a serious defeat for the German Army Group South. It had not only suffered
great losses but had been cut in two. Forces of the 1st Unkrainian
Front, temporarily under the command of Marshal G. K. Zhukov
after the wounding of N. F. Vatutin, had reached the foothills of
the Carpathians. In mid-February the 2nd Ukrainian Front, commanded by Marshal I. S. Konev, acting jointly with Vatutin's front,
had dealt the enemy a "little Stalingrad" near Korsun-Shevchen-
kovsky. Then it had driven on to the Dnieper, forced it over a

length of 175 kilometers, and taken the town and railroad junction of Beltsy. Immediately thereafter, without pausing in their offensive, Konev's forces, over a front of 85 kilometers, reached the national boundary along the Prut River!

We had long waited for that day. As soon as the report from the 2nd Ukrainian Front had reached the General Staff, where at the time I was acting chief of the Operations Department, I informed the Supreme Commander. He ordered that Konev's forces be given a salute of the first category: twenty-four volleys from 324 guns. A. A. Gryzlov (my deputy) and I sat down to write out the order. At nine that evening the rockets of the victory salute lighted up the Moscow sky.

I would not undertake to describe in words the feelings that possessed us at that time. Our cherished, passionate desire to liberate our motherland had been realized. But it was accompanied by another dream, no less lofty: that of helping the peoples who had fallen under the yoke of fascism. We realized that the struggle for the liberation of Rumania, Poland, and other countries had been started by the Soviet people when the first shots were fired on June 22, 1941. But now, when our soldiers had reached the border, the Army was to undertake the direct fulfillment of its liberation mission beyond the borders of the USSR.

The 3rd Ukrainian Front was also advancing successfully under the command of General of the Army R. Ya. Malinovsky. It destroyed the Krivoy Rog grouping of Nazi forces, reached the Southern Bug, and on that same day, March 26, launched the operation that led to the liberation of Odessa and the advance to the lower course of the Dnieper. At the General Staff we learned of the progress of this operation from A. M. Vasilevsky, who was coordinating the actions of the 3rd and 4th Ukrainian fronts as a Stavka representative.

At a press conference on April 2, 1944, the Soviet Government stated that in several sectors units of the Red Army had crossed the Prut River and entered Rumanian territory, and that the Supreme Command had issued an order to pursue the enemy until he was completely defeated and surrendered.

The Soviet Government stated that it had no intention of acquiring any part of the Rumanian territory or of changing the existing social structure of that country. The entry of Soviet forces into Rumanian territory "was dictated by purely military necessity and continuing resistance by the forces of the enemy."[1]

By mid-April the Soviet forces, having crossed the Prut, reached a line running through Rădăuți, Orgeyev, and Dubossary, and occupied an enveloping position with respect to the enemy.

At the General Staff, following the tradition, we prepared materials for the Supreme Commander's May Day Order. Our spirits were high: The day of the complete liberation of the motherland had come. And at the Stavka . . . Well, at a time when we were chasing the enemy out of our house, you'd think the mood would be better.

Such were the thoughts of Antonov (deputy chief of the General Staff) and myself as we went to the Stavka for the routine report. The Supreme Commander was in an excellent mood, as he usually was when things were going well at the front, and he rapidly dealt with all the problems. As we discussed the May Day Order, both Antonov and I expressed confidence that now, beyond our borders, all difficulties would be more rapidly overcome. But Stalin stared hard at us, and our enthusiasm cooled in short order. He said that now the enemy was like a wounded animal who has to crawl back into its lair to lick its wounds. But a wounded beast is even more dangerous. It has to be tracked down and killed in its own lair.

Stalin stressed that the liberation of the peoples under the yoke of fascism was a job no less difficult than chasing the fascist forces out of the Soviet Union. Expanding his idea, he said that beyond our borders our forces would become involved in political contexts that differed radically from our socialist context. That there, in the course of the armed conflict, the interests of antagonistic classes would influence relations with our allies. We had good friends (he said) but also enemies, especially from the milieu of the previously ruling circles and those strata of the population who supported them.

[1] *Vneshnyaya politika Sovetskogo Soyuza v period Otechestvennoi voiny* (Moscow: Gospolitizdat, 1946), Vol. II, p. 105.

The Supreme Commander's May Day Order was restrained, in the spirit of those considerations.

And soon we ourselves were convinced of the correctness of Stalin's warning. Over a considerable period of time, attempts to continue the offensive into the depths of Rumania were unsuccessful. The tremendous fatigue of the troops began to make itself felt. They were weakened by losses, and needed reinforcements and more equipment. On April 17 the 1st Ukrainian Front, on orders from the Stavka, went on the defensive, followed by the 2nd and 3rd Ukrainian fronts. They dug in along a forward line extending from the boundary east of Brody, to the west of Ternopol, Kolomyya, Paşcani, to the north of Iaşi (Jassy), to the east of Kishinev, and from there to the Dniester. The fronts were ordered to be ready to resume the offensive in late May. This date was later set back, since beginning on May 30 the enemy made several mighty efforts to overrun our units and throw them back across the Prut. German units participating in the attack included four armored divisions (the 14th, the 23rd, the 24th, and the SS "Death's Head" Division), the "Gross Deutschland" motorized division, and several infantry units. They had a very strong support, both artillery and air. After ten days of hard fighting, the enemy, although he had suffered great losses, managed to drive wedges into the Soviet dispositions, up to thirty kilometers in some cases.

The enemy's vigorous actions naturally provoked anxiety at the front, the Stavka, and the General Staff. According to our information, the German fascist command then had available the forces to strike a blow not only near Iaşi but in the region of Kishinev, where he had at least seven infantry and five armored and motorized divisions. The enemy might well risk throwing everything he had into an attack so as to wrest the initiative from us in the direction of Beltsy and break into the rear of our grouping of forces to the west of the Dniester.

The threat was very serious, but the Soviet soldiers stood firm on this line as well. A stubborn defense by the forces of the 2nd Ukrainian Front wrecked the plans of the fascist command. R. Ya. Malinovsky, commanding the front, reported to the General Staff that in these battles the enemy had lost a substantial part of four armored divisions. And yet we could not attack at this point: Those hard-fought battles had cost our forces a lot, too.

Since a stalemate had developed in the southwest, especially as regards tanks, and it was impossible to change it in our favor, the General Staff proposed renewing the offensive on this sector of the front only after the enemy had been defeated on other sectors. The Stavka agreed, and the forces began to prepare for Operation Bagration and to carry out other strategic ideas of the Supreme Command. The postponement of operations in the southwest by no means meant that their planning was canceled: It was being worked on both at the front and at the General Staff.

I should like to stress that we did not confine ourselves to military matters. The General Staff, together with the Main Political Administration and the military councils of the fronts and the armies, trained the Soviet soldier for his special position beyond the borders of his own country as a representative of the most advanced social system: socialism. As a soldier of the Soviet Armed Forces.

In Rumania we did not launch offensive operations until August 20. But in Poland our forces kept advancing throughout the summer, reaching the Vistula moving toward Praga, the eastern suburb of Warsaw. In the course of the operations on Polish soil the Polish 1st Army under the command of Gen. Zigmund Berling fought shoulder to shoulder with our troops. By then the Polish soldier had become our loyal adopted brother-in-arms.

Owing to the nature of my duties, I happened to be in on the birth of the People's Army of Poland, and to remain in constant contact with the Polish Armed Forces on the territory of the USSR. In this connection I should like to dwell in greater detail on the Voisko Polskoye[2]: on its origin and development, and the difficult path it negotiated.

On the first day of the Great Patriotic War, a group of Polish officers who were in the Soviet Union appealed to the Soviet Gov-

---

[2] The rather archaic Russian appellation for (roughly) Polish Armed Forces. The author insists that this was a separate organization from the Armia Ludowa (People's Army) (see p. 58) until they were merged (see p. 84). Some historians, however, treat them as the same. (Translator's note.)

ernment. They wrote: "As representatives of one of the peoples oppressed by the fascist aggressor, we feel that the only route to the liberation of the Polish people lies through co-operation with the USSR, within the framework of which our motherland can develop as it should." The officers declared that they would do their duty honorably.

This incident was undoubtedly a symptom of deep processes taking place in the consciousness of those who had suffered from fascism. It made it possible to hope for a military alliance with the Poles against the Nazis.

Their proposals were approved. On July 30, 1941, the Polish Government in London, headed by Gen. W. Sikorski, reached agreement with the Soviet Government on mutual assistance in the war against Nazi Germany. At that time we agreed to create, on our own territory, a Polish army headed by a commander appointed by the Polish Government in London. In that connection, it was stated that the forces created in the USSR would fight against the common enemy jointly with us. The agreement stated: "The Polish Army on the territory of the USSR will be operationally subordinated to the USSR Supreme Command, which will include a representative of the Polish Army."[3]

Details of the command organization and combat application of the Polish forces were specified in a special military agreement between the USSR Supreme Command and the Polish command. It was concluded in Moscow on August 14, 1941, and Major General Vasilevsky was empowered to sign for our side.

As commander in chief of the Polish forces on the territory of the USSR, Sikorski named Gen. W. Anders, who had had experience commanding a group of forces during the Polish-German War of 1939.

By the time the military agreement had been concluded, preparations for forming the Polish Army had virtually begun. Contingents of draftees were established, materials and supplies were allocated, and training bases were built. At the request of the Polish command, preparations were stepped up. We had no objec-

---

[3] *Vneshnyaya politika Sovetskogo Soyuza v period Otechestvennoi voiny*, Vol. I, p. 138.

tions, since General Anders had proposed that as soon as they were ready, the divisions be sent to the Soviet-German front. In early September, trainloads of Polish draftees began to move along the railroad toward the assembly points, and by the eighth of the month the first soldier was on duty at the headquarters of the commander in chief.

At first two infantry divisions were formed, the 5th and the 6th. They consisted of Polish citizens who had reached the USSR as refugees or in some other way. But the influx of volunteers was great, and the originally estimated strength of the Polish Army— 30,000 men—was considerably exceeded: By October 25, 1941, it had reached 41,500, and was still growing. The assembly points were located along the Volga and in the Orenburg area—in Buzuluk, Totskoye, and Tatishchevo. In those very trying times, the Soviet Government provided great material aid to Poland. In particular, the USSR granted the Polish Government in London an over-all loan of 100 million rubles for assistance to Polish citizens. Also, a special loan of 300 million rubles was granted for maintenance of the Polish Army on the territory of the USSR. The Polish troops were provided with Soviet arms and equipment. They were given the same kind and amount of supplies as the divisions of the Red Army then being formed.

All this meant more work for the General Staff. We set up the position of liaison officer for Polish formations in the USSR, and Maj. Gen. of Tank Forces A. P. Panfilov was appointed to it. I knew him from our having studied together at the Red Army Academy of Motorization and Mechanization. He had no staff to speak of. Later, the matter of overseeing the formation of foreign forces was systematized. This bureau was put under the Council of People's Commissars (SNK), since it had to deal with various departments of government. Its chief was called the SNK Representative to Foreign Military Formations in the USSR. He reported directly to the Chairman of the GKO (National Defense Committee) and the Chairman of the SNK, and had in his bureau a special group of officers from the Commissariat of Defense.

By late autumn of 1941, the Polish 5th Division had been formed and trained, and the 6th was successfully completing training. But they didn't get to the front, because in December General Sikorski proposed to the Soviet Government that the contingents of Polish forces be expanded to 96,000, and that six divisions be created instead of two. Yet just before we went over to the counterattack near Moscow on December 4, the Polish Government formally announced that "forces of the Polish Republic located on the territory of the Soviet Union will fight the German brigands hand in hand with the Soviet forces."[4] Despite the very difficult situation our country was in, the Soviet Government agreed to the forming of additional Polish forces. But we had no weapons. The Poles declared that the British Government would supply them, and went on with their work. At Sikorski's request, the assembly points were shifted to Central Asia, where construction was begun on camps, military schools, medical facilities, etc. But even after being trained here, the Polish troops were still not sent to the Soviet-German front. This was due first of all to the selfish and treasonous (vis-à-vis its own people) policy of the Polish Government in Exile, which did not want to fight the Nazis alongside us. Even Sikorski—the most sensible man in that bourgeois government—could not resist the pressure from his colleagues. As the Polish Communists opined at the time, his ideological positions did not correspond to the interests of the people.

British leaders, including the Prime Minister, were also putting on pressure with respect to where the Polish forces should be employed. Those leaders were doubtful of the Soviet state's strength, and as we know did not rule out the possibility of its collapse in the near future. But what disturbed them was not the fate of the Soviet state but their own interests—above all the necessity of defending India against a Nazi invasion. And they intended to do this by using the Polish forces assembled in the USSR. At the same time they wanted to keep the bourgeois regime in Poland, so that close military collaboration between us and the Poles was undesirable.

This double-faced policy explains two tendencies in the sympathies of the Polish forces. The most far-seeing and courageous of the Polish soldiers favored the punctual and consistent perform-

[4] Ibid., p. 352.

ance of contractual obligations toward the USSR in the struggle against the Nazis, fighting together with us. Those with this point of view looked upon the situation of the Soviet state as a transitory phenomenon and had no doubt that the final victory would be ours. And they associated the independence of Poland with that victory. The others—and above all the officers of the Polish command—regarded the alliance with the USSR as a temporary tactical move. They did not want to wage war against the Nazi aggressors shoulder to shoulder with the Red Army. They placed all their hopes in the Western Allies, and wanted to avoid the front in the USSR and to make their way out of our territory.

The Soviet authorities and command did not interfere in the internal matters of the Polish forces, although they knew of the conflict between these two tendencies. Also, since joint operations corresponded to the interests of the Soviet Union and of an independent democratic Poland, we hoped for a turn-around in the attitude of the Polish commanders, and continued vigorously to help them in forming their forces.

Time went by. The hard-fought war continued. . . . Near Moscow we went over to the counterattack, threw the enemy back from the walls of the capital, and forced him to relinquish his plans. The course of the war had changed. The new situation on the front demanded that the Polish command make new decisions. Now, when the Soviet armies were driving the Nazis back and the actions in the area of the capital had developed into a general offensive, we needed every combat-ready unit. An especially great deal could be accomplished by pursuing the enemy. But the Polish Government in Exile did not agree with this, although they had two divisions well trained and equipped with Soviet weapons. The stronger was the 5th Infantry Division, with 12,500 men. Its soldiers and junior officers repeatedly declared they wanted to go into combat against the enemy. And our government proposed the same thing, in accordance with the military agreement. But the answer from Sikorski and Anders was the same as before: "We're not ready."

Even under those circumstances, and at a time when it was experiencing great shortages of literally everything, the USSR punctually fulfilled its contractual obligations vis-à-vis the Polish Government, and continued to help in the training of Polish forces. As for Anders's hopes for help from London, it soon became apparent that the British did not intend to supply the weapons for the remaining divisions. And we could not help: The machine tools for arms manufacture that had been evacuated from the western regions of the country were still on freight trains moving along branch lines in Siberia and the Urals. This was a time when Stalin was distributing weapons for the Red Army almost item by item.

In February 1942 the way things were going in the war compelled the Soviet Government to again ask Anders when the Polish Army would be ready and when it would be sent into combat. It was desiderated that the 5th Infantry Division be sent to the front as soon as possible. Anders replied that the forces would not be ready until June 1, and that he could not agree to using them a division at a time. In his opinion, two divisions would make no great difference at the front, whereas a blow by the entire Army might bring operational success and be of great political importance. As for acquiring combat experience, it would be better if it were acquired by the whole Army at once rather than by individual units.

At another time, and under other circumstances, such arguments might have made sense. But at that particular time, when we were on the offensive, putting individual divisions into action was perfectly sensible. And the appearance of Polish forces on the front would have produced a great effect—especially among the populace of Poland, where every bit of news about the resurgence of the Polish Army was eagerly grasped at. Also, this might have been accompanied by a broader development of partisan and underground activity in Poland. But Sikorski again refused sharply.

Decisive events were in the making at the front, and both sides were preparing for them. But how were the London Poles preparing themselves? In March 1942 General Anders went to London. Ostensibly, he had been summoned there for talks about deliveries to the Poles of those British weapons that he had not yet received.

But he returned with instructions to prepare part of his forces . . . for evacuation from the Soviet Union!

The food shortage that our country was undergoing was the pretext for the evacuation. And everyone understood what that was. The Soviet Government had had no choice but to make a further reduction in rations for forces in the rear area. Naturally, that included the Polish formations. Taking advantage of the situation, Sikorski asked the Soviet Government to permit the evacuation of a part of the Polish forces to Iraq. Permission was granted. Between March 23 and April 3, 1942, 31,488 troops of the Polish Army were sent to Iraq. It was primarily newly formed units, without weapons, that were evacuated.

At the time the real reasons for these measures taken by the Polish Government in Exile were not fully known. But many Polish officers and soldiers said, at the time of the evacuation, that they were being sent to the Middle East as cannon fodder for the British. The command had to maneuver and even declare that the Poles were being shipped out in order to be given training and weapons. Then—when they were combat-ready—they would be returned to the USSR to take part in the joint struggle against the fascist forces.

After the first evacuation, the strength of Anders's army was some 42,000 men. The formation of new units continued, and the 5th and 6th divisions perfected their training. In late May the commanding general again went to London. On the thirtieth he cabled Stalin that he felt it necessary to report to him personally on the results of the talks with the British, and to discuss the further forming of the Polish Army. The General Staff had no doubts that things were coming to a head. The Polish commanding general stated that the British were afraid for their colonies, and wanted the Polish forces to defend them, so to speak, with their own bodies. For this reason the Poles had to be removed from the USSR.

But there was also something new: He stated that the British were expecting, in the summer of 1942, a great offensive by the enemy on the eastern front. According to British intelligence, the main blow was to be struck in the direction of the Kuban and the

Caucasus. It was plain that Sikorski's Government in Exile, under pressure from the British, had welched on its earlier commitment to put its forces into action on the Soviet-German front; and was saying it felt it was necessary to evacuate those forces to Iraq. Despite all this, the Polish Prime Minister continued to prevail upon the Soviet Government to call up more Poles and go on forming divisions. Anders told of all this at the Kremlin.

Such a provocative and unjust policy brought about a corresponding reaction. Since the Poles had not met their commitments, and since we were very short of weapons for the Red Army and a very trying situation had developed at the front, the Soviet Government informed the Poles (in July 1942) that it considered the further forming of Polish units in the USSR not feasible, and posed the question of their complete evacuation.

In August 1942 another 44,000 Polish troops were sent to Iraq. They were accompanied by more than 25,000 civilians—most the families of military men. But the most progressive and socially conscious of Anders's officers and soldiers refused to be evacuated, and remained in the Soviet Union. Their number was relatively small, but the role they played in the liberation of their native Poland was very great. Of this, more later.

Thus ended our first attempt to help the brotherly people of Poland from, on Soviet soil, the military forces necessary to offer armed resistance to the occupying troops. It was not wholly successful; and the responsibility for that lies entirely on the shoulders of the Polish landowners and manufacturers who formed the Government in Exile in London. But it should not be regarded as totally fruitless. It had an effect on the activeness of the genuinely revolutionary forces of Poland, who expanded their work for the creation of a people's army, functioning in both the Polish underground and the USSR. And even Anders's soldiers, fighting for Poland far from their motherland, could think things over and correctly evaluate the friendly help from the Soviet land.

In Poland, meanwhile, political developments had led to the creation of the Polish Workers' Party (PPR), to its elaborating new modes of political strategy, and to an intensified struggle for merging patriotic forces into an anti-Nazi national front. The PPR called upon the Polish people to merge their efforts with the struggle of the anti-Nazi coalition—primarily, with that of their nearest neighbor, the Soviet Union. And the People's Guards (Guardia Ludowa), an armed organization headed by Communists, arose in Poland.

The situation on the Soviet-German front had also changed with the crushing defeat of the German fascist forces at Stalingrad, which meant that the tide of the war had turned in our favor. Among the Polish patriots in the USSR, this stepped up the process of unifying the forces of liberation and realizing the practical necessity of fighting on the side of the Red Army.

I remember the spring of 1943 very well. It was a time when the Soviet Supreme Command was preparing the decisive operations near Kursk. The operational plans were being worked out, the forces were being concentrated, the reserves and matériel were being built up. In a word, we were doing everything necessary to bury the plans of Hitler's strategists once and for all, and to put Nazi Germany on the brink of catastrophe.

It was then that the loyal sons of Poland, her Communist leaders who were in exile in our country, spoke out about forming a Union of Polish Patriots in the USSR. In full conformity with the aims of the national front created by the Polish Workers' Party, this organization had the function of uniting for the duration of the war those Poles on Soviet territory—regardless of political, social, or religious views—into a single camp to strive for the defeat and destruction of the enemy. The Union decided that one of its main tasks was to form Polish military units to fight jointly with the Red Army against Nazi Germany.

The Soviet Government received from the democratic forces of Poland a request to create a Polish infantry division in the Soviet Union. The National Defense Committee considered it; and on May 6, 1943, it passed a decree on creating the Tadeusz Kościuszko Polish 1st Division. By June the units and subunits of the new formation were already training in the Seletsky camps near Ryazan. Many Polish Communists took a large part in organizing the planned training of the division.

The Soviet General Staff discerned a special meaning in the creation of the Kościuszko Division. It laid the groundwork for the large-scale formation of the regular people's Armed Forces of Poland. On July 15, 1943, in a ceremonious setting, the division was given its colors, which bore an eagle. The personnel swore an oath of allegiance to the blood-soaked Polish land and to the people fighting against the yoke of fascist occupation. The soldiers of the division solemnly promised to remain loyal allies of the Soviet Union. In the ranks of this division stood the youth of the future People's Army of Poland. Many prominent military leaders of People's Poland began their career here.

On September 1, 1943, the division completed its build-up and training; and on that same day it set off for the Soviet-German front. On October 12, near the small Belorussian hamlet of Lenino, it received its baptism of fire.

Forces of the Western Front had advanced up to this point only a few days before, after two months of fierce battles. Acting jointly with the Kalinin Front, they had driven the enemy out of the so-called Smolensk Gate (from where he had made air strikes against Moscow), barring the way to Poland and, farther on, to Germany. The enemy also realized the importance of this area. Consequently, they fortified it strongly, and concentrated many troops there. General Kurt von Tippelskirch, who in 1944 was commanding the German 4th Army, wrote: "This defensive line ran along before the Dnieper and covered the last great railroad and highway main line before the Pripet Marshes. If the Russians managed to gain control of the highway and the railroad line from Gomel through Mogilev to Orsha, defense east of the Pripet Marshes would hardly be feasible."

The troops of the Thirty-third Army of the Western Front, including the Polish division, had stopped in front of this new defensive line along the approaches to the Dnieper. The line had to be broken. The command of the Thirty-third Army counted on a successful breakthrough; but there were many difficulties facing the troops. In order to ensure success, an extremely high density of artillery was created: 206 guns and mortars per kilometer of front, and 52 tanks. The commanding general hoped to break through the enemy's defense with a frontal assault on a sector directly adjoining Lenino on the north. For this purpose, it was decided to put three rifle divisions in the line in the first echelon. In the center, room was made for an attack by the Polish 1st Infantry Division. To the left, the 42nd Rifle Division would attack; and to the right, the 290th Rifle Division.

The positioning of the more experienced Soviet forces on the flanks was due to the fact that facing the 42nd Rifle Division was a strongly fortified height (217.6), while across from the 290th Division was an accidented terrain with heights and lowlands, made very swampy by streams flowing into the Merei River, impassable for tanks, which ran in front of the enemy's defenses. It was assumed that the 42nd and 290th rifle divisions would quickly take Height 217.6 and the marshy area on the left flank, after which they would move ahead and assure the successful actions of the Polish formation. The job of the Poles was to dislodge the enemy from Height 215.5 and, supported by the success of the Soviet divisions, to break through the enemy's defense to a tactical depth. The plan was to develop the advance of the Soviet and Polish forces by throwing in the 5th Mechanized Corps.

But the battle didn't go as planned: The enemy's forces and possibilities proved to be greater than anticipated. The attack of the 42nd Rifle Division was beaten off. Although it dug in in Height 217.6, it could not take it. The enemy inflicted heavy losses on the attackers and forced them to stop at the edge of the defense-line. The division attacked over and over, but without success. In the sector facing the 290th Rifle Division, the Soviet forces took the swampy flood lands of the stream west of Lenino and captured the hamlet of Trigubov. But the Nazis counterattacked and drove our forces out of the eastern edge of the hamlet. The battle continued, with extremely fierce fighting, but no progress was made here, either. The Polish 1st Infantry Division, attacking in the center, had the greatest success, and broke through to a depth of four kilometers. Eyewitnesses and those taking part in the attack testified to the courage and daring of the Polish soldiers who were carrying out this military mission jointly with Soviet troops. The Polish soldiers and officers displayed unusual firmness and greatness of spirit. On more than one occasion, there was hand-to-hand fighting. . . .

The critical situation on the flanks of the army's attack zone could not be changed in our favor. This was bad for the situation of the Polish forces, who had advanced in the center. They had to beat off repeated counterattacks with strong air support. Our 5th Mechanized Corps was moved up but lost a great many tanks and had no marked influence on the course of the battle. In the sectors of the other armies, too, the attack was beaten off. The enemy's defense line held.

At that time, no real breakthrough was made in the battle of Lenino. The Kościuszko Division and the Soviet divisions had to grind to a halt. But the significance of that first baptism of fire for Soviet-Polish friendship went far beyond that of the usual tactical measures and such notions. Here is the kind of thing engraved upon the memories of those Polish warriors who survived the battle:

> From every hand (recalls W. Zalewsky, at the time an officer in the 3rd Company, 2nd Regiment) we heard shouts of "Hurrah for the Poles—the eagles!" I looked at my men. You'd have said that in their hearts they were still in the forward line, tensed and ready to attack. . . . I remember the first glass of tea I drank at a Russian battery. I remember how they crowded around us—how they embraced us and kissed us and congratulated us.[5]

The battle of Lenino confirmed how great was the readiness of Polish and Soviet soldiers to fight jointly until Nazi Germany had been completely defeated. It made plain their boundless courage, and strengthened even more the Soviet-Polish military alliance. From that battle alone emerged three new Heroes of the Soviet Union who were Polish soldiers.

The order of the day, issued and read to all troops on October 14, testified to the fact that the Polish volunteers were capable of sacrifices for the sake of the great goal before them: the liberation of their motherland. They showed that Poland was alive, was

---

[5] Cheslav Podgursky, *The Poles in the Battle of Lenino* (Warsaw, 1971), p. 109 (in Polish).

striving for freedom, was fighting for it, and would beat the Nazi occupiers. Glorifying the fallen heroes, the order of the day stated: "Now and in the future, victory will be ours."

October 12—the day marking the difficult but glorious starting point of the path to common victory over the enemy—became the holiday of the People's Army of Poland, Voisko Polskoye.

Historical incidents incline one toward reflection. And even then, in 1943, we at the General Staff often went back in thought to the difficult path of the Polish soldiers during the war. In various ways, they returned to their homeland victoriously. But the path chosen by those who fought shoulder to shoulder with the Red Army was closer to the homeland than that of those who were sent to the Middle East.

The Polish forces evacuated from the USSR did not go into combat for a long time. They were stationed in Iraq, in the area of Kerkuk and Mosul, until the Nazis no longer threatened the "pearl of the British crown," India. In July and August of 1943 the Polish 2nd Infantry Corps, commanded by that same General Anders, was formed from these troops and other Polish forces stationed nearby for the same purposes. The time of the corps' formation is remarkable, because it coincided with the battle of Kursk. At that time the turn in the tide of the war was not only established, it was reinforced by the Red Army in several subsequent operations. After that, the situation in the Middle East caused no anxiety in anyone. And so the corps was sent through Palestine to Egypt, and from there (in the first months of 1944) to Italy, where it became part of the British 8th Army. The fighting strength of the corps was almost 50,000 officers and men, and when rear-area services were included it amounted to 60,000 men.

The Polish soldiers fought on the Sangro River, at Monte Cassino, and near Ancona. They showed great valor and genuine soldierly heroism in breaking through many of the enemy's defensive lines. This is borne out not only by the emplacements and trenches won from the enemy on the Gustav Line (the main defensive line of the Nazi forces in Italy) but by the monuments to the soldiers who fell here. The end of the war found the corps in Bologna, which they had liberated on April 21, 1945.

The 2nd Infantry Corps represented only a part of the Polish Armed Forces in the West. With the aid of the Allies, the Government in Exile had formed, in the west, air units, Navy units, and units and formations of land forces. For example, the 1st Armored Division, formed in Scotland and having a strength of 15,500 men, functioned successfully with the opening of the second front in Normandy. As a part of the Canadian 1st Army, it was in the middle of the fighting until the end of the war. Nazi Germany's surrender found this division on the shore of the North Sea, at Wilhelmshaven. The 1st Airborne Brigade, numbering about 2,000 men, was among the Allied forces that carried out the large-scale airborne operation "Market Garden." The brigade showed great heroism in the region of Arnhem.

The foregoing examples could be multiplied, since there were other Polish formations and units among the land forces that fought valorously and made their contribution to the cause of victory. Likewise familiar are the actions of the Polish pilots flying with the RAF. At the war's end there were fourteen divisions of them, each of which corresponded roughly to one Soviet squadron. To their credit were about 1,000 enemy aircraft shot down and damaged, and a great many bomb hits on enemy targets. The small Polish naval forces fought boldly in the Atlantic, the North Sea, the Norwegian Sea, and the Mediterranean, taking part in battles and landings, and escorting convoys.

On the day Berlin surrendered, Polish forces in the west numbered 194,500 men. After the war, about 120,000 returned to their homeland. All of them were joyously welcomed and found their places in the building of a People's Poland. And that was only natural: The great majority of the Polish citizens had fought bravely for the liberation of the motherland. Blood shed in the name of freedom commands the greatest respect for soldiers, no matter where they have fought; and People's Poland appreciated the feats of its sons. It understood the vastness of the gulf separating its soldiers from the grandees of the London clique, whose chief aim was to restore the regime of the landowners and capitalists.

In our country, meanwhile, the process of forming new Polish units and formations had gone on. The man in charge of this important operation was one of Poland's most outstanding revolutionaries and military figures, a fervent patriot and bold internationalist, Gen. Karol Sweszczewski. By late 1943 there were already three infantry divisions, an artillery brigade, an armored brigade, and other necessary units and subunits. Like the 1st Infantry Division, they had been equipped and supplied gratis by the Soviet Union, and in their military training had profited from the experience acquired in the Great Patriotic War. Since Anders had taken most of the Polish officers away with him, the Poles were now short of officers of their own. It became necessary to put a good many Soviet officers at the disposal of the Polish forces—above all, specialists. The divisions that were formed were combined into the 1st Army Corps. In mid-March 1944 it was transformed into the 1st Polish Army. This army was commanded by General Berling, who had previously commanded the Kościuszko Division.

Now this army was positioned near Kovel, making ready to fight on its native soil. Its commanding general was able to get into personal touch not only with the General Staff but with the Supreme Command. We had already been ordered to send a special representative to the 1st Polish Army, and had designated Col. (later Maj. Gen.) N. M. Molotkov, together with a group of officers: Cols. A. S. Evseyev and M. F. Dubrovsky and Captain Eropkinov.

We received information on the armed struggle on Polish soil. We knew that Partisan detachments of the Guards had been formed under the leadership of the People's Polish Workers' Party, and that a vigorous struggle against the aggressors was developing. The military actions of the Polish people's avengers were especially intensified in early 1944, when the Red Army began to break through the enemy's front. The supreme organ of fighting Poland, the National Council of Poland (Krajowa Rada Narodowa), had arisen in the Polish underground upon the initiative—and with the direct participation—of B. Bierut, W. Go-mulka, and other leaders of the Polish Workers' Party. The Soviet Supreme Command, putting great hope and trust in the liberation forces of Poland, learned that the National Council of Poland, acting in the name of the Polish people, had on January 3, 1944, decreed the merger of the People's Guards with units of the armed detachments of other left-wing organizations into a united People's Army (Armia Ludowa) commanded by Gen. Michal Zymierski, known as Rola.

At the request of the Polish command the Soviet Union also furnished assistance to this part of the Polish People's Armed Forces, who were compelled to fight in the enemy's rear. Weapons, ammunition, medical supplies, and other indispensable stores were delivered. Soviet partisan units and detachments under the command of P. P. Vershigora, I. N. Bokov, V. A. Karasev, G. V. Kovalev, M. Ya. Nadelin, V. P. Pelikha, N. A. Prokopyuk, S. A. Sankov, V. P. Chepiga, V. G. Shangin, and I. P. Yakovlev crossed over into Polish territory. The Polish and Soviet partisan detachments did not always operate separately. There were also joint operations against the German fascist occupiers, including some in the (Kraśnik) Lubelski area close behind the enemy's lines. The results strengthened belief in the imminent victory. By the summer of 1944 the People's Army included thousands of soldiers fighting jointly with the attacking Soviet and Polish forces.

On the threshold of decisive events in the western strategic direction, contacts with political and military leaders of the democratic forces in Poland were strengthened. In mid-May 1944 representatives of the National Council of Poland came to the Soviet Union. On May 22—the day when the Stavka of the Soviet Supreme Command discussed the plan for Operation Bagration for destroying the Nazi forces in Belorussia—the Soviet Government received the representatives. The guests gave detailed information to the Supreme Commander and the Union of Polish Patriots on the situation in Poland, including certain matters concerning the creation of the People's Army. The friendly, confidential talk went on for two hours. The Soviet Government recognized the council as the only representative of the Polish people, and satisfied all its demands with respect to material assistance.

During the representatives' sojourn in the USSR, they were given an extensive tour through the Ukraine and were taken to visit Polish military units. They returned to their homeland with a feeling of deep satisfaction at the strengthened friendship between our peoples.

Meantime, preparations were being made for the Soviet attack near Kovel. K. K. Rokossovsky, commanding the 1st Belorussian Front, regarded the huge and very complex area of Belorussia, including Polesye and Kovel, as sufficiently favorable for carrying out bold operations in depth. One could envelop the enemy's group of forces in Belorussia from the southwest (from Polesye), and then, acting jointly with forces attacking from north of the Pripet Marshes, destroy the enemy's forces in the forests and swamps.

To a certain degree, the plan for the offensive operation of the left wing reflected that intention of the outstanding field commander. It was planned to begin the attack on the left sector of the front just when the enemy's defenses north of Polesye had been fundamentally shaken but he had not yet lost all capacity of resistance on the western boundary of Belorussia. It was intended that the blow delivered at Kovel, coming from both the flank and the rear, would crush the enemy's last hopes of being able to hold firm on Belorussian soil.

The aim of this offensive was first of all to destroy the Kovel grouping of Nazi forces which, according to our estimates at the time, consisted of at least ten divisions with means of reinforcement. After breaking through the tactical defenses it was planned to exploit the success in a northerly direction along the eastern and western banks of the Western Bug, enveloping Brest from the southeast, the west, and the north. After the capture of Brest, mobile forces were to drive forward, either toward Pruzhany and Slonim or Bielsk and Białystok. It was not difficult to see that if the operation were successful the Nazi forces would be hit by two assault forces of the First Belorussian Front moving toward each other. The enemy's defeat in this area would open up very good prospects for the liberation of Warsaw.

According to the plan for the operation, in the first phase three mixed armies (Gen. N. I. Gusev's 47th Army, Gen. V. I. Chuikov's 8th Guards Army, and Gen. V. Ya. Kolpakchi's 69th Army) would break through the Germans' tactical defenses. Then we would put in S. I. Bogdanov's 2nd Tank Army and Gen. V. V. Kryukov's Mechanized Cavalry Group, which would develop the offensive. The mixed armies (except for the 47th) would drive on westward to the edge of Lublin, where they would take up defensive positions, thus securing the front from that direction. It was roughly estimated that the operation would be completed by August 3.

Thus the Kovel operation by forces of the left wing of the 1st Belorussian Front was conceived as a decisive phase in our forces' actions in the way to Warsaw. It did not provide for the capture of Warsaw nor for the forcing of the Vistula; but actually the defeat of the enemy's largest grouping in the Brest region was the key that opened the gate to Warsaw.

However, military and political events that occurred soon after the plan was approved by the Stavka necessitated several very substantial changes in it. This started with the military events. The new commander of Army Group Center, Field Marshal Walther von Model (he had replaced Field Marshal Ernest von Busch), did not wait for our Kovel offensive. On the night of July 5 he left Kovel, which is located in the lowlands, and withdrew his forces some distance west to a previously prepared defensive line running through Paraduby and Targovishche which was based on advantageous heights. Also, units of the SS Viking Motorized Division, which had been put under Model's command, were secretly moved up to this line. In this way Model created a special kind of fortified zone that our forces knew nothing about. His scheme was simple: He figured that the Soviet commanders, when they noticed his withdrawal, would immediately rush in pursuit but, encountering unexpected fire from the dug-in and covered tanks, would suffer heavy losses. Sad to say, our commanders did fall for this simple ruse. Their mistake can be attributed to a certain "dizziness from success"[6] in the course of the battle for Belorussia.

Noticing the enemy's withdrawal General Gusev immediately ordered the advance detachments of three divisions to push ahead. They easily brushed aside the enemy's weak coverage and took Kovel and several other populated places. At the same time, General Gusev reported the situation to the front commander (Rokossovsky), who was in the Kovel area, evaluating it as a general withdrawal of the Nazi forces. In his turn, Rokossovsky reported to the Stavka representative, Zhukov. Zhukov did not deny the feasibility of such a maneuver, but he felt it was necessary to establish the fact of a withdrawal with complete certainty. In the event that the withdrawal of the enemy's Kovel grouping was a reality, his orders to the front commander were to go over to the attack immediately, putting in the 47th, 69th, and 8th armies, the 11th Tank Army, and both cavalry corps.

The next day the Nazi forces continued to withdraw. By July 6 the armies of Gusev and Kolpakchi had advanced nine kilometers. A map taken from a dead officer of the 342nd Infantry Division showed that the defensive line for that unit ran to the Western Bug. Now Rokossovsky and Zhukov had no more doubts. But now another question came up. Since the withdrawal had substantially changed the situation and opened up new possibilities, what plan should be used for the forces' operations? All our military regulations said clearly that when the enemy withdrew he should be pursued with all available forces, and this was being done. But now the operations plan had to be adjusted. So Marshal Zhukov, personally, and the Military Council of the front set about doing it.

Meantime our forces were pursuing the enemy. Gusev, the commanding general of the 47th Army, demanded that Maj. Gen. P. N. Rudkin, commanding the 11th Tank Corps, which had been put at Gusev's disposal, make some immediate bold strikes. But Gusev had not carried out reconnaissance in adequate depth or variety, and had not provided the corps with artillery and air sup-

[6] The title of a famous article published by Stalin in the thirties. (Translator's note.)

port, since he had hastily assumed that the Nazis were really on the run. In their turn, the commander of the corps and the commanders of its brigades assumed that the enemy was virtually in flight, and in view of the little time available they hastened to put their units into combat without thinking of artillery and air support, and without having made adequate reconnaissance. At 1100 hours on July 8 the corps jumped off. The two tank brigades were deployed over areas that had not been reconnoitered and, in effect, they functioned blindly. It was not even considered necessary to deploy the corps' self-propelled artillery. The infantry did not advance in the wake of the tanks. As a result of such inadmissibly bad tactical planning by the corps, its tank brigades unexpectedly ran into a solid defensive line. They tried to break through on their own while under short-range fire from the dug-in tanks, but suffered great losses and were unable to complete their mission.

It was a harsh lesson. The "wounded beast" had snapped viciously. And it showed that the slightest negligence in tactical planning—the slightest underrating of the enemy—could cost dear.

When Zhukov heard of what had happened, he immediately ordered an investigation and reported to Stalin. "I consider," he concluded his report, "that the commanding officer of the corps, Major General Rudkin, should be removed from his command and replaced by a more competent and conscientious commander. For his negligence, Gusev should be given a reprimand by order of the Stavka."

The Supreme Commander demanded additional information on the causes of the failure, and this was furnished by Gen. G. N. Orel, commanding the front's armored troops. The corps commander was removed from his post.

The news of this negligence was painful for us at the General Staff—especially for me, since Philip Nikitich Rudkin had been my classmate at the Red Army Academy of Motorization and Mechanization.

Since neither Zhukov nor the Military Council had any sure knowledge of what the enemy would do next, it was necessary to propose different versions of the way in which the operation should be developed. If the enemy was dug in along the heights east of the Western Bug, we would stick to the earlier operations plan, with some slight adjustments. But if the Nazi forces withdrew (which was more likely), it would be better to aim the main blow at Dęblin, advance to the Vistula, and develop the offensive along its eastern bank to the Warsaw suburb of Praga. It was planned to establish bridgeheads beyond the Vistula which could be used in the future for a drive to the west. The secondary thrusts were to be made toward Siedlce (forces of the 47th Army supported by armored and cavalry corps) and in a northerly direction toward Brest (70th Army), rolling back the enemy's defenses facing the front's right-flank armies.

In this plan, which was carefully and thoroughly studied by the General Staff, the mission of advancing to the Warsaw region—assigned to part of the left-flank armies of the front—happily coincided with the aim of a deeper encirclement of the enemy in the region of Brest. This we reported to the Supreme Commander. On that same day (July 7), Antonov had sent Zhukov a telegram saying the plan had been approved by the Stavka.

From the sad experience of the 11th Tank Corps one could conclude that the enemy's defenses were not simply to be broken through on the run. We had to set about making planned preparations for a breakthrough, with every angle covered. And that took some time. The start of the operation in the Kovel region was postponed until July 18, since by that time the forces of the 1st Ukrainian Front would have gone over to the attack in the direction of Lvov, would be breaking through the enemy's defenses, and in the region of Vladimir-Volynsky would have created favorable conditions for actions by the left-flank armies of Rokossovsky's 1st Belorussian Front. In order to avoid coming back to this subject, let me say that the offensive by the 1st Ukrainian Front was launched successfully on July 13, 1944.

For the right flank of the 1st Belorussian Front—in the direction of Brest—problems were not solved so easily. The General Staff and the front command were concerned because the advance of our forces had slowed down in this area. In the region of

Baranovichi—an important railroad junction and a major strong point in the enemy's defense line—the Nazi forces were fighting furiously, trying to deny our armies access to Brest, where we intended to encircle the enemy.

In order to speed up the process of eliminating the annoying bottleneck, Zhukov flew to the Baranovichi region. By agreement with Rokossovsky, who had remained near Kovel, he organized a maneuver using troops from I. A. Pliyev's mechanized cavalry group to bypass Baranovichi from the north. He co-ordinated this movement with actions in this area by P. I. Batov's 65th Army, and sent A. A. Luchinsky's 28th Army to cut the railroad from Baranovichi to Slonim. On July 8 Baranovichi was taken by our forces.

During the Soviet forces' successful drive toward the borders of Poland, an event took place which was very important for the liberation mission of the Soviet and Polish armies. On July 21, at a session of the National Council of Poland in the town of Chełm—the first piece of Polish land liberated from the Nazi occupiers—the Polish Committee of National Liberation was created as a provisional government for democratic Poland. On the second day the committee issued a manifesto to the Polish people calling for struggle for the nation's complete liberation from the Nazis and for strengthening co-operation with the world's democratic countries—above all, with the Soviet Union.

The manifesto listed the priority tasks for a democratic transformation of the foundation of the Polish state. The revolutionary regime considered that one of the most urgent was the creation of a Voisko Polskoye.

It was during those days, so crammed with important events of various kinds, that we got a bit of news from the enemy camp: On July 20, at the German GHQ, an attempt had been made on Hitler's life. The motives of the plotters had not yet been made clear; but the very fact of a plot testified to a revision of values and deep differences among the military men of the Third Reich. A. A. Gryzlov told me of the attempt in a telephone call to the 3rd Baltic Front, where I was at the moment. Both of us were sorry that things had come out relatively well for the main criminal.

Soon people back in Germany began writing about the plot in letters to the front. We came into possession of a great many such letters that never reached their addressees. This was because our offensive was developing so rapidly that the Germans bringing the mail, not knowing where the front line was, often rode their motorcycles right into our positions.

On the fourth day of the offensive by the left-wing armies of the 1st Belorussian Front, when the Western Bug (forming the boundary with Poland) had been forced, Zhukov, Rokossovsky, and Nikolai Bulganin (the member of the Military Council)[7] received an order from Stalin: to take Lublin no later than July 26 or 27. To this end it was proposed to use mainly S. I. Bogdanov's 2nd Tank Army and M. P. Konstaninov's 7th Guards Cavalry Corps. Since the order changed the front's plan to some extent, the Stavka explained that the capture of Lublin was demanded by the interests of an independent democratic Poland.

On July 23, forces of the 1st Belorussian Front liberated Lublin. The provisional government set to work in the city. It had the job of restoring the Polish state and, jointly with the Red Army, of organizing the people's armed struggle against the occupying forces.

That same day Stalin sent Churchill a message explaining the Soviet position on the governing of Poland. "We do not want to set up—nor are we going to set up—our own government on the territory of Poland, since we do not want to interfere in the internal affairs of Poland. This [the setting up of a government] must be done by the Poles themselves."

The General Staff received instructions on relations with the Polish authorities, and the Soviet forces received corresponding instructions.

The destruction of the Nazi Army Group Center and the advance of the western fronts to the borders of the Soviet state meant that the Soviet forces' basic missions in the battle for

[7] In Soviet parlance, *"the* member" of Military Council is the "first member" or the political member; viz., the commissar, the others being the commander, the chief of staff, etc. (Translator's note.)

Belorussia were virtually completed. As always in such situations, there arose a need for a new strategic orientation or for adjustments to the fronts' plans for their operations.

On July 19, 1944, in a special communication, Marshal Zhukov reported to the Supreme Commander his ideas for the further operations of the Belorussian fronts, where he was Stavka representative:

1. The chief strategic goal of the 1st, 2nd, and 3rd Belorussian fronts in the next phase must be to advance to the Vistula as far up as the Gulf of Danzig, and to seize East Prussia, or at any rate cut off East Prussia from central Germany simultaneously with the advance to the Vistula.

As the reader can see, the Deputy Supreme Commander (Zhukov) assumed the complete feasibility of destroying Army Group Center and liberating eastern Poland. But the operation against East Prussia struck him as more complex and difficult:

2. Because of its fortified zones, engineering structures, and natural features, East Prussia is a very serious obstacle. The approaches to Königsberg from the southeast and the south are covered by five fortified zones; and on the east, moreover, a flooded region has been prepared west of Insterburg.

Zhukov felt that the most advantageous directions for attacking East Prussia were:

First direction: from the region of Tilsit along the littoral in the general direction of Königsberg through Libots;
Second direction: from the region of Kaunas and Alitus through Gumbinnen to Königsberg, necessarily bypassing on the south the flooded region and the Lettsensky fortified zone;
Third blow: from the region of Mława through Hochenstein and Allenstein to Braunsberg.
Also, a strong force must be sent east of the Vistula in the general direction of Marienburg to cut off East Prussia from the Danzig region.

Noting that the thrust from the region of Tilsit could be made only when the enemy had been cleared out of Lithuania, Zhukov figured that the second and third directions could be used if the offensive of the 3rd and 2nd Belorussian fronts were developed.

> Chernyakhovsky could make the thrust through Gumbinnen. But a part of his forces must advance north of the Augustów Forest through Suwałki to Gołdap.
> The thrust from the region of Mława must be made by the 2nd Belorussian Front in the following directions:
> (a) one group to Allenstein;
> (b) one group to Marienburg, advancing to the Gulf of Danzig;
> (c) one group must advance to the Vistula, deploying over the sector Grudziądz-Nieszawa, where it must dig in.
> To the left, along the dividing line between it and the 1st Ukrainian Front, the 1st Belorussian Front must advance, and must by all means secure good bridgeheads on the west bank of the Vistula.

Other ideas, too, were set forth in this memorandum. Marshal Zhukov reported that the 1st Belorussian Front needed another three hundred tanks and one hundred self-propelled guns. Also, that the 2nd Belorussian Front needed, in addition to the three armies it already had, another mixed army consisting of nine divisions and a three-division rifle corps, one tank army or two or three tank corps, and other reinforcements, including cavalry and aircraft.

In conclusion, Zhukov offered suggestions as to the demarcation lines between the fronts. The memorandum ended with this sentence: "I feel it would be very useful to consult with you personally on these impending operations, and that it would be good to call in Vasilevsky."

Antonov, who had received a copy of the memorandum, reported to the Supreme Commander that in his opinion one should review impending operations not only on the Belorussian Front but on all fronts from the Baltic to the Carpathians. Stalin agreed with him, and summoned Zhukov and Vasilevsky. The meeting was scheduled for July 27–29.

The time had come for new, crushing blows at the enemy in the southwest. It was necessary once again to define further the missions and direction of the main thrusts of the advancing fronts, to check and correct where necessary, and here and there to determine the nature of their interactions, to establish the fronts' grouping of forces, and the procedure for creating Stavka reserves, their positioning, and their use.

Also, the Supreme Command had to find new solutions for certain problems of controlling our forces, co-ordinating the thrusts of the different fronts, and monitoring their actions. It was necessary to keep closer tabs on the course of military operations, and how well they were supported. The fact was that the great successes of our forces had engendered here and there an excess of self-confidence and a disdain for the enemy. As a result there was somewhat less exigence toward, say, carrying out reconnaissance, following the principle of concentrating forces and action by assault forces. Occasionally there was a dispersion of forces and means; for example, of mobile forces, aircraft, and artillery to some extent. Even I. S. Konev, that master of classical massed thrusts and the rapid development of a successful breakthrough, did not avoid that mistake in preparing for—and during —the Lvov operation.

Owing to the fact that P. S. Rybalko's 3rd Guards Tank Army had penetrated to the rear of the enemy's grouping in Lvov, the Stavka representative (Zhukov) and the front commander (Rokossovsky) assumed that the enemy would abandon Lvov and begin to retreat. On July 23 they reported to the Supreme Commander their decision to further move up the tank armies of Katukov, Rybalko, and Lelyushenko, and Baranov's cavalry corps, which were to advance fanwise toward Częstochowa and Kraków without a clearly defined main grouping.

But the Supreme Commander and the General Staff thought otherwise. Of course it was possible that the enemy would abandon Lvov, and then everything would be all right. But what if he tried to hold it? In that case, in the rear of our forces—behind our backs—the Germans would have a very important communications hub and a very important defense area, plus on our flank the region of Stanislav, still defended by the enemy. The Soviet forces would be cut off from supply lines and would be without ammunition and stores.

The directive issued on that head by the Stavka on July 24 read:

> The Stavka of the Supreme Command considers your plan for using tank armies and cavalry corps premature and dangerous at this time, since right now such an operation cannot be materially secured and would lead only to the weakening and scattering of our striking forces.
>
> On this basis, the Stavka of the Supreme Command directs that you first of all destroy the enemy's Lvov grouping and interdict its withdrawal to the San River or to Sambor, for which purpose you will:
>
> 1. Use Katukov's 1st Guards Tank Army and Baranov's 1st Guards Cavalry Corps to seize the region of Jarosław (Yaroslav) and Przemyśl (Peremyshl) with a view to cutting off the basic communications of the enemy's Lvov grouping to the west;
>
> 2. Use Rybalko's 3rd Guards Tank Army and Lelyushenko's 4th Tank Army to destroy the enemy's Lvov grouping and take Lvov, acting jointly with Kurochkin's 60th Army.
>
> Bear in mind that if we do not take Lvov, an important railroad hub, we cannot develop a substantial offensive toward the west in the direction of Kraków.
>
> 3. Use Sokolov's 6th Guards Cavalry Corps to strike at the flanks of the enemy's Krasnystaw grouping in the general direction of Tomaszów and Kraśnik, and to destroy it acting jointly with Gordov's 3rd Guards Army and the left wing of the 1st Belorussian Front.
>
> 4. The advance to the west in the next few days will be limited to reaching the San River and seizing crossings and bridgeheads on the western bank of that river.

In this way did the Stavka solve the problem of using mobile forces and crushing the enemy in the Lvov region, and determine the way in which the 1st Ukrainian Front's break-through would be developed. If (getting a bit ahead of the story) one recalls how hard was the fighting to hang on to the Sandomierz bridgehead, even though our rear was completely secured, the Stavka's foresight becomes even plainer.

Not just in this case but at all times, the Soviet Supreme Command tried to prevent unwarranted headlong advances. The tendency to make sweeping advances without adequately securing lines of supply became especially dangerous on foreign territory. Here the enemy was closer to his own bases and had good communications lines for bringing up whatever he needed. We, by contrast, were far from our bases, and had to repair and build railroad lines. Under such conditions, one had to take all precautions against mishaps.

During the days of the conference at the Stavka, a complex political and military situation was developing on the territory of Poland. On the evening of July 25, units of Bogdanov's 2nd Tank Army and Chuikov's 8th Guards Army, after taking Dęblin and Puławy, reached the eastern bank of the Vistula. Meantime, Kryukov's 2nd Guards Cavalry Corps had engaged the enemy in a battle for the southern outskirts of Siedlce, from where (as it seemed to us) a direct route would be opened up to Warsaw. But Kryukov could not develop his attack, since the German command had brought in fresh forces. And two days before, the enemy had launched counterattacks by infantry and tanks on the right flank of our front, hitting especially hard in the zone of Batov's 65th Army. These counterattacks were beaten off, but our offensive was considerably slowed down.

On July 27, blows struck by General Luchinsky's 28th Army from the east and General Popov's 70th Army from the west and southwest had the result that in the Brest region we encircled a considerable enemy grouping, and it required two days to liquidate it.

As a result of rapid operations, Kolpakchi's 69th Army reached the Vistula to the south of Puławy. Its advanced detachment forced the river and, after seizing a small bridgehead, began to widen it.

Especially heavy fighting began on July 27 in the region of Siedlce. Attacking here were the main forces of the 47th Army, then commanded by General Gusev, and of the 2nd Tank Army. The tankmen's mission was to seize Praga and the Vistula crossings and bar escape to the west for the entire grouping of Nazi forces still east of the Vistula.

In view of the possibility of further developing the attack toward Warsaw along the western and eastern banks of the Vistula, the front commander ordered the Polish 1st Army to take up a position in the first wave in the sector of Rytsitse (ten kilometers north of Dęblin) and Vlostovitse (ten kilometers south of Puławy). Putting the Polish 1st Army in the first wave was of great importance politically and in terms of morale. The Soviet command had previously spared it, considering that it was not entitled to put it into the line until this point. When this army had crossed the Polish frontier, Zigmund Berling, the commanding general, had sent a brief telegram to the Soviet Supreme Command: "Have crossed the Bug. With all their hearts and souls all soldiers of the army say 'Long live Stalin!' . . . Unprecedented enthusiasm. A mass of volunteers."

News of a different kind came from the "Londoners." The Poles in London did not consider Berling's army to be Polish: They called his patriot soldiers "mercenaries." The "Londoners" wanted to establish their own regime and their old, outmoded order on the territory of Poland. One of their orders openly stated that all attempts "to create left-wing centers of leadership ('governments') will be harshly suppressed, even by means of force." The British Prime Minister gave his full support to the representatives of that camp of bourgeois political hacks.

The Stavka knew that on July 27 the new Premier of the Polish Government in Exile, Stanislaw Mikolajczyk, had left London for Moscow. Apparently he had a lot to worry about: the growing prestige of the Polish Committee of National Liberation and the Polish Workers' Party, the increasingly strong feelings of warmth toward us on the part of the Polish people, and our military successes. Finally, he was disturbed by a declaration issued by the Soviet Government the day before, which stated:

> The Soviet Government does not intend to establish organs of its own administration on Polish soil, considering that that is the business of the Polish people. In view of this fact, it has decided to conclude with the Polish Committee of National Liberation an Agreement on the relations between the Soviet Command and the Polish Administration.

71

And further:

> The Soviet Government declares that it is not pursuing the aim of acquiring any part of the Polish territory or of changing the social system in Poland, and that the military actions of the Red Army on the territory of Poland are dictated only by military necessity and the endeavor to render assistance to the friendly Polish people in liberating them from the German occupation.[8]

The day before the Stavka conference I returned from the 3rd Baltic Front to Moscow. That evening we learned that Stalin had declined to attend a meeting of the Big Three that the President of the United States and the Prime Minister of Great Britain had planned to be held in Scotland during the second week in September. While pointing out the desirability of such a meeting, Stalin wrote to Churchill:

> But at the present moment, when Soviet armies are fighting over such a broad front, and developing their offensive more and more, I am unable to leave the Soviet Union and delegate the leadership of the armies, even for the briefest time. In the opinion of all my colleagues, this is completely unfeasible.[9]

That night was spent in preparing reference materials and draft directives. On July 27 the conference was opened at the Stavka. It was attended by Stalin, Zhukov, Vasilevsky, and Antonov. A. A. Gryzlov and I were also there to put the decisions in the form of directives. As said before, the agenda at this conference included not only the prospects for the offensive by the Belorussian fronts but a much broader spectrum of questions. At first the conferees went over the general situation on the front, which they found satisfactory. Then they proceeded to analyze the situation and the operational missions in the Baltic area, East Prussia, and eastern Poland.

In the Baltic the actions of the Leningrad Front and the 1st,

[8] *Vneshnyaya politika Sovetskogo Soyuza v period Otechestvennoi voiny,* Vol. II, p. 155.
[9] *Perepiska Predsedatelya Soveta Ministrov SSSR c Prezidentami SShA i Premer-Ministrami Velikobritanii vo vremya Velikoi Otechestvennoi voiny, 1941–45* (Moscow: Gospolitizdat, 1957), Vol. I, p. 247.

2nd, and 3rd Baltic fronts were developing successfully, so that all the Stavka did was to make some adjustments in the plans for their offensive. Especially close scrutiny was given to the situation on the approaches to East Prussia and toward the west. The conferees concluded that the enemy would be extremely stubborn about holding on to East Prussia. It was decided that there was little possibility of launching a successful offensive in a hurry. It would have to be carefully and thoroughly prepared, using basically the forces present in that area.

In the west, where the enemy did not have such strong defenses, we were to achieve great successes in the next few days. The defeat of the enemy near Lvov, of which the Stavka learned during the conference, opened up possibilities for moving on Warsaw from the south. In this connection, very great importance attached to the Sandomierz region in the zone of Konev's 1st Ukrainian Front: It was the gateway to central Poland and the key to the enemy's defenses beyond the Vistula.

As before, the forces of the 1st Belorussian Front were functioning as two wing groupings. As has already been said, the two mixed armies of its left wing (the 8th Guards and the 69th) had already reached the Vistula and begun to force it on July 27, soon seizing small bridgeheads in the regions of Magnuszew and Puławy. The Polish 1st Army had also reached the Vistula. The 2nd Tank Army was successfully advancing up the eastern bank of the Vistula to Praga, a suburb of Warsaw. This army was commanded by Maj. Gen. A. I. Radziyevsky, its chief of staff, since the commanding general, Bogdanov, had been wounded and brought back to Moscow on orders from Stalin. The other forces of the front's left wing were advancing toward the region of Siedlce. There had been no alarming news from that quarter.

The situation on the right wing of the 1st Belorussian Front was not so good: It was lagging by some 200 to 250 kilometers. But Białystok had been taken, and our forces were approaching Brest, which would soon be liberated. The conferees did not see any particular threat in the fact that the general rate of the offensive had been slowed down. True, the forces of the 1st Belorussian Front were weakened and their supply services were in disorder owing to a solid month of forward movement during the Belorussian operation. But the conferees all agreed that they could break the enemy's resistance in the regions of Brest and Siedlce and, taking advantage of the break-through made by Bodganov's tankmen, in the north, gain back what they had lost.

The conferees concluded it would be best if the drive on Warsaw were made by the right wing of the 1st Belorussian Front. It was decided that after taking the regions of Brest and Siedlce, the front's right wing should, without pausing, develop the offensive in the general direction of Warsaw. No later than August 5–8 it was to take the suburb of Praga, and also seize a bridgehead on the Narew River in the region of Pułtusk and Serock along the left flank of the 2nd Belorussian Front. The front's left wing was to seize bridgeheads on the Vistula in the region of Dęblin, Zwoleń, and Solecs.

The 1st Ukrainian Front was to force the Vistula no later than August 1 or 2 and seize a bridgehead in the region of Sandomierz. Then it was to drive in the general direction of Częstochowa and Kraków.

Next the conferees discussed the situation on the Carpathian flank. What had happened there was that since the beginning of the operations in Rumania, there had been an inevitable bifurcation in the thrust of our main groupings. Some had driven west, advantage of the break-through made by Bogdanov's tankmen, in the southwest. Meantime the Carpathians were still in the hands of the enemy. From there he could strike at the flanks and rear areas of both strategic formations. This threat had to be dealt with. At the Stavka meeting on July 27 it was decided that Gen. A. A. Grechko's 1st Guards Army and Gen. E. P. Zhuravlev's 18th Army could cover the flank adequately. Nonetheless, the conferees ordered the General Staff to make sure this was the case. After the General Staff had made precise calculations and asked Konev's opinion, it became plain that the two armies would not suffice. Three days later, therefore—on July 30—the Stavka decided to form a 4th Ukrainian Front, to include the 1st Guards Army, the 18th Army, and 8th Air Army, and artillery, engineering, and other forces.

Thus on July 27 the Stavka, with great thoroughness and clarity, laid down the strategic missions corresponding to the particularities of the situation in the Baltic and in the west. Provisions were made for cutting off the Baltic area from East Prussia and East Prussia from Germany, and for crushing the German Army Group North. The Stavka warned the fronts against driving headlong into East Prussia without adequate preparation. In the west —which had been the main sector in the course of the war—it was proposed to destroy the enemy's defenses on the banks of the Vistula and move on westward.

The directives for the execution of these missions were written up, approved, and signed on the spot; and at 2400 hours they were sent out to the fronts.

The next day the Stavka discussed the procedure for controlling current and impending operations, and for interaction among the fronts. Up to that time, Stavka representatives had had the right to co-ordinate the actions of forces. At this session, Zhukov declared that the Stavka representative must also have the right, where necessary, to conduct operations directly. If the truth be told, Zhukov, with his imperious character, had often exercised that right already. The question now was whether such a state of affairs should be legitimized. And it was all the more pressing in that some front commanders had complained when Stavka representatives took it upon themselves to conduct operations. One could well understand those commanders: In the final analysis, it was they who were responsible for everything. But it was also realized that commanders think primarily of their own fronts, and are not inclined to pay special regard to their neighbors, assuming that they can take care of themselves. In such cases a Stavka representative had to correct the commander promptly.

On July 29 the Stavka passed a special resolution on the authority of Vasilevsky and Zhukov to command the forces on those fronts where they were representing the Stavka: "The Supreme Command empowers Deputy Supreme Commander, Marshal of the Soviet Union Zhukov, not only to co-ordinate but to conduct the operations carried out by the forces of the 1st Ukrainian Front, the 1st Belorussian Front, and the 2nd Belorussian Front."

Vasilevsky was empowered to conduct the operations of the 1st and 2nd Baltic fronts and the 3rd Belorussian Front.

The conference had its piquant moments. Even before this session was over, the 1st Belorussian Front and the 1st Ukrainian Front were asking for explanations of the directives they had just received. In particular, they asked if armies not mentioned in the directives could force the Vistula. The question made sense, since the commanders were trying to get from the Stavka all the bridging equipment they could, explaining their request by saying that the forcing was going on over a broad front.

When Stalin learned of these requests from Antonov and myself, he puffed on his pipe and dictated the following answer:

> The Stavka's order on the forcing of the Vistula River and the seizure of bridgeheads by those armies named in the order is not to be understood to mean that other armies should sit on their hands and not try to force the Vistula. The front commanders are obliged to supply a maximum of bridging equipment to those armies in whose tactical zone the Vistula must be forced in accordance with the Stavka's order. However, other armies must also force the Vistula, if possible. Since it attributes great importance to the matter of forcing the Vistula, the Stavka hereby instructs you to inform all commanding generals of your front that the soldiers and officers who distinguish themselves in forcing the Vistula will be given special decorations up to and including the title of Hero of the Soviet Union.

After the conference—as often happened in such cases—the Supreme Commander invited all present to dinner. Antonov and I were up to our ears in work, and for this once we asked permission to get back to our offices. Stalin waved his hand to show he had no objections.

In this connection I should like to tell about one of the most memorable dinners at Near House. According to a long-established custom, on the table before the host (Stalin) there always stood a beautiful long-necked carafe full of a colorless liquid, with moisture-beaded sides. Before dinner, Stalin usually drank one or two glasses of cognac, after which he would drink only dry Georgian wine poured from bottles with typewritten tags on them. He would pour his goblet about three-fourths full of wine, then leisurely add the other one-quarter from the crystal carafe.

The first time I was at this dacha I carefully observed everything around me, and immediately noticed the carafe. It was silly, of course, but it interested me to know what was in it. I thought it must be some kind of special vodka to give the wine extra strength. And I determined to try it when I could. For a long time my plan was frustrated, since my place at the table was far from the carafe.

One ill-starred evening at the dacha I was late in coming to the table because I had been on the telephone in the next room. (On instructions from Stalin, I was checking on the situation on one of the fronts.) When I came back into the dining room and reported, everyone was already seated at the table, and my usual place was occupied. Noticing this, Stalin indicated with a gesture that I should take the empty chair next to him.

The dinner got under way. As usual, the talk was about matters at the front. Everyone served himself. When the time came, he went to the buffet for the next course.

"Now," I told myself, "is the time to sample that vodka." And when Stalin got up, along with everyone else, to get the next course, I quickly grasped the carafe and poured myself a glassful from it. For the sake of decency, I waited until the next toast was proposed, then drank it off. It was water! And extremely cold. I was embarrassed. Although I quickly realized what I should do, and took a bite of something like everyone else, I plainly could not hide my surprise.

The boss, restraining a smile and screwing up his eyes, cast me a glance. Then after a moment he asked quietly, so that no one else could hear: "Well, was it strong?" The blood rushed to my face, so embarrassed I was. And all that evening I felt like a fool and cursed my improper curiosity.

3

TOWARD WARSAW

The enemy was not asleep. What was Mikolajczyk up to? Adventurists and heroes. How best to aid the uprising? The Czerniakow bridgehead. Communications are broken off. The tragedy of Warsaw. The struggle continues. Co-operation in combat. The Polish 1st Army enters Warsaw.

When planning a military action, commanders at any level take into account first of all the enemy's counteraction—his possible countermeasures. But in wartime it often happens that even though all possible developments have presumably been foreseen, in the course of combat a new and completely unforeseen situation will arise—one that demands adjustments in the plans made before.

Naturally, the Stavka and the General Staff knew that the Nazi command was seeking methods of stabilizing the front—especially in zones of Army Group North and Army Group Center, whose situation might prove to be catastrophic. True, at that time we did not have definite knowledge of the enemy's strategic intentions. But we had already begun to get reports that perhaps the enemy had shifted part of his forces—above all, panzer formations—from Rumania to other fronts. And in fact he had effected a regrouping in an attempt to stabilize the forces of Army Group

Center and to restore its communications with the Baltic area. We soon ran up against fresh units in the Warsaw sector.

It should be remarked that the measures taken by the Nazi command were like the efforts made by Trishkin, the character in the Krylov fable who kept trying to patch his coat: In strengthening the center, they weakened the southwest front. Rumania was soon out of the war, and the Soviet forces there were racing toward the Balkans and Hungary. But near Warsaw, where the fresh enemy forces withdrawn from Rumania had been put into the line against the weary troops of the 1st Belorussian Front, our situation was seriously complicated. And this complexity was deepened by mistakes in reconnaissance.

On the first day of the Stavka meeting the 2nd Tank Army, developing its attack on the left flank of the 1st Belorussian Front, had unexpectedly encountered strong enemy forces. As was discovered later, these forces consisted of four panzer divisions: the 19th Division, the SS "Death's Head" Division, and the SS "Viking" Division (all three brought up from the south), and the "Hermann Göring" Division just arrived from the Italian front, plus several infantry units of the German 2nd Army. In the hard-fought battle that began a few days later along a line running from Siedlce to Mińsk Mazowiecki, it proved impossible to beat off the enemy's counterattacking tanks. In a narrow sector of the front the enemy achieved a considerable superiority in forces, inflicted losses on the advanced corps of the 2nd Tank Army, and then roughed up its other corps.

These bloody and very fierce battles went on for several days. As a result, the enemy's defenses, based on the Warsaw fortified zone, acquired a relative stability for a considerable time. Our break-through to Praga proved impossible.

This circumstance was very important. The failure of the 2nd Tank Army's maneuver—intended to cut off escape routes to the west for the German forces east of the Vistula—had an unfavorable effect on the whole situation in this area. Now the forces of the 1st Belorussian Front's right wing, exhausted by their long and uninterrupted advance across Belorussia, could not quickly advance to Warsaw. Also, the relative stability of the Nazi forces along the Siedlce-Mińsk-Mazowiecki line posed a new threat to those forces reaching the Vistula south of Warsaw.

As Rokossovsky said to a correspondent for the French newspaper *Le Monde,* Henri Magnon, any attempt by the Soviet forces to force the Vistula could lead to defeat. And the front commander concluded his interview with the journalist by saying: "We are under the threat of a blow to our flank. That is the whole problem."

It must be admitted that the events in the Warsaw region were not promptly accorded their due importance. At first, neither Zhukov (the Stavka representative), the front command, nor the General Staff attributed any special importance to them, figuring that the enemy would soon be crushed. But day after day went by, and the situation did not improve. Not only that, but the date for forcing the Vistula was put back, and first priority was given to holding on to such advanced positions. In the opinion of the commander of the 1st Belorussian Front, the enemy had about twenty divisions for a north-south strike along the eastern bank of the Vistula against the front's left wing forces which had reached the river; and we expected that the enemy would deliver such a blow without fail.

This does not at all mean that the Soviet command was sitting on its hands while awaiting the attack on that flank. Beginning in early August 1944, Zhukov, Rokossovsky, and the General Staff made vigorous attempts to destroy the enemy's grouping on the approaches to Warsaw. This is borne out both by the several discussions at the Stavka of the further actions of the 1st Belorussian Front and by the continuing long battles that frustrated the enemy's vigorous and even dangerous countermeasures. But this did not result in changing the situation in the Warsaw region in our favor.

It is not merely because they are interesting in themselves that I am discussing the ups and downs in military affairs: They are also important in connection with the uprising in German-occupied Warsaw.

Whereas the Soviet Government, in its declaration of July 26, 1944, had clearly and openly set forth its views on Poland,

Mikolajczyk and his London cronies were playing a double game. It turned out that as early as July 24 the Government in Exile and the Polish Home Army (Armia Krajowa)[1] had decided to order an uprising in Warsaw with the understanding that it should take place before the Soviet forces reached the city. The purpose of this decision by the adventurists was, once the capital had been seized, to establish their own organs of power and oppose them to the provisional government of democratic Poland.

It is significant that the time of the Warsaw uprising (code name: "Storm") had been discussed a long time previously. And at the time the commander in chief of the Polish Home Army had reported to London that the uprising could not possibly be successful. But when organs of the people's regime appeared on liberated territory, the so-called delegates of the Government in Exile and the command of the Polish Home Army changed their minds. On July 25 Gen. Tadeusz Bor-Komorowski, commander in chief of the Home Army, reported to London: "Ready at any minute for the battle for Warsaw."

Neither the Soviet Government nor the command of the Red Army nor the organs of the people's regime in Poland nor the Voisko Polskoye was apprised of the uprising, nor did they have any information as to the preparations for it. And if the Allied military command (SHAEF) is to be believed, they knew nothing of it either.

The command of the Polish Home Army, subordinated to the Government in Exile, tried in every way to isolate the region of Warsaw from the Soviet forces. On orders from Bor-Komorowski, a part of the underground Home Army refused to make contact with our forces and co-ordinate actions with them. Rokossovsky informed us of this as soon as Lublin was taken.

The command of the Home Army, representatives of the Government in Exile, and a group of their close collaborators kept very close check (in their own way) on the course of the fighting on the Soviet-German front, especially near Warsaw. They real-

[1] The Polish Home Army was an armed organization created on the territory of occupied Poland by the Government in Exile with the view to restoring the bourgeois regime in Poland.

81

ized that the scales would soon tip in favor of the Red Army. And in order to prevent the establishment of a people's regime in Warsaw, they tried to set up their own government there—one dominated by the bourgeoisie and the landowners. For fear of being too late, those who organized the uprising repeatedly advanced the day and hour for the beginning of the action in the capital. They hoped to gain control of the situation in Warsaw before the arrival of the Soviet troops and the Polish 1st Army, which was already becoming part of the People's Army.

Quite possibly, they hoped that the Western Allies would help them make an airborne landing[2]—something that would have provided some leverage for the Government in Exile. But as early as the autumn of 1943 the Supreme Command of Great Britain and the United States had told the Government in Exile quite definitely that it could not count on an uprising being supported by the Anglo-Saxons in any way—especially from the air.[3]

Of course the British reactionaries—those calculating politicians—realized that the Warsaw uprising was aimed against the Soviet Union. But they could not risk such an undertaking as helping the insurgents. After all, [to continue] to help them with their Air Force meant endangering the lives of British pilots and possibly losing their own aircraft. The powerful German AA defense was putting them out of commission. So the British decided to discontinue the flights.

The plotters did not intend to start the uprising at the time when the Soviet forces were still back near Minsk or east of Kovel. They waited until the front was close to Warsaw. This enabled them to hope that if the insurgents got into a critical position, our armies would get there in time to rescue them.

The success of any operation, from the biggest to the smallest, depends on many factors. Not least among them is the plan of action. And such a plan is especially important for an uprising—a very complex form of armed struggle. Also, everyone knows that even a plan that is excellent in terms of its intent and aims is doomed to failure if it does not correspond to the situation and is

[2] I.e., by Polish paratroopers based in England. (Translator's note.)
[3] Cf. Adam Borkiewicz, *The Warsaw Uprising* (Warsaw, 1957), p. 19 (in Polish).

not adequately provided for. I have never seen a copy of the plan for Operation Storm—the plan that the C. in C. of the Home Army intended to follow in effecting the uprising of his detachments in Warsaw. But there is firm evidence that Bor-Komorowski, on the eve of the decisive events, advanced the time of the upising from August 2 (or a later date) to 1700 on August 1. The command of the Home Army made this critical decision without taking into account the real possibilities for taking the necessary steps to assemble the insurgents, to arm them, or to organize military actions. As was pointed out by one of the historians of the Warsaw uprising, Adam Borkiewicz, instead of the twelve hours previously provided for getting the insurgent forces into a state of combat-readiness, there were now only five hours (in certain areas and for certain detachments). This decision disorganized the uprising from the outset, and canceled out everything that had been done over a period of many years. All that was left was the insurgents' high morale.

Under these conditions, it became impossible to carry out the missions whose timetables and objectives had been worked out on paper. At the outset of military operations, there was not even elementary communication among the different insurgent forces.

On the appointed day (but at different times, because of different conditions) the Home Army's underground detachments began the uprising. Many soldiers went looking for their commanding officers. Neither they nor their officers knew where their arms and ammunition were stored. The element of surprise was lost, and the enemy was able to seize all the key points for communications, transport, and electric power. Because of the aforementioned circumstances, the insurgents were unable to act purposefully or strike any powerful first blow. Their attack was weak. After all, the Home Army had only 16,000 men, of whom only 3,500 were armed. (They were armed with rifles and pistols, since there were virtually no other weapons available.)

At the same time, the uprising took on a scope and character that its planners had not at all expected. The hatred that the inhabitants of Warsaw felt toward the occupation troops now found an outlet. Most of them joined in the uprising. People began to build barricades; and they joined the military detachments even though they had no weapons. They were convinced that the uprising had been planned jointly with the Soviet command. Even the appeal from the delegates of the Government in Exile to the Warsovians, in which no mention was made of the Red Army, did not shake this conviction.

The mass support given to the uprising by the inhabitants of Warsaw resulted in a certain degree of success for a brief period at the outset. But the Home Army did not manage to take the entire territory of the city; and a day later events began to develop in a manner very different from what the plotters had expected. The enemy had not suffered any great losses. He held the key points in the city; and he quickly coped with the situation and compelled the insurgents to go on the defensive. But they had made no preparations for that. They lacked the strength for it. And they were badly in need of ammunition, communications equipment, and medicines.

The brief action by the Home Army, conceived with cold political calculation, had become an uprising of the popular masses. But it had not been provided for; and ultimately the blows struck by the Nazi command crushed it utterly.

Marshal Rokossovsky recalls that on August 2 he received an intelligence report that some kind of uprising had been launched in Warsaw. But attempts to get more precise information proved fruitless. Neither the Polish Committee of National Liberation nor the National Council of Poland nor the command of the Voisko Polskoye knew anything about the uprising. Later it turned out that not even the command of the People's Army, or Armia Ludowa,[4] detachments in Warsaw had been informed of the uprising. However, as soon as the broad masses of Warsovians rose up, the Communists and their detachments of the People's Army immediately decided to join in the uprising and put their forces at the disposal of the Home Army command. This decision prevented a possible schism among the anti-Nazis in Warsaw and substantially strengthened them. With the blood they spilled on

[4] The Armia Ludowa was an armed organization headed by Communists and created as a force of the people in the interests of liberating Poland from the Nazi aggressors. It became an integral part of the Voisko Polskoye. Cf. p. 58. (Translator's note.)

the barricades, the soldiers and officers of the People's Army proved their devotion to the cause of liberating the people from the German fascist occupying troops.

Mikolajczyk, Prime Minister of the Polish Government in Exile, who had just arrived in Moscow for talks, offered no meaningful information on the events in Warsaw. Indeed, on July 28, on his way from London, he had met in Cairo with emissaries from Warsaw, but they had been unable to tell him anything about the uprising. On July 31, at a reception at the Commissariat of Foreign Affairs, Mikolajczyk stated that a plan of action had been worked out and that his government was now mustering its forces. With respect to Warsaw, he said that the Polish Government had "thought out" a plan for a general uprising and wanted to ask the Soviet Government about bombing airfields near the city. Thus up to that point, everything was described in very general terms as something not scheduled for the near future. Obviously, the Prime Minister of the Polish Government in Exile had no intention of talking about the first days of fighting in the capital of Poland. Thus through the efforts of the Nazis occupying the city and the "solicitude" of the bourgeois commanders of the Home Army, Warsaw was isolated from all those who could actually have helped the insurgents win a victory!

The commander of the 1st Belorussian Front (Rokossovsky) tried in every way to establish contact with the insurgents, including the military leaders. But he received no reply to the telegram he sent to General Bor-Komorowski.

The situation on the Soviet-German front worsened sharply on August 2. Near Warsaw the enemy launched a strong counterattack against the 1st Tank Army and the 47th Army, and they had to fight a hard defensive battle under unfavorable conditions. Their units were deployed in a line. The front commander had no reserves; and it was expected at any minute that the enemy tanks would break through and drive south along the Vistula so as to crush the forces of the front's left wing, who were busy forcing the river. Meantime, Warsaw was burning. The smoke was seen by those Russian commanders who had gone to the area of the enemy's counterattack to direct operations, and by Rokossovsky himself.

A few days later the heroic actions of the Soviet troops and the skill of their commanders put an end to the enemy's temporary success vis-à-vis the 1st Belorussian Front. He had not succeeded in throwing back our armies, or in pressing them really hard. On the other hand, we were unable to overcome the Nazi defense.

Warsaw was bleeding. Yet neither the command of the Home Army nor the Polish Government in Exile at any time requested of the Soviet Government or the Soviet command that it help the insurgents. They did not even consider it necessary to inform us of the uprising. Only later did it become clear that neither requesting nor informing was included in the political calculations of the Mikolajczyk group or of the Home Army command, even when the Nazi troops were starting to drown the uprising in blood.

At this time Stalin received a cheerful message from Churchill in which the Warsaw uprising was mentioned for the first time. Churchill said that the Home Army had requested that the British urgently supply arms and ammunition to the insurgents, and that this request would be granted. By way of an aside, he said the fighting in Warsaw was fierce. The Prime Minister also wrote that the insurgents had asked for help from the Russians, and hoped it would arrive soon. According to Churchill, the insurgents were being attacked by one and one-half German divisions. The message ended with the significant phrase: "This may be of help to your operation."

Stalin doubted, first of all, the reliability of the information Churchill had received. The next day he replied to the British Prime Minister, saying that all his data were greatly exaggerated and not plausible. He was particularly skeptical of the insurgents' intention to take Warsaw.

> The Polish Home Army [Stalin wrote] consists of a few detachments which are incorrectly called divisions. They have neither artillery nor air support nor tanks. I cannot imagine how such detachments can take Warsaw, into whose defense the Germans have put four panzer divisions, including the "Hermann Göring" division.[5]

[5] *Perepiska Predsedatelya Soveta Ministrov SSSR c Prezidentami SShA i Premer-Ministrami Velikobritanii vo vremya Velikoi Otechestvennoi voiny, 1941–45*, Vol. I, pp. 252–53.

As for the last sentence in Churchill's message, it was quite laughable: as if the Warsaw uprising had been an action intended to help the Red Army!

But Churchill's message was not simply filed away. Stalin ordered Zhukov, Rokossovsky, and the General Staff to report on their ideas concerning the capture of Warsaw.

On August 6 the Stavka representative and the front's Military Council reported to Moscow: "1. A strong enemy grouping is operating in the sector Sokołow-Podlaski-Ogrudek (ten kilometers north of Kałuszyn)-Stanisławów-Wołomin-Praga. 2. We do not have enough forces to crush this grouping." They asked permission to take advantage of one last possibility: to put in the 70th Army (it consisted of four divisions, and had just been assigned to the reserve), and to be given three days to prepare for the operation. The report stated: "We cannot go over to the offensive before August 10 because prior to that time we shall not have been able to bring up the requisite quantity of ammunition." The General Staff agreed. The Stavka granted permission and the time for the preparation, and the army was put in; but there was still no decisive change in the situation.

Our failure to break through to Warsaw right away, the fact that because of the exhaustion of the attacking forces it was impossible to turn the tide of the battle (whose timetable the enemy had upset), and the necessity for sharply improving the armies' security in the rear—all these things compelled the Soviet Supreme Command to organize a new offense with a view to liberating Warsaw. In this connection it should be borne in mind that the Stavka had no large reserves, so that the 1st Belorussian Front had to get along with the forces it had on hand.

So far as I know, very little has yet been written about the operations plan for liberating insurgent Warsaw. Yet it would certainly seem worthwhile to give a detailed account of it. Things went as follows.

On instructions from the Stavka, Zhukov and Rokossovsky gave Stalin their ideas on actions in the Warsaw operation. They reported:

. . . 1. The front can launch its Warsaw operation after the armies of the right wing have reached the Narew River and seized bridgeheads on its western bank in the sectors of Pułtusk and Serock. These armies are positioned some 120 kilometers from the Narew. It will take ten days to cover that distance.

Thus the offensive by the armies of the right wing of the front, which will carry them to the Narew River, must be effected between August 10 and August 20.

2. Meantime, on the left wing of the front, using the 69th Army, the 8th Guards Army, the 7th Guards Cavalry Corps, and the 11th Tank Corps, we must carry out a separate operation with a view to expanding the bridgehead on the western bank of the Vistula so that these armies can reach a line running through Warka, Stremets, Radom, and Wierzbnik.

For purposes of carrying out this operation it is necessary to transfer Katukov's 1st Tank Army from the 1st Ukrainian Front to the 1st Belorussian Front and send it from the region of Opatów through Ostrowiec to Sienne with the mission of striking in a northerly direction and advancing to the front at Zwoleń and Radom, and thus helping the 69th Army, the 8th Guards Army, the 7th Cavalry Corps, and the 11th Tank Corps to destroy the enemy facing them.

Also, the line of demarcation between the 1st Belorussian Front and the 1st Ukrainian Front must be moved northward so that it runs Krasnystaw-Iłżanka-River-Opoczno-Piotrków. This will make for a greater density of troops in the armies of the 1st Belorussian Front's left wing, and will increase the striking power of our forces in the direction of Radom.

3. When these operations have been carried out and the armies of the front's left wing reach the line of the Narew River, while those of the left wing reach the Warka-Radom-Wierzbnik line, the troops will need at least five days so that the air bases can be moved up and artillery rear-area services brought up, along with ammunition, fuel, and lubricants.

4. Taking into account the time required for preparation, the Warsaw operation may be launched on August 25, using all of the front's forces, with a view to reaching the defense line Ciechanów-Płońsk-Wyszogród-Sochaczew-Skierhiewice-Tomaszów and capturing Warsaw.

In this operation, to attack north of the Vistula we shall use three mixed armies, the 1st Tank Army, and the 1st Cavalry Corps, and to attack south of the Vistula, the 69th

Army, the 8th Guards Army, the 1st Tank Army, the 2nd Tank Army, two cavalry corps, one tank corps, and one mixed army to be taken from the right wing of the front.

In this operation the Polish 1st Army will advance along the western bank of the Vistula with the mission of taking Warsaw jointly with the forces of the front's right wing and center.

Thus in order to crush the enemy's Warsaw grouping it was planned to use the forces of both wings of the 1st Belorussian Front in a pincers movement. At the same time, one of the armies that had forced the Vistula was to strike north along the western bank of the river and cut off the enemy grouping. The jumping-off areas for these forces were to be as follows: on the right wing, the bridgeheads which were to be seized on the Narew River in the region of Pułtusk and Serock, and on the left wing the bridgeheads on the Vistula at Magnuzew and Puławy that had already been built up by the 8th Guards Army and the 60th Army. Even under the most favorable conditions, the operation could not have been launched before August 25.

At this time, S. Mikolajczyk was having talks with Stalin and Molotov about the state of affairs in Poland and about Soviet-Polish relations. On occasion, Antonov was summoned from the General Staff to take part in the talks. Stalin firmly declared that Polish matters would be decided by the Poles themselves, and that talks must be held with the Polish Committee of National Liberation. The "London Poles" agreed. And B. Bierut, chairman of the National Council of Poland, E. Osubka-Morawski, chairman of the PKWN (Polish Committee of National Liberation), and others came from Lublin to Moscow. Gen. Michal Zymierski (Rola), C. in C. of the Voisko Polskoye, also came to Moscow.[6]

In the talks that then took place, each of the parties stuck (as the saying goes) to his own opinion. The last talk between Stalin and Mikolajczyk took place on August 9. In the course of this talk, Mikolajczyk was obliged to tell about the Warsaw uprising in

[6] Cf. p. 58, where General Zymierski is called commander of the Armia Ludowa, or People's Army. (Translator's note.)

greater detail and to state that the insurgents were very short of weapons.

At the General Staff we soon learned that the Supreme Commander had got in touch with Rokossovsky on the high-frequency radio and ordered him to review once again the question of a Warsaw operation. Also, as a first measure, to organize the delivery of weapons to the insurgents and to drop a paratrooper with a portable radio set into the capital to establish communications with the leaders of the uprising. Unfortunately the paratrooper, not knowing the positions occupied by the insurgents, immediately fell into the clutches of the enemy.

When he got back to London, Mikolajczyk did not fail to tell Churchill of his talk in Moscow and of the situation in Warsaw, which was worsening from day to day. Churchill telegraphed to Stalin:

> I have had a distressing message from the Poles in Warsaw, who for ten days have been fighting against strong German forces which have cut the city into three parts. They implore machine-guns and ammunition. Can you not give them some further help, as the distance from Italy is so very great?

From this letter it followed that no one intended to inform the Soviet side in any greater detail. The Allies realized very well that the 1st Belorussian Front was not able to take Warsaw quickly. Hence their fussing about the uprising was taking on the implications of a profoundly political game being played with the fate of the insurgents in the Polish capital. This was borne out by the appearance in the British press of reports referring to the newspapers and radio broadcasts of the Polish Government in Exile. These reports on the Warsaw uprising contained hints that the insurgents were in contact with the Soviet command, which presumably was not giving them assistance. And the Polish bourgeois press in London outdid itself in attempts to put the blame on the Soviet Union for the difficult situation of the Warsaw insurgents.

Stalin reacted to this malicious slander immediately. TASS published in the newspapers, and broadcast on the radio, a statement saying that the Polish Government in Exile, which was responsible for the events in Warsaw, had made no attempt to give warning of them to the Soviet command, or to co-ordinate with the latter any actions in the Polish capital. Therefore all responsibility for what had happened lay with the Polish émigré circles in London.

Not confining himself to this, the Supreme Commander looked thoroughly into everything having to do with Warsaw, and wrote Churchill. In his letter he said that the uprising in the Polish capital was a senseless adventure for which the inhabitants had paid with countless victims. "This would not have happened if the Soviet command had been informed before the beginning of the Warsaw action, and if the Poles had maintained contact with them."

The letter plainly implied that the London Poles were trying to squeeze events into an unrealistic political scheme they had worked out, and had given no thought to the military aspects of the undertaking. The uprising had not been professionally prepared or provided for, and (most important) its organizers had not taken into account the objective role of the Soviet forces. Stalin wrote without beating around the bush: "Under the existing circumstances the Soviet command has concluded that it must dissociate itself from the Warsaw adventure, since it bears neither direct nor indirect responsibility for the Warsaw action."[7]

The Supreme Commander expressed a viewpoint on the ways of liberating Warsaw militarily that differed radically from that of the London Poles. The Soviet command felt that only a front-line assault operation would make it possible to crush the enemy. It did not refuse to help the insurgents by delivering weapons and ammunition; but there were no communications with them, and no accurate information on their position in Warsaw—something that was indispensable to organizing deliveries.

The plan for operations in the Warsaw region, approved by the Stavka, was put into effect promptly. The fighting took on an extremely fierce character, especially on the approaches to the Warsaw suburb of Praga, where the 47th Army and the 2nd Tank

---

[7] *Perepiska Predsedatelya Soveta Ministrov SSSR c Prezidentami SShA i Premer-Ministrami Velikobritanii vo vremya Velikoi Otechestvennoi voiny, 1941–45,* Vol. I, p. 257.

Army were advancing, and in the region of the bridgeheads on the Vistula. But once again the enemy's defenses proved to be very strong. Given our forces' shortage of ammunition, it was extremely difficult to break through them. The German command regrouped some of its forces near the bridgeheads and parried all our attempts to expand them. Our only successes were some slight ones achieved by the forces of the right wing. In late August, at the price of great losses, they seized small bridgeheads on the Narew River south of Różan, in the zone of Gen. P. D. Romanenko's 48th Army, and south of Pułtusk in the zone of Gen. P. I. Batov's 65th Army.

It became obvious that the 1st Belorussian Front's possibilities for an offensive had dried up. In two months of continuous forward movement its forces had covered more than six hundred kilometers in several directions. The troops were tired. The units had suffered losses. Supplies were not being brought up. And a similar situation had developed with the 2nd and 3rd Belorussian fronts and the 1st Ukrainian Front. It became necessary to go over to the defensive temporarily.

The failures of our armies were very distressing; and as if that weren't enough, London saw to it that things went from the frying pan into the fire. Having had the Supreme Commander's reply to his letter on August 16, Churchill persuaded Roosevelt to sign a message to Stalin containing a hint that the reaction of world public opinion would be unfavorable "if the anti-Nazis in Warsaw were actually abandoned."

On August 22 Stalin wrote in reply:

> Sooner or later everyone will learn the truth about the handful of criminals who, for the sake of seizing power, organized the Warsaw adventure. These people abused the trust of the Warsovians, throwing many virtually unarmed people under the German guns, tanks, and airplanes. The result was a situation such that each new day was used not by the Poles to liberate Warsaw but by the Hitlerites to ruthlessly annihilate the inhabitants of Warsaw.[8]

Stalin devoted special attention to the military significance of Warsaw.

[8] Ibid., p. 258.

From the military viewpoint a situation has developed that is fixing the Germans' acute attention on Warsaw and is also very disadvantageous both for the Red Army and for the Poles. Meantime the Soviet forces, who have recently run up against new and vigorous efforts by the Germans to go over to a counterattack, are doing everything possible to beat off these counterattacks by the Hitlerites and mount a new offensive near Warsaw. There can be no doubt that the Red Army will spare no efforts to defeat the Germans near Warsaw and liberate Warsaw for the Poles. This will be the best and most effective kind of aid for the anti-Nazi Poles.[9]

The situation in the Warsaw region was often discussed at the Stavka. Before making not only strictly military but politico-military decisions, we repeatedly estimated how effective different kinds of aid to the insurgents might be, and planned actions by our forces. Beleaguered Warsaw was not forgotten for one minute either at the Stavka or at the 1st Belorussian Front: The insurgents had to be helped, and helped as quickly as possible. Stalin himself came back to that question over and over. On one occasion in early September 1944 during a night report on the situation during the past twenty-four hours, he kept pacing around the room thinking aloud. I do not recall verbatim everything he said then; but since the problem was a very pressing, complex, and burdensome one, I can guarantee fidelity to the general tenor of his remarks.

The Supreme Commander reaffirmed that the members of the Polish Government in Exile in London were responsible for the Warsaw gamble, which was undertaken without informing the Soviet military command and in violation of its operational plans. The Soviet Government would like to see a specially created impartial commission ascertain precisely upon whose orders the uprising in Warsaw was begun, and who was responsible for the fact that the Soviet military command was not given advance notice of it. No military command—neither the British nor the American—would tolerate the organizing of an uprising in a large city ahead of its forces' front lines in violation of its operational plans and without its being informed. Obviously, the Soviet command was

[9] Ibid.

no exception. There is no doubt that if the Soviet command had been asked for its opinion on whether an uprising should be started in early August, it would have objected to the scheme. At the time, the Soviet forces were not in a state of readiness to take Warsaw by storm—all the more so, since by that time the Germans had managed to transfer their tank reserves to this region.

Looking searchingly at everybody, the Supreme Commander went on to say that no one could reproach the Soviet Government for having supplied inadequate assistance to the Polish people, including Warsaw. The most effective form of assistance was the vigorous military actions by the Soviet forces against the German occupying troops in Poland, which had made it possible to liberate more than a quarter of Poland. This had been done by Soviet forces, and only Soviet forces, who had spilled their blood for the liberation of Poland.

There remained another and rather ineffective form of assistance to the Warsovians: dropping weapons, medical supplies, and foodstuffs from aircraft. On several occasions we had dropped weapons and foodstuffs to the Warsaw insurgents, but each time we had been informed that they had got into the hands of the enemy.

Since Churchill and Roosevelt had written Stalin about aiding the Warsaw insurgents from the air, the Supreme Commander said that if the Prime Minister and the President had such a firm belief in the effectiveness of this form of aid and were insisting that the Soviet command organize the rendering of such aid jointly with the British and Americans, the Soviet Government could agree to that. It was essential, however, that the assistance be provided in accordance with a plan previously co-ordinated.

As for the attempts to blame the Soviet Government for the fate of the uprising and the victimization of the Warsovians (the Supreme Commander continued to think aloud), they could only be regarded as manifestations of a desire to shift the blame from where it really belonged. And the same thing applied to the claim that Soviet aid in the matter of Warsaw contravened the spirit of co-operation among allies. There is no doubt that if the British Government had taken steps to see that the Soviet command was given timely notice of the planned uprising in Warsaw, things in Warsaw would have taken a completely different turn.

Stalin also said that a fair exposition of the facts about the events in Warsaw would help public opinion to condemn without qualification the irresponsibility of those who organized the Warsaw uprising, and to understand correctly the position of the Soviet Government. All one could do was try to see that the public learned the entire truth about the events in Warsaw.

Such, roughly, were the ideas Stalin expressed about the uprising in Warsaw.

The General Staff received confirmation of the order to continue attacking near Warsaw and, first of all, to wipe out the enemy's bridgehead before Praga between the Vistula and the Narew rivers. Then on August 29 the three Belorussian fronts and the 1st and 4th Ukrainian fronts were ordered to go over to a fixed defense. The only exceptions were the forces of the 1st Belorussian Front's right wing, who had the mission of liberating the capital of Poland, and two armies of General M. V. Zakharov's 2nd Belorussian Front on the southern approaches to East Prussia: They went on fighting.

The General Staff and the command of the 1st Belorussian Front kept on trying to find a solution to the problems in the Warsaw region. Early in September a reconnaissance party from the 1st Belorussian Front discovered that one of the enemy's panzer divisions and several other forces that had previously been positioned near Praga had appeared before our bridgeheads on the Vistula. Obviously, the German command expected that we would step up our activity there. Now we could take advantage of this transfer of the enemy's forces to strike a blow toward Praga. This was reported to the Supreme Commander, and he issued the appropriate order.

On September 10 the 47th Army jumped off. Right behind it came the Polish 1st Army. The actions carried out by these forces were characterized by great vigor. On the night of September 13 they broke into Praga. That was when the Warsaw uprising should have been started, so as to prevent the Nazis from destroying the bridges, to seize them, and thereby to help the Soviet soldiers cross to the left bank of the Vistula—to the center of the city! But the bridges were blown up by the enemy, and the broad river barred our troops from Warsaw, which had already been a battle-ground for forty-five days. The 47th Army's reconnaissance parties made numerous attempts to force the Vistula and reach the left bank, but they were all beaten off.

The inhabitants of Warsaw's suburb of Praga gave a tremendously enthusiastic greeting to their liberators—the Soviet and Polish soldiers. Women exposed themselves to enemy fire in order to care for the wounded, to give them food and water, and to bury the dead. On orders from Marshal Rokossovsky, that sector of the front on the Vistula before Praga was given to Zigmund Berling's forces, and the 47th Army moved toward the north. The Soviet and Polish forces had reached a point from which a helping hand could be extended to the Warsaw insurgents. Of course those on the other side of the Vistula had learned that the Nazi forces in Praga had been crushed. But the leaders of the uprising from the London camp continued to adhere to their line and did not make one step toward connecting up with us. As before, they remained silent, making no attempt to establish communications, even though (as the British Government had reported) the inhabitants of Warsaw were undergoing incredible hardships.

But the leaders of the People's Army (Armia Ludowa), who had voluntarily joined in the uprising so as to be with the inhabitants of Warsaw at this trying time, promptly sent two girl messengers to the eastern bank of the Vistula, as soon as the Soviet forces approached Praga. At the risk of their lives, these young patriots reached our lines. It was from them that the Soviet and Polish commands first learned the details as to the nature of the uprising, the situation in the city, and the disposition and condition of the insurgent forces.

Now there was only the river between the insurgent Warsovians on the one hand and the Soviet forces and Voisko Polskoye on the other. Or so we thought at the time. Things, however, turned out to be much more complicated, owing to the deceitful political calculating of the rabbles of the landowner state. But we'll come to that a bit later.

On September 13 Antonov reported to the Supreme Commander the latest information on the situation of the 1st Belorussian Front. He had ordered that everything possible be done in this area, including improving the supplying of weapons, ammunition, and other matériel to the insurgents from the air. We had transmitted the orders to the front and to the Air Force. The attempts made that night to drop weapons and ammunition into Warsaw were crowned with success, and the regular supplying of the insurgents began the next day.

After our report, Stalin talked with Rokossovsky via radio. Rokossovsky reported that his front was not at the moment in a condition to liberate Warsaw. Stalin was understanding, and did not insist. To Antonov and me he mentioned once again that it was essential to establish communications with the insurgents, and that moves in that respect had already been made. Also, he ordered Zhukov, who had just returned from the Ukrainian fronts, to go back to the 1st Belorussian Front. "You'll have a free hand there. Look into the Warsaw situation on the spot, and take whatever steps are necessary. Maybe Berling's forces should try to force the Vistula in a special operation. . . . It would make a big difference. . . . Assign the task to the Poles personally, along with Rokossovsky, and help them organize things. They are still inexperienced people."

On September 15 Zhukov flew to the 1st Belorussian Front. On the morning of September 16 he and Rokossovsky went to the Zelen district in Praga, where the headquarters of the Polish 1st Army were located. Berling reported that he had managed to put across the Vistula and into the Czerniakow district of Warsaw a rifle battalion of 500 men, with nine heavy machine guns, sixteen 82-mm. mortars, and one 45-mm. mortar. The battalion was to make contact with the group of insurgents operating in that district, carry out a reconnaissance, and create a bridgehead for securing a crossing over the Vistula. An attempt to put a reconnaissance party across the river to make contact with the insurgents who had seized the northern part of Warsaw had been beaten off by the enemy. The Germans had dug in firmly along the riverbank.

During the day that Zhukov and Rokossovsky spent with the Polish 1st Army, its missions were fixed and measures ensuring their fulfillment were worked out.

As usual, the General Staff representatives (headed by Maj. Gen. N. M. Molotkov) attached to the Voisko Polskoye went where everything was "hottest." They regularly reported to us on the situation, so that we were always up to date on things. That evening Zhukov himself telegraphed the Stavka what had been undertaken, and hence the picture was filled out completely.

> In the near future (Zhukov reported), Berling's main forces will have the mission of taking the southern part of Warsaw, roughly from May 3 Blvd. and Jerusalem Blvd. to the district of Genrikow. After consolidating their position there, they are to carry out an operation to the north, preferably enveloping the city from the southwest.
>
> Also (he continued), if we succeed in making contact with the insurgent group occupying the northern part of the city, we will complement our blow from the south with a blow from the north, enveloping the city from the northwest. . . . If things go well, we will put in a beefed-up rifle corps borrowed from Gusev to secure the bridgehead. I feel that in addition to taking the city of Warsaw it would be a good idea to create a Warsaw bridgehead.

As planned, the forces of the Polish 1st Army began crossing the river at 2100 hours. General Molotkov and Colonel Evseyev went with the first echelon, made up of the Polish 3rd Infantry Division. Colonel Dubrovsky and Captain Eropkinov from Molotkov's group went with the next wave.

Our reconnaissance had been considerably stepped up. Also, we decided to drop two radio-equipped paratrooper scouts from a low altitude directly into the area which, according to our information, was occupied by the insurgents. Guns and mortars were brought up to the bridgehead that had been seized. In the Praga district we created a counter-battery artillery group with over a hundred long-range guns which were to support the crossing to the area of the bridgehead. Most of the Polish 1st Army's artillery and a brigade of 203 mm. guns were deployed as a support group for the infantry forcing the river and expanding the bridgehead.

Air units were given the mission of covering the area of the crossing and supporting the actions of our units on the west bank. In short, we had done everything possible so that we could successfully force the Vistula and, having linked up with the insurgents, crush the Nazi forces in the city and its outskirts. At the same time, the General Staff had made the necessary calculations for the forces which would bypass Warsaw as they advanced.

The General Staff did a great deal of work to make contact with the insurgents. Under the pressure of events, the command of the Home Army finally decided to make contact with us. Acting through London, the General Staff was able to provide Bor-Komorowski with all the documents necessary for that purpose. Home Army detachments in Warsaw were instructed to get into contact with the Polish 1st Army and the headquarters of the 1st Belorussian Front. On September 15 a signals officer from the Warsaw district of Zoliborz reported that he had been instructed to establish radio communication with the Red Army forces in the Praga area. Now we could not only supply the insurgents regularly and intensively but we could drop the stuff they needed in precisely the right area.

The Allies, too, were getting a move on. On September 18, coming from the west, eight groups of Flying Fortresses with twelve planes per group flew over Warsaw at an altitude of four thousand meters. For twenty minutes they dropped parachute-rigged containers of weapons, ammunition, and foodstuffs. Our observers counted almost one hundred parachutes. However, not more than twenty of the parachutes reached the insurgents. Most of them fell on territory held by the Germans, and some of them fell on our positions. On the other hand the Soviet pilots, who now knew where the insurgent detachments were positioned, confidently made night-time drops from altitudes of 150 to 200 meters, being guided by signals from below.

By way of putting a period to this matter of supplying the insurgents, herewith a few figures. From September 14 to October 1, 1944, the aircraft of the 1st Belorussian Front flew 2,243 sorties to make drops into Warsaw. They dropped 156 mortars, 505 anti-tank weapons, 2,667 automatic and semiautomatic rifles, 3 million rounds of ammunition, almost 42,000 hand grenades and other weapons, 500 kilograms of various medical supplies, and more than 113 tons of foodstuffs.

From the right bank of the Vistula—from liberated Praga—the soldiers of the Polish 1st Army could see Warsaw burning. Loyalty to the people summoned them to battle. In his order of the day for September 15, the C. in C. of the Voisko Polskoye faulted the Government in Exile for launching the uprising prematurely. The order of the day stated: "If the uprising had begun right now, it would have been co-ordinated with the command of the Red Army and the Voisko Polskoye. It could have assured the preservation of the bridges, and helped to liberate all Warsaw rapidly and to save the lives of hundreds of thousands of people. Warsaw would not have been subjected to such frightful destruction."

Getting the Polish 1st Army across the Vistula was an incredibly hard job, first of all for technical reasons. We were short on bridging equipment. Because of the river's shallowness on our side, we couldn't bring the heavy pontoons all the way to the bank; and heavy pontoons were what was needed for onloading the artillery and tanks. And the same thing was true on the other side when it came to offloading. The entire bank at the Czerniakow bridgehead and in the Praga area was subjected to raking fire by German machine guns and artillery, not to mention the enemy's strong counteraction against the subunits of the Polish 1st Army that had got a foothold on the left bank of the Vistula.

By September 17 two battalions of the 9th Polish Infantry Regiment (some 1,000 troops) with means of reinforcement were concentrated on the bridgehead in Warsaw. That night it was planned to bring across the third battalion, a battery of 76 mm. guns, and an antitank artillery regiment. Then the 9th Regiment, with support from the artillery of the Polish 1st Army from the right bank of the Vistula and the aircraft of the 16th Air Army, was to launch an attack so as to expand the bridgehead. During that time, other units of the Polish 1st Army (from the 3rd Infantry Division) were to continue crossing the river. The commander of the 1st Belorussian Front and the commander of the Polish 1st Army felt that at first these forces would be enough to fulfill the immediate mission and beat off any enemy counterattacks, including those by tanks.

At the same time, the 47th and 70th armies were continuing operations north of Praga, in the area between the Narew and Vistula rivers. There the Nazis had hung on to an extensive bridgehead from which they could strike a counterblow in the rear of Praga and then develop it toward the south. The vigorous actions by our forces in this area were carried out on direct instructions from the Supreme Commander, who was still worrying about the stability of the 1st Belorussian Front and demanded that any forces enveloping Warsaw from the northwest should render assistance to the troops fighting in the city. We made repeated attempts to advance. However, owing to a shortage of ammunition, strong resistance by the enemy, and his control of terrain that was extremely unfavorable to us, these attempts were failures for which we paid dearly.

For the next two days, there was no letup in the battle at the Czerniakow bridgehead. We had managed to get additional forces across the river at that point, but the results were not heartening. After several subunits of the Home Army, without informing the command of the Polish 1st Army, had gone off in the direction of Mokotowska, the situation in the Warsaw bridgehead became even more complicated. German superiority in troops and ordnance had become considerable in this area. Moreover, they had come into possession of marked operational advantages. Even a slight southward movement by the enemy from the district of the Poniatowski Bridge, which he held, threatened completely to cut off the Polish Army units from the river and, consequently, from the forces positioned in Praga. The river itself and both of its banks were in the zone of raking fire from artillery, mortars, and machine guns. The Germans were using their tanks as concentrated mobile forces acting jointly with strong infantry formations; and it was not easy to resist them without special antitank guns.

The soldiers of the Polish 3rd Infantry Division in the Czerniakow bridgehead had to fight for a very limited sector, which badly hampered their maneuverability. They could not break through to the center of Warsaw or its southern part, since to the west of the bridgehead the enemy had fortified a very favorable slope which dominated our positions, and to the south he had a ramified network of various defenses manned by plenty of troops. Units of the 6th Infantry Regiment of the 2nd Division tried, on the night of September 18, to seize a small bridgehead, but met with huge difficulties. Hard fighting went on for three days, but they could not gain a toe hold.

The situation necessitated major corrections to our earlier plan for the Polish 1st Army's advance into Warsaw. We had to find ways of crushing the enemy in the Polish capital that were different from those we had reported to the Supreme Commander.

"What does the General Staff propose?" he asked after a brief pause.

Antonov said he had nothing to propose other than repeating attacks by the 47th and 70th armies so as to envelop Warsaw from the north and northwest, and reinforcing the Polish 1st Army.

The Supreme Commander demanded information on the strength of the 47th and 70th armies. I gave it to him. When he became convinced that the armies were understrength and that the troops were suffering from fatigue and losses (since they had been engaged in hard fighting continuously since July 18), while the enemy's defenses were strong all along the line, a long silence came over the room. The Supreme Commander slowly paced around the table with his extinguished pipe in his hand. Finally he turned to us and said:

> Tell Comrade Zhukov that he and Rokossovsky are to figure out how to help Warsaw. . . . Isn't it still possible to wipe out the enemy's bridgehead between the rivers (the Narew and the Vistula) and launch an enveloping attack on Warsaw, using forces from Gusev's and Popov's armies? And tell them to think about what can be done about Berling in the city. Can we urgently send him reinforcements—troops with experience in street-by-street fighting?

The order was transmitted; and one day later, on September 20, Zhukov and Rokossovsky conveyed their ideas to the General

Staff. Neither the Stavka representative (Zhukov) nor the commander of the 1st Belorussian Front (Rokossovsky) had any doubts that the struggle to crush the enemy in the Warsaw region should be continued. Antonov and the Operations Department of the General Staff agreed with these ideas. And the Supreme Commander did, too. He ordered that the front make haste with preparations for the operation, and keep careful check on the situation in the Polish 1st Army's bridgehead.

About this time Stalin, the General Staff, and the Main Political Administration received from beyond the Vistula some information testifying to the incredible: The C. in C. of the Home Army had secretly undermined the insurgent forces from within. On September 20, seven officers from the headquarters of Monter, commander of the Home Army Warsaw Area, reached Praga. They had been instructed to get in touch with the command of the Red Army and of the Voisko Polskoye. One of these officers stated that Bor-Komorowski had issued secret orders to use force to compel those armed detachments oriented toward the Lublin government to take orders only from him, and to deal harshly with those who did not comply.

At the beginning of the last ten days of September the Polish 1st Army's situation beyond the Vistula got even worse, although on September 20 they were still hanging on to their position. Also, to the north of Czerniakow the 2nd Battalion of the 6th Infantry Regiment had tried once again to overcome the enemy's defenses and make a penetration in depth. But they were obliged to drop flat under enemy fire at the very edge of the bank.

The next day, the situation in Warsaw became critical. General Molotkov, the General Staff representative, who was on the spot, reported: "Since dawn on September 21, 1944, the enemy, supported by strong artillery preparation and smoke screens, has been attacking units of the Polish Army on the west bank of the Vistula. This has resulted in a loss of communications with the 2nd Battalion of the 6th Regiment, which at 0830 hours called for artillery fire on its own position."

Anyone who has been in combat knows what it means to call for artillery fire on one's own position. It means there is no other way out, and that people in the act of perishing are striving to annihilate the enemy.

The same report stated: "Communications with the battalion of the 8th Infantry Regiment have been lost. As a result of strong counterattacks by the enemy, the group consisting of two battalions of the 9th Infantry Regiment has been pushed back. As of 1800 hours on September 21 it held only a small area in the eastern part of the district."

The concentration of new and very substantial German forces (including tanks) in Warsaw proper decided the outcome of the battle. In the last ten days of September there had been a marked drop in the activity of the scattered detachments of insurgents. On the other hand, the enemy stepped up his attacks in the north, in the center of Warsaw, and in its eastern sections along the bank of the Vistula. Our aircraft and artillery regularly dealt him great losses. And there were days when his aircraft could not put in any appearance above the city at all. But on the ground we could not turn the tide of battle. Owing to the unfavorable circumstances in the city, and especially in the district of Czerniakow, the situation of those units of the Voisko Polskoye in the bridgehead became even worse. Under extremely difficult supply conditions, the battle was continuing in a narrow strip along the bank, in complete isolation from the other district of Warsaw and from the main forces of the Polish 1st Army.

All the foregoing, plus a good deal of information on the political intrigues of the leadership of the Home Army, compelled Marshal Rokossovsky, commander of the 1st Belorussian Front, to declare unequivocally that he favored discontinuing military operations in Warsaw. Zhukov supported his position. In his memoirs, *Soldatskiy dolg* (A Soldier's Duty), Marshal Rokossovsky wrote: "Under such conditions it was impossible to hang on to the west bank of the Vistula, so I decided to call off the operation. We helped the troops that had made the crossing to get back to our side of the river. By September those units of the three infantry regiments of the Polish 1st Army had joined our units."

The Supreme Command agreed with the front commander. The

Sergei Matveyevich Shtemenko.

Marshal B. M. Shaposhnikov of the
Soviet Union.

Marshal A. M. Vasilevsky of the
Soviet Union.

General of the Army A. I. Antonov.

Veteran front-line representatives of the General Staff during the Great Patriotic War meet at the M. F. Frunze Military Academy, April 19, 1967.

Field Marshal Montgomery at a party of Stalin's in the Kremlin, January 10, 1947.

Seeing Montgomery off at the central airport. Center: A. M. Vasilevsky, B. Montgomery, S. M. Shtemenko.

General of the Army Stanislav Gilyarovich Poplawsky (1972).

Russian soldiers listen to a reading of A. T. Tvardovsky's poem, "Vasily Tyorkin."

P. P. Poluboyarov, lieutenant general of the Tank Forces, and Col. N. G. Dushak observe the course of a battle near the town of Zolochev, Poland (1944).

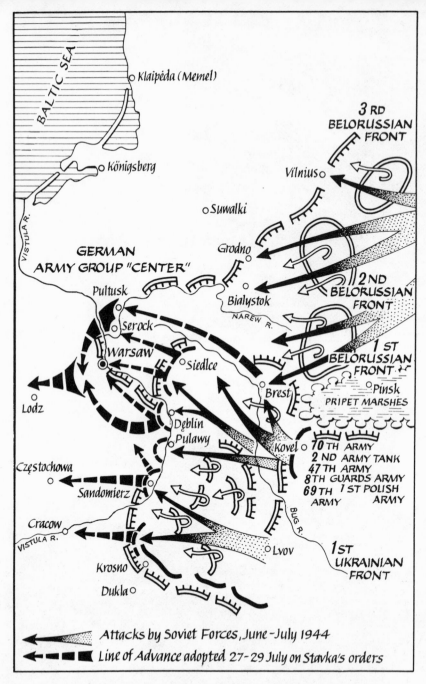

BALTIC SEA

Klaipėda (Memel)

Königsberg

VISTULA R.

3RD BELORUSSIAN FRONT

Vilnius

Suwalki

GERMAN ARMY GROUP "CENTER"

Grodno

Pultusk

Serock

Warsaw

Siedlce

Lodz

Bialystok

NAREW R.

2ND BELORUSSIAN FRONT

1ST BELORUSSIAN FRONT

Brest

Pinsk

PRIPET MARSHES

Deblin

Pulawy

Kovel

Częstochowa

Sandomierz

Cracow

VISTULA R.

Krosno

Dukla

Lvov

BUG R.

10TH ARMY
2ND ARMY TANK
47TH ARMY
8TH GUARDS ARMY
69TH ARMY
1ST POLISH ARMY

1ST UKRAINIAN FRONT

Attacks by Soviet Forces, June–July 1944

Line of Advance adopted 27–29 July on Stavka's orders

The Stavka's plan for routing the enemy in eastern Poland near Warsaw.

Soviet and Polish officers map out a plan of action. Photo taken in a suburb of Warsaw, 1944.

Residents of Praga (a suburb of Warsaw) hail soldiers of the Red Army 1st Belorussian Front, September 1944.

The Prut River at the Rumanian border. 2nd Ukranian Front, March 1944.

Red Army troops enter Rumanian territory, March 1944.

Polish 1st Army was ordered to take up a defensive position on the east bank of the Vistula.

On September 28 the Nazis launched a general offensive in Warsaw. The battles were extremely fierce. For three days the insurgents were on the verge of utter defeat. The last liaison officers from the Polish 1st Army had to leave the insurgents' headquarters, since it had become known that hostile agents were out to annihilate them physically.

During those last days, in various parts of Warsaw, the centers of insurgent resistance were dying out in this last act of the uprising. But even when completely surrounded—even under heavy fire from the Nazis—some scattered groups of insurgents who had lost contact with their commanders did not lay down their weapons. The resistance was especially strong in Zoliborz and Srodmiescie. The Communist officers of the People's Army (Armia Ludowa) had worked out a plan of action—a plan they managed to clear with the command of the 1st Army of the Voisko Polskoye and, through it, with the command of the front—assuring egress for the insurgents from Zoliborz to the bank of the Vistula, and their crossing over to Praga under cover of artillery and air support from the 1st Belorussian Front.

But this plan was sabotaged by the command of the Home Army, which at about 1800 hours on September 30 demanded that the insurgents immediately surrender. Only a small group (headed by Major Shanyavsky) emerged from the battle to the bank of the Vistula and, in boats brought over by soldiers of the Polish 1st Army, were carried back to our side of the river. Two days later, resistance ceased in Srodmiescie.

Such was the end of the uprising in Warsaw. It cast a glow of unfading glory on the insurgent people and covered with eternal shame those members of the so-called Polish London Government who organized the uprising.

In his book *The Warsaw Uprising,* the Polish military historian Jerzy Kirchmayer rightly emphasizes that at the moment when it began the uprising had almost no significance from a military viewpoint. ". . . The uprising did not bring the liberation of Warsaw closer by even one hour," he writes. "It is only in this light that one can realize how grievous was the defeat—unjustified and unnecessary."

The tragedy of Warsaw has become a symbol of the bankruptcy of reactionary bourgeois politicians. At the same time, the barricades of Warsaw bore witness to the whole world that the Polish Workers' Party and the progressive forces it led were ready to serve the people to the uttermost. An eternal flame now burns on the Czerniakow bank of the Vistula as a reminder of the blood shed by Soviet and Polish soldiers in joint battles for the bright future of the Polish people.

In the liberated eastern regions of Poland the people's regime was establishing itself. It was working for the most rapid revival of the country. Many Poles responded to this in a practical way: In the enemy's rear, partisan detachments stepped up their attacks; and in the liberated regions people joined the Voisko Polskoye so that they could take active part in liberating the rest of the country which was still under the heel of the Nazis.

The influx of volunteers was very great. And the possibilities for mobilizing contingents of draftees also increased. This made it possible in August 1944 to set about forming a Polish 2nd Army on the territory of Poland; specifically, in the region of Lublin and Siedlce. Lt. Gen. Karol Sweszczewski was named to command this army. As of October 1 its strength was about 50,000 men. A mixed air corps and other units were also beginning to be formed. Later on, the 2nd Army of the Voisko Polskoye covered itself with glory in the Berlin operation—at Nisa, near Dresden—and ended its military career near the capital of our ally, Czechoslovakia.

Since the possibilities for mobilization in the liberated territory of Poland had by no means been exhausted, the National Council of Poland proposed expanding the Voisko Polskoye still further, and adding, along with the 2nd Army, yet one more army, special forces, and rear-area units. In this connection the General Staff was ordered to keep the question of a third Polish army constantly within our field of vision—which we did. For that matter, we had no doubts as to the possibility of solving that problem. Moreover, Stalin ordered the preparation of a directive on the formation, by November 15, of a Polish Front consisting of three armies. We prepared it, and Stalin approved it—as I reported on October 3 to Vasilevsky, chief of the General Staff, who was in the Baltic area as Stavka representative.

Great difficulties were encountered, however, in carrying out this directive: There were not enough Polish officers. This was due to two causes. These were, first, the grave consequences of the landowner rule, which had not allowed the common people to get an education, and, second, the Nazi aggressors' policy of destroying Polish culture and physically annihilating its representatives. Also, as has been mentioned earlier, many officers in the technical services had gone off with Anders.

The General Staff studied various means of solving the personnel problems of the Voisko Polskoye that arose at that time. Those problems were also studied by our Polish colleagues. But time was passing, and nothing encouraging was found. Ultimately the difficult situation with respect to officer personnel made it necessary to give up the idea of forming a Polish Front, and the officers who had been recruited had to be assigned to existing forces.

The growth in the strength of the Voisko Polskoye was very substantial. By the end of the war against Nazi Germany there were almost 446,000 men in its ranks. By May 1, 1945, it had been issued 303,000 rifles and carbines, 106,500 submachine guns, about 19,000 machine guns of all types, almost 5,000 mortars of all calibers, more than 3,500 field pieces, 673 tanks and self-propelled guns, 630 aircraft of all types, about 12,000 trucks, and many other kinds of weapons and equipment.

The General Staff was getting reports telling of the great destruction undergone by Poland as a result of the long and hard years of Nazi occupation. Everything that could be taken was shamelessly appropriated in a thievish way by the German administration and the Nazi troops, or else destroyed with blind hatred. A vivid example of this was long-suffering Warsaw on the other side of the Vistula. From time to time dull explosions could be heard from the city. What was happening was that the Nazi avengers, following a special timetable, were systematically destroying the buildings of the Polish capital. The very life of the Poles was constantly threatened. It has now been ascertained that in the death camps alone, 3,577,000 Polish citizens perished at the hands of the Nazi avengers. When those who fell on the field of honor are included, the total number of those who perished is 6,028,000. In other words, there were 3,000 Polish inhabitants killed for every day of the occupation. Because of our own experience, we could fully understand the ineffable grief that afflicted the Polish people, and we tried in every way to alleviate the consequences of the fascists' evil-doing.

Although organs of the administrative regime of People's Poland decided all matters of civil life, the military situation and the ruin of the country made it necessary for them constantly to put in all kinds of requests with the military command. This was in the nature of things, and the Soviet troops could hardly help thinking and worrying about the future of Poland. The result was that the three generals who served as (first) members of military councils[10] with, respectively, the 2nd Belorussian Front, the 1st Belorussian Front, and the 1st Ukrainian Front—i.e., generals N. K. Subbotin, K. F. Telegin, and K. V. Krainyukov—were constantly occupied with these matters, and promptly dealt with the problems posed by the immediate situation. They had to make school buildings available for children, help to prepare and print primers, and see that no one interfered with the holding of religious services or laid a hand on Roman Catholic churches and other churches and houses of worship. The organization of hospitals and supplying them with medicines was also a very demanding job.

Taking advantage of the wartime situation, certain groups of shady characters (including the Ukrainian nationalists) bestirred themselves. They murdered officials, stole public property, and destroyed stores of foodstuffs and fodder. The authorities had to combat them, but they could not manage without help from our

[10] I.e., as commissars. Cf. the footnote on page 65. (Translator's note.)

forces. It became necessary to help maintain order on the liberated territory. The tasks were urgent and very difficult, since the fronts lacked much of what was necessary to restore normal life in a land ripped up by fascism.

The Soviet commanders and political workers had a hard time of it, but the work went forward. Our soldiers saw that the Polish people were selflessly setting about restoring their country. The Soviet Government and forces helped them in every way. In this unity and friendship lay the guarantee of a radiant future for Poland.

The Soviet General Staff instructed the commanding general and other commanding officers that in carrying out their missions they should pay special attention to the security of the populace and take steps to preserve industrial installations, towns, villages, and the monuments of Polish culture located therein.

In response to a request from the Polish Government, which stayed in Lublin for the time being, essential freight was brought to various regions of the country along the "green street" created by our truck drivers and railroad men. As early as the end of September 1944, 10,000 tons of flour plus medical supplies were shipped on a priority basis to Praga and the area just around it. Later, when Polish territory beyond the Vistula was liberated, the same amount of flour plus 5,000 tons of sugar was shipped to Katowice. Kraków received 5,000 tons of flour and 2,000 tons of sugar, while Częstochowa and Kielce received 1,000 tons of sugar each. By the end of 1945 the farmers of Poland had received draft animals and more than 138,000 tons of grain from two sources alone:. the 1st Belorussian Front and (later) the Group of Soviet Occupying Forces in Germany. The livestock and stores of foodstuffs and fodder left behind by the fleeing Germans and other bourgeois owners were turned over to the Polish authorities. It was necessary to supply aircraft and trucks to the Polish Government so that they could somehow organize transport and communications. Our troops restored more than 4,000 kilometers of railroad track, and more than 12,000 kilometers of railroad communications. In short, between the Committee of National Liberation and the Soviet forces there arose those genuinely human and brotherly relations of comrades-in-arms which, in April 1945, found expression in the Pact on Friendship, Mutual Assistance, and Postwar Co-operation between the USSR and the Polish Republic.

Despite the fact that the Warsaw uprising had been put down, neither the Stavka nor the General Staff gave up the idea of crushing the enemy's Warsaw grouping. The defense line along the Narew River occupied a special place in our planning. I have already mentioned the plan for an operation starting from the Narew bridgeheads—a plan based on the ideas of Zhukov and Rokossovsky. Preparations went ahead at full speed, and by October 5 the operation was to begin.

But on the morning of October 4 it was reported that the enemy had launched a large-scale attack against General Batov's forces on the Serock bridgehead, and was even pressing our units. Forward movement by the German tanks and infantry was stopped at this point, but hard fighting went on. On October 9 the *Schwerpunkt* of the attack was broken, and our armies tried to counterattack. Unfortunately, they were unable to defeat the Nazi forces. And there was no prospect of doing so in the near future. We had to regroup and build up our forces, while bringing up supplies for future operations.

In late October, Stalin too lost hope for a quick liberation of Warsaw. The forces of the 1st Belorussian's right wing had in fact gone over to the defensive, and a directive on that subject was issued by the Stavka on November 12. The complete liberation of Warsaw and the rest of Poland was associated with our winter offensive toward the west in the victorious year of 1945. As is known, it was very successful, and brought us to the jumping-off points for the final blows against Nazi Germany and its heart, Berlin.

In the course of the winter operations of 1945 the 2nd Belorussian Front literally hacked its way through enemy defenses, beat off his counterattacks, and broke through to the Danzig area. The 1st Belorussian Front, having broken through several lines of defense, reached the Oder. The forces of the 1st Ukrainian Front crushed the enemy in Silesia, liberated that major industrial region for People's Poland, and reached the Neisse. The forces of the 4th Ukrainian Front also carried out successful operations, securing from the south the operations of the main front.

The honor of entering the Polish capital was accorded to the Polish 1st Army, commanded by Lt. Gen. S. G. Poplawski. Its operations depended on the results of the offensive launched by the main forces of Marshal Zhukov's 1st Belorussian Front,[11] to which the Polish 1st Army was attached at that time. Those main forces, led by Katukov's 1st Tank Army and Bogdanov's 2nd Tank Army, drove forward to Łódź and Kutno. After breaking through all the defenses and destroying the resisting units of Army Group Center, they rapidly penetrated into the rear of the Warsaw grouping of enemy forces. The mighty tank wedge of the Soviet units had demolished the stability of the Nazi defense; and the enemy command had to think hard about how best to take to their heels and get out of the long-suffering Polish capital, now lying in ruins. The Polish 1st Army took advantage of this situation, and on January 17, 1945, it fully expunged the enemy from Warsaw.

Konev's 1st Ukrainian Front, like its neighbor on the right, had rapidly crushed the enemy defenses in its zone; and on January 18 both fronts started off in headlong pursuit of the Nazi forces. But whereas the 1st Belorussian Front merely drove straight ahead, the situation faced by the 1st Ukrainian Front was more complex. As I have mentioned, this was the industrial region of Silesia. It was important to preserve it for People's Poland, and the problem could not be solved by a direct blow. It was necessary to maneuver, to lure the enemy out into the field and crush him there. The front command accomplished this brilliantly. The 1st Ukrainian Front's Silesian operation is one of the most interesting and instructive pages in the history of Soviet military science.

Right in the path of the 1st Ukrainian Front's advance lay the ancient city of Kraków, a monument of Polish architecture con-

[11] Zhukov had been appointed commander of the 1st Belorussian Front in early October. (Translator's note.)

taining outstanding works of Polish art. In order to preserve them from destruction, the city could not be bombarded by artillery or bombed by aircraft. And there were many such examples. They testify to the desire and ability to look ahead, to the feeling of friendship lodged deep in the consciousness of the Polish and Russian peoples, to the endeavor to help one's friend under the most complex circumstances of war.

I must again emphasize that on the territory of Poland our forces operated jointly with large partisan forces on a broad scale, especially in the region of Kielce. And the ordinary people, if they could not help us with weapons, nonetheless paid the Soviet troops in a coin that is unforgettable. Many Soviet soldiers were saved from an otherwise inevitable death thanks to the selfless actions of the Polish inhabitants, who subjected themselves to a double danger.

The result of the operations carried out by our forces and the Voisko Polskoye was the complete liberation of Polish territory, from the Baltic to the Carpathians, from the Nazi aggressors. The red Soviet flag and the red and white Polish flag now fluttered over the Baltic shore and the waves of the Oder and the Neisse— the boundaries of a free and independent People's Poland.

Military co-operation between the Soviet and Polish forces continued to grow. Suffice it to say that among the units taking part in the most important of the concluding operations against Nazi Germany, the battle of Berlin, was not only the Polish 1st Army but the 2nd Army, the 1st Armored Corps, the 1st Air Corps, the 2nd Artillery Division, the 1st Mortar Brigade, and others. They formed part of the 1st Belorussian Front and the 1st Ukrainian Front, and included 185,000 officers and soldiers, more than 3,000 guns, about 500 tanks, and more than 300 aircraft. Theirs was a substantial contribution to the great success achieved by our joint efforts.

At no time and in no place was the Soviet soldier's path easy. And it was hard going in Poland, too. Some 600,000 Soviet soldiers are buried in Polish soil. The mournful rows of monuments to the dead remind us of those wartime days—of the Soviet and

Polish people's joint struggle for honor and independence, for the liberation of the Polish state from the Nazi occupying troops. People's Poland honors the memory of the fallen warriors, and is respectful toward the decisive contribution made by Soviet soldiers to the cause of defeating our common enemy, German fascism.

4

THE LIBERATION
OF RUMANIA

On the threshold of Rumania. We make preparations
for the operation. Two opinions. A conference at the
Stavka. The enemy is encircled and destroyed near
Kishinev and Iasi. The gateway to Rumania is
opened. Antonescu's dictatorship loses ground. Our
forces near Bucharest. Events in the Rumanian capital. King Michael in the role of an antifascist. An
uprising by the people. A pleasant surprise. On the
path to a people's regime. The Rumanian Army becomes our ally.

The arrival of Soviet forces on the border between the USSR and
Rumania was associated not only with military operations but
with far-reaching political measures. The Soviet Government already possessed information on the secret talks about Rumania's
situation between Rumanian ruling circles and representatives of
the United States and Britain—talks which had been held with the
aid of Prince Stirbea, the former Prime Minister. While our armies
were approaching the border, foreign journalists and diplomats
were talking about the special conditions allegedly offered by the
Soviet Government to the government of Rumania.

114

The fact that this kind of political gossip was circulating was a reliable symptom of anxiety among the fascist ringleaders of Rumania. The lie was thoroughly refuted by official Soviet organs.

> According to a report in the Swedish press [TASS stated in its rebuttal of March 22, 1944] the Swiss newspaper *Journal de Genève* has published rumors to the effect that "Russian armistice conditions approved by the Anglo-Saxons" were conveyed in Ankara to Prince Stirbea, the representative of Rumania. These conditions allegedly consist of seven points, and contain paragraphs about the Soviet-Rumanian border, the return of Transylvania to Rumania, the Soviet Union's waiving of reparations, etc.
>
> TASS is empowered to refute this report as a fabrication and to declare that no Soviet conditions have been conveyed to Stirbea or to any other representative of Rumania.

I must say that in the early spring of 1944 we at the General Staff were already sensing the wisdom of the Soviet delegation's policy at the Teheran conference (November 28–December 1, 1943), where it was decided to open the second front in Western Europe rather than in the Balkans. Indeed, every day we had reports of foreign-policy maneuvers by the ruling circles of Rumania—of their attempts to draw close to the Anglo-American bloc. Rumanian emissaries were active in Portugal, Switzerland, and Spain. They showed up in Turkey and Sweden, taking soundings of the possibility of a separate peace being concluded between the United States and Britain on the one hand and Nazi Germany and its satellites on the other. Rumania's fascist leaders —especially after the capitulation of Italy—were trying to seize the moment to desert to the Anglo-American camp. The Rumanian "opposition," headed by Iuliu Maniu and Dinu Brătianu, the leader of the "historical" parties, had also been trying for a separate peace since the summer of 1943. All their calculations were based on the hope that the British and Americans would reach Rumania before the Soviet forces did. There were reports that the rulers of Rumania were unstinting in their promises to provoke an Anglo-American occupation.

But when our forces crossed the Soviet-Rumanian border, the Soviet Government—at a press conference on April 2, 1944—issued the statement with which the reader is already familiar, and served notice on the whole world that the advancing units of our army had crossed the Prut and entered Rumanian territory, while the Soviet Supreme Command ordered the advancing units to pursue the enemy until he was completely defeated and surrendered.

On April 10 the National Defense Committee passed a resolution on the behavior of Soviet troops on Rumanian territory. The committee forwarded it to the Military Council of the 2nd Ukrainian Front with instructions to issue an appeal to the Rumanian populace repeating the gist of the Soviet Government's declaration of April 2. At the same time the resolution fixed the procedure for the general supervision, control, and follow-up on activities of civil authorities by the Military Council of the 2nd Ukrainian Front. Personal responsibility for this was made incumbent upon General I. Z. Susaikov, (first) member of the Military Council. The orders were that the Rumanian organs of authority were not to be broken up, and the property rights of citizens and private societies were to be respected. Soviet military government would be introduced on liberated territories. On the basis of this resolution, the military councils of the front and the armies launched a broad campaign of "explanatory" and practical work.

Despite the humanitarian import of the Soviet Government's declaration, Hitler's Rumanian henchmen began to worry, realizing that the Red Army's victories would exercise a great prerevolutionary influence on the Rumanian workers and create favorable conditions for an antifascist conflict. Soon the Allies informed the USSR of new attempts by the Rumanian Government to start talks with them. But now our government entered into talks with the Rumanians. And it presented Ion Antonescu with six conditions for an armistice: rupture of relations with the Germans, and fighting them jointly with the nations of the anti-Nazi coalition; full restoration of the Soviet border with Rumania, and reparations for the damage done by Rumanian forces; return of Soviet and allied prisoners of war; comprehensive co-operation with the operations of Soviet and Allied forces on the territory of Rumania; abrogation of the Transylvanian question; and assistance to Soviet forces in liberating this region from the enemy. Antonescu's government refused the conditions and continued the war.

While the talks were being held, military actions were continuing and developing in their turn. The attempts at a quick advance which we had made from our bridgehead beyond the Prut back in April had been unsuccessful; and on orders from Stalin the three fronts—the 1st, 2nd, and 3rd Ukrainian—took up defensive positions. But this by no means meant a cancellation of the preparations for an offensive: The plan for an operation in a south-westerly direction was being elaborated at top speed at the General Staff and at the fronts.

Both the General Staff and the Main Political Administration had a lot to think about in those days. The job of liberating Rumania was not only very delicate but very complex, since Rumania was an ally of Hitler's Reich, and its ruling circles were accomplices in his crimes. Rumanian soldiers had been among those occupying troops who left behind them on Russian soil the sites of fires whose acrid smoke had still not been entirely dissipated, the blackened ruins of villages and towns, and countless widows and orphans. . . .

As early as the end of March 1944 the Soviet Supreme Command was preparing Soviet officers and political organs for actions in Rumanian territory. The routing of the enemy and his network of agents must be accomplished in the manner demanded by the laws of war, but without infringing on the legal rights of the Rumanian regime in internal affairs. The aims, content, and methods of political work among the troops were spelled out, as were the rules and norms of behavior for Soviet military personnel abroad. Everyone understood how necessary it was ruthlessly to suppress any instance of a violation of the laws, even by irresponsible individuals.

We had a vital interest in close co-operation with the toiling people of Rumania: Only such co-operation could lead to a victory for democratic principles in that country. But here, too, we foresaw great difficulties. The Rumanian Government had declined the humanitarian conditions for an armistice offered by the Soviet Government on April 12, 1944, and blood was still being spilled. The former was trying in every way to frighten the populace with slander about the "horrors of Soviet occupation," exile to Siberia, and other fabrications.

Fascist propaganda combined slander of the Red Army with attempts to discredit the Rumanian Communists and partisans, saying they were plunderers and bandits. But it must be admitted that the Rumanian people quickly figured out who was really fighting for their happiness.

We knew that in a Rumania crushed under the heel of Antonescue's military dictatorship and actually occupied by fascist Germany, the Communists were consolidating their position and influence from one day to the next.

In the spring of 1944, when the crisis of the Antonescu regime began to become apparent, the Communist Party of Rumania emphasized as one of its chief tasks the struggle for the unity of the working class, which was a major precondition to assuring the future success of an armed uprising. Helpful in the accomplishment of this task was the founding, in April 1944, of a United Workers' Party which came out with the May Day manifesto, "To the entire working class! To the Rumanian people!" The manifesto called upon people to use all means to destroy the Nazi war machine. At the same time the Communist Party began to create paramilitary patriotic groups which gradually prepared for an armed uprising. On the territory of the USSR, Rumanian antifascists and former prisoners of war had been formed into the Tudor Vladimirescu Infantry Division and partisan groups. The latter were parachuted into Rumania. In May 1944 the Communist Party concluded an agreement on joint action with one of the national liberal groups; and later the leaders of the National Peasant and National Liberal parties themselves sought contact with the Communists. They were prompted to this by the prospect of Nazi Germany's collapse. In their endeavor to unite the anti-Nazi forces (including the bourgeois parties), the Communists proved very flexible, having the aim of isolating Antonescu's fascist clique and involving in the struggle against it that part of the population that was under the influence of the bourgeois landowner parties. But things had not yet reached the point where a political bloc was formed to oppose the fascist regime.

On instructions from the Stavka, the General Staff was responsible for taking into account the situation in this country or that, including all the complex political problems, and even taking part in their solutions—to varying degrees. Thus at the Stavka we were more than once reminded of the new situation our forces were now entering. Also, R. Ya. Malinovsky, whose front was the basic force in Rumania and Hungary, was often warned of the particular importance of the political task incumbent upon his troops.

The two other fronts—the 2nd and 3rd Ukrainian—were opposed by the Southern Ukraine Group of Nazi armies. It included two German armies (the 8th and the 6th) and two Rumanian armies (the 4th and the 3rd), the German 17th Independent Army Corps, and many other infantry and special units.

The stability of the enemy's forces was very considerable, as had been shown in past battles. For a long time the Southern Ukraine Group had been commanded by one of the most capable German military leaders, Col. Gen. Ferdinand Schörner. (Later he fiercely resisted Soviet forces even after the order for Germany's unconditional surrender.) In late July Schörner was replaced by General Friessner. Hitler's command was hoping that this replacement would be useful. Friessner was known to us as a military leader of great experience and knowledge, although he had had some failures in the Baltic area, where he had commanded the Army Group North. Throughout the Southern Ukraine Group's tactical zone, defense installations were being built around the clock. In some sectors newly created field positions were combined with previously strengthened fortified regions.

There was still one more circumstance that had to be taken into account in planning operations in the Balkans: the likelihood of the so-called Balkan version of Allied operations. This version called for the simultaneous opening of a second front and an invasion of the Balkan Peninsula by Allied forces. As early as the Teheran conference, Churchill had proposed the "Balkan version" in general form; and now he was insisting on its being carried out.

If the Balkan version were put into effect, the Anglo-American forces would play the chief role on the peninsula. The Soviet Union would have to overcome considerable difficulties of a political nature and do a great deal of work in co-ordinating the actions of the Allied armies. It was also possible that our allies would try to reach an agreement with the Rumanian Government behind our back. Incidentally, we soon learned that something of the kind was afoot.

There were also difficulties in co-ordinating the efforts of the Soviet Armed Forces. A mere glance at the map showed that two simultaneous operations were required: one toward the south, in order to liberate Bulgaria and Yugoslavia; and one toward the west, in order to crush the Nazi forces in Hungary, Austria, and Czechoslovakia. Thus for a certain period of time our forces would be scattered. Also, it was plain that they would have to fight over a very broad front under terrain conditions that were extremely unfavorable for an advance, since the mountains, rivers, and many inhabited localities gave the enemy an opportunity to defend himself successfully.

Together with the strictly military and political preparation of the Red Army for its liberation mission on the territory of nations that were Nazi Germany's satellites, diplomatic measures were undertaken—measures that shook the foundations of the Nazi coalition. In particular, on May 13, 1944, the governments of the Soviet Union, Great Britain, and the United States issued a declaration to Hungary, Rumania, Bulgaria, and Finland. It stated that the present policy of the governments of these satellite countries was substantially strengthening the German military machine. At the same time, those nations could cut short the war in Europe, reduce the number of victims among their own citizens, and facilitate the Allied victory. To this end they should get out of the war, cease their co-operation with Germany (which was disastrous for them), and resist the Nazis with all means at their disposal. The satellite nations were warned that they must decide immediately whether they would persist in their present hopeless and disastrous policy or make a contribution to the common victory of the Allies and thus avoid responsibility for taking part in the war on

120

the side of the Nazis. This step taken by the Allied powers had great political effect, since it helped substantially to strengthen the position of the Resistance forces.

As I have said, the commanders of the 2nd and 3rd Ukrainian fronts had received instructions to prepare for the operation back in May 1944. The work was continuing, since the date for launching the operation kept being postponed; and the forces of the fronts changed. Also, with such decisive events impending, changes were made in the command personnel of the fronts. Malinovsky was shifted to the 2nd Ukrainian Front, while command of the 3rd Ukrainian Front was taken over by F. I. Tolbukhin. Konev commanded the 1st Ukrainan Front, while Zhukov returned to his duties as Deputy Supreme Commander, and soon went to the 1st and 2nd Belorussian fronts as Stavka representative. It must be admitted that these personnel changes were very necessary. For example, Malinovsky and the chief of staff of the 2nd Ukrainian Front, M. V. Zakharov, had begun the war in that region and knew it in detail.

The process of detaching from the 2nd and 3rd Ukrainian fronts those forces intended for use in Belorussia and in other directions was completed by early July. The Stavka had been obliged to transfer the 5th Guards Army from the 2nd Ukrainian Front to Chernyakovsky's 3rd Belorussian Front, and to transfer to the 2nd Tank Army to Rokossovsky's 1st Belorussian Front. The 5th Guards Army was attached to the 1st Ukrainian Front, which was making ready for the Lvov operation. The 8th Guards Army and several special units were detached from the 3rd Ukrainian Front so as to strengthen the 1st Belorussian Front's left flank. Since the outcome of the campaign would be decided in the west—the most important front at that time—the Soviet Supreme Command did not hesitate to weaken the forces of the southern fronts to this substantial extent, assuming that the results of the operations in Belorussia and near Lvov would make it possible, later on, to solve whatever problems arose in other directions. By this time it was more or less clear what forces

Malinovsky and Tolbukhin would have available for their offensive in the southwest.

The time for carrying out the general plan of the campaign was approaching. Accordingly, the General Staff instructed the staffs of the fronts to formulate their ideas about an offensive in the region of Iaşi (Jassy) and Kishinev with the aim of destroying the German Army Group Southern Ukraine.

At the time the General Staff officers working on 2nd Ukrainian Front matters were headed up by Maj. Gen. N. V. Postnikov, while those working on 3rd Ukrainian Front matters were headed up by Maj. Gen. K. F. Vasilchenko. They maintained close liaison with the staffs of the fronts and planned operations jointly with them.

It was at the 2nd Ukrainian Front that the planning went most smoothly. With respect to the aim of the operation and the direction of the main blow, the front command and the General Staff rapidly found a common language and firm agreement. In their zone of attack, the front's forces were to cut off communications to the west and south for the enemy's main forces in the region of Ungeny, Iaşi, and Kishinev and, acting jointly with the 3rd Ukrainian Front (their neighbor to the left), encircle those enemy forces. Thus the main blow should be struck in the direction of Huşi, which would make it possible to accomplish all the other missions assigned. The next thing to be done, acting jointly with the 3rd Ukrainian Front, was fully to destroy Army Group Southern Ukraine.

But with respect to the missions and methods of the 3rd Ukrainian Front, there were several opinions. The front's staff and Military Council insisted that in order to encircle the enemy's main forces, the front's main blow should be delivered toward Huşi from the Kitskan bridgehead that had been seized on the right bank of the Dnieper south of Tiraspol. In this direction, there would be no large water or other barriers in the path of the attacking forces. We at the General Staff fully realized this. But we figured that if the offensive were launched from the bridgehead, the element of surprise would be lost and it would therefore be difficult to break through, since the enemy was expecting us to

122

attack from just that area and was prepared to take counter-measures. We proposed that the main blow be struck in the direction of Kishinev, where it would be easier to achieve surprise, although it would be necessary to force the Dniester. We had adequate forces and equipment for forcing the river; and if surprise were achieved, the river-forcing and the break-through could be achieved more easily here (in our opinion) than in any other direction.

During the second half of July the planning continued with special intensity and with the same close co-operation. Again and again, we studied the arguments of both sides in detail. But right in the middle of our work, we got new intelligence enabling us to conclude that the enemy was not expecting our main blow from the Kitskan bridgehead but was looking chiefly to the Kishinev region in his calculations. This was an important conclusion. It now made no sense for the General Staff to defend its viewpoint. We agreed with the opinion held by the command of the 3rd Ukrainian Front: The Kitskan bridgehead must be the jumping-off point.

Meantime, events of decisive significance for the course of the war were taking place on the other fronts. From the west—from the 1st, 2nd, and 3rd Belorussian fronts and the 1st Ukrainian Front—came reports of victories that gladdened the hearts of Soviet men and women. As has already been said, our forces had dealt crushing defeats to Army Group Center and were racing toward the western boundaries of the Soviet Union. Some units had already crossed them and seized bridgeheads on the western bank of the Vistula. At that time Konev's 1st Ukrainian Front was advancing with especially great rapidity. Its forces had successfully forced the Vistula near Sandomierz and were continuing to exploit their success.

The time had come for the final evaluation of plans for operations in the southwest. On July 31 a special conference was held at the Stavka where problems of preparing our forces for the Iaşi-Kishinev operation were discussed. Those attending the conference included Marshal S. K. Timoshenko, Stavka representative with the 2nd and 3rd Ukrainian fronts, the commanders of those fronts, and the (first) members of their Military Councils, I. Z. Susaikov and A. S. Zheltov.

The special significance of the Iaşi-Kishinev operation for the subsequent development of military and political events in Rumania was taken into account at the conference. The Soviet Armed Forces must, in a single mighty blow, destroy the enemy's main forces and at the same time decisively undermine the stronghold of the fascist dictatorship in Rumania.

In this connection I should mention the "piquant" thing about the Iaşi-Kishinev operation. The fact was that the German command was devoting most of its attention to the Kishinev sector, feeling that our main blow would be struck there. Hence the main forces of the best German divisions were concentrated in that area. These formations were positioned compactly in the tactical zone. This indicated that the enemy was counting on beating off our first and most powerful blow before it had made a deep penetration. It is also likely that the enemy figured that if necessary he could pull back his forces to positions prepared in the deep defensive zone. Moreover, the Red Army's blows might be parried by the enemy's main reserves, deployed in this area. But those reserves were not large, consisting as they did of two infantry divisions and one panzer division.

The flanks of the enemy's Kishinev grouping were defended by Rumanian forces. They were not so well armed as the German troops, not so well trained, and not so well supplied. According to our intelligence, their morale was low: Many individual soldiers, and even units, were anti-German. Thus a situation had developed in which the most vulnerable points in the enemy's defense were the flanks of his Kishinev grouping.

At the Stavka conference we came to the conclusion that under these circumstances the best plan would be to encircle and destroy, in a short time, the main forces of Army Group Southern Ukraine in the Kishinev region. The enveloping position of our forces made it possible to break through the enemy's defenses on his weak flanks, then advance by the shortest route to Huşi, Vaslui, and Komrat in the rear of the main grouping of the German forces, so as to encircle them and destroy them.

The primary operational and strategic aim of the Soviet forces was not the taking of the capital but the encirclement and destruction of the German forces in the Kishinev region. After the enemy's defeat, conditions would be favorable for our front to penetrate rapidly into the interior of Rumania and accomplish their next tasks, including the capture of Bucharest and other economic and political centers of that country. In this case we would advance through the "Focşani Gateway"; i.e., through the most favorable terrain. We then planned to advance on a broad front to the Danube and the eastern borders of Hungary and the northern borders of Yugoslavia and Bulgaria. We hoped that as a result of these offensive operations Rumania would soon be removed from its role as a German ally in the war.

We gave special attention to such difficult questions as whether the Soviet forces would be able to prevent a possible withdrawal by the enemy. The logic of things suggested that if Friessner managed to surmise our intent he would immediately pull back his main forces and organize his defense along another line. But just when would he realize what our forces were up to? On the basis of our war experience we figured that the Nazi command would not divine our intent before the second day of the offensive. This was important. In order to avoid the formation of a cauldron, the enemy's forces would have to cover a distance of sixty to eighty kilometers to a crossing on the Prut. But our advancing units, in order to cut off the enemy's escape route, would have to cover a much greater distance (about one hundred kilometers) to that same crossing. Therefore, if the Nazi command managed to pull its forces back, our plans for encirclement would fail, and we would have to carry out a new operation.

Thus the first precondition to our success was achieving surprise and a high rate of advance for our forces. We would have to do a quick job of seizing such advantageous features of the terrain as the Mare Ridge, along which the enemy's second line of defenses ran, prevent him from digging in there, and destroy his reserves moving up from the rear. Also, we had to seize the crossings on the Prut before they could be used by the enemy in a withdrawal.

Our calculations showed that the rate of advance would have to be twenty-five kilometers a day!

From this followed the sequence of our forces' actions. The infantry was to make a quick break-through, which the tanks would then rapidly develop in depth, penetrating to the crossings on the Prut. Thus it was necessary to keep the tanks in a concentrated force and not scatter them in the course of the operation, and to commit them after a break-through in the enemy's defenses. In order to build up forces during the operation, it would be necessary to create a deep operational structure of forces.

The matter of the ratio of forces was also decided at the Stavka conference. We had no great superiority over the enemy, especially on the 3rd Ukrainian Front. The ratios were as follows: in troops, 1.2:1; in guns of various calibers, 1.3:1; in tanks and self-propelled guns, 1.4:1; in machine guns 1:1; in mortars, 1.9:1; and in aircraft, 3:1. Obviously, we would have to compensate for this inadequate superiority by massing our forces on the sector of the main blow. It was decided to solve the problem by stripping all secondary sectors of the front. Here is the striking picture the front then offered. The ratios of forces on the sector of the main offensive were as follows: troops, 6:1; guns of various calibers, 5.5:1; tanks, 5.4:1; machine guns, 4.3:1; mortars, 6.7:1; aircraft, 3:1. This edge of superiority was sufficient for breaking through the enemy's defenses and exploiting the success. All the rest depended on the skill of the commanders and the skill and self-sacrificing spirit of the troops.

At this session the Supreme Commander again talked about the military and political significance of the operation. As we know, he had first pointed out the political aspects of the operation to the commander of the 2nd Ukrainian Front during the initial stage of planning. Now he was talking about it in connection with the density of artillery in Malinovsky's forces. When the front commander reported that on each of the twenty-two kilometers of the break-through sector he could concentrate 220 guns of no less than 76 mm.—i.e., that he could create a very great density of artillery—Stalin said that even that was not enough: We needed more. When it turned out that we lacked the resources to create a greater density on that sector, it was proposed that the break-through sector be reduced to sixteen kilometers, thereby achieving a density of 240 guns per kilometer (and even a bit more). This great density of artillery was one of the guarantees of staggering the enemy, rapidly breaking through his defenses, and exploiting the success in depth as far as the crossings on the Prut and in the direction of Focșani. According to Stalin's thinking, these mighty blows at the defenses of Hitler's ally would have an effect on the policy of the Rumanian monarchy and facilitate its getting out of the war.

Also involved in the 3rd Ukrainian Front's operation were the Black Sea Fleet and the Danube Flotilla, which had just recovered their old bases. Their actions along the Black Sea littoral, in the Dniester Estuary, and on the Danube—the seizure of the enemy's naval bases and ports, landing our assault troops in the enemy's rear, and supporting their attacks—were to become a very important factor in the general success. With the aid of the Stavka representative, the front commander quickly struck up a good relationship with the fleet commander, Adm. F. S. Oktyabrsky, and the flotilla commander, Rear Adm. S. G. Gorshkov (now Fleet Admiral of the Soviet Union and C. in C. of the Navy). They worked closely together. And the same can be said of Gen. I. T. Shlemin, commanding the forces of the 46th Army, which had to force the Dniester Estuary with the help of the Danube Flotilla.

Following the Stavka conference, certain adjustments were made in the plans for the fronts. So far as the 2nd Ukrainian Front was concerned, they may be summarized as follows:

> The aim of this operation: crush the enemy on the Iași sector and, acting jointly with the 3rd Ukrainian Front, encircle and destroy the German divisions of the enemy's Kishinev grouping. On the fifth day the offensive should reach the line Bacău-Deleni-Huși. Then develop the offensive to Focșani with the aim of capturing Rumania's oil-producing regions.
>
> Implementation: Considering the nature of the enemy's defenses, the most advantageous sector for a break-through is

that running from Podu Iloaie to Iași, where no permanent defenses have been put up. The main blow is to be delivered by forces of the 27th and 52nd armies, the 6th Tank Army, and the 18th Tank Corps,[1] jumping off from a sector sixteen kilometers in width and bypassing Iași on the southwest toward Huși.

The main forces were supported by the 5th Air Army, then commanded by Gen. S. K. Goryunov. Three mixed armies were to make secondary attacks on three sectors, both to the left and to the right of the main grouping of forces.

The front had very great reserves. They included the 53rd Army, which was to operate in the attack zone as a part of the main forces of the 52nd Army, the 5th Guards Cavalry, the 23rd Armored, and the 57th and 27th Guards Rifle corps. This structure of the reserve was due to the tasks of exploiting the success from depth. Also, it took into account the front's leading place in the strategic operation.

As we wrote at that time in our report on the actions of Tolbukhin's forces, the aim of the 3rd Ukrainian Front's operation was to "break through the enemy's defenses on the right flank of his Kishinev grouping (where we would be opposed chiefly by Rumanian forces), and with the aid of mobile units rapidly to exploit this success in the general direction of Komrat; then turn northwest toward the region of Leuseni, Lapushna, and Negra, link up with the forces of the 2nd Ukrainian Front, and jointly encircle and destroy the enemy's Kishinev grouping. Simultaneously, units of the 46th Army are to encircle and destroy the enemy's Ackerman grouping."

The main forces of the front included all of Gen. M. N. Sharokhin's 37th Army, and part of the forces of Gen. N. A. Gagen's 57th Army and Gen. I. T. Shlemin's 46th Army. The 7th and 4th Guards Mechanized Corps were to exploit the success. The 17th Air Army, commanded by Gen. V. A. Sudets, would be active in the sector of the main attack.

---

[1] The 27th Army was commanded by Col. Gen. S. G. Trofimenko, the 52nd by Lt. Gen. K. A. Koroteyev, the 6th Tank Army by Lt. Gen. of Tank Forces A. G. Kravchenko, and the 18th Tank Corps by Maj. Gen. of Tank Forces V. I. Polozkov.

128

Since the 3rd Ukrainian Front had only five armies, Tolbukhin could not put much into his reserve: It included only the 10th Guards Rifle Corps.

Thus the characteristic trait of the front commanders' plans was the massing of forces in the sectors of the main blows, and making ample provision for their support. Here they could hit the enemy with an average of more than 240 guns and mortars (76 mm. and above) and thirty to fifty tanks per kilometer of the break-through sector.

A joint directive from the Stavka to the 2nd and 3rd Ukrainian fronts on the preparation and execution of the operation aimed at destroying the enemy in the region of Iaşi, Kishinev, and Bendery was signed on August 2, at 2300 hours. When the fronts had received this directive, they expanded their planning for the operation even further. Forces were regrouped, and the necessary training exercises were carried out. (This was not easy, especially on the small open bridgehead occupied by Tolbukhin's forces.) On instructions from the Stavka, operational camouflage measures were taken. It was very important that our skillful and powerful enemy be made to expect our offensive only in the region of Kishinev. And we succeeded. For a long time the crafty Friessner believed the Soviet command would not strike a blow at him anywhere else. And we also caused him to make a mistake in predicting the scope of our operations.

Misleading the enemy in this way was not easy. To this end, for example, Gen. N. E. Berzarin's 5th Shock Army openly made preparations for an offensive in the region of Serpen. And specially chosen forces, using radio equipment, feigned the concentration of a new army consisting of several corps and armored units, ostensibly intended for the 3rd Ukrainian Front. A feigned concentration of forces was likewise effected in the attack zones of the 40th and 7th Guards armies on the right flank of the 2nd Ukrainian Front. Specially selected trucks pulling various kinds of jerry-built structures to make big clouds of dust created the false impression of columns moving. In the areas that had been occupied by the 6th Guards Tank Army and the 7th Mechanized Corps before their regrouping, dummy tanks and guns were left behind as a matter of course, giving the impression that these forces had not changed their positions.

The forces met the deadlines laid down for them in the timetable. On August 19 both fronts carried out a reconnaissance in force over a broad sector. It showed that there was no need for adjustments in the plans for the impending operations.

Our reconnaissance in force alarmed the enemy. Late in the day, having received a report of it, General Friessner called a conference which was attended by the commanding generals of the 4th and 8th armies and of the 4th Air Force. The Rumanian commanders were not invited. The Nazi generals were all of the opinion that a big offensive by the Soviet forces was to be expected on the next day. In that they were not mistaken. But the regrouping of forces that they hurriedly undertook so as to strengthen their defenses on the threatened sectors could not, by this time, prevent their defeat. The German generals understood this; and that same evening, "just in case" (as Friessner himself wrote later), they considered a plan for withdrawing the forces of Army Group Southern Ukraine.

While this nervous conference was being held at Friessner's headquarters, Marshal Timoshenko (the Stavka representative), Malinovsky, and Air Marshal S. A. Khudyakov, accompanied by the operations officers, went to the 2nd Ukrainian Front's observation post on a height designated on the map as Hill 195. Shortly thereafter, Tolbukhin, commander of the 3rd Ukrainian Front, accompanied by his operations officers, went to his own O.P. Then, on August 20 at 0610, the 2nd Ukrainian Front began its artillery preparation, with the 3rd Ukrainian Front following up at 0800. Thousands of guns were firing, making a breach in the enemy's defenses. The shells literally lifted the enemy's positions into the air. The Iaşi-Kishinev operation had begun.

The military actions of this operation are sufficiently well known, and there is no need to give a detailed account of them. I shall say only that they were very successful, and abounded in examples of great courage, heroism, and valor on the part of Soviet soldiers. The blow by the attacking rifle units was so strong that by noon units of S. G. Trofimenko's 27th Army had broken through the enemy's tactical zone of defenses to a depth of sixteen kilometers and were forcing the Bahlui River. This made it possible to put A. G. Kravchenko's 6th Tank Army into the breach right away, although this move had been planned for the second day of the operation.

In the attack zone of K. A. Koroteyev's 52nd Army the offensive was also developing successfully: By late afternoon these forces had broken through to the approaches to Iaşi and were fighting for the town.

Things were also going well in the 3rd Ukrainian Front's attack zone: In the main sector the enemy's defenses had been penetrated to a depth of ten to twelve kilometers.

According to our estimates at the time, on the first day of the operation our forces crushed six enemy divisions and penetrated to his third line of defense, located at a depth of twenty-five to forty kilometers and running along the wooded Mare Ridge. Here they were halted: The 6th Tank Army was unable to break through the defenses on the run.

The Stavka and the General Staff gave due credit to the heroism of our troops and the successes they had achieved. But in our opinion the results of the first day's actions should, under the circumstances, have been better. This applied especially to the 2nd Ukrainian Front, where in our view the commitment of Kravchenko's tank army should have made it possible to incease the rate and depth of the advance very substantially. Since the offensive had been slowed down, we were apprehensive that the enemy, taking advantage of the favorable terrain, might pull together on the most important sectors as many forces as he could, and hold our forces up for a long time. And this would mean that we would be late in getting to the crossings over the Prut and in cutting off the enemy's escape route to the south, in which case we could not encircle him.

This was what the General Staff reported to the Stavka on the night of August 21. At the time, the Supreme Commander did not think it necessary to issue any more instructions to the fronts, apparently having decided to sleep on it. But again the next morning the 6th Tank Army failed to break through the enemy's defenses, as did the 18th Tank Corps, which had been advancing through the 52nd Army's attack zone in a turning movement around Iași.

This was due to the fact that the German command had organized a counterattack on the approaches to their third line of defenses, using three divisions, including the Great Rumania Armored Division, re-equipped with German matériel. Although this counterattack was beaten off, neither the 2nd Ukrainian Front's tactical air force nor its other forces had been able to nip it in the bud. The result was one more day's delay for our forces attacking up Mare Ridge.

Things were going better for Tolbukhin. His forces had broken the resistance of General Dumitrescu's army group, which was built around the Rumanian 3rd Army.

We at the General Staff were much disturbed by the situation in the sector of the 2nd Ukrainian Front's main thrust. At noon on August 21 we got into telephone contact (as usual) with the staffs of the advancing fronts, and were given the latest information on the situation. Soon we had to go to the Kremlin to report. Zakharov, chief of staff of the 2nd Ukrainian Front, had been optimistic about the situation. He felt that our forces would not be held up long before Mare Ridge and would soon be advancing rapidly. He had also reported that he was expecting news of the capture of Iași from one hour to the next, and he turned out to be right.

At 1500 hours Antonov and I were in the Supreme Commander's office. When the time came to report on the situation in the southwest, Stalin, after carefully studying the map, told us to remind the commanders of the 2nd and 3rd Ukrainian fronts—and the Stavka representative as well—of the main task of the forces under their command: to surround the enemy as soon as possible. He dictated:

> . . . Today the chief task of the forces of the 2nd and 3rd Ukrainian fronts, in which the two fronts will act jointly, is more rapidly to close the ring of encirclement around the enemy in the region of Huși, then to tighten this ring with the aim of annihilating or imprisoning the enemy's Kishinev grouping.

Since a break-through of the enemy's defenses on Mare Ridge might create a temptation to send the main forces of the 2nd Ukrainian Front toward Roman and Focşani in pursuit of the enemy, and to send those of the 3rd Ukrainian Front in the direction of Tarutino and Galaţi, the Supreme Commander emphasized:

> The Stavka orders that the basic forces and resources of both fronts be used to accomplish this main task, with no diversion of forces for other tasks. Accomplishment of the task of crushing the enemy's Kishinev grouping will open for us the road to the main economic and political centers of Rumania.

We paid special attention to these instructions. After all, it was the General Staff's job to follow up on the execution of the Stavka's orders.

In concluding his dictation, Stalin said:

> Both fronts are faced with about forty-four enemy divisions, of which six have already been crushed. You have eighty-seven divisions, plus considerable superiority in artillery, tanks, and aircraft. Thus you have everything needed to accomplish the aforementioned task, and you must accomplish it.

The Stavka representative, Marshal Timoshenko, was instructed to see that this directive was carried out to the letter.

While we were reporting on the situation, new information came in from the front. Iaşi, an important center in the enemy's defense system, had been captured at 1500. And units of General Shumilov's 7th Guards Army, emerging from behind the right flank of the advancing forces of S. G. Trofimenko's 27th Army, had begun to swing to the west in a turning movement around the fortified town of Targu-Frumas. Their task was to break through the enemy's defenses and, from the west, support the actions of the front's main forces. The 6th Tank Army and the 27th Army had driven spearheads through the enemy's defenses to a depth of forty-nine kilometers, broken those defenses, and penetrated to an operational (minor strategical) depth. Now they could cut off the enemy's most likely escape routes toward the west and the south, and destroy those enemy forces trying to avoid the impending encirclement.

The 3rd Ukrainian Front had also advanced a good distance. In the sector of the 4th Guards Mechanized Corps, commanded by Gen. V. I. Zhdanov, penetration went as deep as fifty kilometers. This front had cut off the Rumanian 3rd Army from the German 6th Army.

The Stavka directive came at a very opportune time for organizing the actions of the fronts. By the end of the day, on August 21, the enemy was no longer able to hold the favorable positions he had been occupying on Mare Ridge, and began to withdraw under pressure from the armies of the 2nd Ukrainian Front. With the 6th Tank Army and the 18th Tank Division in the vanguard, Malinovsky's forces raced after him, continuing the pursuit during the night of August 22 and all the next day. The power of the blow struck by the main forces was reinforced by another thrust from I. V. Galinin's attacking 4th Guards Army. Moving along the left bank of the Prut, it secured the front's operation from the east and at the same time split the defenses of the enemy's Kishinev grouping with a blow from north to south. By the end of the day forces of the 2nd Ukrainian Front had penetrated the enemy's defenses to a depth of 60 kilometers, and expanded the break-through to a width of 120 kilometers.

The armies of the 3rd Ukrainian Front were racing from the east toward the crossings on the Prut. Overwhelming the resisting Rumanian and German forces, their mobile units had by the end of August 22 driven wedges into the enemy's positions as deeply as eighty kilometers, and covered three quarters of the distance to their goal. On the left flank, forces of this front, acting jointly with the Danube Flotilla, had successfully forced the Dniester Estuary.

Thus in the course of August 22 one could see the emergent outlines of that huge encirclement that constituted the gist of the operations planned by the Stavka of the Soviet Supreme Command for the destruction of the German Army Group Southern Ukraine near Iaşi and Kishinev.

It was already late in the evening, and the Supreme Commander, after signing the instructions to fire off a salute, ordered that it be fired the next day but that the announcement of the victories (near Iași and Kishinev) be made over the radio immediately. So far as I can recall, this was the only time during the war when there was a lag of twenty-four hours between the announcement of a victory and the firing of the salute.

On August 23 all the armies of the 2nd and 3rd Ukrainian fronts that were in the first wave continued to pursue the enemy. Gen. N. E. Berzarin's 5th Shock Army also took a successful part in the proceedings. In one day of fighting its forces advanced to depths of twenty-four to forty-five kilometers in different sectors. Also successful was the envelopment of the flanks of the German 6th Army, which as has already been said was the basis of the enemy's front in Rumania. The time for encircling Friessner's main forces was drawing near; but on that day our armies did not manage to close the ring.

The German and Rumanian forces were trying to retreat beyond the Prut toward the west and south. Bitter fighting was in progress all along a huge arc running from Vaslui through Huși to Leovo. It was especially fierce near the crossings on the Prut, where the enemy was striving to break out of a trap about to snap shut.

The enemy's efforts at preventing the catastrophe were vigorous and dynamic. Not losing the hope of defeating the Red Army, the German command committed masses of tanks and supported them with strong forces in the air and dense artillery fire on the ground. In some sectors the enemy broke through the lines of the 2nd Ukrainian Front's attacking forces and turned up in the rear of Soviet units. Fighting broke out everywhere, but the enemy's blows were nonetheless beaten off.

By August 24 the main forces of the Nazi armies were surrounded in the region east of Huși. This seemed to spur the enemy on, and the fighting continued—even more fiercely. Friessner wanted at any price to get his forces out and move them west, and he accelerated events. Certain small groups of the enemy managed to break out across the Prut and struck at the rear of our 6th Tank Army and 27th Army, which were in the

135

vanguard. The 2nd Ukrainian Front's situation became even more tense and complex.

One must pay a tribute of great respect to Malinovsky, who in that situation showed unusual self-possession, self-control, and the prudence and ability promptly to make the correct command decisions—the ability to control the actions of attacking forces firmly and confidently. His skill as a commander, which manifested itself so brilliantly on that occasion, was one of the important factors in this outstanding victory of the Soviet forces.

The unshakable foundation of our fronts' successes was the courage and heroism of the Soviet soldiers. It suffices to say that in August 1944, more than eighteen thousand soldiers and officers received medals and other decorations for distinguishing themselves at Iaşi, Kishinev, Vaslui, and Huşi. Many became Heroes of the Soviet Union. Their valor and the victory won over the enemy constituted a worthy contribution to the common cause of defeating the enemy.

In the course of brief, hard-fought engagements, all breakthroughs by the enemy forces were liquidated. By the end of August the 2nd Ukrainian Front, acting jointly with the 3rd Ukrainian Front, had also destroyed the main forces of the surrounded enemy. Out of the twenty-five German divisions in Army Group Southern Ukraine, eighteen were annihilated.

It is difficult to exaggerate the importance of our victory in the Iaşi-Kishinev operation. The destruction of the main forces of Army Group Southern Ukraine produced important military and political results. The Soviet forces had, as it were, opened the gateway to the Rumanian interior, to the boundaries of Bulgaria, and then to Yugoslavia, where the next strategic tasks were to be carried out. The operation created a favorable military and political situation for liquidating the dictatorship of Ion Antonescu, depriving him of an armed force in the form of the Nazi forces and the Rumanian troops loyal to the government. Under these conditions the Rumanian Communist Party instigated an armed uprising of the people, which in the final analysis determined that country's socialist future.

While the fate of the fascist forces was being decided and the encirclement of the enemy's Kishinev grouping was becoming a fact, events that were important to the future of Rumania, and interesting in themselves, were taking place on the other side of the front.

On the night of August 22 a conference was held in King Michael's palace. Ion Antonescu, the chief of the fascist dictatorship and of the government, had not been informed of it. The meeting was attended by the young King, specially empowered persons from his circle, and representatives of the parties of the national democratic bloc: the Communist, Social Democratic, National Peasant, and National Liberal parties.

An anti-Nazi alliance so contradictory in make-up had become possible as a result of the complex and extensive preparatory work done by the Communists—something we mentioned earlier. That work had been done cautiously and patiently. Step by step the Communists strengthened their positions; and on June 20, 1944, the anti-Nazi bloc was formed.

King Michael's court, taking into account the victory of the Red Army, also adhered to the national democratic bloc. Needless to say, the King hadn't the slightest concern for the welfare of the Rumanian people and was merely pursuing his own ends. The members of his court, having sensed that the throne was shaking, were rushing about trying to preserve their own positions.

At this favorable moment for overthrowing the Antonescu regime, the representatives of the allied parties had gathered to evaluate the military and political situation and decide how to eliminate, in a practical way, the fascist government, which was loyal to the Nazis. At this meeting the Communists represented a force that was not merely on a par with its partners but growing. This was due to the fact that under the influence of the defeats dealt to the Nazi coalition on the Soviet front, even greater political shifts had taken place in Rumania. Undermined by the burdens of the war, and having lost a great many soldiers, Rumania was especially sensitive to those defeats. And the contradictions between the working class (whose interests were expressed by the Ruma-

137

nian Communist Party) on the one hand and the fascist regime and the Nazi occupying troops on the other became extremely sharp. Contradictions were also clearly manifested in the relations among the governing classes and the ruling circles, which—like spiders in a jar—were fighting to keep their place in the sun. This struggle now became especially fierce, since it had become plain that the exploiting classes had lost their bet on fascism and the alliance with Nazi Germany.

The Rumanian Communist Party had long been analyzing the contradictions that had arisen within the ruling classes, including those between the monarchical regime and Antonescu's government. It had correctly evaluated the situation, and managed to take advantage of it so that the fascist government might be overthrown and the people's revolution triumph, although in a superficial way the King and his circle took some part in this.

For a better understanding of the course of historical events, it might not be amiss to remind the reader that the crisis in relations between the King and the Antonescu government had begun back in late March 1944. It became especially grave when Soviet forces crossed the Rumanian border and entered Rumanian territory. At this point the King and his advisers realized that a continued alliance with fascism promised nothing good. People close to the King began making plans to save the monarchy. At first no place was allotted, in these plans, to the Communists and the Rumanian people; but reality soon made the courtiers change their tactics and seek contact with the Communists. The monarchists, and even the King himself, realized that only the Communists enjoyed the support of the toiling masses, and that they were the only force in the country capable of overthrowing the fascist regime.

The veteran intriguers around King Michael—including his mother, who when it came to politics by no means took a rear seat —figured that the long-suffering and industrious Rumanian people, who for many years had been doomed by the ruling classes to ignorance and a benighted condition, still believed in the monarchy's good intentions. The former thought they could exploit the patriotic sentiments of the common people who believed that only the fascist dictatorship was to blame for all the wartime tribulations, the death of a great many Rumanian soldiers, and the ruin and impoverishment of the country. The courtiers realized that in the eyes of the people, hatred for Antonescu's pro-Hitler government blocked out the parasitism and class nature of the monarchy. Therefore, they hoped that the people would remain loyal to the King and would preserve the throne—especially if the monarch was among those who rose up against the unanimously hated military fascist dictatorship.

Those close to the King also believed they would be supported by the Rumanian Army. They explained that many Rumanian generals at the front took a dim view of the Nazis and Antonescu's government. In playing their political game, the people around the King also took into account the so-called historical parties—the National Peasant Party and the National Liberal Party—who represented the interests of the Rumanian capitalists and landowners and might serve as an excellent fulcrum and screen for the class policy of the court. At the same time these parties, for quite understandable reasons, by no means avoided alliance with the monarchy.

The Communists attending the meeting approved the idea—advanced by the court—of arresting Ion Antonescu, the head of the fascist dictatorship. Indeed, the King's people—with the knowledge and participation of the CP—had taken advance measures. The plan for Antonescu's arrest had been worked out back in April by people especially close to King Michael; in particular, the King's adjutant, Col. E. Ionescu. Initially the covert circles thought they would confine themselves to arresting the head of the fascist government and no one else. But under the pressure of events they had to change their plans. At one of the conspiratorial meetings the Communists got the court circles to agree to a broader program of action: the overthrow of Antonescu's dictatorship by means of an armed uprising; breaking off the alliance with fascist Germany; Rumania's withdrawal from the war on the side of Hitler; and combating the German forces and the forces of the satellite countries. A military committee, in which Communists assumed the leading role, was elected to handle the technical preparation of the uprising. The King and his followers also agreed as to the time for launching the uprising.

The details of the plan for the uprising were discussed at other conspiratorial meetings attended by representatives of the Communist Party and of the King. For Bucharest they drew up a list of priority objectives to be seized (railroad station, post office, telegraph office, etc.), and they created staffs and commands for the northern and southern parts of the city. It was ascertained which units of the Rumanian forces were ready to support the insurgents.

In the capital the Communist Party had fifty patriotic detachments with an over-all strength of two thousand fighters to carry out the main tasks; and it depended on certain regular troops. All in all, the number of persons armed for the uprising in Bucharest was slightly more than eight thousand.

The Communists made preparations for the uprising in other places besides Bucharest. Much attention was devoted to the oil-producing region of Ploieşti, where paramilitary patriotic detachments and groups were formed.

The question as to when the uprising should begin was especially important: The success or failure of the insurgents depended upon answering it correctly. If the uprising were premature, German forces might well be sent to help Antonescu's dictatorship and might drown the great cause in blood. It would be best to delay launching the uprising until the Red Army had crushed the Nazi forces, deprived the Antonescu government of military support, and thereby created the most favorable conditions for the triumph of the uprising. Rumanian historians have written:

> To assure the success of the uprising, the military plan provided that it should begin after the Soviet Army had launched its offensive on the Iaşi-Kishinev front, so that the German command could not transfer forces from that front and use them against the insurgents.[2]

Ten days before the beginning of the Iaşi-Kishinev operation, the KPR (Communist Party of Rumania) managed to organize

[2] *Annaly Institute istorii partii pri TsK RRP,* 1962, No. 3, p. 133.

the escape of Gheorghe Gheorghiu-Dej from a concentration camp. Then the same thing was done for a large group of other Communist leaders.

But let us return to the events of the night of August 22. At that time it was decided that Antonescu's arrest should be effected in the palace, after he had been summoned to an audience with the King, supposedly to report on the military situation. The job of making the arrest was assigned to a paramilitary detachment trained by the Communist Party—a detachment that had been selected from among the patriotic formations organized in the course of preparing for the uprising. The KPR suggested that a second, reserve group be prepared in case the first detachment did not manage, for some reason, to get into the palace. The King's adjutant formed the second group from among the soldiers of the court's battalion of guards. Also, steps were taken to disarm the private (reinforced) bodyguard that usually accompanied Antonescu.

Antonescu suspected nothing. On August 21 and 22 he twice met with General Friessner at the latter's command post to discuss the threat hanging over the German and Rumanian forces at the front. Friessner expressed apprehension that political intrigues against the Nazis were being hatched among the Rumanian troops. Antonescu categorically denied this, observing that he had taken literally draconian measures against desertion; and he convinced Friessner of his loyalty to Nazi Germany. They both concluded that it was essential to begin pulling the forces back from the region of Iași and Kishinev, and to organize a defense along the fortified line running from the Carpathians through Focșani, Nămoloasa, and Galați to the Danube delta. Antonescu promised he would promptly put all the Rumanian reserves in Bucharest at the disposal of the German command.

Upon his return to the capital, Antonescu immediately called a meeting of his Cabinet, at which it was decided to continue the war, mobilizing all of the nation's resources for that purpose. After the session he asked the King to receive him on August 23 at 1600 hours. And although for the court circles this request was unexpected, it coincided perfectly with their plans to arrest the fascist chief. People close to the King quickly got in touch with the leaders of the KPR. The latter advised carrying out the plan that had been jointly approved; and in their turn, they issued orders to make ready for the uprising. Everything was put into effect.

On the next day, Antonescu came to the palace at the appointed hour. After a lengthy report to the King on the situation at the front, he was dismissed from his post and arrested by guards acting in accordance with the second version of the plan. Together with his namesake, Foreign Minister Michael Antonescu, who had had an audience a half hour earlier, the former dictator was locked up in the royal family's armored shelter. The guards disarmed both of the Antonescus.

Next, the Minister of War, the Minister of Internal Affairs, the Inspector General of Gendarmerie, and the Bucharest Prefect of Police were summoned to the palace by telephone, and arrested. The other members of the fascist government were arrested later.

Antonescu's arrest did not bring peace of mind to the King's advisers. They were afraid the Nazis would attack the palace so as to retrieve their ally. Realizing that in this case things would not be healthy for the King and his people, they asked the KPR to shelter the King. So after midnight he was taken to a safe place far from the capital, where he remained for a long time, going about the same kind of business he usually did.

Meantime, on August 23 events at the palace followed their course. Shortly after 1700, on instructions from the leadership of the KPR, Emile Bodnaras, chief of the Central Command of the Paramilitary Patriotic Formations, showed up at the palace. (This is the same Bodnaras who is now [1973] a member of the Executive Committee and the Permanent Presidium of the CC RCP, and Vice-premier of the Socialist Republic of Rumania.) The eight troopers who accompanied him brought Antonescu out of his bunker and took him to one of the Communist Party's safe houses.

At this same time, representatives of various parties (including the Communist Party and the Social Democratic Party) gathered at the palace to take part in forming a new government. By 2000 they had formed a government consisting mainly of promonarchist military men and some of the technical intelligentsia. Gen. Constantin Sanatescu, who was close to the King, became Premier. In this government the four parties of the National Democratic bloc (including the CPR) had only one representative each—a minister without portfolio. It was plain that the majority of the government's members had no intention of carrying out the will of the people and protecting its interests. Their secret intent was that the development of the revolution should stop with the arrest of Antonescu and his Cabinet, and they were taking their own measures. In particular, General Mihail, a man very close to the King, was named chief of the Rumanian General Staff. For the time being he kept his views concealed and did not openly antagonize the Communists. But the latter saw the direction that would be taken by the majority of Sanatescu's government, and demanded that representatives of all the antifascist parties be included in it.

Also, the new government had to deal with the fact that the Red Army had already broken into the central regions of Rumania. So the government was compelled to conceal its secret designs and proclaim that its most urgent goals were to conclude an armistice with the United Nations, to leave the Nazi coalition, to restore the country, and to struggle for the liberation of northern Transylvania. Shortly before midnight the King went on the air and read a declaration on cessation of hostilities against the United Nations, concluding an armistice and a peace, and forming a new government.

Meantime the military command of Bucharest issued to the paramilitary patriotic forces an order previously drafted by the military committee—where, as the reader will recall, the KPR had the most influence. The uprising was begun in the capital. Armed detachments of workers filled the streets and squares, and military organizations seized the most important institutions and installations. The success of the uprising was assured by the fact that on the front the German forces had been badly defeated by the Red Army, while in Bucharest there was no really strong German garrison: only some AA units, certain other small units, and some specialists. But the Rumanian troops, following Sanatescu's orders, did not take up arms against the Germans although according to the general plan they had the mission of disarming the Nazi units. The KPR circulated a leaflet "The Red Army Is Coming!" which explained to the people the liberating aims of the Soviet forces, and called upon Rumanians to fight for the liberation of their country.

Alarmed by this unexpected turn of events, the Nazi ambassador rushed to the palace. There, together with an answer to his question about the fate of Antonescu, he was informed of the King's demand that the German forces be withdrawn from Rumania, and was assured that no obstacles would be put in their way. As he left the palace, the enraged ambassador swore he would drown Rumania in blood.

The next to come to the palace were the Nazi generals. They had enough sense to realize that things were going badly, and promised to remove from the capital those forces that were stationed there. But when the next day brought Hitler's order to suppress the "impudent" Rumanians, the German generals began to bomb the palace and the most important objectives in the city. Also, certain ground forces were moving toward Bucharest. This was tantamount to a declaration of war against Rumania. Responding to an appeal issued by the Communists, the people and the soldiers who had come over to their side stopped the Nazis at the outskirts of the city. And they rendered harmless those who were still in Bucharest, disarming the German units.

Despite the King's declaration, the statement by the new Rumanian Government, and the direct order from the Rumanian General Staff to cease resistance against the Soviet forces, the Rumania forces at the front did not lay down their arms but continued fighting on the side of the Nazis. There were several reasons for this. Thus on many sectors of the front the Rumanian General Staff had simply lost control of its forces. But this was not the main reason. The fact is that where control still existed, the Rumanian General Staff tried to bring its forces out along a defense line running from Focșani through Nămoloasa and Braila to the mouth of the Danube, so as to prevent the further spreading of the popular uprising. The forces were given a direct order to resist any attempts to disarm them.

Thus in effect the Rumanian General Staff was sanctioning a continuation of the hostilities, since neither the Red Army nor any other army would allow, in its rear, the presence of forces not yet disarmed that belonged to a country with which it was at war. (We had not yet received any word on the conclusion of an armistice.) Also, the Rumanian General Staff had promised to allow the German forces free egress to the west, provided they did not prevent the Rumanian forces from moving to the indicated line of defenses.

Finally, the actions of the Rumanian General Staff were doubly dangerous in that they created the threat of a civil war in Rumania if the Army was used against the people's uprising. All this contravened the intentions of the KPR. Therefore, on August 24 it published an appeal to the people to take up arms against the Nazis. The appeal provoked a lively response, and was very important in spreading the uprising throughout the country.

After evaluating this situation, including the Rumanian General Staff's intention to preserve its forces and withdraw them to the interior of the country, the Soviet Supreme Command ordered the fronts to continue the offensive, going all out, and to destroy the Nazi forces. The Rumanian forces were to be treated in accordance with the way they behaved.

Desirous of giving the new Rumanian Government and its forces an opportunity rapidly and correctly to find their places in the sequence of wartime events, the Soviet Government repeated on August 25 its April declaration that we had no intention of seizing any part of the Rumanian territory or of changing that country's social order or infringing upon its independence. "To the contrary," the second declaration stated, "the Soviet Government considers it essential to restore, *jointly with the Rumanians,* the independence of Rumania by means of liberating Rumania from the Nazi German yoke" (italics mine—S. Sh.).

In the declaration it was stated that the Red Army would not disarm the Rumanian forces. Not only that, but it would preserve their arms and even help them in every way, if they would cease hostilities against us and, jointly with the Red Army, carry on a war of liberation against the Nazis for the independence of their own country and against the Hungarian satellites for the liberation of Transylvania.

At the same time the Soviet Government pointed out that the Red Army could not cease hostilities on the territory of Rumania until the German troops, who were oppressing and enslaving the Rumanian people, had been liquidated. In this respect, any aid rendered to us by the Rumanian forces would make it possible more rapidly to cease hostilities on Rumanian soil and conclude an armistice.

We soon get some important political and military news. The Rumanian radio announced that the Rumanian Government considered itself to be at war with Germany, that Rumanian forces had begun to invade Transylvania, and that Bucharest had been entirely swept clean of German Nazis. The Sanatescu government was asking for the immediate signing of an armistice. This meant that the Rumanian Army had become our ally and, jointly with the Soviet forces, was going to fight for the complete expulsion of German Nazi forces from its country.

The Rumanian Government's decision was dictated by several considerations. First, the successes of the Soviet forces were in fact tremendous. Second, the popular uprising was spreading throughout the country. Finally, all hopes of making a peaceful deal with Hitler had collapsed, since Hitler had ordered that the King be overthrown by a *Putsch* and replaced by a government acceptable to the Germans. So Sanatescu had to turn the arms of the Rumanian Army against the occupying troops. Thus despite his intentions he did what was demanded by reality itself and the interests of a democratic Rumania. It should be noted, however, that the majority of the Rumanian troops at the front had not yet understood everything that had happened, and preferred not to fight the Nazis. Instead, they simply surrendered to the Soviet forces. For example, on August 26 five Rumanian divisions surrendered, down to the last man, to the 2nd Ukrainian Front.

Thus the gateways into Rumania were opened; and in the dis-

146

tance, beyond the Danube, the roads into Bulgaria could already be glimpsed. Meantime, we had to advance as rapidly as possible to all the main strategic points in Rumania, where we would wind up the job of crushing the Nazi forces.

During the Soviet forces' subsequent operations on the territory of Rumania, the Soviet Supreme Command devoted special attention to that country's most important economic, political, and transportation centers—the regions of Ploiești and Bucharest.

As everyone knows, Ploiești lies at the heart of a region that produces crude oil—something desperately needed by the Hitlerite coalition, and especially by Germany itself. Ploiești was also a great proletarian center—a stronghold of the Communist Party —which fact was of great importance in the development of the revolution.

The General Staff took all this into account, plus the fact that Ploiești was located sixty kilometers from Bucharest and more or less covered the city from the north. According to our estimate (which later proved to be very close to actuality), some 25,000 Nazi troops and almost 100 aircraft were concentrated here. The enemy could use these forces to hold Ploiești and destroy the oil fields and refineries; and also as a striking force for operations in the Bucharest region. But there was more to it than that. Ploiești was an important communications hub, including routes running along the Prahova River Valley into the depths of Transylvania, where both Germans and Hungarians were positioned. For an enemy not yet driven out of Rumania, this was an escape route leading directly to the German 8th Army and the Hungarian Army. Meantime, compact enemy groupings held the key points of the oil region, and the most important refineries had been occupied by garrisons.

In planning the enemy's defeat in central Rumania, we did not disregard the help we might get from the Rumanian working class. But of course we did not place any very great hopes in it, since the proletariat of Ploiești would have to fight against regular Nazi troops with all types of military equipment.

The fact that Ploiești was some distance from Bucharest made it possible to isolate the former, cutting the communications lines · between the two cities. We felt that the most suitable kind of offensive would be one involving simultaneous strikes by Soviet mobile forces against the regions of both cities. This would prevent the enemy forces in either city from helping those in the other.

Along with the measures aimed at crushing the enemy, we worked out measures for preserving the oil fields from Nazi strikes —whether from the air or on the ground.

On August 27 at 1700 hours, Malinovsky ordered Gen. A. G. Kravchenko, commanding the 6th Tank Army, to enter Bucharest and Ploieşti. Kravchenko decided to strike at Bucharest with two corps and at Ploieşti with one.

On the night of August 24 the oil field and refinery workers, on instructions from the Communist Party, organized the preservation of production facilities and their defense against the Nazis. And the Rumanian 5th Territorial Army Corps, commanded by General Vasiliu-Reshkanu, came to their aid. In the environs of Ploieşti, the Nazis were hard-pressed. But in the course of the skirmishes they set up a strong blockade around the city and made ready to storm it.

The situation near Ploieşti compelled the Soviet forces to act quickly and decisively. We could not allow the enemy to smash the Rumanian patriots, seize the city, and destroy the oil fields. That would do huge damage to the uprising and to the Rumanian economy. On August 29 concentrating their forces, our tankmen dealt a mightly blow in the Ploieşti region. They were helped by the Rumanian 18th Infantry Division, sent to this area from the front. The Nazis were crushed, and the basis of Rumania's oil-producing industry was saved. With the aid of armed workers, the Soviet forces established firm military and civilian order in Ploieşti and its environs. Rumanian forces completed the mopping-up of Nazi troops in various parts of the oil-producing region.

But at Bucharest things went somewhat differently. On the evening of August 29, the tank corps of the 6th Tank Army deployed in column of route so as to drive toward the Rumanian capital and destroy the Nazis positioned on its approaches. At the same time, King Michael and Prime Minister Sanatescu declared they were ready to accept all the conditions of armistice offered by the Soviet Union on April 12.

Expecting practical action from the Rumanians, we did not hold back our forces' rapid advance into the depth of the country. But what was our surprise when, on August 29 and 30, on several sectors of the front, representatives of the Rumanian Government proposed to the Soviet commanders that they bring their offensive up short on the Danube—along the eastern edge of the Carpathians. This put us on our guard. Once again we could sense the "policy of the fox's brush" that the Sanatescu government, for all its oaths and declarations, was still trying to follow. Upon close examination of the matter we observed that these proposals had been offered with the aim of enabling the rest of the battered Nazi forces to withdraw to the mountains, organize resistance there, and prevent our forces from reaching the depths of Rumania. Obviously, the bourgeois circles of the government were still hoping to preserve, in Rumania, the state of affairs that suited them.

At the same time, Sanatescu asked the Anglo-American command to drop paratroops into the capital. It is not difficult to realize that in this case everything achieved on August 29 as a result of the uprising by Rumania's popular patriotic forces would have been threatened. Fortunately for the Rumanian people, none of this happened. The Soviet forces continued to advance. The Rumanian people manifested great militancy and, in response to the appeals of the Communist Party, spread the uprising throughout the country.

After a forced march, troops of the 6th Tank Army and the 53rd Army approached Bucharest in force. Their appearance guaranteed the inviolability of the people's gains and undid the schemes of the bourgeois politicians. The Soviet troops were accompanied by soldiers from the Tudor Vladimirescu Volunteer Division. That unit merits a few special comments.

The division was formed of volunteers—Rumanian officers and soldiers who had been taken prisoner by our forces. It was neither easy nor simple for them to reach the conclusion that it was essential to fight against Nazi Gemany. A picture of the future collapse of the Third Reich became visible to them during the enemy's defeat at Stalingrad, where two Rumanian armies met their end. The subsequent course of events on the Soviet-German front finally convinced many POWs that the criminal adventure undertaken by Hitler and his minions would inevitably end in failure. On February 2, 1943, a group of Rumanian soldiers asked the Soviet Government to allow them to fight as volunteers along with the Red Army. And in August a conference of Rumanian POWs empowered a number of them to ask Stalin for permission to form a volunteer legion. The POWs were supported by the Rumanian Communists who had sought refuge in the USSR. On October 4, 1943, the National Committee of Defense passed a resolution on the formation of the Rumanian 1st Volunteer Infantry Division. Shortly thereafter it was named after the Rumanian national hero, Tudor Vladimirescu.

The division was formed in the Seletsky camps near Ryazan on a guards TO. The volunteers were commanded by Col. Nikolai Kambrya, and the chief of staff was Yakob Teklu. We kept tabs on the formation of the division through Col. G. M. Eremin, the General Staff representative. The divisions's troops were trained by 159 Soviet officer instructors, who passed on to their Rumanian comrades the best of their experience in the Great Patriotic War.

On May 7, 1944, the Tudor Vladimirescu Division, assembled north of Yampol, was attached to the 2nd Ukrainian Front, and was given combat training. The unit consisted of 9,500 men, and was strongly armed. For example, it had 98 guns and 160 mortars of various calibers, almost 500 light machine guns, and more than 110 heavy machine guns.

The Rumanian volunteers got their baptism of fire during the Iași-Kishinev operation. They honorably endured a hard trial in fighting against a powerful grouping of enemy forces trying to break out of encirclement to the west. The division suffered losses. But it did its job, acquired a fighting spirit, and thus laid a firm foundation for its future military brotherhood with Soviet and Rumanian forces.

On August 31 the inhabitants of Bucharest joyously welcomed

the Soviet troops and the Tudor Vladimirescu Division as they entered the capital of Rumania.

With the defeat of the Army Group Southern Ukraine and the armed popular uprising which had spread throughout the country, great historical prospects opened up for Rumania. An Allied Control Commission was established, and it made sure that the conditions of the armistice were strictly complied with. Soviet troops were on hand. Their presence, plus the work of the Control Commission, stimulated the democratic forces to work toward a new type of government—a people's democracy—and also to avoid civil war. The latter was ruled out, which fact created favorable internal conditions for overcoming the resistance of the counterrevolutionary forces.

It must be said that the Soviet Government and the Soviet military command placed great trust in the toiling masses of those nations that the Red Army had to liberate, including the people of Rumania—a country which of course for a long time had been a satellite of Nazi Germany. There was great respect for the Communist Party of Rumania, the advance detachment of the people, which had been able, under a fascist rule, to keep its ranks intact and to organize and lead an uprising against Ion Antonescu.

Nonetheless, in its work the General Staff realized what strong positions the counterrevolution still held in Rumania, and how difficult it was for the new forces to overcome them. The counterrevolution functioned in a skillful and flexible manner. This was manifested in various ways. Thus as the Soviet forces advanced, in the central regions of Rumania, abundant information on the make-up, condition, and movements of our armies was sent via various channels of communication—especially telegraph and telephone—abroad, for example. This information was plainly in the category of military intelligence. On the basis of a report from the General Staff, the National Defense Committee passed a special resolution on this subject. The committee sent special communications officers to major communications centers in Rumania, and they blocked the sending of such information abroad.

There were also attempts at ideological sabotage, one of which I recall very well. All of a sudden, slanderous reports were circulated about the Tudor Vladimirescu 1st Volunteer Infantry Division. Our enemies claimed that these volunteers were traitors, that after the war they would be condemned, and that Germany would not lose the war. On this occasion, Malinovsky and I. Z. Susaikov sent the following telegram to the division commander:

> The Rumanian division is the most combat-ready unit of the Rumanian people, and is doing a good job of carrying out its missions. The Rumanian people will never let anyone blacken the name of their heroes, who are devoted to their motherland and understood better than anyone else the necessity of fighting for the freedom and independence of Rumania. Don't worry. Fight honorably, and strike at the enemy ruthlessly. . . .

In addition, there were attempts to save the Nazi officials in the country. At this time the Minister of Internal Affairs refused to hand over to the Soviet command the generals, admirals, and other officers of the German Military Mission. For one thing, he claimed that if he handed over German citizens to the Russians, reprisals would be taken against the Rumanian diplomats and the many Rumanian officers then in Germany. For another, he maintained that Bucharest would be bombed out of vengeance. And he offered still more untenable arguments.

Naturally, the members of the mission were arrested, as was widely reported in the Soviet press. The enemy's network of agents in Rumania no longer had a headquarters.

Great was the surprise of our military commanders when they discovered, among the patients in certain Rumanian hospitals, perfectly healthy German soldiers. This bit of camouflage was exposed rather quickly, and the patients had to take their places at assembly points for POWs.

When Soviet officers came to the embassy of Miklós Horthy's Hungary, our enemy, to arrest the Hungarian representatives, they found a sign reading "Swedish Embassy." It turned out that this life-saving sign had been put up by agreement with the Swedish ambassador.

Patently pro-Nazi types, including co-workers of the Sigurantsy, were very often appointed to top positions in the prefectures. And there were attempts—directed against our forces—to wreck trains by sabotaging the tracks. All these hostile acts, along with many others, were nipped in the bud.

The conditions governing the unity of the anti-Nazi coalition and the internal development of Rumania ruled out the methods of immediately "expropriating the expropriators" that had been used in our Revolution. In fact, the situation in Rumania was such that representatives of the bourgeoisie and court circles remained in power for quite a long time. General Sanatescu's government was replaced by the government of another general, Nicolae Radescu, who was perhaps even more reactionary and pro-Anglo-American. Circumstances, however, compelled Radescu to maneuver and give several portfolios to the Popular Democratic Front. In particular, the Communists held two ministries and had one deputy minister.

At that time a prominent role was played by Dr. Petru Groza, head of the peasants' organization, the Plowman's Front, which during the war years had worked shoulder to shoulder with the Communists under the leadership of the Communist Party. Groza vigorously and uncompromisingly opposed the machinations of the reactionary ministers. He followed a policy of friendship with the liberator, the Soviet Union, increasing Rumania's contribution to the cause of victory over Nazi Germany and the democratic development of his own country. Groza did a great deal toward bringing about the fall of the Radescu government in March 1945. For a long time thereafter he headed up the Rumanian Government, and was one of the most prominent builders of socialist Rumania, the people's democracy.

In late August and early September 1944, the Stavka had to decide on the line our military authorities would take toward the young King of Rumania, who was still on the throne. In reporting to the Stavka on the military situation, Antonov and I often remarked that the King's court would inevitably become a center of anti-Soviet activity in Rumania, and we proposed taking decisive steps vis-à-vis the court. As usual, the Supreme Commander listened to us carefully, puffing calmly away on his pipe, and using

153

the end of its stem to smooth down his mustache. Then he said more or less the following. A foreign king is no business of ours. Tolerance toward him would have a favorable effect on our relations with our allies. The Rumanian people, who for the time being trusted the court as an opposition force against the fascist dictatorship, would presumably figure out for themselves the true nature of the monarchy. And there was reason to believe that the Rumanian Communists would not sit on their hands—that they would help the people to understand the situation.

And so we were given a lesson in the grammar of politics. For the sake of objectivity I must record that the King behaved very modestly and did not so much busy himself with matters of state as amuse himself. When it was learned that he was an amateur pilot, Stalin sent him a "Po-s" plane as a gift. The King flew, hunted, and pursued amusements.

But time went by, events unfolded, and by the will of the party and the people the social structure of Rumania moved in a direction that would lead the country to socialism. No one had the slightest intention of interfering with the King and the Queen Mother's choice of residence, and they left Rumania safe and sound.

After the defeat of the enemy in the Iaşi and Kishinev pocket, the General Staff got to work on its dark blue file, containing things that were not terribly urgent but nonetheless important, including promotions and decorations to be handed out. The brilliant victory won by the 2nd and 3rd Ukrainian fronts had provided occasion for just that. In considering the matter, Stalin had said that Malinovsky and Tolbukhin were deserving of the highest military rank—Marshal of the Soviet Union.

"Also," added the Supreme Commander, who was very pleased with the success of the fronts, "this title must be given to the front commanders at a time when the national boundaries of the USSR have been restored."

His proposal was accepted; Malinovsky was promoted to marshal on September 10, and Tolbukhin on September 12.

There had been other instances of awarding high military titles

154

which, to put it bluntly, had been unusual. I recall one such in the autumn of 1943. This is the way things went.

On November 16, 1943, Col. Gen. Ivan Khristoforovich Bagramyan, commanding the 11th Guards Army, was called to Moscow by Stalin. When he reported to Antonov, Bagramyan of course asked why he had been summoned. "The boss doesn't like to announce his intentions beforehand," Antonov replied. "When we go to the Stavka, you'll find out."

The next day, at the time fixed for the situation report to the Supreme Commander, the three of us—Antonov, Bagramyan, and I—went to the Stavka.

At that time the Soviet forces were on the offensive all the way along the front from the Gulf of Finland to the Black Sea. But in the Baltic area, progress was slow. The enemy, resisting fiercely, had managed to create a balance of power in that area.

Stalin was alone, and in a good mood. "What's new?" he asked Antonov.

"There have been no substantial changes in the situation, relative to the daily report," Antonov reported.

Stalin nodded and turned to Bagramyan. "Things aren't going so well for us on the Baltic fronts," he said. "The offensive has slowed down. You can't always advance everywhere, as some people sometimes think you can."

After a brief pause, he went on: "And so we are going to take steps to correct the situation. We're going to beef up the 1st Baltic Front with forces taken from its neighbor on the right [the 2nd Baltic Front—S. Sh.]. But that won't be enough, obviously. Your army is strong, and has given a rather good account of itself. I'm thinking of transferring it to Eremenko's command. . . ."

He fell silent again. Then, turning back to Bagramyan, he rounded out his idea: "And I'd like to appoint you commander of the front to replace Eremenko. How do you feel about that?"

Bagramyan was a bit confused. His words coming a bit slowly, he said, "Thank you for your trust in me, Comrade Stalin. I will try to justify it."

"Good. And to replace you as commanding general of the

Army, I'm naming an experienced commander, Chibisov." Then, quite unhurriedly, Stalin went to the desk to fill his pipe.

Taking advantage of the pause, Antonov put in: "His first name is Nikander, meaning 'conquering hero.'"

Stalin puffed a few times on his pipe until the tobacco was burning. Then he turned back to Bagramyan, who had remained silent. "Why are you keeping mum?" he asked. "Do you have something against Chibisov?"

Bagramyan became even more embarrassed. But then he replied, "No, Comrade Stalin, of course I have nothing against him. He is an experienced commander. When he was a lieutenant general, I was still only a colonel. And now he is a colonel general and a Hero of the Soviet Union. I'd feel sort of awkward with him. . . . Can't you appoint somebody else—Lieutenant General Galitsky, for example?"

Stalin looked closely at Bagramyan. "All right, we'll do it your way." To Antonov and me he said curtly, "Draw up an order assigning commands to Bagramyan and Galitsky." Then he went over to his desk and pushed a button. Soon A. N. Poskrebyshev came in.

Stalin told him, "Draw up an order from the Sovnarkom making Bagramyan a general of the Army."

Poskrebyshev made a note on his pad, but he didn't leave, since he was familiar with Stalin's habit of taking his time in issuing orders. Stalin fell silent again. During this interval he went back to the desk to light up his pipe, which had gone out. Then, puffing on it, he asked Antonov, "Wouldn't it make Shtemenko's work easier if he were given the rank of colonel general?"

"Of course, it would make things easier, Comrade Stalin," replied Antonov. "After all, he even has to deal with marshals, and he is often at the front."

"In my opinion, Govorov, too, should be given the rank of general of the Army. It's not easy for him in Leningrad, either."

We said nothing.

"Draw up an order for all three," the Supreme Commander told Poskrebyshev. The latter nodded and immediately left.

Stalin turned to me and Bagramyan. "Congratulations!" he said.

"Now I'll have to leave you: There's a meeting of the National Defense Committee."

When we got back to the General Staff building, we went to Antonov's office. "On this occasion," he said to us, "let's dine together."

We went into the room behind his office, where he usually slept. He promptly removed the general of the Army's epaulets from his spare tunic and handed them over to Bagramyan. Meantime, Bagramyan removed his own epaulets and gave them to me. With the new epaulets on our tunics, we sat down to eat. Antonov even had a bottle of dry wine which was supposed to be brought out when entertaining high-ranking foreign guests. But in honor of such a remarkable event, we made use of it.

The orders conferring our new ranks upon us were issued in due time. And on November 19 Stalin signed an order naming General of the Army I. Kh. Bagramyan commander of the 1st Baltic Front. K. N. Galitsky was put in command of the 11th Guards Army.

But let us return to the events in Rumania. Naturally, we General Staff officers were primarily concerned with strictly military problems: determining the procedure for utilizing Rumanian forces and the missions they could accomplish; organizing practical mutual assistance. In these matters we depended on the staffs of the 2nd Ukrainian Front and the armies in which the Rumanians were fighting, because they were familiar with the fighting capacity of our new allies.

We had many doubts. In particular, the Rumanian troops had not distinguished themselves when on the Nazi side. Also, they were poorly supplied with technical equipment as compared with the Soviet forces, being especially short of artillery. Hence their military tasks had to be assigned in accordance with their capacity. Moreover, we had to monitor the actions of the officers, since among the generals and other officers were many pro-Nazis who had previously fought on Germany's side. Some people even regarded the Rumanian Army as simply not combat-worthy because of that. Moreover, the rear area on the territory of Rumania

—where vestiges of the fascist dictatorship remained—presented a complex situation.

It was decided to use the Rumanian forces in compact masses. Thus the Rumanian 4th Army (eleven divisions), under the command of General G. Avramescu, would be operationally subordinated to the commander of our 27th Army (Gen. C. G. Trofimenko), and their 1st Army, commanded by Gen. N. Machich, would be subordinated to the commander of our 53rd Army (Gen. I. M. Managarov). This arrangement assured close co-operation between Soviet and Rumanian forces in the two directions most important at that time, Debrecen and Budapest, and made it possible to support Rumanian units with the artillery and striking power of Soviet technical resources.

The aim of these operations was to crush the enemy in these sectors and make it impossible for the German and Hungarian forces to withdraw from the eastern Carpathians to the west. This would clear the way for the 4th Ukrainian Front to cross the mountain ridges. These matters are discussed in greater detail in Chapter 7. Here I need say only that our first joint operations confirmed an old truth: When an army is fighting for a just cause, its troops are capable of valor and prowess. In this case, it proved all the truer, since the Rumanians sensed the presence of Soviet soldiers fighting next to them. The unit that most distinguished itself in the first engagements near Cluj was the aforementioned Tudor Vladimirescu 1st Infantry Division. Later, for its heroism in the Debrecen operation, it was given the honorary title of the Debrecen Division and awarded the Order of the Red Banner.

The campaign trail from Cluj to the approaches to Prague was marked by the joint fighting of Soviet and Rumanian soldiers against the Nazi occupying troops. It was here that the combat camaraderie between the Soviet troops and the troops of the new Rumania broadened, grew, and became stronger. We noticed with particular attention the increasing skills of the Rumanian commanders and soldiers. Certain feats were reported to the Supreme Commander personally. Thus Malinovsky sent Stalin the following telegram:

I ask your permission to award the Order of the Red Banner to two Rumanian fighter pilots, M. Sgt. Georghe Grecu and M. Sgt. Paul Vieru, who on February 10, on instructions from the Soviet command, shot down in the Debrecen region a Haenkel-129 (No. 214) carrying prominent leaders of the underground fascist and Legion movement in Rumania who were trying to fly to Germany. . . .

The General Staff brought the telegram to Stalin's attention, and the permission was granted.

Those ordeals by fire and blood through which the Soviet and Rumanian soldiers passed together in the war against the Nazis must be preserved with particular care in the memories of the peoples. This is demanded by the scarifices brought to the altar of victory. More than 286,000 Soviet soldiers were wounded in the summer and autumn of 1944 in battles for the liberation of Rumania. Some 69,000 of our officers and soldiers perished so that the Rumanian people might be freed of the hobbles of fascist dictatorship—so that they might freely and happily build socialism on their own land. The traditions of friendship and brotherly assistance founded in the battles against the Nazi aggressors must be multiplied on the basis of a Leninist international policy and its principles. Such is the testament of the legendary heroes who freed mankind from the brown plague.

5

ALONG THE TRAIL
OF THE HEROES OF
SHIPKA PASS

The decision to enter Bulgaria. The maneuvers of the bourgeois government. Zhukov in the south. The popular uprising in Bulgaria, and its heroes. S. S. Biryuzov's mission. Just like in a detective story: chasing after the train. A hornets' nest comes to its end. G. M. Dmitrov helps to clear up dissensions. Jointly spilled blood. A lesson in diplomatic tact.

After the defeat of the main forces of Army Group Southern Ukraine, the Soviet Armed Forces were faced with the task of finishing off the remaining enemy forces, which had rapidly retreated into Hungary, the depths of Rumania, and Bulgaria. They had to be tracked down and destroyed.

In late August 1944 the Red Army found itself, like a champion or hero in a fairy tale, standing at a crossroads, not knowing which road to choose. In this case, three roads led off toward the southwest: one to Hungary, one deep into Rumania, and one through Bulgaria. Farther along each road lay difficulties and dangers. But whereas the champion in the fairy tale must choose only one road, the Soviet forces had to move along all three at the same time. And it was our job at General Staff to figure out how that could best be done.

We bore in mind that the enemy still possessed great capacities. Thus he could throw against us the forces he had in Yugoslavia, Albania, and Greece, where there were twenty divisions and seven brigades. Nor could we rule out the possible transfer of some of his forces from Italy, where the German command had about the same number of troops as in the Balkans. The over-all total amounted to more than fifty divisions and brigades. It was a considerable force, and our allies were moving ahead very slowly. Under these conditions, the slightest miscalculation was fraught with serious consequences.

The General Staff took into account all the complexity of the situation in Bulgaria. On the one hand, we knew a lot about the Bulgarian people—a small nation, but one with a glorious tradition of revolution and dedication to freedom, which had long been a friend and brother to our own people. This was the Bulgaria of the bold warriors and courageous fighters against foreign aggressors and their own capitalists, the land of heroic revolutionary uprisings, the homeland of Hristo Botev, Dmitry Blagoev, Vasily Kolarov, and Georgi Dimitrov. On the other hand, we saw the minions of the Nazis heading up a government that had brought Bulgaria into the war on the side of Nazi Germany, putting it into the power of agents of the Third Reich.

It must be noted that the Soviet generals and other officers had a profound belief in the anti-Hitler and antifascist forces of the Bulgarian people, and were convinced they were firmly in favor of our country. We hoped that not a single Bulgarian soldier would raise his hand against the liberating Red Army, and that hope was not blind. It was based on ancient bonds of friendship and the Bulgars' gratitude toward our nation, which had once liberated Bulgaria from the yoke of the Ottoman Empire. Also, on an accurate knowledge of the factual situation in the country. (We at the General Staff had to be able to collate, so to speak, the dictates of the heart against the warning voice of reason.) We knew that a large-scale struggle for national and social liberation had been launched in Bulgaria, that the patriotic forces of the state had combined into a Fatherland Front whose formation was already completed, and that this struggle was headed up by the Bulgarian Workers' Party (BRP).

The slogan of the Fatherland Front was formulated in mid-July 1942 on the initiative of Georgi Dimitrov, the wise and generally respected leader of the BRP. At the time, Dimitrov was working in Moscow, in a building next to the Agricultural Exhibit in Rostokino. For many years, prior to the dissolution of the Comintern in 1943, he was secretary general of its Executive Committee. He also headed up the Foreign Bureau of the CC BRP.

The program of the Fatherland Front was worked out by the Foreign Bureau of the CC BRP. It included first of all nationwide liberation goals: breaking off Bulgaria's alliance with Nazi Germany and its allies, liberating the Bulgarian people from the German Nazis who were lording it over them, and withdrawing Bulgarian occupation troops from Yugoslavia and Greece. The program also spelled out political demands for the democratic restructuring of the country: releasing persons imprisoned for combating the fascists, restoring the civil liberties that had been trampled on, and dissolving fascist organizations. The most urgent task was to overthrow the pro-German rulers and set up a government based on trust in the people and assuring friendship and co-operation with the USSR.

When they learned of this program's contents and slogans, the broad strata of the Bulgarian people—militants of the Workers' Party, Agrarians, Social Democrats, patriotic soldiers, workers, peasants, craftsmen, minor officials, the progressive intelligentsia, and the revolutionary youth—enthusiastically supported the Fatherland Front.

We generals and other officers at the General Staff, in the course of planning the operation in Bulgaria, often had recourse to Dimitrov's writings, or in some cases his personal advice. There was no one else who knew Bulgaria better, or could better judge the paths of its development. I was fortunate enough to meet up with Dimitrov several times at the Stavka, and to be present at some of his talks with Soviet leaders. For me and other younger people, Dimitrov was a living legend—an example of a real revolutionary. After the Leipzig trial[1]—in the course of which, as we know, Dimitrov took the initiative away from his judges and transformed himself into the accuser of Göring, Goebbels, and the entire Nazi system—he became well known to everyone in our country. He in fact acquired unusual popularity as a wise and fearless fighter for the idea of communism. Soviet people knew and loved Georgi Dimitrov as a comrade and brother.

Although presumably there were no direct links between the General Staff and the secretary general of the Executive Committee of the Comintern and the chairman of the Foreign Bureau of the BRP, we General Staff officers recalled that only several hours after the discussion, in the Kremlin, of the new situation created by Nazi Germany's attack on the USSR, Georgi Dimitrov had already called a conference of the secretariat of the Comintern's Executive Committee at which it was decided to launch a massive campaign to aid the Soviet Union, and to organize in Europe a powerful national liberation movement against the German occupation and dependence upon Nazi Germany. We really had the feeling, then, that the Soviet land was not alone; that the Soviet people's struggle was merged in a united front with the struggle of other peoples against the hated enemy.

The Comintern's Executive Committee proposed forming, and subsequently did in fact form, an international unit consisting of political émigrés from various countries. It included Spaniards, Czechs, Slovaks, Poles, Bulgarians, Greeks, Rumanians, Germans, Austrians, Englishmen, and people from other nations. Organizationally, the unit was a part of the Special Independent Motorized Infantry Brigade. Politically, it was headed directly by G. M. Dimitrov.

In October 1941, at the recommendation of Dimitrov, the Bulgarian Ivan Vinarov was named deputy commander of the unit. (Vinarov later became a prominent figure in People's Bulgaria.) The choice had been carefully thought out. Vinarov was a Bulgarian revolutionary who had been compelled to leave his country and emigrate to the USSR. There he was graduated from the

[1] Viz., in connection with the Reichstag fire in 1933. (Translator's note.)

163

Frunze Military Academy and was given the rank of colonel in the Red Army. He next worked on the staff of the Comintern and the Foreign Bureau of the CC BRP. Regularly (no less than once a week), he went to the Comintern and reported to Dimitrov on the internationalists, getting instructions and advice in return.

The brigade was intended for defensive action in Moscow itself, and performed its military duties in the city. Events did not demand that the entire brigade be committed to combat; but certain detachments of its soldiers, including "internationalists," took part in combat on the approaches to the city. Many soldiers of the international unit joined underground groups sent to their own countries, since their homeland required their aid in the struggle against the Nazi occupying troops.

G. M. Dimitrov foresaw an inglorious end for the Nazi aggressors, great social changes in many countries, and the necessity for building new armed forces there. As those on the staff of the secretariat of the Comintern's Executive Committee recall, he once said: "For Communists it is very important to have at least an elementary understanding of military affairs. We go into our own countries, and besides doing political work we have to create an army."[2]

The development of the domestic political situation in Bulgaria permitted Dimitrov, as early as June 1944, to conclude that there would be a worsening of the already-existing crisis in the country. The cause of this was the antipopular policy of Premier Ivan Bagrianov's government. In one of his broadcasts on the "Hristo Botev" radio station, Dimitrov declared that the government was deceiving the people and serving the interests of the Nazis and their Bulgarian minions. But it couldn't manage things "so that the wolves were surfeited and the sheep still untouched." He warned that Bulgaria's domestic situation and the mood of the people and the Army promised nothing good for either Bagrianov or the Nazis,[3] since Bulgaria's rulers were pushing it toward national catastrophe.

[2] *Rabothichesko delo* (*organ TsK BKP*), March 12, 1972.
[3] Cf. G. Dimitrov, *Izbrannye proizvedeniya*, (Sofia, Izd-vo literatury na inostrannykh yazykakh, 1968), Vol. II, pp. 52–53.

At the General Staff we had carefully studied the results of the BRP's very widespread activity, and we knew that a large-scale and well-organized partisan movement was developing in Bulgaria. In 1944 the Fatherland Front had a National Liberation Insurgent Army of 18,000 men in Bulgaria. By Bulgarian standards, this is a lot. This army of insurgents had created a real internal front in Bulgaria throughout the territory of the state, diverting the attention of the monarcho-fascistic forces, the police, and the Nazi garrisons. A network of paramilitary groups amounting to some 12,000 fighters was active at plants, factories, and institutions, in the Army, in towns, and in the countryside. To this we must add another 200,000 partisans' helpers. The partisans had successfully beaten off an attempt by the pro-Nazi government of Bulgaria to put down this movement by force of arms. At the General Staff, we regarded all this as a favorable factor in the situation.

We also had to cope with the fact that, formally, Bulgaria was not at war with the USSR. But the fascist government, although it had not decided on the dangerous step of declaring war on the USSR, was in alliance with Nazi Germany and helping it in every way it could. The Nazi Army made free use of Bulgaria's territory and its transportation system. Bulgarian troops did occupation duty in Yugoslavia and Greece, which enabled the Nazi command to transfer more of its own forces to the Soviet-German front. The clique of Hitler's minions in Bulgaria dealt harshly with partisans and other patriots.

As might have been expected, the greatest burden of work on the plans for the operations in Bulgaria fell on the shoulders of those General Staff officers handling the planning for the 3rd Ukrainian Front. They were headed up by Maj. Gen. K. F. Vasilchenko, an intelligent man who was always ready to proffer a lot of interesting ideas. On one occasion, when he was reporting to me on the plans for the operations, he noted in passing that the German command was not, in his opinion, expecting the Soviet forces to swing into Bulgaria. I asked him to substantiate that view, because if Germany wasn't expecting us in Bulgaia, it would not (obviously) have built a strong defense there. In that case, in

165

launching our attack we could count on the element of surprise, with all the consequences flowing therefrom.

General Vasilchenko called my attention to the secret maneuvers of Bagrianov's government that we had learned about. Some members of that government had had secret dealings with the Anglo-Americans.

"Bagrianov needs all these maneuvers," Vasilchenko said, "to hold back the Red Army from entering Bulgaria. This is also confirmed by the fact that the Nazi officials in Bulgaria have no notion of leaving the country and are calmly sitting there. They think the Soviet Union will not violate Bagrianov's sham neutrality, reinforced by a separate deal with our allies."

All this coincided with my own ideas on the subject. But should I report them to my superiors? From a viewpoint of strictly military analysis, there was little proof to substantiate them. But when I said as much to Antonov, he decided to report the matter to the Supreme Commander.

Meantime, events were continuing to unfold rapidly. The defeat of the Nazi forces near Iaşi and Kishinev had compelled Bagrianov to abandon his hopes of somehow stabilizing the fascist regime in Bulgaria by means of military assistance from Hitler. Any expectation of such assistance had now become utopian. Nor did he have internal resources: The masses of the Bulgarian people hated their loathsome rulers and the fascist system. The time was ripe for a revolutionary explosion. Meantime, the Red Army was driving rapidly through Rumania, where a popular uprising had broken out, and was approaching the northern border of Bulgaria.

August 26, 1944, has gone down in history as the day when the Bulgarian Workers' Party passed a resolution on the direct preparation of an armed uprising by the Bulgarian people. This corresponded to the situation, and was assured by real possibilities. The CC BRP published a historical circular letter, No. 4, obliging all Communists to instigate all antifascist forces to a bold and decisive struggle to drive out the Nazi troops, overthrow the fascist ministers, and establish a Fatherland Front government and a people's democratic regime.

The next day G. M. Dimitrov, who had had many talks with

Stalin, sent a directive addressed to the headquarters of the partisan forces but intended for the CC BRP. The directive ordered that all forces rally around the national Committee of the Fatherland Front, that the Nazi military units and the Gestapo be disarmed, that any resistance to the Fatherland Front or the Red Army be liquidated, and that a Fatherland Front government be formed. One special paragraph stated:

> The Bulgarian people and its armed forces must decisively go over to the side of the Red Army, which is Bulgaria's liberator from the German yoke, and at the same time purge the Bulgarian land of Nazi bandits and their vile minions.[4]

Thus he accurately spelled out the Bulgarian people's program of revolutionary armed struggle against the fascist regime existing in the country. The Bulgarian Communists, heading up the revolutionary forces, immediately set about implementing Comrade Dimitrov's directive on the spot.

Although it was in a hopeless situation, Bagrianov's government continued its policy of co-operating with the Nazis, and it opposed the Fatherland Front. The Soviet General Staff had incontrovertible evidence that reinforcements for the battered German forces were passing through Bulgarian territory to Rumania. This was reported to the Stavka; and on August 30 the Soviet Government proposed to the Bulgarian Government that it immediately block the passage of German troops to Rumania. Bagrianov was between the devil and the deep blue sea. He couldn't wriggle out of the situation, and so he resigned.

For two days, Bulgaria had no government. Then on September 2, 1944, a new cabinet of ministers was formed under Kosta Muravev. When he came to power, Muravev made an announcement on the Sofia radio that was big with commitments, declaring that the government intended to put an end to a policy that the Bulgarian people had never approved. He announced the restoration of all the Bulgarian people's democratic rights and liberties, full and unconditional amnesty for all those who had fought against the dictatorial regime in Bulgaria and against the

[4] Ibid., p. 63.

authorities who had effected the alliance with Germany. Muravev pledged to dissolve all fascist organizations; in the sphere of foreign policy, to follow a policy of strict neutrality; to disarm all German forces that crossed the Bulgarian border, and all those on the territory of Bulgaria. He promised to initiate talks with a view to removing Bulgaria from a state of war with England and America. And he laid special emphasis on one of the government's chief tasks: to establish relations of trust with Russia.

But it soon emerged that this statement by the government was a lie. The Soviet General Staff had accurate information on German vessels in Bulgarian ports, and on thousands of German soldiers who had sought shelter in Bulgaria from the pursuing Red Army. The enemy, basing his submarines in Bulgarian ports, was still threatening Soviet shipping in the Black Sea, and the maritime flank of the Soviet forces. All these factors compelled us, with no letup in our tempo of work, to prepare for operations by Soviet forces in Bulgaria.

The General Staff's ideas on the operations in Bulgaria were elaborated and reported to the Stavka. The gist of them was that forces of the 3rd Ukrainian Front, the Black Sea Fleet, and the Danube Flotilla should destroy the enemy on the territory of Bulgaria and in its maritime ports. It was proposed that we use the southern part of Dobruja as a jumping-off point, and aim our main blows at Aitos and Burgas. It was proposed that the very important ports of Varna and Burgas, where enemy naval vessels were located, be seized via a combined operation by the Black Sea Fleet and certain units of the front's striking force. In reporting to Stalin on the idea of the operation, Antonov did not neglect to mention the possibility of achieving surprise if the enemy was not expecting us in Bulgaria.

While he did not reject the General Staff's ideas, Stalin said that it would be necessary to get more information on the situation locally, and put the final touches on the operations plan there. For that purpose he ordered Zhukov to visit the 2nd and 3rd Ukrainian fronts. There, he was to work with the front commanders and Marshal Timoshenko, the Stavka representative with those fronts. Stalin suggested to Zhukov that before leaving he should have a talk with Dimitrov and listen to his advice. In the meantime, he himself had a talk with Dimitrov on the telephone, relative to Zhukov's visit. Dimitrov's approval was obtained, and a very useful meeting took place.

As usual, Zhukov went off on his new assignment without delay. When he reached his destination, he got promptly to work. Following the classical rule of military science, he began by clarifying the information on the enemy, and it turned out that the situation faced by Tolbukhin's forces had not been studied thoroughly enough. Bulgaria was somewhat off to one side from the main highways of the war, and was not formally our enemy, so that we were more familiar with the German forces than with the Bulgarian Army. All we knew was that the main body of Bulgarian forces was in the center and western part of the country, while considerable forces were stationed in Greece and Yugoslavia. But as for the situation in the northern part of the country, neither the front nor the General Staff knew as much as they should have. Naturally, steps were soon taken to rectify this situation.

There was no time to be wasted in preparing for the operation. Whereas earlier the German command and the pro-Nazi Bulgarian Government had not expected the Red Army to enter the territory of Bulgaria, by this time (early September) it was easy to notice that considerable formations of Soviet forces were moving in that direction. To delay meant losing the element of surprise. Yet, as often happens in war, the situation at that particular moment compelled us to postpone things for a certain time. Fuel had to be brought up; otherwise the tanks and trucks could not move. In fact, for lack of fuel, one of the army's artillery was lagging behind. Also, we had to regroup forces to a certain extent.

The operations plan was completed by September 4, and it basically reflected the thinking of the General Staff. (Timoshenko had fallen ill and did not take part in this work.) By that time, the situation in Bulgaria had become even more complicated. Battered units of Army Group Southern Ukraine were retreating across Bulgarian territory without any hindrance whatsoever by the Bulgarian authorities. Several dozen German naval vessels had found

169

shelter in Bulgarian ports; and Nazi forces were concentrated in the regions of Sofia, Breznik, and Slivnitsa. The German ambassador to Bulgaria had announced to the Bulgarian Government that the German troops had no intention of leaving Bulgaria in the near future. And the General Staff had received information that at the last moment the Nazis might pull off a coup in Bulgaria and drag that country into war against the Soviet Union.

Since naval actions would be of great importance to the success of the operation in Bulgaria, Adm. N. G. Kuznetsov came to help Zhukov and Tolbukhin. At that juncture, the Black Sea Fleet, commanded by Adm. F. S. Oktyabrsky, and the Danube Flotilla, commanded by S. G. Gorshkov, were put under the operational control of the 3rd Ukrainian Front. The fleet had two main tasks: to prevent the enemy's vessels from leaving Bulgaria, and (in a combined operation with land forces) to seize Varna and Burgas. The fleet was to land marines, who would seize and hold the Bulgarian ports until Tolbukhin's forces arrived. The operation was scheduled to begin on September 10.

The finalized plan for operations in Bulgaria was approved by the Stavka on September 5. On that same day the Soviet Government sent the Bulgarian Government a note stating the following, *inter alia:*

> The Soviet Government cannot regard this Bulgarian policy other than as the factual waging of war on the side of Germany against the Soviet Union—a policy still being continued, despite the sharp deterioration in Germany's military situation, and despite the fact that Bulgaria is now fully capable, without fearing Germany, of breaking with Germany and thus saving the country from ruin.[5]

At seven in the evening the note was handed to the Bulgarian ambassador in Moscow, who forwarded it to its addressee.

Shortly after this news became known in Bulgaria, the Central Committee of the Bulgarian Workers' Party convened in extraordinary session jointly with the staff of the insurgent Army. They approved a plan for carrying out an uprising. The main blow was

[5] *Vneshnyaya politika Sovetskogo Soyuza v period Otechestvennoi voiny,* Vol. II, pp. 182–83.

to be struck against Sofia on the night of September 9. Preparations for the uprising included large-scale strikes and demonstrations by the workers in the capital. Todor Zhivkov, a prominent figure in the BRP, was made responsible for the political and military direction of the demonstrations, and for the demonstrators' security. He was placed at the head of an operations bureau of the party set up to direct the armed forces of the popular uprising in the capital. Other members of the bureau were Comrades Stanko Todorov, Vladimir Bonev, and Ivan Bonev. The strikes began on September 6.

Muravev's government was stunned. On the night of September 6 its representatives asked our chargé d'affaires in Sofia to inform the Soviet Government that Bulgaria was breaking off relations with Germany and asking for an armistice. This was an important declaration.

When the Bulgarian Government's request for an armistice reached Moscow, Stalin—after conferring with other members of the Stavka and with Dimitrov by telephone—called Zhukov and told him that for the time being, until the actual situation was ascertained, he should restrict the advance of the 3rd Ukrainian Front to a line running from Giurgiu through Razgrad, Shumen, and Dylgopol to the northern bank of the Kamen River. He told him about the events in Bulgaria and the doings of the insurgents, saying that a popular uprising was imminent, and that the time had come for Muravev's government to make some basic decisions; that it should have a care for the future.

The Military Council of the 3rd Ukrainian Front established contact with the People's Liberation Insurgent Army of Bulgaria and with local committees of the BRP in the border zone. The Communists' appeal to the people to rid the country of the Nazi bandits, in which action they would act jointly with the Red Army, was heard on Bulgarian soil. At the same time that the uprising was taking form, on Bulgaria's northern border everything was ready for the Soviet forces to enter the country.

On September 7, finding itself in a hopeless situation, the Muravev government officially announced that it was breaking off relations with Germany, and on September 8 it declared war on

Germany. Now the Bulgarian request for an armistice was taken up by the Soviet Government for consideration.

All these events had a direct bearing on the work of the General Staff. I remember that at that time our nightly situation reports were usually given in the presence of many members of the Stavka and the National Defense Committee, since the political and military situation was being discussed, and decisions being made on these matters.

A reply soon came from Zhukov. He said the order to limit the advance of the forces to the indicated line had been conveyed personally to Tolbukhin and Oktyabrsky so that it would be carried out to the letter. He added that the actions of the advanced units would begin at 1100 hours on September 8, and those of the main forces immediately following. Also, that he himself would visit the armies of Gagen and Sharokhin to check on their readiness for the impending actions.

The mentality of a real commander is such that he never confines himself to simply ascertaining the present situation: He always tries to look into the future—to see the long-ranged consequences of an operation. And such, of course, was the case with Zhukov. After reporting that Stalin's orders had been carried out accurately, he tried to look ahead; and he offered his suggestions, based on the actual situation.

> If [he said] the 3rd Ukrainian Front, after reaching the Ruse-Razgrad-Shumen-Varna line does not advance farther, Tolbukhin's front should be extended along the Danube to Turnu-Severin, freeing Malinovsky and his units from defending the Giurgiu-Turnu-Severin sector.
>
> When Tolbukhin's units reach the Turnu-Severin-Kalafat sector, one reinforced army could be put across the Danube to cut the Belgrade-Salonika railroad and occupy a line running from Belgrade through Paraćin and Knjaževac to Lom.

In Zhukov's opinion, this disposition of the forces of the 3rd Ukrainian Front would assure the 2nd Ukrainian Front's operation against Hungary, would help the Yugoslav National Liberation Army, and would compel the Germans to get out of Greece.

The tenor of these proposals coincided with the General Staff's notions as to the future. The Supreme Commander knew about our rough plans; and when Zhukov sent him his proposals, Stalin passed them along to us. These proposals were further developed in working out the plans for operations on the territory of Yugoslavia.

The forces of the 3rd Ukrainian Front jumped off promptly at 1100 hours on September 8. The first to cross the Bulgarian border were the motorized detachments, followed an hour later by the rifle divisions. The Bulgarian border guards did not offer any resistance. And the Bulgarian infantry division positioned in the region of Dobrich did not fire a single shot. Not only that, but the Bulgarian soldiers made many friendly gestures toward the Soviet troops. As for the local inhabitants, they were very hospitable to our officers and soldiers: People came out into the streets to greet the troops of the Red Army. The Bulgarian officers with whom our commanders soon made contact stated that they had received orders from the Bulgarian command not to engage in hostilities with the Red Army.

The 4th and 7th mechanized corps, which were to overtake the infantry during the night, jumped off at 1800. Meantime the Black Sea Fleet started landing marines in the port of Varna.

The bourgeois government of Bulgaria was compelled to break off relations with Nazi Germany in actual fact. As soon as evidence of this factual rupture was received, on September 9 at 1900 hours, the following telegram was sent to Zhukov, Kuznetsov, Tolbukhin, and Oktyabrsky:

> In view of the fact that the Bulgarian Government has broken off relations with the Germans, declared war against Germany, and asked the Soviet Government to begin armistice talks, the Stavka of the Supreme Command, in accordance with instructions from the National Defense Committee, orders: that by 2100 hours on September 9 you complete operations for occupying the populated points indicated in the plan, and that at 2200 hours you suspend military actions in Bulgaria.

On the night of September 9, in Sofia and other key points of Bulgaria, beyond the line along which the Soviet forces were positioned, the decisive events of the popular uprising took place—an uprising led by the BRP. As we know, they resulted in a brilliant victory for the people.

We soon received the news of the victorious popular uprising. At the same time we had a report on the creation of a new government headed by Kimon Georgev. On the morning of that same day Georgev went on the air to announce the make-up of his Cabinet and read an appeal to the Bulgarian people. The government appointed a delegation to conclude an armistice with the USSR. Civil liberties were restored in Bulgaria; and members of the former government who had conducted an antipopular policy were outlawed.

All this was very good to hear. Yet we could not yet get our bearings completely: Information on events in Bulgaria was not sufficient for us to draw any military conclusions. Right then it was very important that Bulgaria, having broken the alliance with the Nazis, should join the great liberation struggle against Nazi Germany. At the same time it was necessary to render harmless the reactionary forces, and prevent them from unleasing a civil war in Bulgaria. Also, the data we had received did not yet permit us to ascertain any of the following: whether the old governmental machine in Bulgaria would be broken; what, at the moment, was the position of the army high command, and what was it going to be in the future; what role was the BRP playing in the Army now, and what role would it take on in the near future. We firmly believed, in any case, that the BRP would keep a strong grasp on the helm of the uprising, and would be able to take steps for the normalization of life in Bulgaria and for setting up a governmental system that would meet the needs of the people.

Certain things were not clear with respect to the make-up of Kimon Georgev's government. For example, we did not have enough details on the past activity of the ministers. Georgev himself was known primarily as a person of anti-German leanings. In our view, this was a big plus. Also, as head of the government after the coup of May 19, 1934, he had established diplomatic relations between Bulgaria and the Soviet Union—something that also spoke in his favor. But at the same time, in that same year of 1934 a violent campaign was waged against the labor movement, and against the Communists in particular. It was, in fact, in the thirties that the last vestiges of parliamentary government and bourgeois democracy were abolished in Bulgaria, and a fascist military dictatorship established.

Also, the Cabinet included such a man as the Minister without Portfolio, Nikola Petkov, a member of the Agrarian Party and a big rentier known for his reactionary views. One might expect from Petkov a very dangerous opposition to the democratic consequences of the popular uprisings. (As the passage of time showed, Petkov proved to be a violent enemy of socialist Bulgaria.) And several other important governmental posts were held by people not regarded as reliable friends of the people. The Stavka necessarily had to take all these things into account, since the main forces of the 3rd Ukrainian Front were still on Bulgarian territory, and in the near future that country would become its rear area.

At noon on September 9, Antonov told me that Dimitrov had telephoned about the delegation from the new Bulgarian Government that was preparing to fly to Tolbukhin's headquarters. Dimitrov had asked how best to organize this flight, and at the same time had told Antonov that the delegation would include Dimiter Ganev, a member of the BRP Politburo. Ganev had been instructed, he said, to tell the front's Military Council about the nature of the government and events in Bulgaria.

We eagerly awaited the report from the front. Finally Tolbukhin reported to the Stavka that a delegation from the Bulgarian Government, properly empowered by the Council of Ministers, had met on September 10 with the Military Council of the front. The delegation included Prof. Dimiter Mikhalchev, former Bulgarian emissary to Moscow, Dimiter Ganev (whom we already knew), and several other persons. The most urgent tasks of the delegation were to get in touch with General of the Army Tolbukhin, commanding the front, to learn the conditions for suspending hostilities, and to discuss with him all matters associated with the beginning of armistice talks.

The delegates also had to reach agreement on the conditions for the Bulgarian Army's co-operation with the Soviet forces in the common struggle against the Nazis, and to discuss the matter of restoring diplomatic relations between Bulgaria and the USSR. As the reader can see, problems of great importance to the country had to be settled first. Other than acting through the front, the Bulgarians had at the time no way of coming to agreement with Moscow and sending the requisite delegation there.

In its talks with the command of the 3rd Ukrainian Front, the delegation led off with the main question: The Bulgarian Government offered Bulgaria's help in a common armed struggle against the German forces, and favored joint action between the Soviet forces and the Bulgarian Army. The chairman of the delegation told Tolbukhin that at the moment it was urgent for Bulgaria to co-ordinate its actions with the Red Army, since (as he put it) the tasks of both armies had become the same. In the name of the Council of Ministers, the delegates asked Tolbukhin to send an authorized representative to Sofia to co-ordinate the efforts of the Bulgarian and Soviet forces.

In the course of the talk the Bulgarian delegates told the front's Military Council that at the moment the Nazis had concentrated considerable forces, with a large number of tanks, in Yugoslav territory in the region of Niš and Bela-Palanka. The Bulgarians opined that this concentration of forces undoubtedly signified an imminent attack on Sofia. They were very worried, and asked for immediate assistance (especially aircraft) for the Bulgarian forces who would be defending the capital. In this connection the delegation gave information on the airfields in the area of Sofia, and said the Bulgarian Army had no fuel for aircraft. In the course of the talks several practical problems arose as regards the combat-readiness of the Bulgarian forces and the communications between Varna and Sofia, in the interests of efficiently accomplishing all kinds of tasks important for both sides.

Tolbukhin promised the Bulgarians that he would forward their requests to the Soviet Government; and in his turn he expressed interest in transport facilities on the Danube and how to go about getting Soviet forces across that broad, deep river. Tolbukhin was usually very cautious in secret talks; but on this occasion he openly declared it was necessary to send Soviet troops through Bulgarian territory to the region of Vidin. The delegation replied that the government and people of Bulgaria would help the Red Army in every way; that they would provide them with railroads and water transport, including German vessels, if they were on the Danube. The Bulgarians promised to help recover German vessels scuttled in the Danube; and they gave information on the possibilities for making railroad shipments in a country where there were but few locomotives, and those badly worn out.

When the official talks were over, Dimiter Ganev asked for a separate audience. He told the Soviet command about the make-up of Kimon Georgev's Cabinet. "This government," he said, "is a Fatherland Front government: a coalition of the BRP, the Agrarian Party, the Social Democrats, the Zveno, and the 'independents' (nonparty people)." He explained the special traits of that government—one in which the Communists, although they did not have a majority, had assured a leading role for the BRP. Then he gave a detailed account of the popular uprising, the partisan forces, and the work of the Bulgarian Communists.

Tolbukhin was of course interested in the mood among the career men in the Bulgarian Army. Ganev knew the Army well, and gave a detailed description of the prevalent attitudes. According to him, the Bulgarian sergeants and rank and file were ready at any time to fight shoulder to shoulder with the Soviet troops. Among the officers there was a reactionary, pro-Nazi element—especially among the forces that had done occupation duty abroad. As for the inhabitants of Sofia, they were impatiently awaiting the arrival of the Red Army.

Ganev provided a lot of useful information on the leadership of the Bulgarian Army. He gave a favorable report of the former Minister of War, Maj. Gen. Ivan Marinov, who in the Fatherland Front government had been given the post of Commander in Chief of the Bulgarian Army. But at the same time, on the basis of personal observation, he noted that Marinov had reacted apathetically to the dangerous situation created by the Nazi forces and the reactionary officers, especially in the region of Sofia. Ganev was also familiar with the Bulgarian General Staff. Without beating around the bush, he said that he had not observed among the staff officers any firm intention to enter into decisive hostilities with the Nazis.

At the conclusion of the talks, Ganev tossed out the idea that the new Bulgarian Government did not yet have a firm guarantee of its security, since the situation in Bulgaria—especially the concentration of Bulgarian troops in the region of Sofia—might be utilized by the reactionary officers in an action against the government. And the German command, in turn, could exploit that development. In his view, there was a very real possibility that the foreign and domestic reactionary forces might combine against the Fatherland Front government.

In the name of the CC BRP, Ganev expressed the wish that aircraft of the Red Army be brought to the Sofia area as a guarantee against possible actions by the reactionary officers. He also asked that the BRP be informed on how to maintain contact and work with the new regime in areas occupied by the Red Army.

The talks with the Bulgarian delegation and the detailed information from Dimiter Ganev considerably clarified the situation in Bulgaria. And the Main Political Administration received one other report—this time from I. S. Anoshin, chief of the front's political administration.

But the fullest explanation of where Bulgaria was headed came from Georgi Dimitrov. The gist of his appraisal was later set forth in his Political Report to the CC BRP (c) at the Fifth Party Congress on December 19, 1948. On that occasion, Dimitrov said:

> On September 9, 1944, political power in our country was torn from the hands of the capitalist bourgeoisie and the monarcho-fascist minority of exploiters and put in the hands of the great majority of the people—the toilers of town and country—under the vigorous leadership of the working class and its Communist avant-garde. The uprising of September 9, having triumphed with the decisive aid of the heroic Soviet Army, opened up the road to the building of socialism in our country.
>
> The combination of the popular uprising of September 9, 1944, and the victorious advance of the Soviet Army into the Balkans not only assured the triumph of the uprising but endowed it with great strength and scope.[6]

[6] Dimitrov, *Izbrannye proizvedeniya*, Vol. II. p. 731.

But for all the success of the uprising, many difficulties and dangers remained. There would be sudden bursts of firing, first from one place, then from another; and snipe shooters would endanger the lives of our soldiers, the Bulgarian partisans, and the Communists. Scheduled departures of important troop trains would unexpectedly be sabotaged. And one day, the entire staff of the German Embassy and the German Military Mission vanished as though they had dropped through the ground. At each step of the way, Soviet soldiers and Bulgarian patriots encountered sabotage by the underground enemy. They had to unmask these plots and fight for the new Bulgaria with all their vigor and revolutionary fervor.

Earlier, when the Soviet forces were advancing farther after having crushed the enemy at Iaşi and Kishinev, the rapid liquidation of the Nazi apparatus for enslaving Rumania became very important to the future of that country. The Rumanians themselves set about this task. But the King and the representatives of the old ruling circles, who were still in power, in everything they did kept an eye on their former German overlords—especially the German ambassador and his military staff. Then the advancing Soviet forces, having discovered a large group of German military personnel, took them prisoner. As a result of these measures, the Nazi network of agents—now disorganized and without a command group—offered only feeble resistance to the development of the popular uprising in Rumania. But in Bulgaria it did not prove possible to neutralize the Nazi hornets' nest in short order, and this caused a certain degree of alarm.

The Red Army had now been marching through Bulgaria for a week, to the accompaniment of a rousing welcome from the people. One day, as Antonov and I were reporting to the Stavka on the situation at the front, one of the members of the Supreme Command bethought himself of the German Embassy staff in Bulgaria, and asked where it was at the present time. Neither Antonov nor I could give a completely satisfactory answer to that question, since our forces were still on their way to Sofia, and Col. Gen. S. S. Biryuzov, chief of staff of the 3rd Ukrainian Front and the representative of the Soviet command, would not be flying

179

there until the morning of September 14. At the moment, his chief task had nothing to do with catching the Nazi agents: It was rather (as the Bulgarians had requested) to co-ordinate the actions of the Red Army and the Bulgarian forces (and, later, to head up the Allied Control Commission). But in war one had to do what the situation demanded. And now Antonov and I, as his deputy, were shown new areas of General Staff work. The General Staff was instructed to send to Tolbukhin, in Stalin's name, orders to seek out and intern the entire staff of the German Embassy and the military mission in the shortest possible time.

These orders were sent to the front; and Tolbukhin, in his turn, ordered Biryuzov to conduct the search, since he (as has already been mentioned) was going to Sofia on September 14, accompanied by Gen. I. S. Anoshin, chief of the front's political administration.

When he got to Sofia, General Biryuzov ascertained that the German diplomatic and military mission personnel were not in the city. When queried as to their whereabouts, representatives of the Bulgarian authorities said they had no information on them. Then where had they disappeared to? Obviously, they could not have vanished without help from their sympathizers. And there was no doubt that they had a sizable network of agents reaching throughout the country and supported by the local reactionaries. This network had to be liquidated in the shortest possible time.

When reporting to Stalin on the situation at the front, Antonov did not neglect to mention this fact, too. The Supreme Commander then instructed him to convey to the 3rd Ukrainian Front orders to step up the search. The latter organized a systematic search for the embassy staff, which could not have vanished like a needle in a haystack. Biryuzov and Anoshin made one more *démarche* to the Bulgarian Government. Little by little, it developed that the disappearance of the Nazi diplomats and military mission had been known to, and directly facilitated by, certain officials of the government. Some of the latter had helped the German officers and diplomatic personnel to get a special train. But no one said where the Germans had gone. We had to organize a thoroughgoing search for the train.

Finally the General Staff received a telegram saying that the fugitives were virtually on the Turkish border near the town of Svilengrad. Tolbukhin and Biryuzov each sent a small airborne force to Svilengrad. Tolbukhin's force, consisting of twenty-five military police from the 3rd Ukrainian Front commanded by Lt. Col. I. Z. Kotelkov, was the first to land near Svilengrad. They rushed to the railroad station, but they were too late. The train had in fact been there, but shortly before their arrival it had departed in the direction of the Greek border. With the help of some Bulgarians it was ascertained that the staff of the German Embassy had arrived a week earlier, and then waited—without leaving the railroad cars—for visas from the Turkish Government. But the latter was in no hurry to accommodate the representatives of Germany, which had suffered one defeat after another on the battle fronts. Also, as we know, on August 2, 1944, the Turks had broken off diplomatic relations with Germany. On this basis they postponed issuance of the visas from one day to the next. When the fugitives had exhausted their stores and food—and when (quite possibly) they had learned they were being sought—they set out for the Greek border.

When the situation had been ascertained, Lt. Col. Kotelkov and his troops went in pursuit of the train. But he had first explained things to the Bulgarian railroad officials and the prefect of the town, and had demanded that the train be held up at the next station. It was stopped at the station of Rakovskaya. The entire embassy staff of thirty-two persons, headed by Ambassador Beckerle and the military attaché, Colonel von Hulzen, was arrested. Along with them in the train were certain persons from the embassy of the now-extinct government of Mussolini, and two staff members from the Swedish Embassy. The diplomats were soon delivered to Dobrich. The hornets' nest had been rendered harmless. This isolation of Nazi Germany's embassy staff and military mission personnel helped to win the struggle against the Nazi network in Bulgaria.

Having detained these patent enemies of the Bulgarian people and the Red Army, our command was nonetheless concerned for the inviolability of other diplomatic staffs, and for the strictest conformity to the law as regards all Bulgarian and foreign citizens. This matter was the subject of a special discussion at the Stavka. Consequently, the following telegram was sent to the staff of the 3rd Ukrainian Front on September 9, 1944:

> The Stavka of the Supreme Command prohibits the making of arrests in Bulgaria and Rumania. In the future, do not arrest anyone without the permission of the Stavka. On instructions from the Stavka of the Supreme Command—Antonov, Shtemenko.

Both the Stavka and the General Staff anxiously awaited news of the Bulgarian Army's turning its weapons against our common enemy, Nazi Germany. This would help in the general cause of defeating the Nazis, especially in Yugoslavia.

From the very outset of planning joint operations for the Soviet and Bulgarian forces and the National Liberation Army of Yugoslavia, we ran up against the consequences of the policy that had been followed by the late and unlamented King Boris. The fact was that Nazi Germany, when it seized the Balkans, had not only installed regimes acceptable to it but had set the peoples at each other's throats. This was the old "divide and conquer" principle of the Roman empire's slaveholders, skillfully utilized by the Nazi politicians. The result was that when the monarchist government of Bulgaria had fallen into dependence upon Germany, it had sent considerable forces into Yugoslavia. The mission of these forces was to help the Nazis put down the liberation movement in that country. The Bulgarian troops were specially selected and were extremely reactionary. Naturally, the Yugoslav populace fiercely hated the accomplices of the Nazi aggressors.

After September 9, there was a firm foundation for relations of genuine friendship between the two peoples. But events showed that it is not all that easy to establish between two peoples the kind of trust required for joint operations. This required not only time but a great deal of educational work, even among the Communists. One especially important thing was to demonstrate the basically new character of the Bulgarian Army—its completely new function.

The help needed at that time to solve this important problem was provided by Dimitrov, who sent Tito a telegram concerning the joint operations of the National Liberation Army of Yugoslavia and the Bulgarian forces against the Nazis. He managed to explain to his Yugoslav comrades the new situation that had developed in Bulgaria, and to the Bulgarian Communists that they must radically improve relations with their Yugoslav brothers (in terms of both class and party), win the trust of the latter, and conclude a military alliance with them. Only under such conditions would it be possible to organize and successfully carry out joint military operations by Soviet, Yugoslav, and Bulgarian forces. Bulgaria's road to the future lay through a purgative war against fascism.

Dimitrov's telegram fixed the BRP's attention on that important matter. The Communists saw to it that the government recalled the Bulgarian troops from Yugoslavia, and worked out a program for their radical reorganization. The pro-Nazi officers and those other ranks who had blemished their records with outrages against the Yugoslavs were discharged from the Army and brought to trial. In this way the reactionary center was liquidated, and the abcess in the organism of the Bulgarian Army was lanced. The units were brought up to strength by bringing in partisans and volunteers. The result of these measures was that the Bulgarian forces about to fight the Germans on the territory of Yugoslavia were not those that had been there before but new armed forces born of the September revolutionary storm in Bulgaria. All of the foregoing made it possible to organize the victorious joint operations of the Soviet and Bulgarian forces and the National Liberation Army of Yugoslavia on Yugoslav soil, of which more later.

The goal of Bulgaria's entering the war against Nazi Germany, and the aim of destroying the Nazi Reich, announced as the program of the Fatherland Front, corresponded to the basic interests of the Bulgarian people and the intentions of the anti-Nazi coalition. But it could not be hoped that this about-face would take place immediately and without difficulty: The heritage of fascism was too heavy, and had to be dealt with seriously.

Our habit of evaluating the likely course of events through the prism of Soviet history suggested to us that we might expect, in Bulgaria, unusual forms of military development. Of course the decision as to the modalities of military development in Bulgaria did not depend on us. But we were obliged to make a prediction about it, and hence to become very familiar with the situation, and constantly to analyze the tendencies in its alteration. This we did very circumstantially. And in September the officers of K. F. Vasilchenko's section were assigned the mission of studying the Bulgarian Army very thoroughly—something they did most conscientiously.

Meantime an unprecedented conflict broke out because of Bulgaria's entering the war on the side of the anti-Nazi coalition. In their striving to throw the Bulgarian Army and all the nation's resources into the fight against Nazi Germany more rapidly than was being done, the Bulgarian revolutionary forces ran up against the secret and very strong resistance of enemies acting on the sly. Foes of the new Bulgaria were discovered not only in the state apparatus but in the Fatherland Front government—in high military posts.

The events took the following course. The Bulgarian Government's wishes (expressed at the first meeting between its delegation and the Military Council of the 3rd Ukrainian Front) to coordinate the actions of the Red Army and the Bulgarian forces in a joint struggle against the Nazis corresponded fully to the requirements of the military situation. The necessity for carrying out joint operations involving the Soviet and Bulgarian forces and the National Liberation Army of Yugoslavia was also clear. It was especially important to remove the threat to Sofia, the seat of the Fatherland Front government and of the CC BRP, which had begun to function legally.

Since the Bulgarian Government had asked us to provide military assistance first and foremost, we sent one infantry corps of the 57th Army, an armored brigade, an antitank artillery brigade, some rocket-projector units, and a motorcycle regiment to the Sofia region. Fighter and ground-attack aircraft from the 17th Air Army were transferred to the Sofia airfield, and the commanding general, V. A. Sudets, moved his headquarters there.

The Bulgarian Government's request for joint action involving the Soviet and Bulgarian forces was also complied with very rapidly and completely. To Sofia, Tolbukhin sent his own chief of staff, Col. Gen. S. S. Biryuzov, a man very gifted in military matters, a good organizer, and an experienced politician. But at that time we could not confine ourselves to just these measures. The situation urgently required that operational control over all forces and resources in Bulgaria be put in the hands of the commander of the 3rd Ukrainian Front. The Bulgarians themselves requested this, since otherwise we could not have unified the will and actions of Soviet and Bulgarian forces in joint operations.

At this point the Stavka instructed Tolbukhin to reach agreement with the Bulgarian Government on the practical aspects of subordinating the Bulgarian Armed Forces to the 3rd Ukrainian Front. This measure corresponded to the norms of international law, since no armistice had yet been signed among the USSR, our allies, and Bulgaria.

On September 16, following the Stavka's orders, Tolbukhin sent the appropriate letter to Damian Velchev, the Bulgarian Minister of War. In it, he proposed that military orders to the Bulgarian Army be transmitted only via the Bulgarian General Staff. From that moment until the end of the war, the Soviet and Bulgarian forces would work in close concord.

Meantime, in Sofia and throughout the country a formative process was engendering the new Bulgaria, where the efforts of friends and the intrigues of enemies were intertwined in a complex knot of often contradictory events. Complete understanding was soon reached with the Communists of Bulgaria and other like-minded people of the same class. But such was not the case with our secret enemies. They disguised themselves very thoroughly, and put on the mask of comrades, so that it was not easy to figure out what they were doing. In this respect, that reliable "class flair" that the Communist Party has always inculcated in Soviet people served as a trustworthy compass for our representatives.

The first area in which the secret enemies gave battle to the new regime in Bulgaria and to the Soviet command was in the matter of allies. The Soviet General Staff felt that on September 1, the day when Biryuzov arrived in Sofia. On that day a group of British and American officers, without prior notice, presented themselves to Major General Marinov, Commander in Chief of the Bulgarian Army. It was obvious that their visit had been previously prepared and organized by the powerful hand of someone who desired to remain in the shadows.

The officers demanded that the airfield be handed over to them, along with the charts of the mine fields along the littoral of the Black Sea, since British vessels were expected to arrive soon in a port in the southernmost part of Bulgaria. As Marinov later explained, an officer and an engineer had already been sent to that port to prepare for the arrival of the ships, although approval had not been obtained either from Bulgaria or from the Soviet command. The visitors also offered military assistance in the Balkans —something the Bulgarian Government had not requested—and stated they would expect an answer on the following day.

Marinov declined any commitments and, having ushered out his uninvited guests, immediately got in touch with Biryuzov so as to decide what to do. He expressed the apprehension that the British and Americans would take further steps which could not be interpreted otherwise than as an attempt to seize objectives important to Bulgaria; e.g., its airfields.

Biryuzov assured Marinov that the allies were not so stupid as to openly aggravate the situation in a country where the forces of an entire front of the Red Army were ready at hand; and he advised him to reply flexibly, saying that the commander of the Soviet forces was in Bulgaria, and that the Bulgarians could not fulfill any request without his authorization.

In and of itself, the visit by our allies was far removed from any generally accepted rules of diplomatic and military courtesy. It was of course a peculiar reflection of the ideas and aims of Churchill's "Balkan variant." Thus was this Anglo-American visit evaluated by us at the General Staff, and by the Soviet military representatives on the spot. And when Marinov met with the Anglo-American officers for the second time, our workers declared they had no need of help from their allies. It was not a gallant answer, but it was utterly clear and definite. And it was properly understood by those to whom it was addressed. The visitors went back to where they had come from.

Thus the special conditions of the Red Army's liberation mission compelled both us General Staff officers and our front commanders to decide certain international questions in the course of our operations. Getting a bit ahead of the story, I note that this very special kind of activity, for which a military organization might not seem fitted, had long ago been reflected in the General Staff's organizational structure. Since the beginning of the war, diplomatic work—of course within the narrow limits of basically military matters—had been an integral element in the General Staff's activity.

Naturally, a telegram about the events in Sofia was sent to Molotov. It soon came back to us with his marginalia. On the substance of what had been done he made no comment; but with respect to the form of our reply to the allied officers, we and our representatives received a reprimand. In the upper left hand corner he had written:

> You should not have said that you "had no need" for our allies. You should have said that the allies had previously discussed such matters in Moscow, and that you would not enter into talks with them in Bulgaria, meantime politely indicating: "You can negotiate in Moscow."

I forwarded these comments to the 3rd Ukrainian Front, meantime reflecting that diplomacy really was a delicate business. Sometimes you wanted to say something pretty forceful, but you had to choose your words carefully and even bow decorously. The Commissar of Foreign Affairs had taught us good manners, and we were guilty of no such lapses in the future.

But that wasn't the end of the story. A few days later, Molotov was on hand when Antonov and I were making our situation report to Stalin. Stalin listened closely. When we got to Bulgaria, he reached for a box of Herzegovina Flors so as to fill his trusty pipe with tobacco from some of the cigarettes. Without raising his voice, he said to the two of us: "General Staff officers, too, should know the basics of international law and the procedure to use when dealing with representatives of other states."

Antonov and I realized what had happened: Apparently Molotov had told Stalin about the "delicate" diplomacy of us military men.

In such situations, it was up to Antonov to speak, since he was senior by rank and position. He replied that the General Staff had a special bureau that handled such matters and maintained close contact with the Ministry of Foreign Affairs. This bureau was the Special Missions Department, which was well known to Comrade Stalin. As for international law, we of course knew military law better than international law.

Stalin was not pleased with that reply. "I *knew* you wouldn't understand," he said angrily, tamping the end of a cigarette against the box. "I'm not talking about that department. For that matter, it mainly handles questions of representation. I'm talking about you—the heads of the General Staff."

Then, speaking somewhat more slowly, he added: "And not just the General Staff. . . . I'm thinking of military men who themselves conduct talks with foreigners or take part in talks, and draw up important military and diplomatic documents. They should know how to do it correctly so that they can represent our country properly. Now do you understand what I'm concerned about? It has nothing to do with formalities at banquets. There you make no blunders. . . . As for 'military law,' a subject you mentioned a moment ago, I've heard a good deal about that. Many military men think that for them the law is only a matter of bayonets."

He fell silent, finally filled his pipe with tobacco from the cigarettes, and then began puffing away on it in leisurely fashion. Everything in the Supreme Commander's expression told us the conversation on that particular subject was over.

I must admit that the demands put on us were justified. At that time, military men—and above all, General Staff representatives —took part in all large-scale talks with representatives of other countries. The conferences at Teheran, Yalta, and Potsdam are striking confirmations of this. At the General Staff we always made thorough preparations for such participation, and of course we studied the basics of international law.

Throughout the war the General Staff maintained very direct

and constant contact with the Ministry of Foreign Affairs. That contact was especially close in the last phase of the war and during the first postwar years, when the guns had fallen silent while the diplomats' voices again resounded in full volume. As for myself, I often had to draw up documents, or perhaps clear them, with such leaders of Soviet diplomacy as Maxim Litvinov, Ivan Maisky, Andrei Gromyko, and others. One could learn something from each of them, although they were completely different kinds of people in terms of character and working methods. We General Staff officers who had contact with them and with others in our diplomatic service are grateful for their understanding and for the great contribution they made to causes of a politico-military nature.

On several subsequent occasions, too, the British and Americans tried to stick their noses into Bulgarian affairs. Groups of officers from those countries continued to visit the Commander in Chief of the Bulgarian Army. One such group of visitors directly asked him to provide information on the Soviet forces. Marinov sniffed out the real nature of the inquiry, and sent his visitors to General Biryuzov, saying that he knew the situation better and could give a more complete answer to the question. The whole thing ended up with the visitors' being politely ushered out of the 3rd Ukrainian Front's battle zone; i.e., out of Bulgaria.

Next, a similar kind of probing was begun among the Bulgarian forces in Greece. A certain major showed up there and demanded that the Bulgarian command transfer authority to the British and not to the Fatherland Front in Greece. And he proffered Allied aid. In a word, our Anglo-American partners in the anti-Nazi coalition were doing intelligence work, trying to strengthen the position of the pro-Western forces and weaken the Soviet influence in the Balkans.

We soon got confirmation that the Anglo-Americans' intelligence activities and solicitations were being supported by people in the Bulgarian administrative apparatus, inherited from the monarchy, and also by Damian Velchev, the Minister of War. For example, the radio stations of the Bulgarian governmental network began to make open broadcasts fully revealing the disposition of Soviet forces. There was some fuss at the front headquarters; and Tolbukhin, via Biryuzov, proposed to the Bulgarian Government that radio broadcasts on the disposition of Soviet forces be made only when cleared by us.

As for Velchev, he tried to pose as a fighter for the Fatherland Front but in actuality was a violent enemy of everything progressive—everything associated with the new Bulgaria. We sensed he was playing a two-faced game when Tolbukhin received his reply to the letter he (Tolbukhin) had written him on September 16 concerning the subordination of the Bulgarian forces. The Minister of War (Velchev) wrote that he was doing everything possible to concert the actions of the Bulgarian and Soviet armies. Actually, however, he was doing just the opposite, and trying to avoid the Bulgarian Army's entry into the war on the side of the anti-Nazi coalition.

On September 19, Biryuzov and Anoshin met with the leaders of the Bulgarian Fatherland Front Government and of the Bulgarian Army. The Bulgarians were represented by Georgev, Marinov, Velchev, and a colonel representing the Army General Staff. The subject was the mobilization of the forces of the people and the Army in a decisive struggle against the Nazi forces.

On this occasion, the reactionary line of Velchev and of certain members of the Bulgarian General Staff was confirmed once again. Whereas the chairman of the Bulgarian Council of Ministers and the Commander in Chief of the Bulgarian Army favored the rapid unleashing of the Bulgarian forces against Germany and their going into combat, the Minister of War and the representative of the General Staff opposed sending Bulgarian forces to the front, claiming that the divisions in Yugoslavia and in Bulgaria itself were not combat-ready and were unreliable.

This rationale seemed convincing. As was mentioned earlier, the Bulgarian forces which until September 9 had been doing occupation duty in Yugoslavia were tainted with pro-Nazi elements, especially among the officers. Naturally, these forces had to be purged of enemies of the revolution and beefed up with former partisans and volunteers. Only then could they be sent into action.

But the process of purging enemies of the people from the Army was already under way, and its tempo was steadily increasing. This work was being done by the BRP through its representatives in the Fatherland Front, with the help of former partisans, members of the underground, and other fighters for the triumph of the people's regime. So that to apply this assumption of combat-unreadiness to the whole Bulgarian Army was mistaken, to say the least. The important thing was not to waste time arguing whether the troops were combat-ready but to speed up the process of restoring them to health: to help bring them up to strength with new recruits from among the people, who hated the whole regime of the minions of both the monarcho-fascists and Hitler in Bulgaria.

General Biryuzov was able quickly to grasp the real significance of Velchev's position, and to understand his practical machinations. He handled things with a complete understanding of the situation. And it should be noted that the Bulgarian Army quickly got through the purging phase, fought courageously against the Nazi forces, and through its selfless struggle made a great contribution to the joint victory over the enemy. Much of the credit for this must go to S. S. Biryuzov.

The position taken by Velchev and his ilk put the General Staff very much on guard, and we pointed this out to Biryuzov and his staff. It was essential to get a clearer picture of the condition of the Bulgarian Army, to help it (if necessary) in every way possible, and to move the forces to the front. This helped to consolidate the gains of the popular uprising in Bulgaria, brought victory closer, and pulled the rug out from under the enemy's network of agents and the would-be restorers of the old regime.

The resistance offered by Velchev and the reactionary officers on the Bulgarian General Staff did not go unnoticed by the BRP and its Central Committee. Special emphasis was placed on strengthening the Army and moving it to the front. At the suggestion of Dimitrov, the CC BRP sent Ivan Vinarov (who is already known to the reader) to visit the troops in order to ascertain the condition of the Bulgarian Army and help it take its place in the anti-Nazi ranks. When he got to Bulgaria, Vinarov immediately set off (with a small group of assistants) to have a look at the troops.

The picture was by no means as hopeless as it had been painted by Velchev and his people. Vinarov's group did not find a single unit that was not loyal to the Fatherland Front. When he got back to Sofia, Vinarov reported his conclusions. He stated that the troops of the Bulgarian Army "will need another couple of weeks to be completely shaped up. They are already combat-ready, but they will unquestionably be more combat-ready after the period of time indicated."

This extract from Tolbukhin's telegram, setting forth the results of the work done by the group from the CC BRP, shows that the issue of the Bulgarian Army's not being combat-ready was, as they say, exaggerated. And after Vinarov's trip it ceased to exist. (The shortcomings of the units could be eliminated in a relatively short time.)

The reactionaries tried to represent the situation in the Bulgarian Army as one of chaos and collapse, citing the stormy meetings which at the time were shaking the barracks in Bulgaria. They might think what they liked, but for the Soviet command the picture of a barracks shaken by strong emotions was familiar from our experience of revolution. It was clear that the incandescence of these riotous meetings was not a sign that the troops were not combat-ready but rather showed that they were searching for that truth that every soldier wants to clarify for himself in the course of a popular uprising, as he defines his place in the flow of genuinely historic events.

Naturally, not all of the officers and soldiers were able to realize immediately all the new developments engendered in Bulgaria by the victorious popular uprising. Some soldiers did not follow the orders of their officers, since they had no notion of their superiors' political views. And there were those who gave more thought to the farms they had left behind them in the countryside than they did to politics. At the time, the new existed alongside the old; and people were not always capable of telling for what and for whom the future stood, since the words and deeds of the Communists had not everywhere had their effect yet.

It was a very difficult task to change, in a short time, the political nature and spirit of an army which had previously served a profascist monarchist regime, and to put it into the service of the gains won by the September uprising. The General Staff also concerned itself with these matters. And more than once we argued whether the soldiers' committees which had been formed in the army units during the uprising helped or hindered the strengthening of order, the mobilization and combat-readiness of the troops, and the building of a new Bulgarian Army.

The BRP skillfully determined the moment when, as the officer cadres were built up with new personnel devoted to the people, the soldiers' committees began gradually to lose their usefulness: when, if they were retained, they might become an obstacle to strengthening discipline and one-man leadership in the forces—to the cause of preparing the Army for actions at the front. The committees were gradually dissolved.

Since the new officers were not always well trained militarily, the idea of providing Soviet military advisers to help the Bulgarian forces arose. It was first expressed by I. S. Anoshin in one of his routine telegrams to A. S. Zheltov, a member of the Military Council of the 3rd Ukrainian Front.

Zheltov supported the proposal. He called Tolbukhin's attention to it and suggested that the question of our representatives be posed before the General Staff. Tolbukhin agreed.

On instructions from Tolbukhin, Biryuzov had a talk on that subject with Georgev and Velchev; and the two of them decided to ask the USSR officially to send Soviet officers to the Bulgarian forces as representatives (or, more accurately, instructors) in matters of combat-readiness.

On September 20 Antonov received a telegram from the 3rd Ukrainian Front in which Tolbukhin posed the problem of advisers in the name of the Bulgarian Government.

The telegram was reported to the Stavka, and soon the Soviet Government agreed to send officers of the Red Army to Bulgarian units—but only to those who were operating jointly with forces of the 3rd Ukrainian Front.

Early in October, seven Soviet colonels took up their duties with Bulgarian troops: Tatarchevsky with the 4th Infantry Division, Kheraskov with the 5th, Titov with the 6th, Galiakberov with the 9th, Grigoryev with the 12th, Shaforost with the 1st Cavalry Division, and Pozhidayev with the 2nd. The Soviet officers did not exercise command: They merely made practical suggestions in cases when these were required. A short time later Maj. Gen. A. V. Blagodatov was named to head up the group of advisers.

Since the commanders of the Bulgarian divisions and regiments had no substantial combat experience, this help from their Soviet comrades came in very handy. Quite literally, our representatives had to look into all problems of organizing military actions and support. In particular need of attention were problems of reconnaissance and control of formations. Reality itself demanded this. For example, in reporting on the state of reconnaissance in the unit to which he was attached, Colonel Tatarchevsky stated: "The division's reconnaissance is not organized. Information on the enemy has been obtained from local inhabitants and partisans. It was improbable and inaccurate." And the situation was no better with regard to other matters.

Soviet political workers greatly helped the new people's Army of Bulgaria in organizing political and educational work. Our Bulgarian comrades willingly greeted the Soviet officers and were very eager to absorb their experience, which had been gained in a difficult struggle against the Nazi armies. The Russians and Bulgars quickly reached fruitful mutual understanding and co-operation, which engendered lasting camaraderie and friendship.

The BRP and the Fatherland Front successfully coped with the reorganization of the Bulgarian Army. They poured into it the revolutionary forces of the National Liberation Insurgent Army. Commanders of partisan units retained their positions as commanders of units in the regular Army. People who had fought in the popular front against the monarcho-fascist regime became the backbone of the new Army.

Taking into account the experience of the Russian proletariat in revolutionary battles, the BRP and its number one helper, the Workers' Youth Alliance, issued an appeal for volunteers. Almost forty thousand vigorous fighters for People's Bulgaria warmly responded to that appeal: partisans, former political prisoners and inmates of concentration camps, and young revolutionary enthusiasts. These were people with a lofty sense of revolutionary duty, an indomitable military spirit, and great competence, who gave the Bulgarian barracks a new look and endowed the troops with firmness in combat and a burning desire to annihilate the enemy on the field of battle at any cost.

Very bold measures were taken in the matter of renewing the officer cadres. Generals and other officers who had bad records as loyal servants of the monarcho-fascistic regime were dismissed from the Army. And command slots, including the highest, were filled with experienced Communists who had previously fought against the King and the fascist clique in the ranks of the National Liberation Insurgent Army, and Communist officers who had done underground work in the regular Army. They included quite a few heroes of September 1923: political émigrés, commissars, and insurgent commanders. Their names are well known: Ivan Vinarov, Georgi Damyanov, Zakhary Zakharev, Ivan Kinov, Ferdinand Kozovsky, Ivan Mihailov, Brandimir Ormanov, Peter Panchevsky. They had served in the Red Army and had been graduated from Soviet military academies. These men had the theoretical knowledge and the practical experience necessary to oversee the building of the Bulgarian Army and military operations.

Certain officers who had previously been put on the reserve list because of their antifascist convictions, were returned to active duty in order to strengthen the officer cadres. They included Vladimir Stoichev, Todor Toshev, and Stoyan Trendafilov. Stoichev became commander of the Bulgarian 1st Army, and the other two commanders of infantry divisions. A good many junior grade officers were replaced by revolutionary-minded noncoms.

All these sources of new officers made it possible to cover the great shortage of officer cadres and endow the new Bulgarian Army with a really popular character.

The institution of deputy commanders with the functions of commissars was introduced into the Bulgarian Army on the basis of the historical experience of the Soviet Armed Forces. In this respect, such prominent Bulgarian Communists as Shteryu Atanasov and others showed their party vigilance and training.

In those days that are so memorable for us and for People's Bulgaria, the reactionaries repeatedly tried to change their tactics of resistance. When their arguments as to the unfitness of the Bulgarian Army were refuted, they began to play for time and sabotage measures for the formation of the forces. They tried to limit the size of the contingents called to the colors. And they put forth the slogan of settling Bulgaria's domestic problems first, relegating to second place the matter of entering the war against the Nazis.

All these tricks employed by the enemies of the people were exposed, and their resistance was overcome. But to combat them cost us energy, attention, and time. It was not possible immediately to tear off from such enemies the mask of friends of the people, since they cleverly camouflaged themselves against the general background of the militant Fatherland Front. The antipopular leanings of these "friends of the people" became especially evident when they linked up with the reactionary Bulgarian émigrés—in particular, with Alexander Tsankov, who had formed the so-called Bulgarian Nationalist Government in Germany. This happened in September 1944, when the Bulgarian forces had been mobilized to carry out joint operations on Yugoslav territory with the Red Army and the National Liberation Army of Yugoslavia.

At this point the Bulgarian Workers' Party (Communists)[7] appealed to the people to take an active part in the war; and Dimitrov wrote that "the future of our country will depend above all on the real contribution that we, as a people and a state, are now making to the general war effort."[8]

The Communists' appeal met with a lively response among the people. The revolutionary process begun on September 9 grew throughout the country. There was an upswing in the mobilization of troops for the holy war against fascist Germany on the side of the anti-Nazi coalition, and by October 1944 Bulgarian soldiers

[7] In late September 1944 the Bulgarian Workers' Party began to call itself the Bulgarian Workers' Party (Communists).
[8] *Istoriya Bolgarskoi kommunisticheskoi partii* (Moscow: *Politizdat,* 1972), p. 470.

were successfully advancing in the direction of Niš, in a joint operation with the forces of the AVNOJ[9] Army and the Red Army.

For the time being, the enemies of the people laid low. But far from ceasing their underground activity, they increased it—especially after the signing of an armistice with Bulgaria on October 28, 1944. Taking advantage of the fact that relations with Bulgaria were now strictly regulated, Petko Stolaynov, the Minister of Finances, and Nikola Petkov, Minister without Portfolio, strongly protested against further expansion of the Bulgarian Army's joint actions on the front with the Red Army.

Naturally, the course of events could not be halted by the opposition of this pitiful group of enemies. The Bulgarians set about organizing a new army-size formation, which was soon a reality. It was given the old name of the Bulgarian 1st Army. But in terms of its functions, personnel, and morale it was an offspring of the revolutionary reforms. On November 21, 1944, the Bulgarian Minister of War issued a directive on the formation of this army, which consisted of six divisions, each with a strength of 12,000 men. As has already been mentioned, it was commanded by Lt. Gen. Vladimir Stoichev, who distinguished himself in subsequent battles. His deputy was Gen. Shteryu Atanosov, a Communist, who was very knowledgeable, with political and military experience. People who had acquired experience in the antifascist struggle were appointed as special assistants in the divisions, regiments, and detachments. Units were beefed up with volunteer antifascists.

Among the troops, a massive educational program was carried out by way of explaining why it was necessary for the Bulgarian forces to fight the Nazi armies—on the side of the USSR, and hand in hand with the Soviet liberating troops. The Bulgarian Workers' Party (Communists) and the Fatherland Front government laid special emphasis on the accomplishment of this task, and endowed it with a strong political cast. They addressed a special manifesto to the Bulgarian people and the Army, saying:

> The war is coming to an end, but it is not yet over. More efforts and more sacrifices are required in order to assure the

[9] AVNOJ: Antifascist Council for the National Liberation of Yugoslavia. (Translator's note.)

freedom of the Bulgarian people and the vital interests of our motherland. . . . We must never forget that at the present moment the place that our motherland will occupy among the freedom-loving and progressive nations is being decided for long years to come. . . .

The reactionaries tried to exploit the difficulties arising in Bulgaria. At one session of the Council of Ministers Stoyanov and Petkov declared that sending new divisions to the front would badly impair the domestic situation and might lead to a popular uprising. One of those who spoke said that the Americans and the British would not go along with an increase in the size of the Army. Both ministers expressed doubts that Soviet policy corresponded to the interests of the Bulgarian people. Unbeknownst to the Communist ministers, Petkov and Velchev rammed through Decree No. 4, in order to provide protection against just revenge in the case of those officers who were known for their pro-Nazi views and had besmirched themselves with crimes against the people. But the BRP(k) exposed the reactionaries' intrigues and sneak attacks in the eyes of the people.

Realizing the importance of Bulgaria's contribution to the common cause of the Allies, the BRP(k) convinced the Fatherland Front government to allocate additional forces to fight against Nazi Germany. On December 14 the Minister of War announced this officially. In order to avoid coming back to this matter later on, let me say at this point that by the end of the war in Europe there were 250,000 men in the Bulgarian 1st Army, which was operating as a part of the 3rd Ukrainian Front.

The guards units and those made up of partisans and volunteers played an important role in building up the Army and in its military successes. They constitute the assault detachment of the Bulgarian forces, distinguished for its high morale and readiness to perform any difficult task.

The people of Bulgaria, as they saw the Bulgarian 1st Army off to the front, wished it success in achieving a quick victory over the hated enemy. The Bulgarian units moved up one unit (or a few units) at a time, depending upon their degree of combat-readiness. The first units to reach the front were the 3rd, 8th, and

11th infantry divisions, followed by the 16th. By late December they were attacking in the area between the Drava and Sava rivers; and in early 1945 they provided the defense which assured the link-up of the 3rd Ukrainian Front with the AVNOJ Army west of Pécs (Hungary). Subsequently, in this region, enemy forces which tried to make a break-through across the Drava and into the rear of the 3rd Ukrainian Front were crushed by the joint efforts of the Soviet, Bulgarian, and Yugoslav troops.

The victorious outcome of the difficult and bloody battles on the Drava and in the region of Kecskemét showed that the organizational and political work done by the BRP(k) when the forces were being built up and during the campaign was of great political and military importance. The Bulgarian soldiers boldly and wholeheartedly served their revolutionary motherland and the common cause of destroying Nazi Germany. Their armed struggle against the Nazi aggressors was universally acknowledged.

6

IN YUGOSLAVIA

On the eve of revolutionary events. Tito in Moscow. Breaking out of a trap. A heroic flight. A good agreement. The miscalculations of the Nazi command. The glory road to Belgrade. Victory. Plans for the future. The last months of the war in Yugoslavia. Camaraderie.

In early September of 1944, when Soviet troops, enthusiastically welcomed by the people of Bulgaria, were moving farther toward the south and southwest, the Supreme Commander instructed the General Staff to prepare materials on Yugoslav matters. He said that Marshal Tito, Supreme Commander of the National Liberation Army of Yugoslavia, had (through our military mission) requested the Soviet Union that the Red Army temporarily enter Yugoslav territory. The officers in the Operations Department of the General Staff immediately got to work on preparing the mission. It proved to be complex, since many questions had to be thought out.

In late September Comrade Tito flew to Moscow for talks, accompanied by the chief of our military mission, Gen. N. V. Korneyev. By then the situation on the fronts in Yugoslavia had considerably improved. Several large-scale offensives undertaken by the Nazis with the aim of destroying the National Liberation

Rumanian and Soviet officers: the start of joint operations.

Artillery of the Bulgarian Army head for the front against Hitler's forces.

Georgi Dimitrov talks with the commander of the 3rd Ukrainian Front, Marshal F. I. Tolbukhin of the Soviet Union, and Col. Gen. S. S. Biryuzov.

Residents of Sofia hail the Red Army.

Flowers for the Russian soldiers.

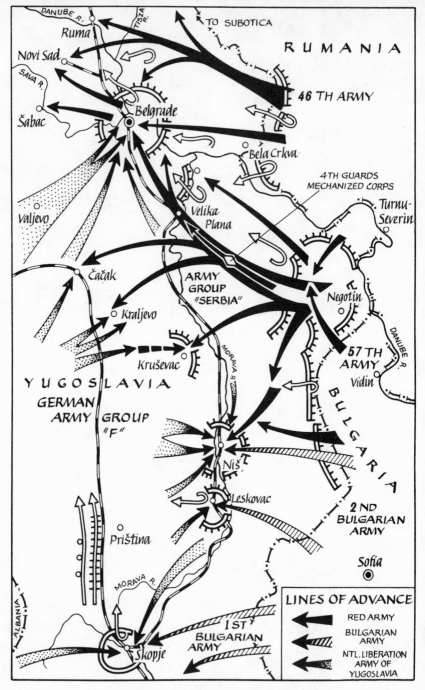

The liberation of Belgrade, capital of Yugoslavia.

Josip Broz Tito, wounded in battle with the Nazi invaders at the Sutesk River. Beside him: Ivan Ribar, chairman of the Presidium of the Antifascist Council for National Liberation, summer 1944.

Kocha Popović, a distinguished military leader of the National Liberation Army of Yugoslavia (1943).

The Soviet Military Delegation arrives in Bosnia to establish liaison and co-operation with Marshal Tito's Stavka, March 1944

Yugoslavian peasants greeting a Soviet pilot.

The Soviet 36th Guards Tank Brigade ready to battle for the liberation of Belgrade, October 1944.

The Danube Flotilla supports the combat operations of the ground forces with the fire of a multi-rail rocket projector, April 1945.

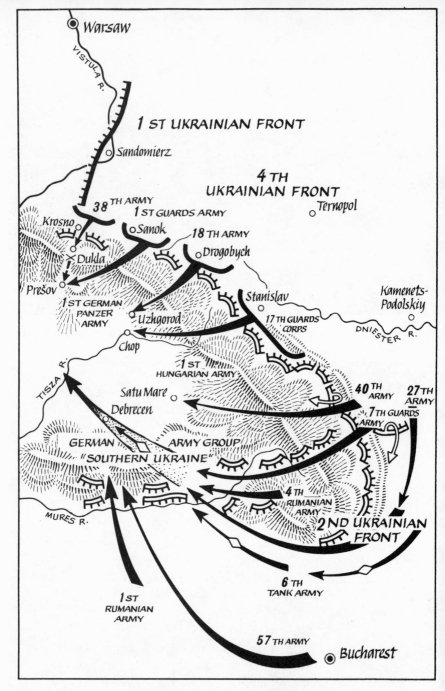

Plan to rout the enemy in the Carpathian Mountains.

In Yugoslavia

Army of Yugoslavia (AVNOJ Army) had collapsed completely.
At the same time the AVNOJ Army had been beefed up, had
acquired much combat experience, and had been restructured.
Now it was no longer a partisan army but a regular modern army
(although it did keep some vestiges of its past). It had fifty divisions, plus many brigades and detachments, amounting to almost
400,000 battle-hardened soldiers. These forces not only fought
defensively but attacked in an organized manner, clearing the aggressors out of one region after another. In early September seven
divisions of the AVNOJ Army broke through into Serbia, linking
up with the five divisions that had already been operating in that
republic. Now twelve divisions were destroying the enemy's garrisons in this area. In the first ten days of the September offensive
the AVNOJ Army liberated ninety-eight towns and inflicted great
losses upon the enemy. The radio station Free Yugoslavia reported that the enemy had lost 24,000 dead and 11,900 prisoners.
The time was drawing near when the forces of the AVNOJ Army
and the Red Army would meet. . . .

Upon the arrival of our Yugoslav comrades, Antonov told me
that at about midnight he would go to Near House, Stalin's dacha
in Kuntsevo.

According to Antonov's later account, the talk at the *souper*
was heartfelt but very practical. Marshal Tito was empowered by
the National Liberation Committee of Yugoslavia to request the
USSR to bring Soviet troops into the territory of eastern Yugoslavia, and to determine the basis of their joint action with the
AVNOJ Army. Our Yugoslav comrades hoped that in the course
of the upcoming operations it would be possible to capture
Belgrade. Stalin, glancing in Antonov's direction, said that the
General Staff obviously would not object. Thus basic agreement
on joint operations was reached at that very time and was
formalized in later talks.

The Supreme Commander of the AVNOJ Army was apprised
of our intentions for the near future. He was told that aid to
Yugoslavia would be provided by the 3rd Ukrainian Front and
the Danube Flotilla. This would be enough to destroy the enemy
in the region of Belgrade. In other regions of Yugoslavia the

201

AVNOJ Army hoped to finish off the Nazi occupying troops on its own. Then Stalin seized the opportunity to remark that the left wing of the 2nd Ukrainian Front would soon have to cross Yugoslav territory in order to invade Hungary. It would be good, he said, if the National Committee would agree to this temporary movement of Soviet forces across Yugoslav territory, since it was necessitated by our struggle against the common enemy. Tito agreed in the name of the National Committee and the Supreme Command of the AVNOJ Army.

In September 1944 the Soviet forces' offensive on the southern flank of the Soviet-German front developed successfully. On September 30 our troops drove the enemy out of more than twenty populated places in Yugoslavia. Each day saw an increase in the amount of Yugoslav territory liberated by the Soviet forces. In their pursuit of the enemy, units of the 2nd Ukrainian Front reached the eastern bank of the Danube. At the same time, armies of the 3rd Ukrainian Front reached the southern and western borders of Bulgaria. In late September Lt. Gen. N. A. Gagen's 57th Army seized the very important region of the town of Vidin on the western bank of the Danube, which made it much easier for our forces to cross that broad and fast-flowing water barrier, and for certain units even obviated that necessity. The Danube had now become our friend: It was an important and convenient route for supplying our forces—a route traveled by the glorious Danube Flotilla under the command of Sergei Georgiyevich Gorshkov.

But in this same sector the enemy had considerable forces. They included 270,000 men: fourteen full-strength divisions and eight understrength divisions, plus many independent regiments and battalions. Besides these, there were five Hungarian divisions—30,000 officers and soldiers—in the northern part of the country. The forces of the local Yugoslav fascist hangers-on amounted to some 270,000 men. So that the total was some 570,000 officers and men—an impressive figure!

The German forces in the southwest were under the command of Field Marshal Maximilian von Weichs. He also had command of Army Group F, occupying Croatia, Bosnia and Herzegovina, Montenegro, and Albania. The troops of Army Group E, under the command of Colonel General Löhr, were positioned on the Greek mainland and in the islands. General Felber's Army Group Serbia was operating in Serbia. Since late August 1944 the enemy's forces in Yugoslavia had substantially increased: In order to counter the successes of the national liberation struggle, the enemy had had to bring in some of the forces from Army Group E. The defeat of the Nazis in Rumania and the Red Army's rapid advance into the Balkan Peninsula had compelled the enemy to prepare for the withdrawal of his units from Greece and Macedonia so as not to be faced with a catastrophe. The order for withdrawal was issued on October 3, 1944. The enemy's forces in Yugoslavia occupied the main political and economic regions and held the railroads and highways, trying to control the situation with the help of garrisons. Special attention was devoted to defending the eastern borders of Yugoslavia and holding onto the routes from Greece to Hungary, Austria, and northern Italy. Apart from Serbia, the enemy's strongest garrisons were located in the region of Skopje, Niš, and Kraljevo.

On more than one occasion, the Nazi command had tried to eliminate the head of the National Liberation Army. In May 1944 the Germans dreamed up the idea of making a strike at the region around the Yugoslav town of Drvar, where the Army's headquarters was located. Tito recounted this during the talk at Near House.

Drvar is located in the western part of Bosnia and is well protected by mountains. The approaches to the headquarters could be covered by relatively small forces. These included a military police battalion of the Yugoslav headquarters, students at the officer candidate school, two or three tanks, and a battalion from an engineer brigade.

The Nazi command worked out a clever plan: to deliver an unexpected blow from the air and to combine it with an attack by sizable ground forces. The Nazis planned to drop sizable paratroop detachments in the region of Drvar and capture the headquarters and Tito himself. Then the paratroopers were to hold on until the ground forces arrived.

The 500th SS Paratroop Battalion and many aircraft were assigned to handle the air operation. The ground forces included units from three infantry divisions and considerable forces of local traitors. The operation was under the direction of the commander of the German 15th Corps.

Early in the morning of May 25, 1944, enemy aircraft made a raid in force in the region of Drvar.

"The date of the attack," N. V. Korneyev observed, "was carefully chosen. It was Comrade Tito's birthday. Apparently Hitler very much wanted to behead the national liberation movement on that very day."

Immediately after the bombing of Drvar, the Germans brought in the first wave of troops—more than six hundred men—in gliders. At the same time, ground troops started moving on Drvar. Each German soldier carried a photograph of Marshal Tito, so that he could recognize him if he met up with him. The troops had also been given a special assignment with respect to the Soviet military mission, concealed under the code name "Moscow." The Nazis had outlawed the mission, meaning that the German troops landed at Drvar could exterminate the Soviet generals and other officers without a trial or investigation.

When the bombing began, followed by the landing of the gliders and the attack by the glider troops, Tito was in a cave seventy meters above the valley floor, equipped for living and working. For emergency purposes, the cave was connected to the valley floor by a solid cable, which it now became necessary to use. Everybody rushed to the previously indicated assembly point.

Those who had organized this surprise attack saw their hopes disappointed. Their soldiers met with strong resistance. When they noticed the landing of the gliders, equipped with special braking parachutes, the Yugoslavs of the military police battalion opened fire. Then the students at the officer candidate school came on the run, and a hard-fought skirmish ensued.

The enemy then dropped about two hundred paratroopers, and they captured Drvar. But Tito, the members of the Politburo of the Central Committee of the Communist Party of Yugoslavia, the generals and other officers of the General Staff, and the staffs of the American, British, and Soviet military missions had already escaped to the east.

At the first alarm signal, Gen. A. P. Gorshkov, deputy chief of the Soviet mission, had rushed to see Gen. N. V. Korneyev. The latter had had a toothache; he had been languishing all night, and only managed to fall asleep in the morning. But in a matter of seconds he had got out of his sleeping bag, and he was soon at the assembly point.

Accompanied by Korneyev and other comrades, Tito went along the mountain path toward Potoci, where an emergency command post had been set up at the suggestion of our military mission. The party got there safely, but later on it turned out that the enemy had cut off all routes in this area, too. His pressure was building. . . .

Night fell. Marshal Tito called a brief conference to decide what to do. It was held beneath a cliff overhanging the path. Opinions varied. Some of the conferees wanted to split up into small groups and break out of the encirclement that way. But the chief of the Soviet mission (Korneyev), recalling similar situations on the Soviet-German front, suggested that they all act together. His suggestion was accepted.

They broke through the encirclement and reached the region of Veliky Shator Mountain. There the situation was eased: They had left the Nazis behind, and troops of the 1st Proletarian Corps arrived to rescue the Supreme Command. From that point they moved on to Kupres, where they paused and surveyed the situation. It turned out that Kupres was not a suitable place from which to direct the operations of the AVNOJ Army. Also, the fact that Tito was out of touch with the Army was fraught with serious consequences. The conferees considered two places from which control might be exercised: Montenegro, which was free of enemy forces and protected by AVNOJ Army forces, and the island of Vis. The latter looked more suitable. But the only way to get there at the moment was via our air base at Bari, with which there were no communications. Also, Comrade Tito, valuing the honor of the Supreme Commander, did not want to entertain for even a moment the notion of leaving Yugoslav soil even for a brief time.

General Korneyev had to use all possible arguments. And he recalled the example of the great Lenin, who was obliged for many years to live abroad but nonetheless did not cease to direct the work of the Communists in Russia. . . .

So Marshal Tito decided to go via Bari to the Yugoslav island of Vis in the Adriatic. But how to get to Bari? There was no plane available; and calling one in was a difficult business, since the mission's transmitter did not reach either Bari or Moscow. Besides, there was no adequate landing strip.

Those were also nervous days at the Soviet General Staff. Antonov reported to the Supreme Commander that there was no news from Yugoslavia. The Stavka instructed the General Staff to ascertain the situation, and if necessary to aid our comrades.

On June 2, 1944, our state of ignorance finally came to an end: We had a telegram from Korneyev. As he told us later, his communications specialist—a sensible and competent fellow named Dolgov—managed to put his transmitter on top of one of the highest mountains, and then put up the highest possible antenna. In a message addressed to both Moscow and Bari (to S. V. Sokolov), Dolgov asked that a plane be sent to Kupres at 2200 hours on June 4. A similar text was transmitted simultaneously to the British command in Bari via the transmitter of the Anglo-American military mission.

The Yugoslavs began preparing a landing strip for the plane. The area was walled around by mountains. Rocks rose up one on top of another, and crevices yawned. Everyone—without one single exception—went to work on preparing the air strip. The chief specialist was P. N. Yakimov, a navigator from A. S. Shornikov's crew. He had come to Drvar before the Nazi attack to help choose a spot suitable for an air strip.

Things were also tense at Bari. On June 2 they had received a part of Dolgov's message. They had managed to figure out that General Korneyev had ordered a plane to be sent to Kupres. But they had not received that part of the message indicating the time the plane should arrive, because communications had failed at that point. They surmised, however, that the flight had been ordered for the nearest possible time—the night of June 4. Then the situation became more complicated when the British command forwarded to Sokolov the message they had received, indicating that the plane should arrive a day later—on June 5. Which date was correct? Under other conditions a query would have been sent out. But at that moment there were no communications, and attempts at restoring them were futile. The base commander decided to send the plane on June 4.

The pilot of the plane sent to Yugoslavia was A. S. Shornikov, one of the most experienced pilots at the Soviet air base at Bari. He flew at night across the sea and through mountains toward an unfamiliar and unequipped air strip among the cliffs. His skill as a pilot was exquisite, and his courage was immense. He had a combat veteran's trust in the buddies who had prepared such an unusual landing strip for him.

The earth was invisible beneath the cloud cover. Shornikov kept circling, looking for a gap in the boundless cloud cover. There was a great risk of smashing into a mountain, but his concern for the fate of his expectant friends kept the upper hand. Finally he found a gap. Down below the signal fires beckoned.

On that first flight on the night of June 4, 1944, Tito, his chief deputies, General Korneyev, and certain officers from the military missions and the AVNOJ Army staff were taken to Bari, where they were joyfully greeted. Shornikov and his crew again flew off to Kupres, followed by some British planes. Together they brought out the rest of the people. A few days later British ships took the AVNOJ Army staff and the military missions to the island of Vis, where the Yugoslav headquarters continued to function.

Such was the collapse of the enemy's attempt to behead the AVNOJ Army. For their feat, A. S. Shornikov, commander of the Soviet aircraft, B. T. Kalinkin, second in command, and P. N. Yakimov, navigator, were awarded the titles of Hero of the Soviet Union and People's Hero of Yugoslavia.

By late summer of 1944 the antifascist struggle of the Yugoslav people had taken on new scope. The ranks of fighters grew from day to day. The Supreme Command of the AVNOJ Army provided firm guidance for the troops in this war of liberation. In Serbia, Croatia, Slovenia, Macedonia, and the Vojvodina, regional general staffs were set up, with the corresponding commanders and chiefs. These organs of military control were put together right there in the partisan regions or on the above-mentioned island of Vis. From the island, a regional headquarters would be transported to the battle zone. This was the way in which the Serbian General Staff, headed by General Kocha Popović, was formed and trained, with the help of Soviet officers. In July 1944, when Popović went off to the battle zone, he was accompanied by Major General Gorshkov.

Our air base in Bari played a large role in transferring the staff to its new base. The Soviet pilot N. A. Girenko and his crew located a landing strip in the region of Kazanchich, twenty-five kilometers south of Niš, and dropped the staff's paratroop group plus a Soviet representative, with radio equipment. On the moonless night of July 12, after communications had been established, Girenko brought in the entire staff, literally under the enemy's nose. Even the partisans—people who had seen a lot in their time —were amazed by such boldness; and such was their joy that they went into a happy dance with the airmen and their newly arrived comrades.

The AVNOJ Army and its leaders were greatly respected by our people, the Soviet soldiers, and the General Staff. They had earned that respect by their uncompromising struggle against the Nazi aggressors, their heroism, and their dedication to the people. In the course of the long and difficult war against the Nazi occupying troops, the AVNOJ Army had learned how to fight skillfully. It had developed its own cadres of commanders and political workers, strong in morale and military science, who knew how to adapt themselves to the conditions of partisan warfare, and were ready to sacrifice themselves for the sake of victory. But we also knew that during this long time, arms had been one relatively weak aspect of the AVNOJ. There was a shortage of artillery and mortars; the tanks were counted by ones; and there were almost no aircraft. As for the AVNOJ Army's small weaponry—rifles, machine carbines, and machine guns—it was a weird mixture of things captured from the enemy: German, Italian, and other weapons. British weapons played a considerable part. Prior to the autumn of 1944, Soviet weapons played a secondary role, since great difficulties were involved in supplying the Yugoslav soldiers over an extensive territory occupied by the enemy.

During Tito's sojourn in Moscow agreement was reached on substantially improving the supplying of Soviet weapons to the AVNOJ Army. The advance of the 2nd and 3rd Ukrainian fronts to the borders of Yugoslavia made it possible to sharply increase deliveries of weapons to our Yugoslav comrades and brothers in the liberation struggle.

The chief subject of discussion between the Yugoslav comrades and the Soviet Government in Moscow in the autumn of 1944 was the organizing of joint operations by the Red Army and the AVNOJ Army. The entering of Yugoslav territory by Soviet forces radically changed the strategic situation in that country and enable the AVNOJ Army forces to create and consolidate for themselves an advantageous position for the impending total defeat of the occupying troops.

Full agreement was reached on joint actions by the Soviet forces and the AVNOJ Army. Serbia was chosen as the region in which the joint offensive would be launched. It would be the object of the main strikes by both the Soviet and Yugoslav forces—something that was justified both by conditions of the over-all strategic situation on the front of the struggle against Nazi Germany and by the situation in Yugoslavia.

In Moscow Tito met Dimitrov, who told him a detail about the Fatherland Front and the new goals of People's Bulgaria and its Army. This meeting had a great influence on the unity of action among the Red Army, the AVNOJ Army and the Bulgarian Army.

The agreement on joint operations by the Soviet forces and the AVNOJ Army which was reached in September 1944 was for the General Staff a very important document. It was the point of departure for planning military operations, with special attention devoted to Serbia, of course. We Soviet General Staff officers stubbornly looked for—and found—some vulnerable points in the defenses of Army Group F and proposed to exploit them to the fullest.

It was observed that Von Weichs had endeavored to organize his strongest defense line along the mountain ridges on the boundary between Serbia and Rumania. Here he had put up engineering structures that were both strong and deeply dug in, and had reinforced the troops of Army Group Serbia. On this sector of the front, the enemy's troop strength and resources were considerable. But along the Bulgarian border, toward which the main forces of Tolbukhin's front were advancing, the enemy had not provided a compact grouping of forces or a compact system of defenses. The Nazi command had not figured that the Red Army would get there that quickly, and it had counted too heavily on the mountainous terrain. And by the time we reached the Yugoslav border, Von Weichs had neither the time nor the means to take counteraction.

Running parallel to the Danube as it did, the German defense line struck us as a convenient objective for simultaneous strikes along the whole front. The enemy was entrenched in the mountains. But he had no great reserves; and in the event of threatened break-through he would either have to withdraw his garrisons to the interior, form them into concentrated forces, and throw them into a counterattack, or else use troops from the defensive lines for this purpose. Thus our task was to see to it that the line of pressure points against the enemy was stretched out as far as possible. Owing to Bulgaria's declaration of war against Germany, considerable Bulgarian forces could be used for this purpose— troops that knew how to operate in the mountains. In the sector of the main attack, of course, we had to use a great concentration of power and the great mobility of the experienced forces of the 3rd Ukrainian Front. They were in a position to break through Army Group F's defenses at their strongest point, and rapidly to destroy the enemy's basic grouping, which would have an immediate effect on the over-all success of the three armies operating in concert.

The forces of the AVNOJ Army and the Bulgarian Army were to deal the enemy a staggering blow, to decoy a good part of his forces, tie them hand and foot, and make it impossible for the

Nazis to create reserves. The Yugoslav and Bulgarian forces would have an especially difficult task if the enemy pulled his main forces out of Greece and sent them north. In that case they would have to take some heavy blows from the enemy, hold the line, and assure the actions of the Red Army. Such were some of the General Staff's ideas while the operations were being planned.

Since forces of the Red Army, the AVNOJ Army, and the Bulgarian Army would all be operating on the territory of Yugoslavia, the General Staff had to come to agreement with the Yugoslav and Bulgarian commands. The main problems in co-ordinating the actions of our forces and of the AVNOJ Army had been settled while Tito was in Moscow. At that time Stalin and Antonov (representing the General Staff) had agreed with the Supreme Commander of the AVNOJ Army that the Soviet Supreme Command would provide a general outline of the joint operations in Yugoslavia, based on the situation on the various fronts, while our Yugoslav comrades would work up that part of the over-all plan that affected them directly. In the course of the talks there was mention of using at least two Bulgarian armies on the territory of Yugoslavia. No final decisions were taken in the absence of the Bulgarians, but agreement was reached on preparatory work in the Soviet and Yugoslav armies.

Meantime, the organizing of the Bulgarian forces' operations was also going ahead. In mid-September Tolbukhin, on instructions from Stalin, met in Sofia with the command of the Bulgarian Army. Soon the Bulgarian command had worked up a preliminary plan for the offensive operations of the Bulgarian forces. Tolbukhin studied them, and reported to Moscow. The Bulgarian command figured that once the Bulgarian forces had been purged of profascist and monarchist elements, they could seize the highway and railway junctions near Kruševac, Niš, Skopje, and Veles, and cut off route for the withdrawal of German troops from Greece to the north, creating at least a triple barrier. The Bulgarians guaranteed that their troops would be ready by late September.

Tolbukhin approved the plan and proposed that our air power be used to support the Bulgarian forces. In view of the general

211

war situation, the Bulgarian command proposed to commit all their available forces comprising up-to-strength infantry divisions, including two guards divisions formed from former partisans and volunteers, a cavalry division and a cavalry brigade, an armored brigade, and two brigades of partisans. Unfortunately, the Bulgarian forces did not possess adequate means of reinforcement.

The decision to move the Supreme Command of the AVNOJ Army away from the island of Vis had been made even before Tito flew to Moscow. The purpose of this very important measure was to ensure stable, uninterrupted control of the military operations carried out by the national liberation forces. The Nazi vultures' raid on Drvar had shown that in Yugoslavia—even in the nearly inaccessible mountains—it was hard to find a place immune to the threat of such a raid. Also, the location of the Yugoslav Supreme Command had to correspond to the new conditions: The AVNOJ Army's operations were now on a broad scale, and required daily and uninterrupted control from a single center. It was also necessary to direct the extensive and complex project of reorganizing the forces (army corps and army groups were being organized), to administer mobilization, and to form reserves. Then, too, joint operations with the Red Army were to take place in the near future. All this put heavy demands on the choice of a site for the most important headquarters for the direction of the war of national liberation, that headquarters being the Supreme Command of the AVNOJ Army. Therefore our Yugoslav comrades took advantage of our offer to locate the Supreme Command of the AVNOJ Army behind our lines in the Rumanian town of Craiova. Even before Tito left for Moscow, the Yugoslav Supreme Command was transferred there—in complete secrecy.

Transfers of headquarters are always carefully prepared in advance and carried out in complete secrecy. Such was the case this time, too. On September 19, 1944, as soon as the darkness thickened over the island of Vis, General Korneyev summoned the pilots P. M. Mikhailov and V. Pavlov from the air base at Bari. Korneyev wanted to talk to them about a very important flight. He heard the pilots' reports as to the readiness of their aircraft, and then showed them an air map on which Craiova was circled in thick red pencil. He told them that a large group of Yugoslav and Soviet comrades had to be flown there, but he did not specify who. And he said the route would be unusual: They would first fly in the direction of Bari; then, before they got there, they would turn around over the Adriatic, fly over Bosnia and Serbia, cross the Danube, and land at their destination. They would take off at 0300 hours.

Everything was being done in great secrecy to assure the security of the flight. Within a few hours the skilled pilots had flown their planes to Craiova. And on September 19, Marshal Tito and other Yugoslav comrades—passengers in Soviet aircraft—had settled not far from the Yugoslav border.

As soon as the headquarters had begun to function in Craiova, Comrade Tito flew off to Moscow as had been previously agreed.

At dawn the allies of the Anglo-American Military Mission, left behind on the island of Vis, found that the Supreme Commander of the AVNOJ Army was missing. Likewise missing were the Soviet aircraft. They began to look around and ask questions. The Yugoslavs answered that Marshal Tito was probably at the front. The chief of the Allied military mission, Maj. Gen. Fitzroy MacLean, began sending urgent telegrams of inquiry to the air marshal, William Elliot, commanding the British zone in Italy, on the assumption that he must know, since Tito could not (or so it seemed to MacLean) have bypassed the base in Bari.

Upon receiving this inquiry, Elliot asked S. V. Sokolov to come to see him.

"What did you do with Tito?"

"I have no way of knowing, Marshal," was the answer.

The commandant of the Soviet air base at Bari was a master at this kind of conversation. He could be extremely dry, polite, and laconic as only a soldier can be.

"As allies, you are well regarded by us," Elliot continued.

"We are grateful to our allies, and have the same feelings of good will toward them," replied Sokolov.

"But the aircraft have left the island of Vis?"

"Unfortunately, I know nothing about it. As you can see, Marshal, I am here beside you."

With that, the conversation ended.

There were no more inquiries forthcoming from the allies: The Soviet Supreme Commander had informed Churchill that Tito was in Moscow to co-ordinate the joint actions of Soviet and Yugoslav forces in the impending operations.

With the advance of our forces to the borders of Yugoslavia, and the transfer of the AVNOJ Army headquarters to Craiova, communications between the Red Army and the AVNOJ Army were simplified. The flow of Soviet aid to the Yugoslav people and its Army was sharply increased. Now our transport planes no longer had to make a long and dangerous trip: Arms, ammunition, and other matériel were delivered to the Yugoslav partisans across the territory of Rumania and Bulgaria.

The work load of the Soviet military mission became much larger at this time. There was an evident shortage of personnel. Our Yugoslav comrades asked us to send Soviet officer-advisers to the general staffs of the republic forces. This request had to be satisfied, and the size of the mission was increased. With the permission of the Soviet Government, Major General Gorshkov was sent to Serbia, where it was planned to launch the basic parts of the Belgrade operation; Col. P. G. Rak was sent to Croatia; Col. N. K. Patrakhaltsev to Slovenia; and Maj. P. M. Kovalenko—who was later named a Hero of the Soviet Union for his heroism and courage in carrying out his military missions—was sent to Montenegro. They were accompanied by several other officers, radio specialists, and technical workers.

The worries of the Soviet generals and other officers increased in proportion to the strengthening of the statehood of People's Yugoslavia. Our mission was officially accredited to a provisional government—the National Committee for the Liberation of Yugoslavia—which fact emphasized not only the military but the political significance of the mission. This naturally imposed a special responsibility on our workers. In particular, they had to deal with complex political, financial, and other problems on a daily basis. Consequently we had to send the mission specialists in foreign affairs and banking (M. F. Fodrov and V. S. Gerashchenko). But as before, the mission's main job was to help deciding operational questions.

During the second half of September, work on the plan for the Belgrade operation went ahead: at the General Staff, at the staff of the 3rd Ukrainian Front, at the headquarters of the AVNOJ Army, and at the headquarters in Serbia. Although this work was done by staffs of different nationalities and in places that were hundreds—and sometimes even thousands—of kilometers apart, its great purposefulness and harmony were worthy of note. That purposefulness was due largely to the great vigor of Antonov and Korneyev. Their solid acquaintanceship and mutual understanding dated back to their days at the General Staff Academy, where they had been classmates. When it became possible for Korneyev to make radio contact from Craiova to the General Staff in Moscow, he wasted no time in taking advantage of it. Antonov gave him the gist of the General Staff's ideas on crushing the enemy near Belgrade, and asked him to clear them with the headquarters of the AVNOJ Army, which was done. The latter approved the thinking of the Soviet General Staff, and forwarded the necessary orders to Col. Gen. Peko Dapchević, commander of the 1st Army Group, who with his staff was working on a plan for the AVNOJ Army operations near Belgrade.

On September 30 the command of the 3rd Ukrainian Front reported to the General Staff its ideas on the campaign, which had likewise been checked with the leadership of the AVNOJ Army. The aim of the joint Soviet-Yugoslav operation was to destroy the enemy grouping of forces in northeast Yugoslavia, seize the most important road junctions, cut off the enemy's escape route from central and southern Yugoslavia toward the north into Hungary, and, finally, liberate Belgrade.

The 3rd Ukrainian Front assigned General Gagen's 57th Army and General Zhdanov's 4th Guards Mechanized Corps to carry out these missions. Air support would be provided by the 17th Air Army.

Our forces were directly opposed by the Nazi Army Group Serbia, which had in its first line at least four divisions, including one motorized division. It was assumed that in the course of the operation they would bring up another two divisions from the region of Niš, and certain units from the German grouping of forces in Greece. Tolbukhin's staff figured it was possible that up to ten or eleven enemy divisions might be concentrated in the 57th Army's attack zone. Thus the Military Council of the 3rd Ukrainian Front asked the AVNOJ Army to divert some of the German forces and bar their route to the north, along with tying up the forces of the fascist toadies Nedić and Mihailović south and southwest of Belgrade. If possible, the Yugoslav forces were to take Niš. All these ideas were conveyed via Korneyev to the headquarters of the AVNOJ Army, which posed the problems to its forces.

Tolbukhin's plans for an attack on Belgrade were based on an accurate knowledge of the situation. He took into account the fact that the forces of the 57th Army were strongly dug in on the right bank of the Danube near the Bulgarian town of Vidin, and had been making preparations, day and night, for a new thrust forward. To the north of Vidin, on a bend of the Danube, the 75th Rifle Corps had successfully fought some hard defensive battles, beating off all the enemy's attempts to throw it back. Now this unit had been transferred from the 2nd Ukrainian Front to the 57th Army.

Since the mountainous terrain made it impossible to bring the Soviet forces together into a concentrated force, and compelled them to advance in separate sectors, Tolbukhin proposed a most unusual solution: to have the main forces (the 64th Rifle Corps and the 4th Mechanized Corps with means of reinforcement) on the left flank of the Army in the region of Vidin to strike in the direction of Zaječar, Boljevac, Ćuprija, Batočina, and Smederevska Palanka. These forces were to destroy the basic grouping of Army Group Serbia and cut off the escape route to Belgrade for what remained of it. At the same time, other Soviet forces would attack along the Danube toward Belgrade (the 75th Rifle Corps) and in the center of the front (the 68th Rifle Corps) in the direction of Slatina, Zagubica, and Zletovo. If the offensive bogged down in one sector, the other corps were to provide help. Once our troops reached the Morava and forced it, it would be possible to direct our main forces directly to Belgrade, with whose capture the operation would be completed. In this phase of the operation our troops were to advance shoulder to shoulder with the troops of the AVNOJ Army. As for the Bulgarian forces, Tolbukhin had given them the mission of tying up the enemy in their own sector.

The General Staff found the ideas of the 3rd Ukrainian Front's Military Council to be basically correct. But it felt it was necessary to commit, in addition, the 10th Guards Rifle Corps of the 46th Army from the 2nd Ukrainian Front. The corps was commanded by Gen. Ivan Andreyevich Rubanyuk. His troops could stagger the enemy in the region of Vršac and undermine the stability of his defenses to the north and east of Belgrade.

Nor did we agree with Tolbukhin on the proper employment of the Bulgarian forces. Since we knew that the Bulgarian commander in chief considered it feasible to go on the offensive, we of the General Staff, in reporting to the Stavka on the plan for the Belgrade operation, recommended that the mission of the Bulgarian Army not be limited to defense but be changed to one of offense.

The Stavka agreed with the General Staff, but suggested that with respect to the Bulgarian Army events not be stepped up until we had reached complete, all-around agreement with the Bulgarian and Yugoslav commands. As for Tolbukhin, he was ordered to begin the offensive on October 13–14, when the concentration of all the forces taking part in the operation was to have been completed. Any delay in launching the offensive would give the enemy time to bring up reinforcements to the region of Belgrade, and to strengthen his defenses.

The orders sent by the Stavka to Tolbukhin said, "Get in touch with Tito in Craiova, and inform him of the operations plan in detail." Tolbukhin did this immediately, and during the night of October 2 our comrades from the AVNOJ Army headquarters worked on the operations plan. In the morning, we at the General Staff received a report setting forth Marshal Tito's scheme. It provided first of all for tying the enemy down south and southwest of Belgrade, and preventing him from moving forces from there

217

against the Soviet troops, for which purpose two corps of the AVNOJ Army, the 12th and the 1st, had been designated. After the enemy had been crushed in this sector, the main body of the Yugoslav forces would move directly against the German concentration in Belgrade, while the rest would turn west so as to operate jointly with the Red Army forces advancing from the region of Negotin.

The mission of capturing Niš, an important railroad and highway junction, was assigned to forces under the Serbian headquarters consisting of four divisions. On October 2–3, Col. Gen. Kocha Popović, commandng these forces, was summoned to Craiova to be given his orders. Marshal Tito asked the Soviet command, in its turn, to provide for thrusts by the 3rd Ukrainian Front for the purpose of linking up with units of the AVNOJ Army so as to cut off enemy forces moving up toward Belgrade from the south.

We called upon the command of the 3rd Ukrainian Front to help us solve the problem of the new Bulgaria's forces entering the territory of Yugoslavia, and to facilitate the joint operations. We telephoned Tolbukhin and explained the nature of the problem, and its ticklishness. Tolbukhin suggested that since the matter was so important, it should be entrusted to General Biryuzov, now commanding the 37th Army in the region of Sofia. (Biryuzov was at the same time chief of the Allied Control Commission in Bulgaria.) On October 4, Biryuzov showed up at Craiova for a meeting with Marshal Tito. At the same time, a large Bulgarian delegation made its appearance there.

Biryuzov visited Tito twice. The first time he set forth our proposals on the plan for the Belgrade operation. The plan was accepted by the Yugoslav command with great satisfaction. In addition to infantry, the Soviet forces had 2,200 guns and mortars, 149 rocket launchers, 358 tanks and self-propelled guns, 1,292 aircraft, and (in the Danube Flotilla) almost 80 naval vessels (mostly gunboats). Agreement was quickly reached on harmonizing the joint operations of the 3rd Ukrainian Front and the forces of the AVNOJ Army.

Then our delegate reported on the Bulgarian forces. He stated that the Army of the Fatherland Front was pursuing only one goal: to make its own contribution to the cause of defeating the Nazi aggressors. And he noted the make-up of the Bulgarian delegation in Craiova: It included several Communists, which fact spoke eloquently of a good and righteous future.

> We all agreed [wrote Biryuzov in his memoirs] that the Bulgarian people could not bear the mark of Cain because of the criminal actions of the former tsarist government. We all understood and firmly believed that the soldiers, generals, and other officers of the Bulgarian Army had genuinely fraternal feelings toward the Yugoslav people.

Comradě Tito gave his permission for the Bulgarian forces to advance in the direction of Niš. And in the course of the next conversation, which included the Bulgarian delegation, he officially announced that decision. Sometime later it was agreed that after the capture of Belgrade, the Bulgarian forces would proceed through Yugoslav territory into Hungary.

This work, which went on simultaneously with the concentration of troops and stores, the preparation of individual operations plans, and organizing control, essentially marked the end of preparations on the highest level. The next thing was to complete preparations all down the line.

By mid-October all preparatory measures had been completed on the army, corps, and division levels. The AVNOJ Army command and the Bulgarian commander in chief reported they were ready for the offensive.

At this point I must make a qualifying remark as to the time when the Belgrade operation was launched, which is usually given as September 28, 1944. Even before (just before) Biryuzov's visit to Tito's headquarters, advance units of three Soviet corps had broken through into the western Balkans and the eastern Serbian mountains, along which ran the first defense line of the main forces of the German Army Group Serbia. The 10th Guards Rifle Corps cleared the Danube's left bank of enemy forces, and advanced in the direction of Bela Crkva and Pančevo. In the 57th Army, General A. Z. Akimenko's 75th Rifle Corps and General N. N. Shkodunovich's 68th Rifle Corps, after bitter fighting, destroyed the German forces they had encircled in the region of Negotin; and General I. K. Kravtsov's 64th Rifle Corps surrounded substantial enemy forces near the town of Zaječar. In view of such a favorable course of events, the Soviet command decided not to halt these forces but, instead, to exploit the successes and not adhere to the date previously set for the beginning of the operation. The Soviet Stavka ordered: "Continue the advance of the 57th Army, and commit the 4th Guards Mechanized Corps no later than October 10–11 to exploit the success." Thus began the very important joint operation involving Soviet, Yugoslav national liberation, and Bulgarian forces.

The fierce offensive that had been unleashed against Army Group Serbia continued successfully. During the next two weeks of fighting, our units drove almost 130 kilometers along the main line of advance. Soon the mountains of eastern Serbia were left behind. On October 10 the Morava River was forced on the run; and the 4th Guards Mechanized Corps, which had reached this point safe and sound after a complex march with fighting along the way, was put across the river to a bridgehead that had been seized in the region of Velika Plana. On October 12 the corps' tanks headed for Belgrade at top speed.

Along with the Soviet forces, our Yugoslav comrades and the soldiers of the Bulgarian Army fought valiantly. As soon as Soviet forces attacked the enemy in the region of Negotin, the 14th Corps of the AVNOJ Army struck at the enemy's communication routes leading through the mountains to the rear area.

Bitter fighting developed near the town of Zaječar. Here, Maj. Gen. P. E. Lazarev's 19th Rifle Division (a part of the 64th Rifle Corps), besieged the enemy's garrison. The enemy dug in along favorable defensive lines and fought stubbornly. The division was reinforced by a motorcycle battalion of the 4th Guards Mechanized Corps. By the morning of October 8 the German forces had been completely crushed, and 1,600 POWs were taken. The way through the mountains was open.

Close co-operation among the Soviet, Yugoslav, and Bulgarian forces was realized in the Niš sector. The Bulgarian Army pressed the enemy from the east, from the north he was under pressure from Soviet units and the Yugoslav 45th Division, while from the west and south he was being hit by units of the AVNOJ Army's 47th and 24th divisions. The help provided by the AVNOJ Army when Soviet forces had crossed the Morava at Velika Plana was especially appreciable. Units of the 1st Proletarian Corps of the AVNOJ Army were also advancing in this area, and they helped to hold and consolidate the bridgehead we had seized. They vigorously co-operated with Soviet troops in the region of Topola and Mladenovac, which lay along the main line of advance by the main body of Soviet forces toward Belgrade. The camaraderie between Soviet and Yugoslav soldiers was sealed in the blood spilled in those hard-fought battles to crush the enemy in the region of Topola, and in other battles.

The matters decided in the course of the Belgrade operation included not only very important military problems but questions of international friendship and camaraderie between peoples jointly fighting against the Nazi occupying troops. Stalin and Tito agreed that Belgrade would be taken by forces of both the Red Army and the AVNOJ Army: that they would enter the city together. Unfortunately, we at the General Staff did not allow for the fact that the Soviet tank's rate of advance was considerably faster than that of the Yugoslav forces, which at the time had neither tanks nor trucks. Nor did the front and army staffs take this sufficiently into account. So the tanks of the 4th Guards Mechanized Corps, pushing on ahead, began to suffer losses from the enemy's fire, since the corps had few infantry of its own, and the Yugoslav infantry could not keep up with it. We of the General Staff were reminded of these discrepancies in the advance of the Soviet and Yugoslav forces by a telegram from General Korneyev dated October 13, to which the Yugoslav telegraphist had affixed a not altogether usual notation: "By radio, very express." This telegram was forwarded to the Stavka. The 3rd Ukrainian Front then received a telegram ordering that Yugoslav infantry be put on our tanks, and that the joint capture of Belgrade be effected more quickly.

Meantime, Tolbukhin had also noticed a certain disparity in the forward movement of the forces, and got in touch with Marshal

Tito. Both of them wanted to smash the enemy's defenses and prevent him from pulling back his forces. Inside Belgrade, using structures in the city, he could organize a solid defense and compel the attacking forces to besiege the city. And everyone knew what that would mean: Not only would time and lives be lost but the city itself would be destroyed. Thus both tanks and infantry had to move ahead rapidly—not separately, but together.

In accordance with Stalin's instructions, Tolbukhin asked Tito to put his infantry on Soviet tanks and trucks so that they could take Belgrade jointly, and thus speed up the development of the operation. Tito of course agreed immediately. And by October 14 the first Soviet tanks, carrying Soviet soldiers with machine carbines and fighters from the 1st Proletarian Corps, unleashed the battle for Belgrade.

Much has been written about the battle of Belgrade, both in Russia and in Yugoslavia. One can only note that the enemy was able to bring in some reinforcements, and that the fighting in Belgrade was very hard. The Germans offered especially strong resistance in the area of the old fortress of Kalemegdan. Units of AVNOJ Army's 1st, 5th, 6th, 11th, 16th, 21st, 28th, and 36th infantry divisions fought in Belgrade, in close co-operation with the Soviet infantry and the tanks of the 4th Guards Mechanized Corps.

To a considerable extent, the enemy's defeat was due to the fact that no matter how hard he tried to bring up to Belgrade, from the south and southeast, a grouping of his forces numbering 20,000 men, he did not succeed. While the battle for the capital of Yugoslavia was getting under way, other hard-fought battles were in progress on the southeastern approaches to the city. Attacking here, in close co-operation, were the 75th Rifle Corps of the 57th Army, the Yugoslav 14th Corps, units of the 5th Shock Division of the AVNOJ Army's 1st Proletarian Corps, and our 5th Independent Motorized Rifle Brigade. They managed to cut the enemy off, and squeeze him in pincers; then they set about destroying him. Two guards mechanized brigades of the 4th Mechanized Corps distinguished themselves: the 15th, commanded by Guards Col. M. A. Andrianov, and the 14th, commanded by Guards Col.

N. A. Nikitin. The valorous deeds of these brigades were reported to the Main Political Administration by General I. S. Anoshin, chief of the Political Administration of the 3rd Ukrainian Front, who came into Belgrade with the advance units.

On the approaches to the capital the enemy abandoned about two hundred guns of various calibers and fifteen hundred loaded trucks. Vestiges of the defeated German forces scattered through the forest south of Mt. Alva, where Yugoslav soldiers continued to mop them up.

On October 20 Guards Lt. Gen. of Tank Forces V. I. Zhdanov, commander of the 4th Guards Mechanized Corps, and Lt. Col. Gen. Peko Dapchević, commanding the 1st Proletarian Corps of the AVNOJ Army, reported to the command that the capital of Yugoslavia had been liberated. Next a city-wide meeting was held. The commanders of heroic troops who had just emerged from combat—the Soviet general, Zhdanov, and the Yugoslav general, Dapchević—made warm speeches to the inhabitants of Belgrade, and embraced. Thousands of people loudly welcomed their comrades-at-arms. And in Moscow, that same evening, an artillery salute thundered out in honor of the brave soldiers of the 3rd Ukrainian Front and the troops of the AVNOJ Army.

On October 21 Marshal Tito sent a letter of thanks to the commander of the 3rd Ukrainian Front. He wrote:

> Please convey the following to the troops under your command who fought in the Belgrade sector: I express my gratitude to the soldiers, generals, and other officers of the Red Army units who, jointly with units of the AVNOJ Army, liberated the capital of Yugoslavia.
>
> The heroism and tenacity you manifested in the hard fighting for the liberation of Belgrade will always be remembered by the people of Yugoslavia as the unforgettable heroism of the Red Army's troops. Your blood and the blood of the AVNOJ Army's fighters, spilled in the joint struggle against our common enemy, will eternally strengthen the brotherhood between the peoples of Yugoslavia and the Soviet Union.

Many Soviet soldiers received Yugoslav decorations, and General Zhdanov was awarded the title of People's Hero of Yugoslavia.

During the battle for Belgrade, officers at the Soviet General Staff, the AVNOJ Army headquarters, and the headquarters of the 3rd Ukrainian Front were already figuring how to develop the operation after the liberation of the city. The German command was trying to withdraw to the north the main body of its forces in Greece and southern Yugoslavia. Those troops were moving via railroad and highway west of Belgrade and along the Adriatic littoral. The shortest and most convenient route was along the valley of the Western Morava River.

On October 15 the Military Council of the 3rd Ukrainian Front communicated to the General Staff a proposal for cutting off the enemy's escape route to the north. Tolbukhin, V. M. Laiok, and A. P. Tarasov reported that the line west of the Southern Morava that had been occupied by the 3rd Ukrainian Front, the AVNOJ Army, and the Bulgarian Army made it possible to take Čačak and Kraljevo, the capture of which would block the route of the German forces. It was proposed that some of the forces of the 57th Army should strike in the direction of Gornji Milanovac and Čačak, and then develop the attack toward Kraljevo. At the same time a blow would be struck at Kragujevac.

The front command's opinion was shared by the headquarters of the AVNOJ Army and by Marshal Tito personally. And our Yugoslav comrades suggested that after the capture of Čačak and Kraljevo the enemy would have only one escape route from Albania and Greece: through Montenegro and the Sonjok to Sarajevo.

On October 18, Tito wrote to the commander of the 3rd Ukrainian Front:

> In order to deprive the enemy of this opportunity, I consider it [necessary] that the main body of your forces in Belgrade should be sent through Lazarevac, Valjevo, Zvornik, and Vlasenica, to capture Sarajevo. . . . For joint operations with units of the 3rd and 5th army corps of the AVNOJ for the rapid capture of Sarajevo, I suggest sending units of the 4th Guards Mechanized Corps.

At the same time it was reported that the regions through which the joint Soviet-Yugoslav forces were to move had been cleared of German units.

A monument symbolizing the gap in the German defense at Dukla Pass.

A "conveyor belt" in the Carpathian Mountains passes along the ammunition.

Marshal I. S. Konev of the Soviet Union (at the stereoscopic telescope), commander of the Ukrainian Front; Col. Gen. K. S. Moskalenko, commander of the 38th Army; and Lt. Gen. S. Shatilov, chief of the Political Directorate of the 1st Ukrainian Front, at an observation point of the 38th Army near Krosno, September 8, 1944, the first day of the Dukla operation.

Col. Gen. A. A. Grechko, commander of the 1st Guards Army, with staff officers on the Árpád Line.

The Árpád Line.

Standard of the 1st Czechoslovakian Battalion, Buzuluk, 1943.

On the eve of the attack in the Carpathian Mountains, Col. L. I. Brezhnev, chief of the Politica[l]
Division of the 18th Army, addresses the soldiers and officers.

Visiting L. Svoboda, President of the Czechoslovakian Socialist
Republic, in 1971.

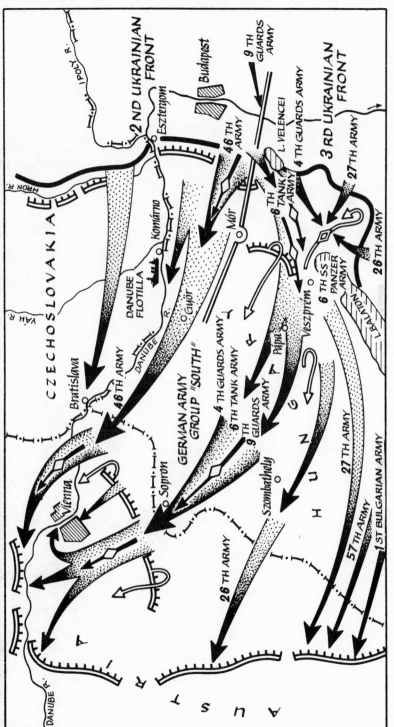

On to Vienna.

Soviet troops enter Vienna, April 1945.

Street fighting in Vienna.

General A. V. Blagodatov, Soviet commandant of Vienna, talking to workers, April 1945.

At a monument to the great composer.

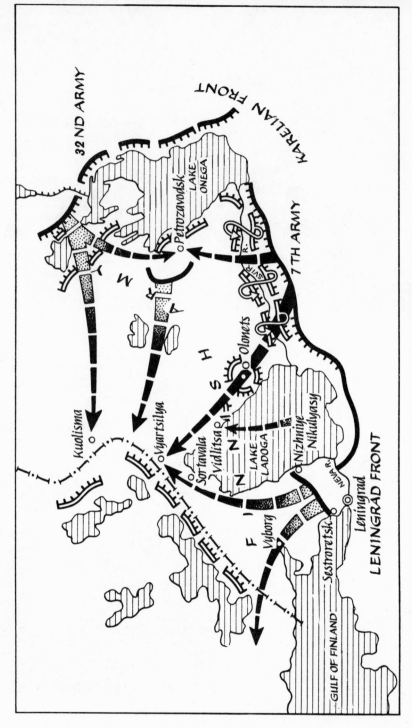

The Stavka's plan to rout the enemy in southern Karelia.

But neither of these plans was put into execution. The problem of cutting off the enemy's escape route was solved in a third way: by means of joint Yugoslav-Bulgarian operations in the region of Priština—a region traversed by the last railroad used by the enemy to evacuate his forces from Greece to the north. Agreement between the Yugoslav and Bulgarian headquarters was quickly reached on the operations plan and the joint action, and then a successful operation was carried out.

In late October 1944, having carried out their mission on the territory of Yugoslavia, the units of the 3rd Ukrainian Front went off on a new campaign. The only Soviet forces left behind to give further assistance to our Yugoslav friends were our pilots, who were continuing in worthy fashion the military and international traditions that had developed during the glorious days of the Belgrade operation. The pilots' job was to support the AVNOJ Army in its mopping-up operations, since there were still at least ten German divisions in Yugoslavia, along with the forces under Pavelić, Nedić, Rupnik, and Mihailović, which totaled almost 200,000.

In October 1944 the intentions of the Nazi command in Yugoslavia became even more clearly apparent. It was not only withdrawing its forces rapidly to the north but stepping up the construction of defensive lines along the Drava, Sava, and Drina rivers. Those lines were apparently intended to cover the withdrawal of Nazi forces from Italy and Yugoslavia into Hungary and Austria. Also, well-fortified positions—or, as the Germans themselves called them, "lines of firm resistance"—were rapidly being built along a line running from Trieste through Maribor to Bratislava. They were to assure a solid front of German forces from Italy to Hungary. The enemy was expecting the Soviet command to drive a wedge into that front, and was preparing for counteraction.

At the General Staff we saw that if the enemy succeeded in deploying his forces in a line of defense from Trieste to Bratislava, this would assure good interaction between the Hungarian and Italian groupings, and an advantageous flank position with respect to the 2nd Ukrainian Front, which was driving northward. Also, between Malinovsky's left flank and Tolbukhin's front there was a considerable area, roughly from Sombor to Novi Sad, of slight troop density. In order to prevent the still-separate German groupings from combining into a solid front, it would be necessary for the 3rd Ukrainian Front to go over to the offensive before the fall season of muddy roads set in. The most likely direction for the offensive was the valleys of the Drava and Mura rivers (negotiable by all types of forces), where conditions were most favorable for creating the very wedge that the enemy was so fearful of. That is why, in sending the corps of the 57th Army to the Sombor region, we briefed the commanding general on the possibilities of an offensive toward the west.

In the first half of November, at the Stavka, the results of the 1944 operations were toted up, and a general plan was worked out for the 1945 campaign. Great attention was paid to the forces of the 3rd Ukrainian Front, which constituted the left flank of the Soviet-German front. At that time Tolbukhin came to Moscow with his operations officers, and worked with them on November 7 and 8.

At the Stavka, two viewpoints were considered. The first, which Tolbukhin initially supported, was that we should drive toward Vienna. It was expected that when we had made such a deep thrust, the enemy defending the region of Budapest would pull out of Hungary, because of the threat that Soviet forces would break into his rear area. According to the other view, an offensive in that direction was not necessary under the circumstances. Its proponents (including the General Staff) held that it was first of all necessary to supply direct assistance to the 2nd Ukrainian Front near Budapest, so as to encircle and destroy the enemy there. In that case the way would be opened not only to Vienna but to Czechoslovakia, and from there through the Ore Mountains, the Sudetic Mountains, and the Elbe Valley into Germany. The second view prevailed. Tolbukhin was given time to work up his ideas in connection with this plan.

The very closest contacts were being maintained with the headquarters of the AVNOJ Army. Our Yugoslav comrades were also thinking of how best to destroy the enemy in the northern part of their country, to which new Nazi troops had been brought. On November 1, bitter fighting broke out in the region of Čačak and Kraljevo against large enemy forces withdrawing to the north. The fierceness of the fighting in this area was due to the fact that the Nazis still held the railroad that ran through here. In these engagements, the 17th, 23rd, 25th, and 2nd Proletarian Infantry divisions of the AVNOJ Army covered themselves with glory. They beat off large-scale attacks by enemy infantry and tanks and then went over to the offensive, throwing the enemy back, seizing him in a mortal grip, and making an orderly retreat impossible.

With the defeat of the enemy's Belgrade forces, the AVNOJ Army had acquired an extensive and advantageous territory for bases. From there it could exercise a decisive influence on the course of operations in the northern part of the country, where the enemy forces were located. Now the AVNOJ Army could act even more vigorously. One typical example of its growing military skill was the encirclement and destruction of considerable German forces in a short period of time. Thus the Yugoslav Maritime Group and the 3rd Infantry Division first encircled and then destroyed the enemy in the region of Danilovgrad, Skadar, and Podgorica. The 8th Army Corps created a cauldron for the enemy in the region of Knin, where it wiped out a German infantry regiment. And the 25th Division of the AVNOJ Army surrounded and destroyed the enemy in the region of Guča.

The advance of AVNOJ Army units into Herzegovina, which began in February 1945, was of great importance. At that time the AVNOJ Army headquarters was faced with the necessity of liquidating the enemy's defenses in the area of Mostar, the main city of Herzegovina. Having dug in here, the enemy was blocking the southwestern approaches to another and even more important city and communications hub, Sarajevo, from which there were routes into Croatia. Between February 6 and 15, the AVNOJ Army's 8th Corps and 29th Division successfully carried out a well-planned and -organized operation near Mostar. A Yugoslav tank brigade took an active part in the offensive. The enemy suffered heavy losses: His 369th Infantry Division was battered, and more than 1,200 officers and soldiers were taken prisoner.

Mostar was liberated, along with a considerable part of the territory of Herzegovina. Fearful of losing Sarajevo, the Nazi commander refused to transfer to Hungary the Prinz Eugen Division, reinforced after recent battles. The Soviet General Staff greatly appreciated this help from our Yugoslav comrades-in-arms.

From November 1944 through May 1945, the Soviet pilots of Gen. A. N. Vitruk's Air Group provided substantial assistance to the forces of the AVNOJ Army. This group was organized after Comrade Tito's talks in Moscow, at which time he asked for air support for the AVNOJ Army. The National Defense Committee considered this request well founded, and decreed that People's Yugoslavia be provided with an air group consisting of two divisions (the 10th Guards Ground Attack Division and the 236th Fighter Division). Yugoslavia was also provided with the necessary service units (the 9th Air Base Services District), and economic and technical resources. The agreement on turning these divisions over to the AVNOJ Army was signed in Belgrade in November 1944.

General Vitruk's group was not merely a strong military unit (244 planes) but a center for training personnel and for developing new organs of control for the Yugoslav Air Force.

The pilots of this group carried out their military missions heroically. (General Vitruk himself was awarded the title of People's Hero of Yugoslavia.) They fought selflessly in Yugoslavia until the final victory over the fascist occupying troops.

The defeat of the Nazi forces in Yugoslavia was helpful to the success of the national liberation forces in Albania. More than once, on instructions from Moscow, our pilots based at Bari supplied the Albanian patriots with arms, ammunition, medical supplies, and other equipment. In the autumn of 1944 units of the AVNOJ Army managed to establish rather firm contact with the National Liberation Army of Albania. In certain cases the armies of these neighbor nations operated jointly. On November 17 the National Liberation Army of Albania drove the German troops out of Tirana. It pursued them into the mountains, where they were either destroyed or compelled to leave the country. By November 29 Albania was swept clean of occupying troops.

On November 17, 1944, the Bulgarian 1st Army, attacking jointly with the 46th and 42nd Infantry divisions and the 3rd and 2nd Kosovska brigades of the AVNOJ Army, captured the big enemy communications hub of Priština. A few days later, units of the Bulgarian 2nd Army, together with the Yugoslav 22nd Infantry Division, liberated Mitrovica and thereby blocked the enemy's route to Novi Pazar.

United States and British aircraft based in Italy became involved in the military operations in Yugoslavia by agreement among the allies. Their missions were assigned via our General Staff—something we quickly agreed on with our allies. In case forced landings in the mountains might be necessary, the requisite landing strips were sought out in regions controlled by partisans and equipped insofar as possible. In this respect, much help was forthcoming from the Soviet air base in Bari, whose pilots (as we have said) often flew to Albania or Montenegro and used landing strips prepared by the local inhabitants and the partisans.

The Soviet pilots were always given a joyous welcome, especially in Montenegro. The partisans and mountaineers had tale after tale to tell about the skill of the men who flew the airplanes marked with the Red Star. It once happened that two aircraft—one Russian and one English—set down on the same landing strip near a village high in the mountains. They were both C-47s, hence identical except for their markings. As they stood side by side on the landing strip, the entire population of the village, from youngest to oldest, gathered around them. And while the crews conferred with each other, the peasants tried to determine which plane was better, and which pilot was the more skillful. Finally an aged peasant stepped forward. While everyone watched, he paced off the length and wing span of the planes, and gave each fuselage a businesslike whack. Then, after pondering, he loudly declared that the Russian plane was a half-meter longer, so it was harder to land in the mountains than was the British plane. Thus was the argument settled to the satisfaction of all present.

It turned out, however, that it was one thing to agree at general staff level on the use of aircraft, and another to organize such use properly in the field. We were made aware of this in November

1944, when twenty-seven American aircraft appeared above a column of the 6th Guards Rifle Corps, marching through Yugoslavia. The aircraft were recognized, and since they were allies, they were welcomed with a waving of caps. But suddenly they turned around and made a heavy bombing attack. Unfortunately, it was accurate: The corps commander, Lt. Gen. Grigory Petrovich Kotov, was killed, along with thirty-one other officers and men, and there were thirty-seven wounded. Since the planes' maneuvers indicated they were going to make a second attack, nine Soviet fighters were sent up. A dogfight ensued. The result was that along with the human lives, three American and three Soviet planes were lost.

On November 9 a representation was made on this subject to the chief of the American military mission in Moscow, and on November 10 an American general arrived in Sofia. He expressed regrets to the Soviet command, and those regrets were taken into consideration. But from then on the troops paid due regard to the sky whenever aircraft appeared, and the general staffs checked and rechecked the recognition signals.

As a result of the joint work done by the Stavka, the General Staff, and the 3rd Ukrainian Front's Military Council and Staff, a plan was worked out for the operations in Hungary. On November 12 Tolbukhin presented his ideas, which were considered by the General Staff, and then reported to the Stavka, which approved them. The plan stipulated, as the next objective, that the main forces of the front should advance to the region of Subotica, force the Danube, and seize an operational bridgehead near Pécs on the western bank of the river.

The next stage of the offensive against the Nazi forces was characterized by broad co-operation among the armies of the USSR, Bulgaria, and Yugoslavia. During the first phase of the offensive by the 3rd Ukrainian Front, when its left flank was close to the right flank of the AVNOJ Army, it was important that the Yugoslav forces continue vigorous actions in the area between the Drava and Sava rivers. Later, when the main forces of the 3rd Ukrainian Front had headed north, there would be a spreading gap between the flanks of the Soviet and Yugoslav armies. This gap could be filled by forces of the new Bulgarian 1st Army, which was being formed by the Fatherland Front.

Thus the plan for further operations assumed the participation of three friendly armies which would jointly solve the problem of breaking up the forces of the enemy's Hungarian and Italian groupings. Also assumed was close co-ordination on all matters of planning and carrying out the operations.

The Stavka instructed Tolbukhin to negotiate personally, on this score, with Comrade Tito and the Bulgarian command. Between November 17 and 20, Tolbukhin visited both Belgrade and Sofia. General agreement was reached on the actions of the Yugoslav and Bulgarian forces. Also, the Yugoslavs made it possible for the Bulgarian Army to supply itself, in Yugoslavia, with straw, wood, and hay—things indispensable to the Bulgarian forces at that time. Since the Bulgarians had not yet moved their 1st Army up to the front, the Yugoslav command agreed to advance along the Sava River Valley in the general direction of Zagreb, and prior to the beginning of operations to assign an army corps to the Bulgarian Army so as to secure the left flank of the 57th Army.

In the second half of November 1944 the forces of the 3rd Ukrainian Front swung toward the north, while the AVNOJ Army, which had gained in strength, prepared for an offensive under the leadership of the Communists. But Yugoslavia was still suffering great shortages—especially of foodstuffs. Our country came to the aid of our comrades-in-arms. In December 1944 more than 50,000 tons of grain and flour were sent to Yugoslavia. On March 10 a Yugoslav tank brigade (sixty-five T-34 tanks), formed in our country, set off via railroad from the Tula region. On April 1, in the vicinity of Šid, it went into action against the enemy. Until the day of victory the members of this brigade fought valiantly, advancing in the direction of Zagreb. March 1945 witnessed the beginning of a massive transfer to the AVNOJ Army of Soviet arms and arms captured by our forces. Included were twenty fully armed and equipped infantry divisions, three artillery brigades, two tank brigades, two air divisions, several communications regiments, and engineering and transport units. On this score the National Defense Committee issued a special decree dated February 10, 1945. History has shown that the arms were turned over to the brave and valorous defenders of People's Yugoslavia.

Time is the best measure of the stability of what was done in the past. The peoples of the Soviet Union and of Yugoslavia are true to the friendship forged in the selfless struggle against the enemy hated by both. This friendship was sealed in blood spilled by both nations on the fields of battle near Belgrade and in dozens of big and little towns and villages in Yugoslavia. Some 6,500 Soviet soldiers are buried in Yugoslav soil. The gravestones glorify those who came to Yugoslavia through the flames of battle, from the walls of Moscow, from the ruins of Stalingrad, Kiev, and Minsk, to save the peaceful homes of our Yugoslav brothers from fire and destruction.

7

IN THE CENTER
OF EUROPE

The Hungarian knot. A directive from the Stavka. Commotion in Horthy's camp. Pressure from Hitler. A secret mission. A letter from officer POWs. Clumsy maneuvers. Col. Gen. Béla Miklós. The battle for Budapest. Churchill and Eden in Moscow. A report from Marshal Timoshenko. The death of the Soviet truce envoys. The birth of military co-operation. Near Balaton. "Don't drag out the war."

The success of the Iaşi-Kishinev operation meant that one of the practical problems now facing the Soviet forces was the liberation of Hungary.

As is generally known, Hungary is located in the geographical center of Europe—at the crossroads of the continent's main thoroughfares. During the years of World War II its rulers, headed by the Regent, Nicholas Horthy, had become loyal minions of Hitler. They had transformed the country into a satellite of the Third Reich, and one of its bases of support. Hungary sent Germany crude oil (which after the loss of the Rumanian sources had acquired the preciousness of an elixir of life for the Wehrmacht),

233

grain, meat, and agricultural raw materials. It also supplied troops.

In our calculations, we at the General Staff took all this into account. But that was not all. We had not forgotten that Hungary occupied a special place in the calculations of the Anglo-American bloc. We knew, for one thing, about the Western powers' two-faced attitude toward Hungary. For example, they had reacted rather oddly toward Hungary's entering the war against the USSR. Britain had not declared war on Hungary until the end of 1941, and the United States did not do so until even later—in June 1942. Such attitudes were fraught with all kinds of surprises; and, as we shall see, this had an effect on the plans of the parties.

The liberation of Hungary promised marked military gains for us. Once having liberated that country, the Soviet forces would enter our allied country of Czechoslovakia, which was on Germany's southern border, and would move into Germany from the south. From there it was only a few hundred kilometers to the center of the Nazi lair. And we had other ideas in mind, as well. For example, the liberation of Hungary would substantially change the military situation in Italy, Yugoslavia, Greece, and Albania. It would pose the threat of our striking at the enemy's rear area in those countries, and cutting off his routes for withdrawal into Germany. This situation would be a new and very important element in the strategic picture in Europe.

The enemy understood the directions in which military events might develop, and strove stubbornly to hang on to Hungary. We felt this the moment the Soviet forces drew near to Transylvania.

The defeat of the enemy near Iaşi and Kishinev had made it possible to take a somewhat different approach from that used previously to the problem of overcoming the defenses that the Germans and Horthy's forces had set up in the Carpathians. The General Staff and the Stavka began to have second thoughts. Was it really necessary to break into Hungary over the mountain ridges, using the kind of head-on blow the 4th Ukrainian Front was preparing to deliver? Such an attack would involve great losses of both lives and matériel. Wouldn't it be better to develop an operation in the southwest so as to put our armies in regions located beyond the mountains; that is, to go around the mountain ridges from the south through Rumania? Of course there was no way of dispensing with an offensive in the mountains, and dealing the enemy head-on blows. But the main mission would be carried out much more simply, more economically, and certainly more decisively.

At the General Staff we studied the situation very carefully; and on August 25 Antonov reported to the Stavka on a possible variant for the operations of the 4th and 2nd Ukrainian fronts. It was proposed to the General Staff that it consult with Petrov, commanding the 4th Ukrainian Front, and somewhat later with Malinovsky, commanding the 2nd Ukrainian Front, and Deputy Supreme Commander Zhukov, who at the time was in Rumania.

Without delay, we got on the high-frequency voice radio and talked to General of the Army Petrov. In his sector, troops and equipment were moving slowly as ants along all the roads and paths climbing the foothills of the Carpathians, pushing on through forests and clearing themselves a path with either gunfire or hand-to-hand fighting. The front was advancing, getting ready to force the eastern Carpathians from the east. But the troops had no mountain equipment. And the results of the advance were not especially encouraging. Although the enemy had pulled back somewhat to the summits and passes on the main mountain range, he had not given up any key positions. Meantime, our forces had suffered heavy losses in both human lives and matériel.

Petrov agreed with all of the General Staff's arguments. But he said that, pending a final decision by the Stavka, it wouldn't be a bad idea to bring the 4th Ukrainian Front to a halt. Time was needed to train the troops in mountain operations, improve the supply situation, and give the troops at least a bit of rest, since they had been advancing for a long time. The General Staff did not object, since going over to the defensive would make it easier for the front to prepare for new offensive operations. We hoped that the Supreme Commander would agree with us and Petrov. Also, we at the General Staff had received some information on plans for an anti-Nazi uprising in Slovakia. That information was neither very clear nor very reliable, but it was not to be ignored.

As it happened, the 4th Ukrainian Front almost did not manage to go over to the defensive; but of that, more later.

On the night of August 26 we reported to the Supreme Commander on our ideas and those of General Petrov. We had previously prepared a draft directive for the 4th Ukrainian Front to go on the defensive. Stalin signed it; but with a view to the future offensive, he ordered the front to create strong reserves, since these are necessary in mountain warfare. In order to emphasize still more the importance of the decision that had been made, Stalin told us to add to the directive the words: "Postpone the operation you have scheduled [the forcing of the Carpathians —S. Sh.], and do not undertake it without authorization from the Stavka." This addendum was also necessary because if there should be an uprising among the Slovaks, we would have to weigh very carefully the military and (especially) the political consequences of that important document. We had not for a moment forgotten the example of the Warsaw uprising: The Red Army had helped Warsaw in every way possible, but was not able to rescue it from disaster.

General Petrov issued an instruction to the forces of his front in which he explained to his commanders the reason for going on the defensive:

> Pursuant to a directive from the Stavka of the Supreme Command, the forces of the front have taken up on a fixed defense, while at the same time maintaining strong reserves.
>
> This transition to the defensive was occasioned by the successful operations of the 2nd and 3rd Ukrainian fronts, and the resultant possibility of performing our assigned missions with less difficulty and by more effective means.
>
> Consequently, this change-over to the defensive must be understood as a phase in preparation for a subsequent offensive with decisive goals.

On September 4 the Stavka received a report from Zhukov and Malinovsky. They wrote: "It is not to be expected that the 40th Army and the 7th Guards Army can rapidly break through with a frontal assault." These armies, commanded by Gen. F. F. Zhmachenko and Gen. M. S. Shumilov, respectively, were already headed toward Hungary, and were supposed to go around the southern end of the Carpathians.

As we expected, the report suggested advancing into Transylvania, combining attacks from the east and south, sending the 53rd Army, the 27th Army, and the 6th Tank Army from the Danube to this area, and capturing the region of Cluj, Oradea Mare, and Hațeg. "By taking this region," Zhukov and Malinovsky went on, "we will pose a threat of encirclement to the Germans and Hungarians opposing the armies of Zhmachenko and Shumilov, and we shall be able more rapidly to reach the defensive line of Cluj–Satu Mare, for joint operations with the 4th Ukrainian Front."

Thus the General Staff's opinion was very authoritatively confirmed.

On the evening of the following day, after having closely studied all these considerations, the Stavka ordered the 2nd Ukrainian Front to make some corrections in the operations plan presented the day before. The gist of the corrections was that the front should, in going around the southern end of the Carpathians, combine frontal and enveloping movements by several armies; should help General Petrov's front; and should not disperse its forces.

This swing by the 2nd Ukrainian Front put a stop to all conjectures and chitchat abroad to the effect that the Soviet Union would pursue the old goal of tsarist Russia with respect to the Bosporus and the Dardanelles. Hitler, in particular, was convinced that the Red Army would throw all its forces in that direction, and had left only a small covering force in the Carpathians. This is confirmed in the book *Lost Battles,* by General Friessner, who commanded Army Group Southern Ukraine, which was smashed by our forces. This mistake by the enemy was very critical, since it had an effect on the grouping of his forces and, in particular, resulted in his strengthening the sector south of the Carpathians rather than that to the west, which was more important strategically.

So far as I can recall, this was the first directive to mention

Debrecen—on this occasion, as an objective for the cavalry it was planned to use in developing the front's offensive. An advance as far as Debrecen would put our forces in a position advantageous for further advance in any of several directions: to the east and northeast, in the rear of the enemy forces in the Carpathians; to the north, to cut off the enemy's withdrawal route; to the northwest, to help the possible uprising by the Slovaks; and to the west, to strike at Budapest. The maneuver worked out by the Stavka was more far-reaching than the commander of the 2nd Ukrainian Front had assumed. It held many possibilities for developing subsequent operations, and posed a threat of encirclement for the enemy forces dug in both in the Transylvanian Ukraine and in Transylvania.

In this directive the Soviet Supreme Command spelled out the bases for co-operation between the Soviet forces and the Rumanian forces, which had now turned their weapons against Nazi Germany. The Stavka proposed to the Rumanian command that it assign two or three infantry divisions for the defense of the Danube, and no fewer than three divisions to defend the sector of Szeged–Turnu-Severin. These forces would be provided by the Rumanian 1st Army. As for the forces of the Rumanian 4th Army, under the command of General Avramescu, and the other Rumanian units in the region of Brașov and Transylvania, it was planned to use them jointly with the Red Army in the offensive toward Cluj.

Pursuant to Stalin's orders, the forces of Malinovsky's left flank made a swing to the north. In their center was Gen. A. G. Kravchenko's 6th Tank Army, with 262 tanks and 82 self-propelled guns. On September 14, on the approaches to Turda, the enemy launched a strong counterattack so as to frustrate our operation. As a result, the 6th Tank Army fought some fierce engagements with enemy tanks and infantry in this area.

The crushing defeat of Army Group Southern Ukraine near Iași and Kishinev had had a considerable effect on the political situation in Hungary, and on that country's military posture. The pillars of the fascist regime were beginning to feel the earth quake under their feet. Although Hungary had been occupied by German troops since March 1944, this fact would not now guarantee the strength of its defenses against the Soviet forces. The policies of reactionary ruling classes and counterrevolutionary governments—a policy of betraying the national interest and oppressing the people—had brought the country to a catastrophe. At the very time that the Nilashists were shouting (and foaming at the mouth as they did so) about "final victory" and "Hitler's miracle weapon," Hungarian workers were being forcibly evacuated to Germany, and plant equipment was being shipped there, along with reserves of raw materials, agricultural implements and foodstuffs. And the country was in even greater military dependence upon the German dictatorship than ever, since Hitler had sent several German divisions into Hungary while withdrawing the main body of the Hungarian combat-ready forces.

As soon as the Soviet forces had completed the liquidation of the German forces encircled at Iași and Kishinev and began to advance toward Hungary, Yugoslavia, and Bulgaria, the people in Horthy's camp began feverishly to look for a way out of a situation that threatened disaster for Hungarian fascism. But even now, when the blind faith of the Hungarian ruling circles in the strength of German weapons was undermined, Horthy and his clique did not give a thought to unconditional surrender. Rather, they proposed to avoid collapse by increased orientation toward England and the United States. Horthy and his followers thought that sooner or later the Western powers would make a deal with Nazi Germany behind the back of the Soviet Union, whereupon the Germans would let the British and Americans into Hungary before the Soviet forces had got across the Carpathians. And there were grounds for such hopes. In Churchill's own words: "I was very anxious to forestall the Russians in certain areas of Central Europe. The Hungarians, for instance, had expressed their intention of resisting the Soviet advance, but would surrender to a British force if it could arrive in time."[1] Horthy and his followers thought that throwing themselves on the mercy of Britain and America would be a lesser evil than surrendering to the USSR.

[1] Winston Churchill, *Vtoraya mirovaya voina*, Vol. VI, p. 146 [p. 148 in the English-language edition—translator's note].

They were betting on the instability of the anti-Nazi coalition. At this point their chief concern was to hold back the Soviet forces and gain time—to enable the Anglo-Americans to forestall the Red Army and become masters of the situation in Hungary.

The members of the Hungarian Cabinet also knew that certain prominent Nazis would not object to throwing open the western front to the Anglo-American forces so that all the forces of the Third Reich could be concentrated against the Red Army in the east. This would of course have facilitated the Anglo-Americans' advance into Hungary, while the Red Army troops would have shed much blood as they slowly overcame the stubborn German-Hungarian resistance. The Hungarian fascists figured that their country's occupation by the Western powers would not entail retribution for their crimes, and would enable them to continue the fight against the Soviet Union. As for the Wehrmacht, Horthy and his clique hoped that with the patronage and presence of the Anglo-American forces, they could manage the Wehrmacht rather easily.

Thus in the autumn of 1944, Hungary was in the center of military and political events in Europe.

When the Red Army began to operate beyond the borders of the USSR, it of course became more difficult for us to conceal the direction of our attacks: The enemy learned of the movements and concentration of our forces. Thus we could not conceal the swing to the north made by the left flank forces of the 2nd Ukrainian Front. When the members of Horthy's Cabinet learned of this, they sounded the alarm, figuring that the Soviet armies were taking up their jumping-off positions for an offensive against Hungary. There was a great "flap" in Budapest. A session of the so-called Royal Council was held on the evening of September 7. Horthy, the Regent, discussed Hungary's military and political situation with the government and representatives of the High Command of the Hungarian Army. Their evaluations were very unfavorable.

Lt. Gen. János Voros, the chief of staff, had information on the situation at the front indicating beyond a doubt that the Red Army intended to strike powerful simultaneous blows from two converging directions: from the east, from Rumania; and from the north, through the Carpathians. Voros did not conceal the fact that such actions by the Soviet forces might result in a gigantic pincers which could cut off the main forces of the Hungarian Army (fighting in the eastern Carpathians) from the center of the country, and pose a direct threat to Budapest.

At this session, not a single word was said about surrender. But those present agreed that with only its own forces, Hungary could not hold out against the Red Army. Since contact had not yet been made with the Anglo-Americans, circumstances compelled the Hungarian Government to demand help of Hitler. Literally to "demand," and not "ask," since Nazi Germany had a great interest in preserving its last ally, Hungary. In case of a refusal, the Hungarians could frighten their German patrons by saying that Hungary would be compelled to make a deal with the Soviet Union on an armistice.

An extraordinary session of the Hungarian Cabinet was held on the next day, September 8. Once again they talked about finding a way out, but none of the ministers had anything new to propose: Everything had been said the evening before. Not only that, but as was reasonably observed by Count Béla Teleki, a landowner and professor at Cluj University, a convenient opportunity for armistice talks with the Soviet Union had been lost several weeks before. The question of the possible occupation of the country by Anglo-American forces seemed to have been settled. The reason for this was the German Government's reply [to the request for help]. In its eagerness to prevent a collapse on the eastern front, it was willing to transfer forces from the western front. Also, Greiffenberg, the Nazi emissary to Hungary, promised in the name of the German High Command that an armored division and an SS police division from the region of Belgrade would come to the aid of Hungary within five days, to be followed by the 18th SS Infantry Division from Györ and the 22nd Infantry Division and an armored brigade from other regions.

Thus it seemed that Horthy and his followers had got all they had been hoping for: The German Government had said it might leave the western front open, hence the Anglo-Americans could rapidly advance into Hungary; German forces were on the way, and this would make it possible to organize strong defenses on the borders, stop the Red Army, and gain precious time. And then . . . Nobody said a word about intervention from the west, but everyone was thinking about it. In vain did the chief of staff of the Hungarian Army demonstrate to the government that Hungary must basically count only on its own forces: The German promises had prompted the ministers to decide, irrevocably, to continue the war against the USSR. And so one more opportunity to prevent needless sacrifices of victims, and to shorten the war, was lost. The Horthy government did not want to see that it hadn't the faintest hopes of success.

The German command correctly evaluated the situation that had developed in Hungary. Friessner, who was commanding the German forces, rushed back and forth between his own headquarters, the palace of the Hungarian Regent, and Hitler's headquarters. The new forces were brought up on schedule. As Friessner wrote later: "The command of the army group took several steps to ensure the security of its rear area in case of an unforeseen change in Hungary's policy." Large tank forces were concentrated in the region of Turda for a counterattack: The Nazis wanted at all cost to frustrate the plans of the Soviet command.

On September a special conference dealing with the situation in Hungary was held at Hitler's headquarters. Present were a limited number of high-ranking German and Hungarian officers, and such civilians as were necessary. General Friessner was given what amounted to dictatorial military powers. Literally all civil and military organizations were to be subordinated to him henceforth. "In that respect, no demands on the part of Hungary were to be taken into account," Friessner himself wrote later. Thus the Hungarian General Staff found itself in the position of a secondary organ of control over its own forces, and had in fact lost any authority over them.

At the end of the session the army group was ordered to hold on until the last man. Later, on September 20, the German Government confirmed, in an ultimatum to Hungary, its decision to consolidate the kind of regime it wanted in that country. Thus Hungary was caught in the vise of a regime that predetermined a bloody war on its own territory.

After swinging to the north in the direction of Debrecen, the forces of the 2nd Ukrainian Front regrouped and encountered the enemy in new engagements. The Nazi command was expecting this: An additional Hungarian mechanized corps and a German armored division were concentrated against the 40th Army, the 7th Guards Army, and the 27th Army. All attempts at a breakthrough by our forces and the Rumanian units operating jointly with them proved unsuccessful. The fighting was especially heavy in the area of Turda, where—as I have said—the German command tried to regain the advantage by a counterattack. Inspired by the recent order to fight to the last man, the enemy fought with frenzied violence.

The 27th and 6th tank armies also became involved in the fighting, which lasted for several days. Neither side achieved any notable success. This put us General Staff officers on our guard; and we repeated to the Stavka our doubts that it was possible to achieve, in the Turda region, any favorable shift in the situation.

Things were a bit different in the sector through which General I. M. Managarov's 53rd Army was advancing on the left. Here the enemy's defenses were weaker. Our forces broke through them rather easily and reached the area northwest of the town of Arad. In the opinion of the front command, favorable conditions had been created in this army's battle zone for a massive blow by Soviet forces in the direction of Oradea Mare and Debrecen.

In the opinion of the General Staff, a thrust in the direction of Debrecen was very promising. It would make it possible to bypass, on the west, Turda and the entire Transylvanian and Carpathian grouping of enemy forces. But it also involved difficulties. If the main Soviet forces drove toward Debrecen, they would have to keep a close watch on their flanks, which might be threatened by very large enemy groupings: one from the Carpathians and Transylvania, and the other from Yugoslavia. And no one could guarantee that these groupings would not be moved, as per a single plan, in the general direction of Budapest. This consideration became an important operational factor because of the extension of our communications, the fact that our rear area in Rumania had only recently been put in order, and the relative weakness of the 2nd Ukrainian Front's mobile forces.

We at the General Staff kept close track of both enemy groupings, and in making our advance drafts of the Debrecen operation, we tried to make it coincide with blows against the enemy's forces in Yugoslavia. Our calculations showed that we would be able to tie down the German forces in the Balkans by joint operations conducted by the 3rd Ukrainian Front and the AVNOJ Army, who would launch offensives on September 28–29, 1944. As for the enemy groupings in Transylvania and the Carpathians, which posed a direct threat to the right flank of Malinovsky's forces advancing toward Debrecen, they would be the first target of joint actions by the 4th and 2nd Ukrainian fronts. And if necessary, we could also throw in certain forces from Konev's 1st Ukrainian Front (which is what happened at Dukla Pass).

Thus the Debrecen operation was operationally sound, but it nonetheless demanded of the front commanders great precision in controlling their forces, and flexibility and speed in maneuvering.

The General Staff reported to the Stavka on all these matters, but we were advised once again to consult with the front commanders in question. They supported the plan. On September 23 the General Staff received a reply from Zhukov which read as follows:

> In view of the nature of the terrain and the enemy grouping facing Malinovsky and Petrov, I feel that it would be better for Kravchenko's army to be concentrated north of Arad immediately, with the mission of striking toward Debrecen; i.e., into the rear of the basic grouping of Hungarian units.
>
> With the capture of the Debrecen area the Hungarians' entire defensive system will collapse, and they will be compelled more rapidly to pull back from the Cluj region and from the Carpathians.
>
> A frontal attack by Malinovsky would lead to a prolonged battle and would enable the enemy to build up his defenses in the Tisza sector undisturbed.

Thus the General Staff's ideas, based on the proposals of the 2nd Ukrainian Front's Military Council, were supported,

The Debrecen operation was launched on October 6 and continued almost until the end of the month. It was characterized by great stress and complexity. Since so much has been written about it, there is no need to describe it in detail once again. I shall mention only that in the course of that operation the enemy was badly defeated in the regions of Oradea, Debrecen, and Szeged. The Soviet forces liberated Transylvania, reached the Tisza, forced it on the front's left flank, and advanced to the Danube, having established beyond the Tisza an extensive operational bridgehead along the line Chop–Baja–eastern bank of the Danube–King Peter Canal.

As a result of a very powerful blow by the 2nd Ukrainian Front, the enemy forces facing the 4th Ukrainian Front lost much of their stability. Our calculations had been right: The enemy could not hold the Carpathians, and in the course of bitter fighting he was thrown back to the west. Petrov's forces, going over to the offensive, drove ahead, overrunning one defensive line after another. South of Chop they linked up with forces from the 2nd Ukrainian Front.

The time had come for a new and mighty offensive by the Soviet forces—this time toward Budapest. While planning it, the Stavka did not abandon the hope that the Hungarian Government would realize what the situation was on the front and in Hungary itself, be sensible, and take Hungary out of the war by peaceful means. On September 29, 1944, Stalin wrote to Roosevelt that together with liquidating the enemy in the Baltic region, the Soviet forces had "two immediate tasks: to take Hungary out of the war, and to feel out the German defenses on the eastern front by means of attacks by our forces." A peaceful initiative by the Hungarians was not ruled out, and there was no intention of disregarding its manifestation.

The situation on the front left the Hungarian Government in no doubt as to the resolute intentions of our command. Horthy's fear of vengeance compelled him promptly to sound out the British and American positions on the occupation of Hungary. On September 22, 1944, unbeknownst to the Nazis, Colonel General Nadai, Horthy's agent, flew to the vicinity of Naples, where an Allied headquarters was located. This headquarters was not chosen at random. The Hungarian fascists were expecting the arrival of the Allies via the Istrian Peninsula and Austria in accordance with a plan that was well known, since Churchill's government had made no secret of it. But the trip ended in failure. The British and Americans were making extremely slow progress on their fronts, and they realized that the Red Army, which had already entered the territory of Hungary, would not stop at some halfway point. So they sent the general back where he had come from, having advised him to deal with the Russians. The plans laid by Hitler's Hungarian minions to straighten out their affairs behind the back of the Soviet Union had collapsed.

Now there was only one thing left for the Horthy clique to do: to initiate talks directly with Moscow and ask for an advantageous armistice. In late September 1944 a special delegation of the Hungarian Government headed by Gen. Gábor Farago, a former Hungarian military attaché in Moscow, set out for Moscow. Along with Farago, the delegation included the aforementioned Teleki, and Sent-Ivani, a representative of the Hungarian Ministry of Foreign Affairs. Needless to say, the delegation was sent off without the knowledge of the leaders of Nazi Germany or its military command.

The Farago group was allowed by our troops to pass safely through the lines, and reached Moscow on October 1. This fact was communicated to our allies, and their representatives soon joined in the talks.

The man in charge of taking the delegation to Moscow, arranging for their reception, and handling the preliminary talks was Col. Gen. F. F. Kuznetsov. A few days after the delegation's arrival, Kuznetsov told me that Farago was very worried about his hogs. He was breeding hogs on his estate somewhere near Debrecen. He requested that when the Soviet troops had captured this area, they not lay a hand on them. Farago was told that Soviet troops not only refrain from taking other's property but even protect it if the owner is absent. At this, he relaxed. Getting a bit ahead of the story, I note that after our troops had fought their way into the Debrecen area, there was no need to protect the hogs on Farago's estate because the Nazis had eaten every last one of them.

The Hungarian Government's maneuvers threw Hitler into a fury. Striving to hang on to Hungary at any price, the Nazis put additional armored forces and infantry into the country. All radio and land-wire communications between the Hungarian forces and the authorities were monitored, and measures were planned to counter any possible anti-Nazi actions.

Since the Horthy clique feared the Red Army's entry into the country, the measures taken by the Nazis command were not adequately countered by the government. But a considerable number of the higher-ranking and other officers in the Hungarian Army felt that the intensification of the occupation controls—which had been humiliating in the first place—was a new act of violence and harsh infringement on the sovereignty of Hungary. The deep dissatisfaction with the country's great dependence upon Nazi Germany was aggravated by bitter experiences in connection with the great losses suffered by the Hungarian troops at the front, and by the realization that an unavoidable military defeat was impending.

As a protest against the punitive measures of the German command and the humiliation of their country, many Hungarian officers surrendered to our troops, and openly expressed dissatisfaction with the position of their government. The prisoners reported that Col. Gen. Béla Miklós, commanding the Hungarian 1st Army, which had defended the Carpathians, was likewise opposed to the policy being followed by the government, and very unhappy with the Nazis' moves.

The Stavka and the General Staff considered it feasible to utilize the mood of the officers and soldiers to take Hungary out of the war. The Hungarian officers' anti-Nazi, patriotic feelings would serve as the basis for measures taken in this direction. In this connection, Stalin talked on the telephone with Petrov and L. Z. Mekhlis, and told them to think about what might be done.

Mekhlis soon reported to the Supreme Commander that it might be possible to send a collective letter—via certain officer

POWs unhappy about the occupation of Hungary—to General Miklós, the commander of the Hungarian 1st Army, urging him to take action against the Nazi occupying troops and thereby help preserve the independence of Hungary. The idea of the letter was suggested by the prisoners themselves, who were informed of Miklós's anti-Nazi views. Stalin agreed with this idea.

The prisoners promptly drew up the letter, and it was signed by forty Hungarian officers. The letter stated that Nazi Germany was undergoing a decisive military defeat, and would also undergo political collapse; that all its satellites except Hungary had not only broken with Germany but had taken up arms against the German forces. It further stated that as a result of the aggressive war unleashed by Hitler, Hungary was in the worst situation it had been in throughout its thousand-year-long history, and was now on the brink of ruin.

The officers expressed the conviction that Hungary would not perish. They noted, however, that it could be saved only by driving out the Nazi occupying troops, and that this could be done only by acting jointly with the Red Army.

> Today, when the whole world is fighting against Hitler, military action by the Hungarian Army would win independence for Hungary at a small cost in lives, and would put the Hungarian people in the ranks of the world's freedom-loving peoples. Right now [the letter emphasized] is the time to decide the question: To be, or not to be?

The prisoners had appealed to Miklós, since the 1st Army could effectively act in the interests of the entire Hungarian people and the state.

> We have reached a turning point in the history of our motherland [they wrote]. If at this critical juncture Your Excellency understands the requirements of the hour, the Hungarian 1st Army will immediately cease hostilities against the Russians, go home, and turn its weapons against the Germans. In this way it will save the motherland from otherwise inevitable catastrophe. The motherland and the nation expect this of Your Excellency and your soldiers.

Three officers—Maj. Emile Gallai, Capt. Mihai Dyulai, and 2nd Lt. Pál Neubauer—volunteered to deliver the letter to its addressee and then return. On September 20 the Stavka representative approved the plan for carrying out this measure in the sector of the 4th Ukrainian Front. At 0600 on September 24, in the battle zone of the 351st Rifle Division, the delegation, bearing an unfurled national flag, safely crossed to the advanced positions of the Hungarian 16th Infantry Division. On the evening of September 28, Captain Dyulai returned to the Soviet lines. He brought a note from all members of the delegation saying that they had arrived safe and sound, had been well received, and had delivered the letter to its addressee. Since the questions posed in the letter were very important, General Miklós could not answer them immediately: He wanted to get in touch with Budapest first. But it was indicated that an affirmative answer would be forthcoming in a few days.

It should be noted that at this point the talks with Farago in Moscow had gone rather far, although they were not easy. The Hungarians were empowered to sign an armistice agreement only if the Soviet Union agreed to "the participation of the Americans and the British in the occupation of Hungary," and to the "unhampered withdrawal of the German forces."

In reply to this, the nations of the anti-Nazi coalition declared firmly that the independence of Hungary could be guaranteed only under one condition: that Hungary break off all relations with Nazi Germany, and the Hungarian Army turn its weapons against the Nazi forces. Only then could Hungary make a worthy contribution to the anti-Nazi coalition's victory over the enemy. Also, the Horthy government must set about withdrawing Hungarian forces from Rumania, Yugoslavia, and Czechoslovakia.

Finally, all these demands were accepted by the Hungarians.

In its turn, the Hungarian Government asked that the advance of the Soviet forces on Budapest be held up, pleading the necessity of concentrating enough Hungarian forces in the vicinity of the capital to counteract any attack by the German Army. Our government agreed to comply with this request, and the General Staff issued the necessary instructions on that head.

Thus by the end of the first third of December the preliminary conditions for an armistice had been worked out by the contracting parties. The news of the favorable course of the talks was sent

249

to Budapest, and quickly became known to the Hungarian Army. But the Hungarian forces continued to resist, and no withdrawal of troops was observed. Nor did we get any word from Budapest.

Pursuant to the agreement with the Hungarians, the Soviet side sent Malinovsky, commander of the 2nd Ukrainian Front, to Szeged for talks on the Hungarian Government's compliance with the preliminary conditions for the armistice. But what was Malinovsky's surprise when he saw that the Hungarians had sent, as their delegation, a colonel and a first lieutenant who were quite unprepared to conduct any talks on matters of substance. The colonel—he was a section chief on the Hungarian General Staff, handling matters of POWs and internment—was in no position to engage in talks, and conveyed no information on the disposition of the Hungarian and German troops. But he did state that the Hungarian 1st Army had received orders to withdraw from the Debrecen region toward the region of Miskolc and farther, apparently to Budapest.

Malinovsky tried to find out why the Hungarian forces had not withdrawn from the defensive line along the Tisza River, but got no sensible reply. He had the impression that the Hungarians "want to play for time, so as to get their forces out of the trap they fell into in Transylvania." He dictated the following terms to the Hungarian Government:

> 1. Proceed immediately to withdraw the Hungarian forces from the Tisza River to Budapest, and with a part of those forces strike a blow at the German forces opposing the front in the vicinity of Szolnok;
> 2. Immediately order the Hungarian forces, after establishing contact with the Red Army, to undertake military actions against the German forces;
> 3. By 0800 on 16/10/44 deliver to Szeged full information on the disposition of the Hungarian and German forces, and in the future, provide full information on military actions in their zones.

When Stalin had received Malinovsky's report, he instructed Antonov to make a representation to the head of the Hungarian delegation on this score, and dictated the text. It stated:

The Hungarian delegate sent from Budapest to Szeged—the truce envoy, Col. Utasi Laurend—is an absolutely uninformed person and hence could not engage in talks with representatives of the Soviet command on matters of the Hungarian Government's compliance with the preliminary conditions for an armistice.

The Hungarian Government had requested the Soviet Government to hold up the advance toward Budapest so that the Hungarian Government might withdraw its forces from that sector and send them to Budapest.

The Soviet Government complied with this request from the Hungarian Government. But the latter not only failed to withdraw its forces from the Tisza River and send them to Budapest but stepped up their activity, especially in the vicinity of Szolnok.

The facts cited above indicate that the Hungarian Government has apparently chosen not to fulfill those prearmistice conditions that it pledged itself to fulfill.

Such being the case, the Supreme Command of the Soviet Forces demands of the Hungarian Government that within forty-eight hours of receipt of this representation it fulfill the prearmistice conditions that it pledged itself to fulfill, and most urgently:

1. To break off all relations with the Germans and initiate military actions against their forces;

2. To proceed to the withdrawal of Hungarian forces from Rumania, Yugoslavia, and Czechoslovakia;

3. By 0800 on October 16, via the link used earlier (i.e., via Szeged), to provide the representatives of the Soviet command with full information on the disposition of the Hungarian and German forces, and at the same time to report to the aforementioned Soviet representatives on the progress in fulfilling the prearmistice conditions.

By the authority of the Supreme Command of the Soviet Forces: General of the Army Antonov, Deputy Chief of the General Staff of the Red Army.

October 14, 1944, 1925 hours

On the following day, apparently having realized the hopelessness of further procrastination, Horthy made an appeal to the Hungarian people in which he pointed out the state's factual subordination to Nazi Germany, and the latter's direct attempts to destroy the independence of Hungary. *Inter alia,* he wrote: "I have received reliable reports that special German detachments intend to put their own people in power by means of a coup, and to convert the territory of Hungary into an arena for the rear-guard battles of the German Reich."

Horthy declared he was resolved to defend the country against the Nazis.

> In this connection [he wrote] I have informed the repre-sentative of the German Reich in Hungary that we have con-cluded a preliminary agreement for an armistice with our ene-mies, and for the cessation of hostilities on our part against them. . . . I have issued the corresponding orders to the mil-itary command. Therefore, in accordance with their oath and my orders to the Army, all military units are obliged to sub-ordinate themselves to the commander I have designated.

This order to the Armed Forces was likewise dated October 15, 1944.

We did not know Horthy's real intentions. But one thing was clear: The break with the Nazis had been organized about as badly as possible, and perhaps only for appearances' sake. The Regent had not established the necessary contacts between politi-cal and military circles. Even the military people devoted to him had not been warned, and reliable military units had not been concentrated in the capital.

Present in Budapest at the time was the powerful German 24th Armored Division, with a large number of Tiger tanks. Naturally, it was the factual master of the situation in the city. So when Hitler learned of Horthy's rebellion, steps were taken immedi-ately. An armed *Putsch* was carried out in Budapest. The Regent was removed from office, and his appeal to the people declared null and void. At that point he asked for asylum in Germany and was sent off with his family in a special train going to the Reich. Hitler's follower, the Hungarian fascist Ferenc Szálasi, was named head of the new government.

"These political measures," wrote General Friessner, "which were carried out in the rear of the army group, were the work of the chief of the police and the SS in Budapest, acting on direct in-

252

structions from the German Government, with the help of such 'specialists' as Skorzeny and Bach-Zelewski."

Instead of a decision to cease hostilities against the Soviet forces at the front, the Hungarian Army received a categorical order to resist stubbornly. Operational control of the forces was definitively taken out of the hands of the Hungarian General Staff. The headquarters of the Germany Army Group South now worked up all plans and issued all orders. Protests by those who favored calling off military actions against the USSR and its allies were put down by force of arms. The war continued, with fighting as fierce as before.

All this had its effect on Colonel General Miklós, commanding the Hungarian 1st Army. On October 16, accompanied by part of his staff, Miklós crossed over to the Soviet lines in the defensive sector of the Hungarian 16th Infantry Division, commanded by Major General Vasvari. Miklós declared to General Petrov and L. Z. Mekhlis that he was deeply worried about the future of his country, and that as a patriot he could not go along with the Nazi occupation of Hungary; that he did not want the Hungarian people to pay with their blood for Nazi interests.

In one of his talks with Petrov, Stalin had suggested that it might not be bad if Miklós ordered his army to cease hostilities against the Soviet forces and start fighting the Germans. Petrov had a talk with the Hungarian general, and the latter pondered the matter. It was not easy for him to decide to turn his weapons against the Germans. Nonetheless, he began to work on an order, and on October 17 he showed Petrov his "Order to Cease Hostilities Against the Russian Army and Initiate Actions Against the German Army." It mentioned the talks Gábor Farago had had with the governments of the USSR, Great Britain, and the United States about an armistice, "so as to put an end to this unhappy war as quickly as possible and take advantage of our last opportunity to assure a better future for the people of our country"; and it stated that the draft agreement on the armistice provided for the independence of Hungary, and that "no Power would interfere in its internal affairs." Next came the words: "The Royal Hungarian Army will keep its weapons so that it can turn them against the

German occupation troops and combat troops that are still in Hungary."

Employing his authority as commanding general, Miklós ordered his Hungarian troops immediately—no later than 0600 on October 19—to cease hostilities against the Soviet forces and, jointly with them, to begin waging war against the Nazis. Those forces on the defensive were ordered to begin on that same day, at 1000 hours, to withdraw from their positions to specified points. "All German units encountered en route must be destroyed. In this respect, the Russian Army will help us. At this moment, when the question whether to be or not to be is being decided for our beloved motherland, I personally make those who shall receive this order responsible for its execution."

Ten Hungarian officer POWs were immediately sent through the lines with Miklós's order. When they received it, the officers and soldiers of the Hungarian forces were disoriented. First they had received Horthy's address of October 15 calling upon them to cease hostilities against the Soviet forces. Then, on the very next day, they had had an ominous order from the military command of Szálasi's government telling them to resist at any price. And now came Miklós's order.

We at the General Staff patiently waited to see what effect Miklós's order would produce. But our hopes for an armistice and for Hungary's bloodless exit from the war were not justified. Szálasi threw against our positions all the forces remaining in the country, and the Nazi command helped him in every way possible. Striving to achieve greater stability of defense, the Nazi command began everywhere to incorporate Hungarian units into German forces. Certain Hungarian generals commanding divisions and armies were replaced by men more loyal to the Nazi regime. Many German officers were "attached" to Hungarian units to serve as political spies and informers. This had some effect: The enemy's defenses—especially in the sectors of the Hungarian units—remained strong.

In the last ten days of October, we at the General Staff received reliable information on the punitive measures Hitler had carried out in Hungary, the replacement of Horthy, and the order to the

Hungarian Army to resist the Soviet forces stubbornly. Military actions showed that the Hungarian units were carrying out the orders of the new government.

On October 20 Malinovsky sent in—for personal perusal by the Supreme Commander a heartfelt request that his front be provided with more tanks. He wrote:

> Apparently the enemy has correctly judged that the forces of the 2nd Ukrainian Front are advancing in a direction that is very important both operationally and strategically, and he has thrown eight panzer divisions into the battle against this front. . . . From now on, the front is faced with some very hard fighting. The enemy will not easily yield Hungary, since it is his most vulnerable spot. And under the leadership of Szálasi, the Hungarians are continuing to fight stubbornly. . . .

At the same time, he reported that the enemy had lost up to four hundred tanks in recent engagements, but that we had also lost three hundred.

All these things meant that an armistice was not to be expected.

On October 24 we reported to the Supreme Commander that Miklós's order had not produced sufficient effect on the enemy. On the evening of that same day, the following directive went out to the 2nd and 4th Ukrainian fronts and to Timoshenko:

> In view of the fact that the Hungarian forces have not ceased hostilities against our forces and are continuing to maintain a common front with the Germans, the Stavka orders that on the field of battle you act toward the Hungarian troops just as you would toward German troops. . . .

Now, after the completion of the Debrecen operation, our fronts in their forward movement ran directly up against the German and Hungarian forces defending the region of Budapest. A defeat of the enemy here would open the road to Vienna and make it possible to organize subsequent operations in Czechoslovakia and Germany itself.

At first only the forces of the 2nd and 4th Ukrainian fronts were assigned to make the drive on Budapest. But later the 3rd Ukrainian Front was also brought in. It might seem that we had more than enough forces. But the situation was such that the enemy could bring up reserves from the depths of Germany, and troops from Italy, from the Balkans, and even from the west. We expected that the grouping of German forces would grow, and that Hungary might become an arena of fierce fighting.

In the region of the Hungarian capital, the Nazi command and the Szálasi people had created very strong defensive lines which, in the form of broad half-arcs, covered Budapest from the south, with their bases on the Danube. The great city was prepared for a long siege. Here the Nazis had concentrated the main forces of Army Group Center, units of the Hungarian forces, and sizable reserves of arms, ammunition, foodstuffs, medical supplies, and other stores. All this was done in order to tie our forces down here for a long time and prevent them from crossing the Reich border toward the west.

At the General Staff we made an in-depth study of the impending actions by Soviet forces in the Budapest operation: their nature and the methods to be employed. The gist of our thinking as regards maneuvers was that we should move around the city on the north and the south, using minimal forces in frontal attacks. The operation demanded long and careful preparation—all the more so since the autumnal season of bad roads had set in, and the rain was heavy. There was virtually no air action, and artillery often had to be dragged along by hand. Any kind of transport would bog down the washed-out roads. Under these conditions it was very hard to supply the front with all it needed, and even harder to effect regrouping and turning movements.

Meantime, the enemy was striving in every way to block our maneuver and our forward movement. It was important for him to compel us to make a frontal attack—the least promising for us, and fraught with heavy losses—and to provoke us to attack on the run without the requisite preparation. Such is the logic of war, when two forces with diametrically opposed aims come into conflict.

The enemy's defenses covering Budapest from the east along the line of the Tisza River were very strong. There were well-built engineering structures of the field type in this area; fresh reserves had been brought up to this zone; and the forces we had squeezed out of Transcarpathia and Transylvania had taken up positions here. The enemy was stubbornly hanging on to terrain that was advantageous for defense and was snapping back with counterattacks. The latter were especially vicious along the juncture between the 4th and 2nd Ukrainian fronts, where General F. F. Zhmachenko's 40th Army was advancing, together with General Avramescu's Rumanian 4th Army. The engagements were hard-fought, and the results were negligible. The generals and other commanding officers had frayed nerves. Even the imperturbable Malinovsky sometimes lost his equanimity. On one occasion Gen. I. M. Managarov, likewise a very even-tempered individual, asked Malinovsky to assign him additional traction equipment because of the bad weather. The front commander replied curtly and nastily, "Get your traction equipment from the enemy!"

Our hopes that we would have time to make thorough preparations for the operation were not fulfilled.

In mid-October Churchill and Eden, accompanied by their political and military advisers, came to Moscow. They had talks with Stalin, Molotov, and Antonov. I, too, had occasion to attend some of the sessions, along with other General Staff officers and officials from the Commissariat of Foreign Affairs.

Antonov was assigned to prepare the report on the situation at the front, which as usual was drawn up in the Operations Department of the General Staff. Together with a survey of the operations on the Soviet-German front, the report contained a discussion of the difficulties involved in carrying out offensive actions, and of the Soviet command's plans for the future.

On the eve of the first day of talks, the Supreme Commander sent for the report so that he could look it over. He told Antonov, "Let Shtemenko bring it," and so I set out for Near House. It was a short trip, and our car was soon following the winding road I knew so well.

Stalin was alone. Without asking any questions, he greeted me, took the report, and went into his office. He filled his pipe, started puffing at it, and sat down at his desk quite unhurriedly. He glanced through a few pages. The text was supposed to take close to a half hour to read, allowing for the fact that from time to time Antonov would have to point things out on the map.

I sat down not far away, ready to answer questions; but Stalin proceeded to correct the report, snuffling and grunting as he did so, without asking any questions.

When he had almost reached the end, the Supreme Commander indicated a passage in the text with his red pencil, and said, "Right here, Comrade Shtemenko, we'll describe our plans a bit more forcefully than in the draft report. We'll say that we'll strive to reach the German border sooner, and for that purpose we'll first smash Hungary. Our main interest will lie here, in Hungary. As an operations officer, you should know that."

The talks with Churchill and Eden went off successfully. The agenda, previously agreed upon, was adhered to with absolute accuracy, as always. Many complex questions were settled, including that of the USSR's entering the war against Japan. Events in southeastern Europe were discussed in detail.

As he was leaving Moscow, Churchill expressed satisfaction with the results of the talks, and reacted in his own way to the insertion Stalin had made in Antonov's report as to aiming the main thrusts of the Soviet Armed Forces toward Hungary. The British Prime Minister expressed the hope that the Anglo-American forces would reach the Ljubljana Gap in Yugoslavia in the shortest possible time. Naturally, the thought that Churchill had uttered had been carefully weighed in advance. His remark could signify only an intention to break into the center of Europe through Ljubljana, going around the southern end of the Alps, and to reach Hungary and Austria before the Soviet forces did. Once again we could sniff the "Balkan variant," served up under a different sauce. Needless to say, the Supreme Commander noticed this immediately.

Very shortly thereafter our allies tested our intentions. In late October Lieutenant General Hammel, a representative of the Allied command in the Mediterranean theater, paid a visit to the General Staff. He met with Antonov and asked him to tell about our plans for future actions in the Balkans. At the same time he requested information on the AVNOJ Army's plans as regards actions to the west of Belgrade, and about its forces.

Antonov flatly refused to give Hammel any information on the Yugoslav forces. He told him, "We do not intend to move any farther in Yugoslavia. The task of fighting the Germans west of Belgrade is being handled by Marshal Tito's army, so it would be better to get the information you want from him."

As for Soviet plans, Antonov repeated what had been said during the talks with Churchill and Eden. "Our chief task is to take Hungary out of the war as quickly as possible, and our main thrusts will therefore be in that direction."

As had been the case when entering other countries, the Soviet troops moving into Hungary were faced with very complex and multifaceted political problems. It was essential to establish correct and just relations with the Hungarian populace. Here, as in Rumania, it would be necessary to draw a fine line between the laboring population of Hungary and the policy of the ruling circles who had involved the country in a criminal war on the side of Nazi Germany. Meantime the Hungarian fascists were trying to frighten the populace by spreading myths about the Soviet troops.

And so on October 27 the National Defense Committee passed a special resolution on the Soviet troop's line of behavior in Hungary. It instructed the Military Council of the 2nd Ukrainian Front to publish an appeal from the Red Army command to the population of the liberated part of the country explaining the purpose of the Soviet troops' mission of liberation and the goals of their operations on Hungarian soil. This appeal was immediately drawn up by Gen. I. Z. Susaikov, the (first) member of the Military Council, and distributed among the Hungarian populace.

The appeal stated that the Red Army had no intention of acquiring any part of the Hungarian territory or of changing the existing social order. The Soviet forces' entry into the country was due strictly to military necessity and the continued resistance by German forces and military units of Germany's ally, Hungary. The Soviet troops had only one purpose and that was to defeat the hostile German armies and destroy Nazi Germany's rule in the countries it had enslaved. Not only was citizens' private property being preserved in Hungary: Soviet military authorities were protecting it. Local organs of authority and civil self-government were continuing to function. In conclusion, the Hungarian populace was called upon to help the Red Army and thereby shorten the war.

The GKO (National Defense Committee) directive and the appeal issued by the command became the basic guideline documents for military councils, political sections, and troops during the entire period of military actions in Hungary.

The situation demanded that we move faster in unleashing an offensive in the Budapest area: We had to reach a point from which we could advantageously strike at the heart of Germany. Also, the capture of the city would have a great effect on the situation of the political forces in Hungary.

One factor which to some extent figured in our hurrying up the attack on Budapest was the jingoistic optimism of the reports that L. Z. Mekhlis sent in on the breakdown and demoralization of the Hungarian forces. He did a particularly good job of throwing the fat on the fire with his telegram of October, addressed to Stalin personally:

> The units of the Hungarian 1st Army opposing our front are in the process of a breakdown and of demoralization. Every day our troops take from 1,000 to 1,500, 2,000 or more prisoners. On October 25, 1944, the 18th Army took 2,500 prisoners, with whole units surrendering at a time. . . . Owing to the turning movements of our front's forces, many Hungarian units are quite simply scattered; and individual groups of soldiers wander through the woods, some with arms and some without, while some have put on civilian clothes. . . .

With his reports, Mekhlis managed to stimulate Stalin's imagination, and the latter asked the General Staff how we might best attack Budapest so as to take it as quickly as possible. Suspecting nothing, we replied that the best way would be to utilize the extensive bridgehead that had been seized by the left flank of the 2nd Ukrainian Front in the area between the two rivers: the Tisza and the Danube. Here it would not be necessary to force a river, and the enemy had fewer forces in this area than on other sectors.

Also, the 46th Army, which had advanced to that point, was relatively fresh. After breaking through, it could roll back the enemy's defenses beyond the Tisza on the north, and thus facilitate a direct thrust toward Budapest by Shumilov's 7th Guards Army and the Rumanian 1st Army coming from the east.

Having thought over the General Staff's idea, Stalin called Malinovsky and ordered that the 2nd Ukrainian Front should immediately capture Budapest. Even Antonov, who gave the Supreme Commander an unvarnished report on the situation, could not prove to him that the reports from Mekhlis did not correspond to the facts—especially in the area of Budapest.

I mention this episode because in the technical literature there have been frequent mentions of the fact that on October 29, 1944, the 2nd Ukrainian Front launched an offensive toward Budapest without adequate preparation or troop build-up. The first to write about this was Malinovsky, who had personally received from Stalin the order to take the Hungarian capital in the shortest possible time, "literally in a matter of days." Malinovsky asked for five days in which to set about accomplishing the mission, but the order he got was: "Mount the offensive toward Budapest tomorrow."

We confirmed this verbal order from the Supreme Commander by a Stavka directive dated October 28 at 2200 hours.

At 1400 on the next day, Gen. I. T. Shlemin's 46th Army, reinforced with the 2nd Guards Mechanized Corps, jumped off. As Marshal Timoshenko soon reported to the Stavka, strong resistance and counterattacks by the enemy prevented this army from advancing more than four to six kilometers the first day of battle. Malinovsky must be given due credit: He did everything possible so that his forces might succeed. In particular, he rapidly moved the 4th Guards Mechanized Corps, borrowed from the 3rd Ukrainian Front, up to the battle zone.

During the next four days the 46th Army's advance speeded up a bit, since Shumilov's 7th Guards Army and the Rumanian 1st Army were committed to the offensive. A lot of help was supplied to the front command and the armies by Marshal Timoshenko, the Stavka representative, and Air Marshal G. A. Vorozheikin.

They skillfully shifted a good part of the Air Force to the battle zone of the 46th Army, which was playing the leading role at the moment. The pilots attacked the enemy's battle formations and knocked out his fire points in front of the advancing forces. The aircraft with the Red Stars were used massively, and the enemy could not manage or organize a viable defense. By the evening of November 3 the 4th and 2nd Guards mechanized corps, commanded by V. I. Zhdanov and K. V. Smiridov respectively, were within ten or fifteen kilometers of Budapest on the south and southeast.

But with that, the advance of the Soviet forces came to an end. As our reconnaissance units reported, the enemy had taken advantage of the temporary halt in the operations of the 4th Ukrainian Front west of Uzhgorod and near Chop, to transfer three panzer divisions from there to the battle zone of the 46th Army. And we were soon made aware of this: Our attacks in the relatively narrow zone beyond the Tisza met with resolute resistance. They were repeated, but got nowhere. As it turned out, the enemy's defenses in this sector had been doubled, and no one could guarantee they would not be increased even more. After all, the Budapest area was not isolated from the rest of the country or the other sectors of the front, hence the enemy was able to bring up his reserves to this area.

Thus the situation became unfavorable for us. The relatively narrow attack zone of the Soviet forces made it easy for the enemy to execute successful counteractions, and the configuration of the front line enabled him under certain conditions to make counterattacks on the battle formations of the mechanized corps and the 46th Army, which were far extended toward Budapest. This threatened to frustrate our measures and augured a rough time for our troops.

At the General Staff, we were pondering. The decision to strike beyond the Tisza had been made by the Supreme Commander personally, and no one would dare to cancel it or correct it. But we had to save the situation.

The way out, as we saw it, was to expand the front considerably and increase the vigor of the offensive by Malinovsky's forces.

Whereas according to Stalin's decision the offensive was to be made chiefly by the 46th Army on the front's left flank, the General Staff's thinking called for the forces of the center also to increase pressure on the enemy and break through his defenses. Thus while we General Staff officers did not dispute the substance of the Supreme Commander's decision, we figured that it would be much more difficult for the enemy to organize a strong defense on a broad front than on a narrow one. Also, an offensive on a broad front would open up possibilities for taking Budapest not only with the forces of the front's left flank alone (the 46th Army) from the southwest, as had been planned earlier, but with forces in the center, coming from the east and northeast. Under the circumstances this pincers movement would be more effective. Also, stepping up pressure in the middle of the 2nd Ukrainian Front's zone of attack would help Petrov's armies to break through the bottleneck at Chop and improve conditions for their advance.

Malinovsky agreed with the General Staff's suggestions—they coincided with his views—and said that the front's Military Council would support us vis-à-vis the Supreme Commander.

On November 4 the General Staff reported to the Stavka on its ideas. In so doing, we cited the suggestions of the 2nd Ukrainian Front's Military Council, which had just been sent to Moscow.

Stalin did not object. He instructed us to issue a directive and to step up execution of the measures aimed at the capture of Budapest. The directive stated:

> . . . The offensive toward Budapest, on a narrow front and using only two mechanized corps and a negligible quantity of infantry, may lead to unjustified losses and expose the forces advancing in this direction to a blow on their flank from the northeast. . . .

Since the date set by the front command for launching the attack by the 53rd Army, the 27th Army, and Pliyev's and Gorshkov's mechanized cavalry formations, was no earlier than November 10, the Stavka ordered:

> You will more rapidly bring up the front's right wing (the 7th Guards Army, and the 53rd, 27th, and 40th armies) to the western bank of the Tisza River, so as to carry out the

offensive on a broad front and crush the enemy's Budapest grouping with a blow by the front's right wing from the north and northeast, combined with a blow by the front's left wing (the 46th Army, and the 2nd and 4th Guards mechanized corps) from the south.

Pliyev's Mechanized Cavalry Group was ordered—no later than November 7—to strike toward the north from the region of Szolnok, roll back the enemy's defenses on the Tisza, and bring the front's right wing to the river. Although Pliyev had no infantry, Stalin gave this mission to his group since he had no other reserves available.

Near Budapest, hard fighting broke out again. Our troops fought very heroically, but for a long time they could not achieve a decisive success. This was due not only to the enemy's strong defense but also to the fact that after the Rumanian operation certain commanders had become, so to speak, "dizzy with success."

Marshal Timoshenko, the Stavka representative, who was constantly with the troops, reported to Stalin on November 24:

> The 2nd Ukrainian Front is one of the most powerful fronts, with huge forces to crush an opposing enemy, yet recently it has not been successful.
>
> The following are the basic causes of the lack of success in these actions:
>
> 1. Having a relative superiority in numbers, the front command is trying to destroy enemy groupings in several sectors at the same time (Miskolc, Eger, Hatvan).
>
> 2. Such attempts to overcome the enemy in all sectors leads to a dispersion of forces and makes it impossible to obtain the requisite advantage. For example, the front's main grouping (the 7th Guards Army and the 27th and 53rd armies), with twenty-four rifle divisions, three mechanized and armored corps, and two cavalry corps, is positioned as follows:
>
> (a) in the direction of Miskolc, the 27th Army (with eight rifle divisions) over a sector of fifty kilometers;
>
> (b) in the direction of Eger, the 53rd Army (seven rifle divisions) over a sector of forty-five kilometers;
>
> (c) in the direction of Hatvan, the 7th Guards Army (nine rifle divisions), over a sector of fifty-five kilometers. Three mechanized and armored corps, and two cavalry corps, are operating in this same sector.

Thus the rifle units are distributed evenly among the armies and sectors. The only army to have any superiority is the 7th Guards Army, since the Pliyev group and the 2nd and 4th mechanized corps are operating in its zone. But since both the Pliyev group and the mechanized corps are battle-weary, they do not provide any particular superiority in numbers in Shumilov's sector. Moreover, in the event of breaking through an organized defense, these mobile groups act independently without the support of sufficient artillery or interaction with the infantry.

3. Commanders and their staffs have been somewhat spoiled by the successful actions in Rumania and Transylvania, and do not properly organize co-operation among types of forces.

In view of the foregoing, I consider it useful to require the following of the command of the 2nd Ukrainian Front:

(1) to revise the previously accepted plan so as to create groupings with absolute superiority over the enemy on two sectors:

(a) Hatvan-Balassagyarmat, considering this to be the main sector;

(b) Miskolc, considering it to be secondary. . . .

The Stavka agreed with the opinion of its representative, and on November 26 it ordered that the front commander create a decisive superiority over the enemy in the main sector, and concentrate here the artillery "break-through divisions" and armored units. The main direction of the front's actions led through the attack zone of the 7th Guards Army, enveloping Budapest from the north.

The Stavka ordered:

1. To assure the success of your planned offensive, concentrate no fewer than two break-through artillery divisions in the sector of Shumilov's 7th Guards Army.

2. For the attack in Shumilov's sector, commit Kravchenko's 6th Guards Tank Army. To reinforce the 46th Army from the sector of the 7th Guards Army, transfer not two but only one mechanized corps.

3. Use the Pliyev group to develop the attack immediately behind the 6th Guards Tank Army.

4. Increase the density of the battle formations of the 7th Guards Army's infantry, for which purpose you will expand to the southwest the attack zone of the 53rd Army. . . .

It was ordered that the attack be launched no later than December 2 or 3.

This time, near Budapest, the 2nd Ukrainian Front's operations would be conducted jointly with those of Tolbukhin's 3rd Ukrainian Front. In October the forces of the 3rd Ukrainian Front had completed their chief liberation tasks in Yugoslavia, and now they could be used in Hungary. In early November the General Staff felt it necessary to use this front to crush the enemy in western Hungary so that it could then advance toward Vienna along with Malinovsky's forces.

During the October holidays, several commanders, including Tolbukhin, came to Moscow. As usual, before reporting to the Stavka on the situation and on his suggestions for using the forces of his front, the commander discussed these matters with us at the General Staff. We talked about the general plan for actions by Soviet forces in the region of Budapest, about the front's regrouping in Hungary, and its subsequent tasks. Vasilevsky, Antonov, and the Operations Department of the General Staff favored using the forces of the two fronts first to encircle and then to destroy the enemy in the Budapest area. Tolbukhin firmly supported the General Staff. And the Stavka, too, agreed with us. But Tolbukhin asked us not to issue a directive to him yet, since he wanted first to check the situation on the spot.

Important news was forthcoming from the zone of Tolbukhin's front. On November 7–9 forces of the 57th Army under the command of M. N. Sharokhin had forced the Danube in the vicinity of Batina and Apatin, using whatever equipment they could get their hands on. Both bridgeheads had been expanded, and after two weeks of fighting they had linked up. In this bridgehead, to the right of the 57th Army, General I. V. Galanin's 4th Guards Army had established itself. Thus the 3rd Ukrainian Front had got a foothold beyond the Danube.

In view of this, Tolbukhin messaged us on December 10 that to take his forces into western Hungary would not be correct. He felt they should be used to encircle and crush the enemy's Budapest grouping.

In view of this situation [the marshal emphasized] I consider it advisable that the front's attack be made in a northerly direction toward Komárno, with some of the forces moving on Györ. This will make it possible, jointly with the left wing of the 2nd Ukrainian Front, to cut up the enemy grouping and, when it has been destroyed a piece at a time, to advance to the Danube Valley and then on to Vienna.

He asked that the 46th Army be included in his front. This army had forced the Danube southeast of Budapest, and the bridgehead it had seized on the western bank of the river could serve as a good jumping-off point for the front's forces in the impending operation.

Bitter fighting went on in the vicinity of Budapest throughout the first half of December. Our forces improved their jumping-off areas, and the staffs of both fronts worked on the plans for the upcoming operation intended to encircle the enemy. On December 15 the 3rd Ukrainian Front reported its operations plan to the Stavka, and the 2nd Ukrainian Front followed with its plan two days later. The plans were approved, but the 3rd Ukrainian Front was ordered not to divert forces in the direction of Vienna.

According to the plan the fronts' main forces were to encircle Budapest in turning movements, Malinovsky's forces from the north and Tolbukhin's from the southwest. They were to close the ring on the stretch of the Danube between Esztergom and Nesmai. The 30th Rifle Corps of the 7th Guards Army, the Rumanian 7th Army Corps, and the 18th Independent Guards Rifle Corps were to march directly on Budapest. It was planned to create an outer ring of encirclement to beat off attempts at raising the siege of Budapest. The offensive was to begin on December 20.

The General Staff devoted special attention to the artillery support for the impending operation. This was necessary primarily because of the enemy's well-prepared defenses, saturated with a great many pillboxes. It would be impossible to get through those defenses without massive artillery preparation. Also, the enemy had many tanks. According to our intelligence at that time, Tolbukhin's forces were opposed by five panzer divisions (three German and two Hungarian) and one mechanized division.

Malinovsky's front was also opposed by many tanks: Four panzer divisions and three motorized divisions was our estimate at the time. And here again, artillery was our basic means of dealing with tanks.

As for Budapest proper, the Supreme Commander ordered that the greatest possible density of artillery be provided in this area. There were 224 guns per kilometer of front in the break-through sector in the attack zone of the 7th Guards Army, which was attacking along the 2nd Ukrainian Front's main line of advance, and 170 per kilometer of front along the 3rd Ukrainian Front's main line of advance.

Both fronts went on the offensive on December 20, 1944.

In my first volume of memoirs I mentioned the mistake made by the Nazi command when, in beginning the summer campaign of 1944, they assumed that the Red Army would make its main thrust toward the southwest. Apparently even now, on the threshold of 1945, the Nazis had not given up that illusion—all the more so, since the Soviet troops in that sector were dug in. And so the enemy substantially increased the number of troops and tanks on the outer front of the encirclement of Budapest. Obviously he was counting on maneuvering. He did not intend to abandon the western regions of Hungary, and he figured he would extricate the troops that had been caught in the cauldron. Strong counterattacks were to be expected from the Germans. Indeed we encountered such attempts on the second day of the offensive in the battle zone of Shumilov's 7th Guards Army and of Kravchenko's tank army: in the region of Nemtse, Sakalos, and Shakhty. Here the enemy tried to cut off and destroy our units; but he himself was hit on the flank and in the rear, and was thrown back with heavy losses.

Along the 3rd Ukrainian Front's line of advance the enemy also prepared a counterattack, operating from the "Margarita Line." But his timing was wrong, and his intentions were frustrated at the very moment when he was concentrating the forces of the group that was to counterattack. This was made clear by two maps belonging to the German 2nd Panzer Division that were seized by forces of the 3rd Ukrainian Front in the region of Székesfehérvár.

They told our experienced staff a great deal. Tolbukhin reported to the General Staff at the time:

> One of them [this refers to the maps—S. Sh.] bears a legend for a large number of inhabited localities on our territory southeast of Lake Balaton. The other shows the location of the headquarters of the 3rd and 57th panzer divisions, the headquarters and units of the 3rd, 6th, and 23rd panzer divisions, and of the 130th RGK Panzer Regiment. All this shows clearly that the Germans were preparing for vigorous actions to the east of Lake Balaton.

It was later learned that the 8th Panzer Division and individual battalions of tanks were also in this area.

The General Staff shared the opinion of the front's Military Council, and we reported to the Supreme Commander. He ordered us to warn the front as to the necessity for special vigilance and constant readiness to beat off the enemy's countermeasures. And in fact the German and Szálasi forces counterattacked many times daily. The battle was very fierce: Our forces kept tearing at the enemy's defenses, with heavy losses. After six days of uninterrupted fighting the 2nd and 3rd Ukrainian fronts linked up on the Danube in the area of Esztergom, and solidly encircled Budapest. Caught in this pocket were almost 190,000 enemy officers and soldiers.

We promptly set up our outer front. As we shall see, this proved to be badly needed.

The most important events, however, were yet to come. The enemy had beaten off the thrusts by our forces driving toward Budapest. And he continued to improve his defenses in the city itself and its outskirts. As of January 1, thirteen panzer divisions, two motorized divisions, and a motorized brigade were concentrated in this area. In the enemy's own words, there had never before been such a high density of armored forces on the eastern front. These measures were taken under the direction of General Wehler, who upon Friessner's dismissal had replaced him as commander of Army Group South.

In the Budapest area, at that time, it was not just two mighty military forces that collided. The enemy had transformed the

269

beautiful capital of Hungary into a network of trenches, with no regard for the things of historical value in Budapest, rich in monuments of culture and art, with no concern for human lives. The Soviet command tried to avoid needless bloodshed, and to preserve for the Hungarian people everything that had been created by the outstanding masters of the past. On December 29 the enemy, surrounded in Budapest, received an ultimatum from the commands of the 2nd and 3rd Ukrainian fronts offering humane conditions of surrender. (For example, it contained a guarantee that the Hungarian officers and soldiers could go home immediately.) But the truce envoy of the 2nd Ukrainian Front, Capt. M. Steinmetz, was fired on and killed. Capt. I. A. Ostapenko, the truce envoy of the 3rd Ukrainian Front, met with a refusal to surrender; and as he was returning to our lines he was shot in the back. Such was the way in which these Soviet truce envoys, who were bringing salvation to many thousands of people in the besieged city, and to monuments of culture, were foully murdered.

On the night of January 2, 1945, the Nazi command launched a vigorous action against the Soviet forces on the outer front of the Budapest ring. For almost a month—until January 26—our soldiers kept beating off violent attacks by tank formations striving to liberate the forces encircled in Budapest. But in this battle—which abounded in dramatic moments—our troops held firm. Their strength, courage, and tenacity spelled the doom of the Nazi command's plan. Also, our commanders (at all levels) and staffs demonstrated great military skill at this time. They did not let the enemy achieve a victory, although at times forces of the 3rd Ukrainian Front found themselves in critical situations. This was the case, for example, on January 20, when the enemy's tanks, after breaking through to the Danube in the region of Dunapentel [Dunapataj?], split the front's forces for a moment. But the regiments of self-propelled artillery shifted to this sector eliminated the danger with crossfire from the north and south.

The crushing of the enemy encircled in Budapest was accompanied by the first signs of Hungary's rebirth. We at the General Staff knew, for example, about the actions of Hungarian partisans in various parts of the country, especially the mining regions. We did not exaggerate the military significance of those actions, but at the same time we realized their tremendous influence on the people. The existence of the partisan groups testified to the concealed anger and hatred that the people felt toward the Hitlerite regime. Naturally, the most attention was attracted by the work of the Hungarian Communist Party, which had initiated and inspired the struggle for the rebirth of national independence on a democratic basis. We knew that in the summer of 1944 a single central organ for the Resistance movement—the Hungarian Front—had been created on the initiative of the Hungarian Communists. In September of that same year the Communist Party's appeal telling of the liberating mission of the Soviet troops made its appearance among the people. The party called for a struggle, to be waged jointly with the Soviet Union, to drive out the German imperialists and crush the Hungarian reactions: a struggle for peace, and for a free, independent, and democratic Hungary. November 1944 witnessed the formation of the Committee for the National Liberation of Hungary, which began preparations for an uprising in Budapest. Under the direction of a military committee set up by the Communist Party, partisan groups in Ujpest, Kispest, and other parts of Budapest blew up shipments of matériel, killed Nazi officers and soldiers, and wrecked railroad tracks. On December 1, 1944, the Budapest Municipal Theater, where a meeting of Hungarian fascists was being held, was blown sky-high. And we knew of many instances when Hungarians, at the risk of their lives, had saved Soviet soldiers.

A big milestone in the history of this state emerging from the ruins was the convening of the Provisional National Assembly of Hungary in liberated Debrecen. This was the result of work done by the Communist Party, which was striving to unite the nation's democratic forces on a basis of its "Program for the Democratic Restoration of Hungary." The assembly met on December 21 and 22, and formed a Provisional National Government headed by Col. Gen. Béla Miklós.

The make-up of the government reflected all the contradictoriness of the situation in the country. It included representatives of the Communist Party, Social Democrats, the National Christian and Independent parties of the small landholders, and representatives of the fallen Horthy government; in particular, Gen. Gábor Farago, Count Géza Teleki, and Col. Gen. János Voros, all of whom we have already met.

The Provisional National Assembly had predetermined the next steps to be taken by Miklós's government. His first act was to break off relations with Nazi Germany and declare war on it. Then he approached the governments of the allied nations with whom Hungary was at war on the subject of an armistice.

The conclusion of an armistice as a central task of the Provisional National Government was of course tied in with Hungary's taking part in the war against Germany. The Provisional National Assembly's address to the Hungarian people, dated December 21, spoke of the future of a democratic Hungary, and of liberating the rest of the country from the German occupation.

> We must not stand idly by while the Russian Army liberates our country from the German yoke. We shall have really earned the right to freedom and independence only when we take part—with all our strength—in our own liberation. Let us rise up in a holy war against the German oppressors for the liberation of our motherland!

The Provisional National Assembly made a special appeal to the troops.

> Soldiers! For you there is no other command to be obeyed than the command of the nation. In the name of the Hungarian nation, the Provisional National Assembly orders you: Turn your weapons against the German oppressors. Help the Red Army—our liberators. Join the people's struggle for liberation. Join the new national armed forces now being created!

Thus the new Hungarian Government declared its readiness to stand shoulder to shoulder with the United Nations in the war against Nazi Germany. At first it asked for time to ascertain its potential for creating a new army. Later it undertook to form no fewer than eight divisions. The Soviet Union, the United States, and Britain agreed with this; and on January 9, 1945, Colonel General Kuznetsov met with General Voros, Minister of War in the Provisional National Government of Hungary. (Voros, former chief of the Hungarian General Staff, had come over to our side after the Szálasi *Putsch* and the coup d'état.)

The Minister of War declared to the Soviet representative that the Hungarian Government considered it necessary to take an active part in the war against Nazi Germany on the side of the United Nations. But he said right off that the creation of an army would depend upon the dates fixed for turning over to Hungary the officers and soldiers who had been taken prisoner by the Russians. Voros figured the POWs would be best utilized in the new Hungarian Army, since they had uniforms and footwear—something which, in his opinion, would greatly facilitate the organization of the forces.

He was convinced that many of the volunteers would join this army. Some of them were old reservists with military training; others were young and needed training. He said that while the National Assembly was in session they had received detailed information from representatives on the spot about how the people were ready to repay, weapon in hand, the Nazi occupying troops for all their crimes. He asked that the officers and noncoms in Russian prison camps be turned over to the Hungarian War Ministry as soon as possible so as to create a framework on which the Army could be built. This was also necessary so as to purge the officer corps of what Voros called the "Swabian" elements. He further requested that the Army be equipped with captured German arms and ammunition, since the Hungarian troops had been trained in their use. And he asked that the Soviet command undertake to supply the Hungarian Army, since it possessed the necessary resources and rear-area service organization.

Kuznetsov told Voros that the Soviet Government had already authorized the formation of one Hungarian division (instructions on this score had been sent to Malinovsky), and he affirmed that military assistance would be provided to Hungary. As to choosing the structure of the Hungarian divisions, the Soviet representative offered no advice, since that was a matter for the Hungarians themselves. "Adopt any structure you like," Kuznetsov told him. And he emphasized that the Hungarians themselves would have put the Army together, and that much depended upon how successfully the first division was formed.

"I guarantee," replied Voros, "that democratism and a new spirit will be instilled in the Army, and that the friendship and co-operation between the Russian and Hungarian forces will be strengthened in battle. After all, friendship and co-operation are born not at the dinner table but on the field of battle."

One could hardly disagree with this. So that our representative felt it necessary merely to emphasize that words must be backed up by deeds.

It must be recorded, however, that the deeds were not forthcoming. Miklós, Voros, and the other cabinet members who had formerly belonged to the Horthy clique tried in every way to frustrate the development of the new Hungary's Army. And they managed to drag out the time required to form combat-ready divisions. Only one division was sent to the front, and it did not get there in time to see action.

But along with the official trend (so to speak) in the military development of the new Hungary, which as fate would have it was under the control of former Horthy men, on the fields of battle a genuinely democratic trend was being born in the form of combat camaraderie between Soviet soldiers and Hungarian volunteers. This camaraderie was manifested during the fighting in February, when the enemy encircled in Budapest was liquidated.

The war had done its work. The rank-and-file Hungarians serving in the Nazi forces in Budapest did not want to fight for Germany; and it was only under the threat of a court-martial and physical reprisals that they continued to wage defensive battles jointly with the Germans. But the senior Hungarian officers still believed Hitler's promises that he would send reinforcement to Budapest and break through the ring that the Soviet forces had formed. The contradiction between the Hungarian officers and the rank-and-file was due for a solution—and was in fact solved—in the course of the fighting.

Within Budapest, the Soviet forces advanced step by step toward the Vara (or fortress), the central part of Buda, to where the center of the enemy's resistance had gradually shifted. On

February 8 General Pfeffer-Wildenbruch, commanding the Budapest garrison, ordered that within the next few days the Hungarian units should concentrate on the territory of the Vara, and continue to resist there. Reactions to this order varied. The officers tried to follow it, but the soldiers made their own decisions; and many of them, rather than go to the Vara, dispersed through the city.

The great majority of the soldiers wanted to surrender and thereby bring the war to an end so far as they were concerned. But some of them were firmly resolved to fight—against the Nazis this time. There were various motives for coming over to our side; but the chief ones were the anti-Nazi sentiments and the urge to get even with the Germans for their crimes vis-à-vis Hungary and the Hungarian soldiers. Many POWs told of the contempt the Nazis had for their ally, and how they deprived Hungarian soldiers of their last chunk of bread.

The number of Hungarians taken prisoner by the 2nd Ukrainian Front grew from day to day, and by this time amounted to many thousands. Since the POWs repeatedly declared they wanted to fight the Nazis, groups of Hungarian volunteers were formed within our own units, giving them a chance to prove themselves in battle. The experiment was successful: The Hungarian volunteers fought bravely and skillfully.

After this, rifle companies of Magyar volunteers were formed in various Soviet units fighting in Budapest. Units including such companies included the 83rd Marine Brigade, the 108th Guards Rifle Division, the 180th, 297th, 320th, and other rifle divisions. Later, some of these companies were combined into detachments. Thus the 320th Rifle Division had such a detachment entirely officered by Hungarians. It was commanded by First Lieutenant Vereb.

It must be said that the Russian way of handling soldiers during the period of forming subunits was to the liking of the Hungarians. The soldier was first fed, then sent for a bath. Finally, when he had been fed, bathed, and had on a new uniform, the master sergeant issued him his weapons. The Hungarian soldiers, who had been exhausted by fighting, who had had nothing to eat

275

for several days, and who merely smiled when asked when they had last had a bath, willingly accepted the Russian way of doing things and often praised it.

Because of the military situation, it was necessary to send these newly formed subunits into combat quickly. But insofar as possible, our command tried to make such an event a ceremony, employing a military band to give reinforcements (including Hungarians) a send-off when they were on their way to the front line.

On their very first days of combat, February 8 and 9, the Hungarian detachments showed that the volunteers were keeping their word. Thus the chief of the 320th Rifle Division's Political Department reported:

> During these two days, the 1st Magyar Volunteer Detachment under the command of First Lieutenant Vereb has fought well. It has carried out the missions assigned to it by the command. The company has cleared the Germans out of five districts and killed thirty enemy soldiers. It has taken fifteen soldiers prisoner, and has captured matériel. . . .

Military camaraderie was born in the ruins of Budapest, in the joint fighting against the Nazis.

The 83rd Marine Brigade, in which Hungarian volunteer companies were fighting, reported that the enemy's defenses had been breached. The eighty Hungarian soldiers captured on this occasion simply joined a company of the Hungarian Volunteer Army. During the days that followed, we continued to get new reports of successful actions by the Hungarian elements fighting alongside the Soviet troops in Budapest.

Not long before the fall of Budapest, when the enemy was making ready for his last attempt to break through the ring of encirclement, the Hungarian companies began to combine into battalions—four companies to each battalion.

On February 11, Lt. Col. Oscar Varikhazi, commanding the 6th Infantry Regiment of the Hungarian 10th Division, came over to us. He brought with him his staff and the remnant of his regiment —three hundred men. Varikhazi had been born in Budapest into the family of a noncommissioned officer in the regular Austro-Hungarian Army. His mother was a dressmaker. Varikhazi had fought in World War I, and in 1919 he was in the Red Army of Hungary. After the suppression of the Hungarian Soviet Republic, he was discharged from the Army, and was not recalled into service until sometime later.

In the course of the current war he had learned a lot, especially on the Soviet-German front. Because of his anti-Nazi sentiments he was scheduled to be court-martialed and had avoided it only because of an illness. In October 1944, as commander of the 18th Infantry Regiment of the 1st Army, he refused to take the oath to the Szálasi government and was removed from his position. During the fighting in Budapest, however, the situation grew so critical that he was given command of the remaining troops of the 6th Infantry Regiment. It was with these troops that Varikhazi came over to the Red Army. They served as the nucleus for forming that really viable unit of Hungarian volunteers known in military history as the Buda Hungarian Volunteer Regiment, which reached a strength of 2,500 men. This regiment fought well against the enemy forces encircled in Buda in the region of South Station, the Gellert Hills, and the Vara. Here the Soviet, Rumanian, and Hungarian troops came together in joint fighting against the Nazis. It was here that their military camaraderie was strengthened.

The assault on Budapest continued until February 13. That day witnessed the final crushing of the enemy, who had defended himself with such ferocity.

After the cessation of hostilities in Budapest, the Buda Regiment had five battalions totaling 2,534 men, including almost 1,200 artillerymen, about 400 riflemen, more than 100 tankmen, more than 300 signal men, plus combat engineers and other specialists.

The elimination of the enemy in Budapest would seem to have opened up favorable prospects for offensive operations in the direction of Vienna. In seizing Austria and its capital, our forces would deprive the enemy of an important military-industrial base; and they would then move on to another military-industrial region: the Prague region. In this case the enemy's potential for producing armaments would be seriously undercut. Also, the capture of the Prague industrial region would have political importance, since the Czechoslovaks were our allies.

The offensive toward Vienna was likewise very important in helping our forces driving on Berlin from the east: It would pose a threat to the enemy from the south. The Stavka and the General Staff controlled and co-ordinated the front's actions in such a way as to assure the element of surprise in our attacks, to put the enemy in a difficult position, to compel him to scatter his forces, and to use disadvantageous methods of conducting military operations.

In February 1945 the Stavka and the General Staff were giving special attention to the relationship between the western and southwestern fronts. It should be remembered that the 1st Belorussian Front, after reaching the Oder, had to stop and carry out an operation in eastern Pomerania so as to eliminate the threat from the north. Now it was essential to step up the advance toward Vienna. This was facilitated by the successful operations of the 4th Ukrainian Front in Carpathian Poland and in the Transcarpathia. Therefore, on February 17—three days after the fall of Budapest—the Stavka issued to the 2nd and 3rd Ukrainian fronts a directive on planning and carrying out the drive on Vienna. The chief role was assigned to Malinovsky's forces. The main body of those forces was to advance north of the Danube, where the enemy (according to our intelligence) had no tanks so that his defense was based largely on infantry. Our intelligence reports further told us that Tolbukhin's forces, operating farther to the south, would be opposed by seven panzer divisions. Initially, these forces were assigned a modest task: to assist their neighbor on the north, the 2nd Ukrainian Front.

Certain changes were made in the composition of the fronts by way of mutual transfers of forces. Gen. V. V. Glagolev's powerful 9th Guards Army was pulled out of the Stavka reserve and put under the command of Malinovsky (in the Szolnok region). The Bulgarian 1st Army, put under the command of Tolbukhin, was given the mission of securing the front's operation from the south, operating along the northern bank of the Danube.

D-day was March 15.

As always happens in war, the enemy tried to make things go his way: to bring about a shift in the situation that was favorable to him. In this case, he attempted to batter the Soviet forces in Hungary, throw them back across the Danube, and prevent them from reaching the southern borders of Germany.

On the day the Stavka's orders reached the forces, the German command moved large panzer forces into Malinovsky's sector. The attack was launched from the region of Komárno along the north bank of the Danube against Shumilov's 7th Guards Army, which had occupied an operational bridgehead west of the Hron River—a bridgehead very important for the offensive toward Vienna. The 7th Guards Army offered stubborn resistance for several days, but was nonetheless compelled to withdraw to the eastern bank of the Hron.

In the course of the fighting we managed to find out that one of the German units operating in the Komárno area was an armored division of the 6th SS Panzer Army. That army, which had previously been fighting in the west, was known as the best shock army the Nazis had. It was commanded by Sepp Dietrich, a favorite of Hitler's, and had three types of tanks: Panthers, Tigers, and Royal Tigers.

The appearance of the 6th Panzer Army on our front was a very serious new element in the situation. No one had expected it to show up there, since our allies had given special notice to the Stavka that it was on the western front. Obviously, this regrouping of armies in the east was associated with some important enemy plan. Such was our evaluation, at the time, of the intelligence we had from the 2nd Ukrainian Front. But for the time being we could not ascertain the Nazi command's intentions.

Using only a part of the SS 6th Panzer Army's forces, the enemy had rushed headlong against Shumilov's army. True, he had deprived us of the bridgehead across the Hron, which was a good jumping-off point for the drive to Vienna. But at the same time he had lost the element of surprise—an important factor in success. Our attention was now fixed on the panzer armada; and in the final analysis this made it possible to determine the German command's intentions. Soviet intelligence, using various means, constantly brought in new information on the enemy.

Purposeful reconnaissance gradually made it possible to ascertain that southwest of Budapest, in the region of Lake Balaton, the enemy had concentrated a very large grouping of troops and equipment, with panzers as the nucleus. As we later found out, there were thirty-one divisions here (eleven of them panzer divisions), along with certain other forces. The over-all strength was more than 43,000 officers and men. The armament included almost 900 tanks and self-propelled guns, more than 5,600 guns and mortars, and 850 aircraft. In all likelihood, the only reason for concentrating such a large grouping of forces there was a counteroffensive.

The Stavka immediately instructed the General Staff to warn the forces and keep a close eye on the enemy. But preparations for the drive on Vienna were not held up. Rather, they proceeded at full speed.

Gradually, the enemy's intentions became clear. His most likely lines of advance were laid down on the reconnaissance maps. The main one was from a jumping-off point between Lake Balaton and Lake Velencei, driving southeast to split the forces of the 3rd Ukrainian Front and reach the Danube by the shortest route (thirty kilometers). It was expected that the main forces of the 6th Panzer Army would be used here. Opposing the enemy was Gen. N. A. Gagen's 26th Army.

We also expected two secondary thrusts: one by the 2nd Panzer Army, attacking eastward from the Nagykanizsa region with the aim of crushing Gen. M. N. Sharokhin's 57th Army; and one by forces of Army Group F, moving from the southern bank of the Danube against Gen. V. Stoichev's Bulgarian 1st Army. These three lines of advance converged in the area of Szekszárd.

And now the enemy's ultimate aims began to emerge. After the loss of Budapest, the most obvious one was to hang on to the last big oil fields in Hungary and the Vienna industrial region, which was still supplying various kinds of armament, including tanks, aircraft, and ammunition. Nor was it ruled out that the Nazis would shift their center of resistance to the mountainous regions of Austria and Czechoslovakia. This territory was the easiest to defend. Moreover, if resistance proved impossible, the Germans could—in this area—surrender to the Anglo-Americans rather than to the Red Army. All the foregoing purposes could be served by positioning the 6th Panzer Army in the region of Lake Balaton.

It was plain to see that the forces of the 3rd Ukrainian Front were in for some hard fighting, and careful preparations were made for it. The Stavka ordered the creation of a defense in depth, with especially strong antitank weaponry. By the time the enemy launched his offensive the 3rd Ukrainian Front had about 400,000 officers and soldiers, 400 tanks and self-propelled guns, almost 7,000 regular guns and mortars, and about 700 aircraft. Thus while the number of troops on both sides was about the same, the enemy had a more than twofold superiority in tanks and self-propelled artillery, but had less regular artillery and aircraft[2] than we did. This enabled the Stavka to opt with confidence for a defensive operation.

Tolbukhin spent a good deal of time among the troops: He checked on the preparations for defensive battles, to be followed by an immediate transition to the offensive. He also visited the left flank of the front, where both of the enemy's secondary offensives were anticipated. On our side, a regular "International" was put together, consisting of Soviet, Bulgarian, and (south of the Drava) Yugoslav troops. In the town of Szigetvár Tolbukhin called a conference of the commanders of the Soviet 57th Army, the Bulgarian 1st Army, and the Yugoslav 3rd Army, at which cooperation during the impending operation was discussed.

On March 6 the enemy launched the counteroffensive we had been expecting. It was especially massive along the main line of advance. The fighting went on continuously for nine days and was extremely fierce. Although the German forces were very numerous, they could not break through to the Danube—even though for that purpose they at times concentrated as many as 450 tanks in one sector of the front.

[2] But cf. the figure of 850 German aircraft cited on page 280. (Translator's note.)

The defensive battle of Balaton was one more example of the Soviet soldiers' magnificent courage, unwavering stability, and heroism. In only two days' fighting—March 6 and 7—the enemy lost almost 100 tanks and self-propelled guns, and in the course of the entire battle (March 6 through 15), he lost almost 500! The mass heroism of the troops of the 3rd Ukrainian Front dissipated the enemy's last hopes of restoring the situation in the center of Europe. Our victory also helped the Anglo-American forces in Italy and helped to complete the crushing of the occupying troops in brotherly Yugoslavia.

Not for a moment did the General Staff and the Stavka lose their conviction that the enemy's counteroffensive in the Lake Balaton region would be beaten off. We had a very clear idea of how hard the fighting was on the west bank of the Danube, and what extraordinary difficulties the Soviet troops were overcoming. In the course of the battle the Stavka reinforced the 3rd Ukrainian Front with troops borrowed from its neighbor on the right. But the Supreme Command did not cancel the front's mission to go resolutely on the offensive when the defensive fighting was over. And it had fresh troops ready for that action.

It is impossible to forget those anxious March days of 1945, when the Soviet strategic leadership often weighed the enemy's chances under various possible sets of combat conditions. We projected possible conditions and the outcome of the battle, especially in the case of a fixed defense on the right bank of the Danube, where our troops had the job of hanging on to their bridgehead. All indications were that the fighting would be especially hard and bloody in this area. And we discussed still another variant: withdrawal from the right bank of the Danube to the left, abandoning the bridgehead. In this case, with the shelter offered by a water barrier, retention of the position beyond the river could be guaranteed.

But the question inevitably arose: What should we do then? After all, we had to bring the war to an end by dealing the enemy the most crushing blows and advancing farther to the west. In view of this, it became plain that defense on the right bank of the Danube was much more advantageous and promising than on the left. From the left bank, it would be immeasurably more difficult to go over to the offensive, since the enemy would be sheltered by the river. And of course we would lose time.

At the Stavka and the General Staff we weighed all the pros and cons, and decided to use the first plan: defense on the right bank of the Danube, and going over to a counteroffensive the moment the defensive battle was over.

This question involved another: that of General V. V. Glagolev's 9th Guards Army. On March 9 Tolbukhin had telephoned the Stavka for permission to use this army—which had just been attached to his front—for defensive purposes. He also asked whether it would not be a good idea to withdraw his forces—or at least his headquarters—to the left bank of the Danube so as not to lose control.

At the time, Antonov and I were in the Supreme Commander's office. Stalin listened to Tolbukhin's proposals, thought a moment, and then said in an even voice, "Comrade Tolbukhin, if you're thinking of dragging out the war for another five or six months, then of course you should withdraw your forces beyond the Danube. It will certainly be quieter there. But I doubt that that's what you're thinking of. So you should dig in on the right bank of the Danube, which is where you and your headquarters belong. I'm convinced the troops will do their difficult duty, if only they're well led."

Then he said he thought it was essential to knock out the enemy's tanks during the defensive operation. He said we should not give the enemy time to dig in at the points he had reached and organize a solid defense. "Consequently," the Supreme Commander went on, thinking aloud, "we'll have to go over to the offensive as soon as the enemy is stopped, and crush him entirely. For that, we'll need a good many fresh troops. And we have them in Glagolev's army. General Kravchenko's 6th Guards Tank Army is also in the vicinity. As of now it belongs to Malinovsky, but if necessary we can transfer it to your front. Draw your conclusions from that."

Then, after looking at Antonov, he added, "The General Staff agrees with me."

Tolbukhin said he understood the orders, and hung up.

The General Staff was instructed to confirm these orders in a directive, which we did. The directive stated:

> The commander of the 3rd Ukrainian Front is ordered to wear down the enemy's panzer grouping advancing from the region of Székesfehérvár, after which—no later than March 15 or 16—the front's right wing is to go on the offensive with the aim of smashing the enemy north of Lake Balaton and developing the thrust in the general direction of Pápa and Sopron. *The 9th Guards Army is not to be involved in the defensive engagements but is to be used to develop the counteroffensive and to crush the enemy definitively* [italics mine —S. Sh.].
>
> The commander of the 2nd Ukrainian Front is ordered to go over to a fixed defense north of the Danube, and in the zone where the front is directly adjacent to F. I. Tolbukhin's shock forces, to advance his left flank toward Győr.

Thus the Stavka had outlined in general terms the actions aimed at crushing the main enemy forces in the vicinity of Lake Balaton. The idea was that the groundwork for the Vienna operation was to be laid here. And I note that the preparations for that operation continued even during prolonged and heavy defensive battles.

As we had anticipated, the enemy's forces were completely worn down; and on March 15 he called off the offensive. Now our hour had struck. On March 16 Tolbukhin's forces, reinforced by the 6th Guards Army from the 2nd Ukrainian Front, began to advance. Thus the drive on Vienna—in the course of which very great results were achieved—was begun immediately after the defensive battles, without any operational pause.

One of those results was the complete expunging of Nazi troops from the territory of Hungary. Since then, April 4 has been observed in People's Hungary as a great national holiday. And on that spring day, as is the custom, people bring flowers to the common graves of the more than 140,000 heroes of the 2nd and 3rd Ukrainian fronts who gave their lives for the freedom and independence of Hungary.

On that day people do not think only of the military victory won on Hungarian soil. They also think of the great change in the course of Hungary's history—a history that goes back a thousand years. They recall that the heroic victories of the Red Army made it possible for Hungary's toilers to throw off the yoke of social and national oppression, to liquidate the exploitative system, and to put the nation on the broad highway of national progress—of a material and spiritual flowering.

8

THROUGH THE CARPATHIANS
INTO SLOVAKIA

The Carpathian Mountains loom ahead: How can
we get over them? The origin of the Czechoslovak
National Army. Ludvík Svoboda. The situation in
Czechoslovakia. The Beneš Plan: aiming for a military Putsch. The Stavka's decision to aid the Slovak
uprising. Konev and Petrov go into action. Through
fire to Dukla Pass. On the other side of the mountains. Heroes and enemies of the people. A breather.

In history, 1944 has gone down as a year of remarkable strategic
operations by the Red Army, which during that time won decisive
victories over fascism and thereby hastened the liberation of many
peoples of Eastern Europe. I remember that at the beginning of
the year, when almost everywhere on the front our forces were advancing, Antonov (our deputy chief of the General Staff) asked
me to come to see him. Gathering up a file case full of materials
(as usual) for briefing purposes, I hurried to his office. But I
didn't have to brief anyone: Antonov himself did the talking.

As usual, he did not waste words. He explained cursorily that
Eduard Beneš's Czechoslovak Government had reported the pos-

sibility of armed resistance on their part against the Germans in Slovakia. They needed help and were asking us for it.

This appeal for aid was legitimate: The Czechoslovak Government was an ally of the USSR, and it had a military mission in Moscow, headed by General Pika. And yet the request indicated that a radically new phenomenon was involved, because this was no doubt the first time that the Beneš government had mentioned the possibility of armed resistance against the German dictatorship in Slovakia. Up to that time we had not encountered such an idea, either in talks with Czechoslovak officials from London or in correspondence with the military mission under General Pika, who had several times got in touch with the General Staff on various matters. Previously, all the representatives of the Beneš government had invariably striven (covertly) to prevent the Czechoslovak antifascist movement from breaking out on a large scale. Beneš and the members of his Cabinet were far-seeing, experienced people who realized very well that the activization of the people's forces meant a great class danger for a bourgeois republic. In order to prevent the people's wrath from overflowing, these bourgeois politicians had tried to solve the problem of their country's liberation without a general armed uprising by the people. But in that case, what were they hoping for?

As though answering that question, Antonov said that Beneš and his Cabinet regarded the Slovak Army as the chief center of armed resistance in Slovakia, and they probably did not intend to stir up the popular masses against the Nazis. Apparently they were afraid that the people, once armed, would themselves achieve liberation. In that case the bourgeois ministers would be threatened with the loss of their leading political position, and the unenviable prospect of lagging behind the liberation struggle in their own country. Meantime, Beneš's followers figured they could reach agreement with the higher-ranking officers of the Slovak Army without any great difficulty.

But the divisions of the Slovak Army were understrength and badly armed. Plainly, they could not successfully oppose the Nazi forces. That is why the Czech Government had asked the USSR to supply equipment and troops. Antonov told me that they had asked that we deliver to Slovakia, before the uprising was to begin, 50,000 rifles plus ammunition, a Czechoslovak paratrooper brigade trained in the USSR, and two Soviet rifle divisions.

Beneš and his Cabinet had made no mention of the other Czechoslovak forces trained in the USSR, which had fought alongside us against the German invaders. By January 1944 those Czechoslovak formations had already acquired a glorious military record. The first unit to be formed was a Czechoslovak battalion, which received its baptism of fire in a hard-fought battle near Kharkov at the village of Sokolovo in March 1943. The battalion was commanded by one of the men who had helped to create it: Comrade Ludvík Svoboda, later the President of the Czechoslovak Socialist Republic. In the autumn of that same year, Svoboda was given the command of a Czechoslovak infantry brigade which had been formed on the basis of the battalion. The soldiers of that brigade distinguished themselves in the liberation of Kiev, for which the brigade was awarded the Order of Suvorov, second class. Later, there were so many Czechoslovak patriots eager to liberate their country from the fascists that one brigade couldn't hold them. Getting a bit ahead of the story, I note that on April 10, 1944, the Czechoslovak 1st Army Corps was created in the USSR (in the region of Chernovtsy). One of the brigades in that corps was commanded by Ludvík Svoboda, who had received the rank of general. These first Czechoslovak combat units and formations became a very important part of the national liberation struggle in their homeland, and formed the basis for the future Czechoslovak National Army.

But at the time, the Beneš government had its own special plan for operations in Slovakia. According to this plan, after the Slovak divisions had risen up against the Nazis, a defense line against the latter would be formed along the mountain passes in the north, where the national boundary follows the High Tatra Mountains, and where the Czechoslovak command was counting basically on the inaccessibility of the terrain. In the plans for defending the western part of Slovakia, the emphasis was likewise on advantageous natural defense lines: the Morava River, and the mountains and heights along the Váh and Hron rivers. As for the common boundary with Hungary, where the terrain was everywhere accessible to enemy invasion, the Czech generals from London planned to stop the enemy with the help of the American and British air forces: They figured that high-level bombing would prevent the enemy from invading Slovakia. But on the basis of three years' war experience, it was plain to both Antonov and myself that the enemy would stop this plan from being carried out.

And yet Antonov instructed me: "Think hard about the Czechoslovak Government's request for aid. Estimate the realistic possibilities on paper and, most important, determine the best ways of supplying such aid practically. Study the plan of action they have suggested. We are obliged to reply convincingly and frankly, even if we cannot share the hopes of our allies for the success of this plan."

There was no doubt that we would necessarily have to help our ally, Czechoslovakia, and on a considerable scale. The Soviet Government had made a basic decision on the matter; and Stalin, the Supreme Commander, had ordered that the Czechoslovaks be informed of our agreement—which was done. Now General Gryzlov and I were analyzing the Czechoslovaks' request and plan of action they had proposed. Our conclusions were not optimistic. Our calculations showed that the Czechoslovak Government was mistaken in its intention to try to keep the basic part of Slovakia by using the forces of the Slovak Army. Stopping the German forces at the border was an impossibility, not only with the aid of Anglo-American bombing but even if two of the Red Army's rifle divisions were put into Slovakia. Analysis of the actual situation showed that an incursion of a great many German forces into Slovakia along a great part of the Hungarian frontier might be expected.

Again, the problem of airlifting two Soviet divisions into Slovakia was not an easy one. We had no more than 170 transport planes available, each of which could carry only twenty troops with their equipment. Thus all the planes would have to make at least five or six trips apiece in order to put two rifle divisions and their equipment into Slovakia—without artillery or rear-area organizations. And the airlifting of any heavy equipment weighing more than two tons was ruled out entirely.

And there were other difficulties. For example, the normal functioning of that many aircraft required five air strips with enough gasoline on hand to refuel them for the return trip, plus reliable fighter cover. None of this existed in Slovakia.

Furthermore, if the first wave of the airlift was successful, the enemy, having figured out our intent, would put up strong resistance in the air. In such a case, heavy losses could not be avoided, since the distance made it impossible to provide fighter cover from our territory.

On the ground, too, a complicated situation might very well arise. If two rifle divisions were to be got into Slovakia in this way, they would have to be supplied with everything necessary for combat and survival. This meant that after the forces had been concentrated, they would have to be supplied by air—something that would require a considerable number of transport planes.

But the most important consideration was that the Czechoslovak Government seemed to be closing its eyes to the fact that the Soviet forces could not yet make a direct incursion via the Carpathians. We still had to move up to the mountains. And the way was barred by a strong enemy defense line set up on the eastern approaches to the main Carpathian range. This had to be overcome. Only then could we force the mountains through the passes and enter Slovakia. And in the Carpathians the enemy was our equal both in numbers and in matériel. Especially important lines of advance were covered by the so-called Arpad Line, jam-packed with a great many permanent fire points and all kinds of obstacles.

Thus arithmetic and logic had shown that the plan proposed by Beneš's generals was based on what they would like to do rather than on what could actually be done. Without the participation of the people, there were no hopes for success in combating the Nazis in Slovakia. Bearing in mind that we must state everything frankly to our allies, we at the General Staff proposed to Antonov that the Slovak matters be regarded only as a possibility for creating an extensive bridgehead for an active partisan struggle on the territory of Slovakia. Antonov fully agreed with this viewpoint.

But the General Staff did not rule out the possibility that for political reasons the Czechs' proposal would be accepted nonetheless, and that our army would be ordered to go to the aid of Slovakia before everything was ready for the Soviet advance through the Carpathians. The General Staff recommended that in this case we put one Czechoslovak and one Soviet airborne brigade into Slovakia, along with the rifles, ammunition, and other matériel necessary for an uprising. Moving the troops and matériel in would be difficult. It would require a good many transport planes, and heavy losses would be unavoidable. (True, there would be less need of air strips in this case.) Simultaneously with airlifting of the troops and matériel, the forces of our fronts were to launch operations where the opportunity presented itself.

As for the modus operandi against the German forces in Slovakia, the operations officers at the General Staff felt it was not advisable to have a fixed defense of the entire country—in the initial phase of the operation, at any rate. There were too few forces and resources for such a defense, especially since the enemy could utilize numerous approaches—particularly in the south—to break through it. Also, the enemy had great air superiority. Under these circumstances it would be better to use the airborne brigades mentioned earlier as a nucleus for developing a large-scale partisan movement throughout the country by means of mobilizing the people and arming them. Given those conditions, this method of fighting was better.

In late March and early April of 1944 our advance to the eastern Ukraine was completed: Kolomyya was liberated by an assault force of the 1st Ukrainian Front. In and of itself, the fact that a small peripheral town had been seized was not remarkable. But on March 29 Moscow fired a salute in honor of the victorious forces, since an important strategic result had been obtained. By advancing to this point, our armies had split the enemy's Army Group South; and now one part of it was being chased westward, while the other had been thrown back to the south within striking range of the 2nd Ukrainian Front's forces which had reached the approaches to Khotin. Immediately afterward, General Zhmachenko's 40th Army, in the right wing of the 2nd Ukrainian Front, reached the foothills of the Carpathians to the west of Botoșani. Now any interaction between the enemy's strategic groupings in the west and southwest was seriously complicated, since the broad massif of the Carpathians lay between them.

Although it proved impossible at that time to create a second Korsun-Shevchenkovski cauldron on the Dnieper, the results of the Red Army's spring offensive were spectacular: Important regions of our country were cleared of the invaders, and millions of Soviet citizens were freed from enslavement. In the course of the offensive (including the advance in the Crimea), huge enemy forces were defeated: Eighteen divisions and brigades were destroyed, while sixty-eight divisions lost half or more of their troops. Field Marshal Erich von Manstein, who was commanding the forces of Army Group South, was late in surmising our intent. And for all his efforts to get out from under our blows, he failed —especially with regard to the German 1st Panzer Army.

These successes on the southern flank of the Soviet-German front decisively altered the situation in our favor. Von Manstein had to give up the post of commander of the army group. True, the bitter pill was sugar-coated: The defeated field marshal was given an award—a sword for his Knight's Cross. While accepting it, Von Manstein heard the Führer acknowledge in a melancholy tone that the time for large-scale operations on the eastern front— the kind of operation for which Von Manstein was especially suited—had passed. "Now it is important in this area simply to hang on to positions stubbornly. The initial phase in this new method of commanding forces must be associated with a new name and a new motto."[1]

At that time our operations could not be further developed, owing chiefly to the weariness of the troops (who had been driving ahead for a long time under the very bad springtime road conditions) and to the enemy's growing resistance. The troops of the 1st Ukrainian Front took up defensive positions in mid-April, and those of the 2nd Ukrainian Front in early May; and they stayed on the defensive until autumn.

[1] Erich von Manstein, *Uteryannye pobedy* (Moscow: Voyenizdat, 1957), p. 545.

At that time the Soviet command had no intention of forcing the Carpathians directly. A head-on attack could be very costly. The mountains had to be skirted. This idea was basic in plans for future operations in the Carpathians, where we proposed to use only small forces. The 4th Ukrainian Front, commanded by Col. Gen. I. E. Petrov, was created on July 30, 1944. It consisted of two armies: Col. Gen. A. A. Grechko's 1st Guards Army and Lt. Gen. E. P. Zhuravlev's 18th Army. Later the front was also given Maj. Gen. A. I. Gastilovich's 17th Guards Rifle Corps. The front was short on both troops and munitions. The two armies comprised eighteen divisions, but the strength of each formation did not exceed 4,500 men. Available ammunition amounted to only a fifth to a third of the standard supply.

The ratio of forces favored the enemy. Intelligence reported that facing the front, in a defensive zone of almost four hundred kilometers, there were ten German infantry divisions from the 1st Panzer Army and eleven divisions from the Hungarian 1st Army. The enemy's main forces held well-fortified positions, including the Arpad Line along the watershed of the main range of the eastern Carpathians. He controlled wooded mountain passes and mountain roads. His line of defense had no apparent weaknesses.

The Stavka, however, was hoping that the defeat dealt to the German 1st Panzer Army had so weakened it that the enemy would not be able to hang on in the mountains. So it ordered the forces of the new front to continue the advance with the mission of seizing the passes in the direction Humenné, Uzhgorod, and Mukachevo, and then reaching the Hungarian Valley. But its attacks were beaten off.

By August 1944, great changes had taken place in Slovakia. The successes of the Soviet forces left no doubt that the outcome of the war would be in our favor, and this stirred up an underground struggle by the Slovak people against fascism.

The resistance movement was headed by the Slovak National Council representing a people's front for combating the Nazis and their minions within the country. The organizer of this front was the fifth illegal CC of the Communist Party of Slovakia, headed by

Comrades Karol Smidke, Gustav Husák, and Laco Novomesky. The SNC began to prepare for a popular uprising. By August 1944, this had also helped launch a partisan movement. The number of paramilitary groups grew; the strength of each group increased; and their actions became more organized. Several partisan groups developed into brigades. And the Soviet Union increased its aid. This work was handled directly by the Ukrainian staff of the partisan movement, headed by T. A. Strokach. Comrade A. Sram was permanent representative of the Communist Party of Czechoslovakia. On Soviet territory, a large group of Czechoslovak citizens were trained at special short courses to become partisan organizers. From this group came such famous partisan commanders as Comrades L. Kalina, Ya. Usak, T. Pola, A. Sahat, S. Kamčak, and others. Soviet specialists—staff workers, sappers, radio operators, etc.—were assigned to help them.

The so-called organizer groups, set up on the basis of the Soviet partisans' experience, were of great importance. The strength of the organizer groups for Slovakia was about two dozen persons each. They were under the command of Soviet officers: P. A. Velichko, E. P. Volyansky, I. I. Dibrov, K. K. Popov, A. S. Yegorov, D. B. Murzin, and others. In the last half of 1944 alone, fifty-three such groups were put into Slovakia.

These groups were air-dropped. Each formed a nucleus around which a partisan of local inhabitants was rapidly formed, and they played an important role in resisting the fascists. One such force was the M. Stefanik 1st Czechoslovak Brigade, which consisted mostly of Slovaks. Another was the Jan Zizki "For the Freedom of the Slovaks" 2nd Czechoslovak Brigade. Soviet partisan units and detachments under the command of L. E. Berenshtein, V. A. Karasev, V. A. Kvitinsky, M. I. Shukayev, and a few others were shifted to the territory of Slovakia.

It must nonetheless be admitted that the General Staff had no objective, accurate information on the situation in Slovakia. The reports we got from the partisans mostly had to do with their combat operations. There was no reliable, specific information on preparations for a mass uprising: The underground CC of the

KSČ (Czechoslovak Communist Party) was preparing the uprising in the greatest secrecy.

The information we were getting from the Czechoslovak Military Mission was distorting the situation. The London Government in Exile was still giving all its attention to the aforementioned unreliable action involving the use of the Slovak Army's weak forces. This action was beginning to resemble the prelude to a military coup.

The Czechoslovak Military Mission in Moscow was working with great vigor and persistence. Every other day—and sometimes more often—we got letters from Pika. They said a lot about the Slovak Army and its readiness for the operation, but there was not a word about the Slovak National Council or the people's resistance forces. Furthermore, the chief of mission invariably emphasized that actions by the Slovak forces against the Germans were conceivable "only under a foreign Czechoslovak command." Presumably, at the General Staff we were to conclude from this that Beneš's followers exercised undivided sway over the Army. In the name of the Ministry of National Defense, Pika asked us to propose a feasible timetable for joint actions by the Slovak divisions and Soviet forces.

All of the matters touched upon were contained in a briefing we gave at the time to the Stavka. In that briefing we reported on the Beneš government's confidence that the Slovak Army was ready to advance in order to seize passes in the Carpathians along a line from Medzilaborce to Bardejov in a zone of about forty to fifty kilometers. At the same time we noted that the liberation of Slovakia was being viewed merely as a task for the Army, without involving the broad popular masses—something that had not even been mentioned. The request for a timetable was likewise suspect: It looked like an attempt to feel out the plans of the Soviet Supreme Command. Our forces were facing a powerful enemy line of defense, which so far had allowed us to entertain no realistic hopes of a quick forcing of the Carpathians. And this was well known both to Pika and to the Czechoslovak politicians in London.

In the late summer of 1944 yet another claimant to the role of ruler of Slovakia's destinies made his appearance on the scene. This was General Chatlosh, Minister of Defense in Slovakia's profascist puppet government. Having foreseen the imminent collapse of the Third Reich, General Chatlosh decided to try to establish contact with the USSR on his own, and to propose to us that we act jointly against the Germans. He intended to set up a military dictatorship in Slovakia, and head it up himself. His idea was to send a secret personal letter to the Soviet Union via one of his aircraft, obviously figuring he would dupe the Czechoslovak politicians in London.

His intentions became known simultaneously to the underground Central Committee of the KSČ and to agents of Beneš's London Government in Exile. The Central Committee decided to make use of Chatlosh in the interests of the uprising as a figure possessing real military power. At the time, it was looking for ways to get in touch quickly with the Soviet Government and the Soviet military command so as to inform Moscow of the preparations for the uprising in Slovakia, and the state of the Slovak National Council and the KSČ. Chatlosh's airplane, ready to take off, offered just such an opportunity.

The Beneš government's agents in Slovakia were sent into a tizzy. They sent a report on Chatlosh "upstairs," to London. It was accompanied by the observation: "Chatlosh could wreck our plans."

In London, the alarm was sounded. A suitable cable was sent to the military mission in Moscow; and Pika informed Soviet military authorities of the arrival of the plane. In so doing, he suggested that the plane be given a proper reception and Chatlosh's authority utilized so that it would be easier to bring about an uprising by the Army, but that Chatlosh then be dumped. . . .

The Slovak Defense Minister's plane flew to the USSR on August 4, 1944. But the pilot, Major Lisitsky, who was to engage in talks and deliver Chatlosh's message to the Soviet command, was not the only person aboard. The Central Committee, the KSČ, and the Slovak National Council had succeeded in sending along their official delegation, consisting of Karol Smidke, secretary of the undergound CC CPS, and Lt. Col. Ferenčik, representing the Military Center of the Slovak National Council.

The approach of Chatlosh's plane was reported to Stalin, and he ordered that it be allowed to enter our airspace. It landed near Lvov. The General Staff got documents from the Slovak National Council and information from Karol Smidke that gave us a complete picture of the situation in Slovakia. We now learned that broad antifascist forces were active in that country, and that the time for a mass uprising was ripe. It became clear why the politicians in London had felt it important to effect the liberation of Slovakia without involving the Slovak resistance forces, and to foment an uprising only in the Army.

Jan Golian, chief of staff of the Slovak Land Forces, who had worked with the National Council, sent a detailed report on the military situation in Slovakia and the disposition of the Slovak forces, information on their weaponry, a note on the Arpad Line, and information on the Hungarian forces. He reported that the mood of the Slovak troops was anti-German and pro-Soviet; that the great majority of the officers, although not strongly in favor of the operations plans, would follow the orders of those leading the uprising. It was proposed that the Germanophiles be rendered harmless. He felt that at the last moment Chatlosh could be of help, so that the uprising and the advance by the Soviet forces would go smoothly, without resistance or delays.

Then Golian spelled out his plan for the Red Army's advance into Slovakia. Without going into detail, I note that the plan was unrealistic. It did not allow for the possibility of countermeasures by the Nazis. Even more important, it was drawn up as though there were no strong line of defense across the approaches to the Carpathians. It assumed that the Soviet forces would make use of the passes seized by the Slovak Army, and would be able in one night to seize a considerable part of the country. In his conclusions, Golian naïvely affirmed: "There exists the possibility of a surprise penetration by the Red Army forces into eastern Slovakia, without the slightest resistance, as far as is possible in one night, before the German and Hungarian commands find out about it." And nothing was said about an uprising of the people!

The documents we got from Slovakia had not changed the state of affairs. It was fifty or sixty kilometers to the passes in the Carpathians; and there was no way to help the Slovaks, other than by smashing the enemy in his strong lines of defense. That was the gist of the problem.

Meantime the delegates from the Slovak National Council were received at Soviet governmental and military offices; they met with officials from the Czechoslovak military mission and with representatives of the Czechoslovak Ministry of War, of whom there were quite a few in Moscow at the time.

The Beneš government repeated its earlier demands: Literally everything, from interaction between the Red Army and Slovak units to the demand that any attempt by any politician from Slovakia to hold talks in the USSR, must be approved in London.

On August 20, 1944, forces of the 2nd and 3rd Ukrainian fronts launched their crushing offensive near Iaşi and Kishinev. The successes we achieved fostered hopes that we could outflank the enemy's defense line in the Carpathians by going through Rumanian territory. We hoped that we could then come within striking range of the enemy's rear in the Carpathians, and either destroy him or force him to withdraw. Consequently, in accordance with an order of the Supreme Commander dated August 26, the forces of the 4th Ukrainian Front went on the defensive. At that same time we had also achieved a certain stabilization of the situation north of the Carpathians in the zone of the 1st Ukrainian Front, where a bridgehead had been seized on the left bank of the Vistula near Sandomierz.

In the meantime, Hitler had decided to occupy Slovakia very quickly. His occupation plan became known. On August 27 Pika reported that three SS divisions would soon start moving into Slovakia. The most probable date was August 27.

The situation had taken a turn for the very worst. The enemy was starting his invasion of Slovakia just when a popular uprising was about to take place there, and only a few days before we had ordered I. E. Petrov to go on the defensive. Moreover, his forces lacked the matériel to launch an offensive. The forces of the left wing of Konev's 1st Ukrainian Front (the 38th Army) were in about the same condition. Thus the uprising could not be effectively supported by us.

Meantime events were snowballing. On August 30, while I was making a report to Antonov in his office, he had a call from the 4th Ukrainian Front. They said they had had a request from Martynov's partisan detachment in Slovakia to indicate a course and air strip for a plane carrying three Slovak envoys who wanted to make contact with the Soviet command. No other details were communicated.

Antonov ordered that the course be indicated to them.

"Could this be the uprising?" he asked.

We called Petrov, but he told us nothing new. But we did not have to wait long. The Council of Commissars' liaison officer for foreign military personnel informed the General Staff that he had had a meeting with Pika at the latter's request. Pika had told him that on the night of August 30 the Czechoslovak Government had called upon the populace of Slovakia and the Army to rise up in arms. The uprising had already begun. The insurgents had seized four towns, including Ružomberok, and two airfields: St. Peter's and Tri Duba (near Zvolen). Pika asked that we expedite the process of airlifting the two Czechoslovak airborne brigades into Slovakia, and make air drops of arms and ammunition for the insurgents.

That night was one filled with dramatic events. In Rumania the Soviet forces were mopping up the enemy encircled near Iaşi and Kishinev. At the General Staff we were working on plans for operations in Transylvania, through which the southern end of the German defense line in the Carpathians extended. As I said earlier, successes achieved here might have a decisive effect on the stability of the enemy forces facing Konev and Petrov. But the enemy's line of defense in Transylvania was very strong, and we had not yet been able to break through it.

The following is what really alarmed us. If an uprising had been launched in Slovakia, the insurgents obviously needed prompt, effective help. But we had no information on what the German command was actually trying to do in Slovakia. Had it sent forces into that country? If so, what forces, and how many? What kind of resistance were they meeting? It was extremely important to find out these things.

At 0600 on August 31 we had a report from the 4th Ukrainian Front that three aircraft, carrying officers and soldiers of the Slovak Army, had landed. Next we received a report from Konev: Slovak aircraft carrying officers and soldiers had flown to his zone, too, and landed there. All these aircraft had taken off from the airfield at Prešov. No one yet knew why the flights had been made.

Finally we had a telephone call from Gen. F. K. Korzhenevich, chief of staff of the 4th Ukrainian Front, who had something specific to report. The Slovak officers who had arrived on the plane said that German forces were beginning to occupy Slovakia. Four enemy divisions were advancing: one from the vicinity of Košice toward the north, two from near Kraków toward the south, and one from the Brno region toward the southeast. Units of the Slovak Army, together with detachments of insurgents and partisans, were offering resistance, and were hanging on to several communications hubs.

At the General Staff we took careful account of this information. It was plain that the enemy now had a marked superiority in numbers. But could he defeat the people?

That same day the Czechoslovak military mission informed our command that Slovak divisions were holding the mountain passes through the main range of the Carpathians, and were making ready for operations aimed at a link-up with the Red Army. Their surprise attack behind the defense line of the enemy facing Konev's and Petrov's forces might be the decisive factor in a mutual success.

When he learned of this, the Supreme Commander ordered the General Staff to render assistance to the insurgents and to instruct our forces to carry out an offensive operation. "Write up a directive for Comrade Konev," he said. "His front achieved great successes at Sandomierz, and he has consolidated his position. Then, too, he has lots of experience in offensive actions. But for the time being, Petrov must wait and get the lay of the land."

Stalin himself talked on the phone with Konev and told him to report in short order his opinion on using forces of the 1st Ukrainian Front to help the Slovaks.

But the following day, September 1, brought very different news. According to the Czechoslovak military mission, the insurgents were involved in hard fighting with the advancing German forces, and the enemy had already managed to seize Prešov. (The headquarters of the Slovak forces that had taken part in the uprising was located at Prešov.) Contact with the Slovak 2nd Division had been lost, and the Slovak 1st Division had been ordered to break through from the Carpathians into central Slovakia to link up with the insurgents.

By now the situation was very alarming. It had turned out that in all likelihood the passes through the Carpathians would not be open for the Soviet forces, and that the main insurgent forces were concentrated in central Slovakia and would not be able to strike a blow behind the defense line of the enemy facing our forces.

Under these circumstances the Red Army's forces were faced with bitter fighting for each step across the Carpathian range, and even fiercer fighting in the passes. And in Slovakia itself they would have to fight no less hard to link up with the insurgent army. In a word, the path ahead was long and difficult.

In the meantime, at the 1st Ukrainian Front headquarters, Konev had had a talk with Col. V. Talsky, deputy commander of the "Army Group" of the Slovak Army. He had been on one of the planes that crossed the lines and had come, so he said, to get instructions on the actions of the Slovak forces.

Konev gave the Supreme Commander a telephonic report on the talk and reported his own ideas on the offensive operation to aid the Slovak uprising. He proposed to launch the operation in seven days, since it would take that long to bring up the necessary troops and matériel.

On the night of September 2, when Antonov and I were giving the Stavka our daily report on the situation at the front, special interest was shown in the southwestern sector and the Carpathians. The Supreme Commander went up to the table at which several members of the Politburo and the National Defense Committee were seated, and there was a brief exchange of opinions on aid to the Slovak uprising. This aid was regarded not merely as a military task but as the performance of our obligation, as an ally, toward the peoples of Czechoslovakia; as a manifestation of proletarian internationalism—of the international solidarity among toilers of all countries. I did not take down verbatim what was said by the comrades who briefly expressed their views on that occasion; but their tenor was that we should render aid as quickly as possible. At the same time it was plain that a quick success in the Carpathians was hardly possible, so that it would cost many lives to break through the enemy's line of defense. Taking all this into account, the Supreme Commander nonetheless ordered the General Staff to organize the supplying of arms and ammunition to the insurgents, and to write up a directive to the 1st Ukrainian Front to carry out an offensive operation in the Carpathians, incorporating Konev's suggestions in that directive.

That same day Gen. N. I. Chetverikov, chief of the Organization Department of the General Staff, together with the chief of the Czechoslovak military mission, considered the arms and matériel requisitions for Slovakia. As for me, I drafted a directive to the 1st Ukrainian Front and read it over the telephone to Stalin, who told Antonov to sign it. Here it is:

> In view of the activization of the partisan movement in Slovakia and the fact that certain regular units of the Slovak Army have undertaken an armed struggle against the German aggressors, the Supreme Commander orders:
> 1. You will prepare and carry out an operation along the line of demarcation between the 1st and 4th Ukrainian fronts in such a way as to strike from the region of Krosno and Sanok in the general direction of Prešov, reach the Slovak border, and link up with the Slovak forces.
> 2. Permission is granted to bring the Czechoslovak Corps into this operation, and to make use of the Slovak forces positioned northeast of Prešov—something on which agreement must be reached with them beforehand.
> 3. The responsibility for carrying out this operation is yours. If necessary, the line of demarcation between your front and the 4th Ukrainian Front can be changed.

Since the circumstances were very pressing, and since Konev

was in fact already working on his operations plan, September 3 was set as the time for him to submit his suggestions. The General Staff's position was very ticklish. The directive for the operation in the Carpathians—which on Stalin's orders had been issued only to the 1st Ukrainian Front—could put the forces in a difficult position. The farther forward they moved, the more their southern flank would be exposed; and it would require increasingly more troops and matériel—which were already in short supply. This was a direct violation of Red Army regulations as regards securing a formation's flanks in operations. No wonder that when Konev received the directive he immediately called Antonov. He said the left flank of his front would be threatened, and he expressed himself quite bluntly on the subject of our "not very quick wits." Antonov had to explain to him just how ticklish the situation was. Konev understood; and when he submitted the plan for the Carpathian operation that Stalin had called for, he added a diplomatic marginal note: "In view of the usefulness of the operation's direction for the 4th Ukrainian Front's drive toward Miskolc and Budapest, it is most essential that the 4th Ukrainian Front's right wing (i.e., at least four divisions from the Sanok area) be brought into the operation, or else that four rifle divisions be transferred to me from the 4th Ukrainian Front."

For the task of breaking through the enemy's defenses in the Carpathians, Konev had assembled a grouping of forces in the region of Krosno. The main line of advance was to be in the direction of Dukla, Tylyav, and Prešov. What we were counting on most was making a rapid break-through. It was figured that on the third day of the operation the Slovak divisions and the partisans would be brought into it to link up with our forces.

We at the General Staff promptly informed the Stavka of the proposals of the 1st Ukrainian Front's Military Council. Stalin approved the operations plan and ordered Antonov to instruct the forces of the 4th Ukrainian Front to go over to the offensive as well.

At 2230 of that same day, Petrov had already sent the Stavka his proposal. The right-flank formations he would provide for the operation were 107th Rifle Corps and Gen. A. A. Grechko's 1st

Guards Army, reinforced with the requisite special forces and artillery.

Time was pressing, and only a few days were allowed to make preparations for the operation. And the mission was very difficult. The nature of the terrain enabled the enemy to oppose each step of the attacking forces with relatively small forces of his own, especially since there were but few roads on the approaches to the defense line. Under those conditions, maneuvering—the basis of mountain warfare—was very restricted, and in some cases ruled out entirely. The situation was further complicated by the lack of special equipment and the fact that our troops lacked experience in mountain warfare.

Preparations were made in minimal time. Of necessity, the operation took the form of a frontal, head-on assault, which (as mentioned earlier) threatened under the circumstances to turn into a process of gnawing through the enemy's position at a tremendous cost in lives. Yet if we managed to keep a step ahead of the enemy, to achieve surprise, and to retain freedom of maneuver, a frontal attack might be the fastest way to achieve our goal.

Both the General Staff and the Stavka were thinking hard about how to diminish the unfavorable effects of the attack's being a frontal one; how to use the forces in other sectors to help our forces in the Carpathians to succeed. Countless times during those few days, the Operations Department worked up different plans for organizing such interaction. I remind the reader that in the north, such aid was ruled out: The main forces of Konev's front were involved in hard fighting for the Sandomierz bridgehead. For that matter, his front had already done more than could easily be believed. But aid could be furnished from the south—from Rumania. And so on September 5 the Stavka, after consulting with Zhukov and Malinovsky, diverted the main forces of the 2nd Ukrainian Front in the direction of Debrecen so as to threaten the enemy forces in the Carpathians and cut them off from the rest of Hungary and from Germany. This was intended to help the 4th Ukrainian Front to overcome the enemy's defenses in the mountains.

Such was the scheme for interaction between the 2nd Ukrainian

Front and the operations of the 38th Army (from the 1st
Ukrainian Front) and Petrov's forces. Naturally, this substantially
improved our chances for a successful offensive across the Carpathians in order to aid the insurgent Slovaks.

General K. S. Moskalenko, commanding the 38th Army,
planned to break through the German defenses with a frontal assault from the region north and northwest of Krosno in the direction of Dukla and Prešov. It was proposed to develop the success
with mobile forces, to take Dukla Pass, and to link up with the insurgents on the territory of Slovakia. The 38th Army (the 52nd,
67th, and 101st rifle corps) had been reinforced by Lt. Gen. V. K.
Baranov's 1st Guards Cavalry Corps and Maj. Gen. F. T. Anikushkin's 25th Tank Corps. It also included the Czechoslovak 1st
Army Corps under the command of Gen. Ya. Kratokhvil. (That
corps's first brigade was commanded by Ludvík Svoboda.) As
Konev had emphasized, the main thing was to secure the element
of surprise and great rapidity of action.

The plan for a break-through in depth by means of a frontal assault was based primarily on the operations of Grechko's 1st
Guards Army of the 4th Ukrainian Front. Its main line of advance ran close to that of the 1st Ukrainian Front's main forces
(on their left) in the 38th Army's zone, and passed through
Bukovsko and Komanch.

The 38th Army jumped off on September 8, and the 1st Guards
Army on September 9. Although the showers, the washed-out
roads, and the poor visibility all took their toll, the Soviet forces
moved ahead and dealt the enemy a hard blow on the approaches
to the main range of the Carpathians. But the enemy acted with
skill and decision. He had managed to spot our preparations, and
was anticipating active operations. During the first days of the
offensive he regrouped forces in the sector of our *Schwerpunkt,*
having bolstered his forces with a great many tanks and field
pieces which tried to block off, with fire and counterblows, the
possible routes along which the Soviet forces could advance.

From the very outset of the offensive, we at the General Staff
waited tensely for information from beyond the Carpathians. The
situation was not clear to us. Where were the two Slovak divi-

sions, and what were they doing? If the Czechoslovak military mission were to be believed, they were both fighting successfully. And this, by the way, explains the fronts' being authorized by Stalin (in the Stavka directive) to use the Slovak forces.

But we soon received information that both of the Slovak divisions, instead of fighting, had already been disarmed by the enemy. This had happened as a result of out-and-out treason committed by General Malar, the commander of the Slovak Corps. He had divulged to the enemy the plans for seizing the passes in the Carpathians, and then had abandoned his troops and gone over to the Germans. The troops he had left behind had laid down their arms without having put up any noticeable resistance. Only a few units went over to partisan methods of fighting.

As a result the Nazis were able to bring up large forces on all sectors of importance, to secure the passes and gain full freedom of maneuver in depth. The farther we advanced toward the passes, the stronger the enemy's resistance, so that the 38th Army's and the 1st Guards Army's rate of advance was slowed.

Such was the collapse of the hopes that the Czechoslovak Government in Exile had placed in the Slovak Army. We didn't come out of it any better than they, since for the Soviet forces the operating conditions had become even more difficult and complex. And yet our mission had not changed: The people had risen up, and they must be given assistance. All the thinking of the General Staff, the Stavka, and the military councils was directed toward that end.

In the course of the fighting, the command of the 1st Ukrainian Front and the 38th Army tried to make a break-through by committing the 25th Armored Corps, the 1st Guards Cavalry Corps, and the Czechoslovak 1st Army Corps. But in the mountains, neither the cavalry nor the tanks could get ahead of the infantry. They went abreast of the latter, forming a long column on a single road. They were not able to maneuver at all. Also, they were very extended and were under heavy flanking fire from the enemy. Under such complex conditions, none of the commanders could rapidly develop the attack.

Yet the bitter fighting on September 10 and 11 gave us some

306

hope: Our forces not only got through the enemy's first line of defense but, in one sector, they partially broke through the second line. The break-through was made in a narrow sector no more than one or two kilometers wide. The command of the 1st Ukrainian Front and of the 38th Army decided to take advantage of this chink in the enemy's armor so as to prevent the operation from becoming a slow process of gnawing through the enemy's defense positions. General Baranov's cavalry was sent into the breach.

It took great courage to make such a decision at such a time. Both the commander of the front and the commander of the 38th Army were faced with the necessity of finding and taking at least one chance to break through and help the insurgent Slovaks. And the cavalry troops had to go into a corridor of fire. Owing to the lack of time and the difficulties involved in regrouping the artillery and mortars along the narrow mountain paths, artillery support would be inadequate to neutralize the enemy's fire weapons on the flanks of the corridor: A considerable part of them would no doubt continue to function with great effectiveness. Nor could we hope that our aircraft would be able to silence the enemy's fire weapons: We had too few aircraft, and their targets were well concealed in the accidents of the terrain. So that instead of delivering continuous mass blows, our aircraft would have to act in small groups; and this would not provide any real, immediate support. Moreover, there was a shortage of fuel. But there was no alternative.

At that point—as always at difficult, critical moments—the Communists moved into the front rank of the warriors. The others looked at them and "dressed right." The political workers of the front and the Army—Generals K. V. Krainyukov, A. A. Epishev, S. S. Shatilov, and many others—were with the troops day and night: inspiring them, helping them, and assigning party personnel. For us this well-organized political work was a mighty force which ensured that the Soviet soldiers' morale would be at a high pitch for the attack. In those days of hot fighting in the autumn of 1944, Maj. Gen. Leonid I. Brezhnev—chief of the political section of the 18th Army, then advancing in the Carpathians—wrote in one of his reports from the front: "The Carpathian operation was a real test for all the army's personnel, from soldiers to generals. They passed that test successfully."

In order to diminish the effectiveness of the enemy's fire, General Baranov's corps advanced at night. The darkness was our ally: It prevented the enemy from using aimed fire, and this gave hopes for success. But at the same time it sharply reduced our accuracy of orientation and the cavalry's rate of movement. Yet in twenty-four hours the corps managed to advance twenty kilometers. The guards cavalrymen did not stop: They next covered another twenty kilometers, and their scouting parties reached Slovak territory.

But the enemy was raging, and fierce fighting was going on along the sides of the corridor. On September 14 the enemy succeeded in closing the corridor and cutting the corps off from the main forces of the 38th Army. All attempts to re-establish contact with the corps were failures. Meantime, the cavalrymen had exhausted their small reserves of ammunition, provisions, and forage. The horses were worn out, and the corps lost its mobility—something the enemy quickly took advantage of. He began to block the mountain passes and roads, and gradually enveloped our units with his forces. The General Staff had to organize air drops to the cavalry.

For me, personally, the days of the 1st Cavalry Corps' battle behind the enemy lines were especially anxious ones. I knew many of the cavalry officers very well and realized what it meant for a cavalry unit to be fighting in the mountains while surrounded. The battle went on under these difficult conditions day and night. Here and there it developed into hand-to-hand fighting.

In a week of fighting the soldiers of K. S. Moskalenko's army had broken through the enemy's defenses over a sector of twenty-two kilometers, and had penetrated an equal distance in depth. These actions prompted the enemy to send in sizable forces. Our front commander reinforced the 38th Army, putting in first P. P. Poluboyarov's 1st Guards Armored Corps, then General V. E. Grigoryev's 31st Armored Corps. True, they were considerably understrength. Thus Poluboyarov's corps had only fifty-nine tanks and nine self-propelled guns. But at the same time, this was a considerable boost for the advancing 38th Army.

Poluboyarov's tankers were put in along the army's left flank, almost on the boundary line with the 4th Ukrainian Front. In the opinion of the front and army commands, this was the weakest spot in the enemy's defenses. Also, on this flank there was some possibility of maneuvering along the wing of the enemy's basic grouping. The tankers drove ahead resolutely, their actions well co-ordinated with those of the forces moving down from the north along the main line of advance. After two days of heavy fighting the 4th Guards Armored Corps broke through to the hamlet of Dukla. At the same time, the main forces of the army, including the Czechoslovak 1st Army Corps, were approaching Dukla from the other direction. The Czechoslovak soldiers became our adopted "brothers-in-combat." In the very first engagements in the Carpathians, they showed themselves to be loyal, steadfast comrades-in-arms. The conditions during this offensive were just as hard for the Czechoslovak 1st Army Corps as for our own soldiers.

Before continuing my account of the break-through across the Carpathians, I shall take the liberty of making a brief disgression —one which, however, is related to the above-mentioned events.

In the autumn of 1971 I chanced to spend my vacation in Karlovy Vary. I stayed at the Bristol, where I met up with Marshal Ivan Stepanovich Konev, who had also come to the spa to improve his health. As it happened, both of us were invited by Ludvík Svoboda, then President of the Czechoslovak Socialist Republic, to have lunch with him at the old hunting lodge of Lana near Prague. (This lodge has long been used by presidents of Czechoslovakia as a place to relax and entertain friends.)

We set out in plenty of time, and soon noticed that at the rate we were going, we would get there a bit early. As a punctual man, Konev had given the estimated time of his arrival with military precision. So when we drew near to Lana, he slowed down our car, then stopped altogether in the shade of the trees along the road.

When we pulled up at the gates at 1200, we met squarely up

with the President's car. It turned out that he, being an equally punctual man, had done the same thing enroute that we had done.

After warm greetings and a few jokes about military habits, Konev got into Svoboda's limousine, and we went on.

The woods were filled with silence and the fragrance of fading flowers and grass. Our host suggested we visit a part of the forest where a herd of reindeer wandered freely among the ancient oaks. After some roving through the woods, we came to the hunting lodge. It was almost one o'clock, which is lunchtime according to the Czech custom. The President invited us to the table.

When comrades-in-arms meet up with one another, regardless of what their rank is, the talk is always free and unconstrained. There is always something to recall, something to mention with approval, or something to keep silent about—which is sometimes more eloquent and effective than words. Such was the case this time, too.

The President turned to Marshal Konev. "Do you remember, Ivan Stepanovich, how you got angry at me when I was already a corps commander?"

"How could I fail to remember? That was not the kind of occasion a man forgets. The going was very hard for the Czechoslovak soldiers right then. They were advancing toward Dukla. The enemy had brought all the roads under his fire, and tank attacks were frequent. But there was almost no command control of the corps. General Kratokhvil, the corps commander, was twenty-five kilometers behind the front lines. What kind of command control is that?"

I pricked up my ears. The conversation at the table, as though by prearranged plan, was perfect for the book of reminiscences I was just then finishing, at Karlovy Vary. Of course I had already learned a lot from documents and from Konev's reports to the Stavka. But documents are one thing and accounts by eye witnesses—especially such eye witnesses as these two—are something else.

The general Konev had been talking about—General Kratokhvil—had been appointed commander of the Czechoslovak 1st Army Corps on the insistence of the Beneš government. But he had not coped with the tasks assigned to him. While the soldiers and officers of his corps were in the Carpathians storming the defenses of a powerful, stubborn enemy with great losses, he was sitting safely behind the lines ingesting excessive amounts of the English whiskey he had brought with him. Konev therefore removed him from command of the corps, replacing him with General Svoboda, and then reported what he had done to Stalin. The Supreme Commander approved the decision taken by the front's commander. But with regard to the cashiering of Kratokhvil, he said that in this case we were dealing with an officer commanding the forces of a nation which, although our ally, was nonetheless a different nation, so that the removal of Kratokhvil and the appointment of Svoboda would have to be formalized juridically. This was soon done, after talks with the Czechoslovak Government.

As a result of Marshal Konev's action, there was a substantial improvement in the condition of the Czechoslovak Army Corps. General S. S. Shatilov wrote as follows to A. S. Shcherbakov of the Main Political Directorate: "After the removal of Kratokhvil and the appointment of General Svoboda, things have improved considerably. Svoboda has tightened discipline and standards. There is now more order in the corps."

At that moment the Czechoslovak soldiers were fighting shoulder to shoulder with the Soviet soldiers as they advanced toward the border of Slovakia. On September 20, 1944, the corps, acting jointly with Poluboyarov's and Anikushkin's tank corps, took the aforementioned hamlet of Dukla. A few days later the corps, still fighting, crossed the Czechoslovak border. It was a glorious victory for the Czechoslovak patriots. But then why did Konev get angry at Ludvík Svoboda after the latter had become corps commander? Here is what the former President of Czechoslovakia, now gray with age, had to say in reminiscence.

"At the time," Svoboda said, "I had to see the battle zone with my own eyes. I don't understand how you can command forces without having an idea of the terrain along the line of advance. So I went directly through the forward units to the attacking forces. And there I saw that it was essential to inspire the troops—to set a personal example in combat. And it was just then, Ivan Stepanovich, that you called me to the field telephone."

"As for me," Konev said with a smile, "I had to know exactly what the situation was in Dukla Pass. Moscow had demanded it. I tried to find you, but I was told the commander was in the forward positions. 'Exactly where?' I asked. Finally they found you. I was in a fit of temper, so I said, '*Gospodin* General, I forbid you to be a rifleman. We need a corps commander, not a soldier.'"

To which our hospitable host replied, "And I took offense at your '*Gospodin* General,' and asked why not 'Comrade General'?"

"Yes, I remember that. But then I cooled down a bit and answered: 'Remember, Comrade Svoboda, that you are valuable to us, and you mustn't risk your life like that. Besides, a corps commander shouldn't do that.' And that was the end of it."

A good many other interesting things were recalled that day, as the President played host to us. But from all that was said, I singled out that episode near Dukla that neither Svoboda nor Konev had forgotten. In my view, that incident does not merely show the personal courage of the man who was then commander of the Czechoslovak Corps: It also shows how difficult and nerve-wracking things were for all those taking part in the Soviet offensive and the storming of the Carpathians—from privates to generals. Because Svoboda's going up to the forward positions was not bravado. The same thing was done by many senior officers, who were bending every effort to see that our very difficult breakthrough across the mountains into Slovakia was crowned with success.

At 0600 on October 6, 1944, General Svoboda's forces, together with the 67th Rifle Corps of the Red Army (this corps was commanded by Gen. I. S. Smygo), took Dukla Pass by storm. Here the Czechoslovak soldier crossed the boundary into his native land, and began its liberation.

In honor of these glorious events, October 6 is now celebrated as Czechoslovak People's Army Day. One of the chief slogans in the political life of contemporary Czechoslovakia—"With the Soviet Union Forever!"—was born on the shell-scarred way up to Dukla Pass.

Today I sometimes have occasion, in the course of my official duties, to meet with Comrade Svoboda in Prague. Each meeting brings me joy and renews our strong friendship. And each time my memory goes back to those days when that friendship was born and matured on the fields of those battles in which the first Czechoslovak military unit took part. That unit was an infantry battalion formed on the territory of the USSR through the efforts of its commander, Lt. Col. Ludvík Svoboda, Staff Capt. Yaroslav Prokhazka, a Communist and political worker, Sr. Lt. Otakar Rytirzh, Sr. Lt. Otakar Yaros, and other Czechoslovak patriots.

In those wartime days the Soviet leaders showed great concern for our Czechoslovak friends in deciding how to make use of the young and still inexperienced Czechoslovak military unit. Everyone wanted it to emerge intact from the hard fighting—to win the banner of freedom and bring it with honor to the motherland. To the best of my knowledge, the Supreme Commander ascribed great political importance to that battalion. During discussions at the Stavka on the situation at the front, he expressed himself on this score more than once. He was inclined not to throw the Czechoslovak battalion into battle against experienced and well-equipped German forces, on the assumption that in that case it would inevitably suffer heavy losses.

The question was settled during a talk between the Supreme Commander and Ludvík Svoboda, commanding officer of the battalion. Stalin frankly explained to the lieutenant colonel his viewpoint and all his apprehensions. The battalion commander replied no less frankly and sincerely. He said that the Nazi aggressors were the chief enemy of his country, and that therefore he and his comrades-in-arms felt they must fight their hardest against them. They regarded it as their duty to their country. As a result of this talk, the Czechoslovak unit was soon sent to the front.

After the battles in the Ukraine, the storming of the Carpathians and the taking of Dukla Pass were the victories the Czechoslovaks had longest looked forward to. But paradoxically, the battle of Dukla had unpleasant consequences for Svoboda.

Right at that time, President Beneš sharply criticized the commander of the Czechoslovak Corps for its heavy losses. This criticism was in the nature of a direct accusation, although by virtue of his position Beneš must have been adequately informed as to the extremely difficult conditions facing the corps, and all the Soviet forces, during that offensive. Svoboda countered these offensive and unjust charges by the head of state, and proved that he was in the wrong.

But the then Minister of War, Ingr, and several other Czechoslovak officials and military officers (including the recently cashiered General Kratokhvil) became involved in the business. From London, General Pika at the Czechoslovak military mission got instructions to disband the corps, since (it was claimed) there was no possibility of beefing it up. Svoboda received a similar cable. Rather than building up the corps, Ingr proposed disbanding it and using its units to form three or four infantry battalions, making them into an individual brigade. Both the artillery regiment and the tank brigade were to be disbanded. In a word, the nucleus of the formation would be destroyed. Ingr did not ask Svoboda's opinion: He ordered and demanded.

The Soviet Supreme Command was duly informed of all this. But in this instance the policy of the government in exile was not supported. The Supreme Command of the Soviet Armed Forces got in touch with the commander of the 1st Ukrainian Front and asked his opinion as to building up the corps with more troops and more matériel. The Military Council replied that the corps had an adequate basis for expansion and further growth. Our units had already reached Slovak territory, where there were many volunteers. In the near future, with the liberation of the region beyond the Carpathians, where there were many Slovak inhabitants, that base would expand even more. The Military Council categorically opposed disbanding the corps.

The Stavka agreed with the proposal by the Military Council of the 1st Ukrainian Front that the Czechoslovak Corps be retained and expanded by means of recruiting volunteers, while acquiring the arms and other matériel it needed from Soviet reserves. This was done.

With the authorization of the Soviet Government, Svoboda sent a small group of his people into the Transcarpathian Ukraine (which had been liberated in late October) to recruit reinforcements for the corps. The group worked very vigorously, and along with doing its main job, helped to organize people's committees.

Thus was the Czechoslovak 1st Army Corps preserved. It was a glorious military formation consisting of patriots, and it served as the basis for creating the Armed Forces of socialist Czechoslovakia.

Colonel General Grechko's 1st Guards Army (from the 4th Ukrainian Front) advanced on the left flank of the 38th Army. Here, too, the rate of advance was affected by the same difficulties in the operational situation: the mountainous terrain and the stubborn resistance of the enemy, who had built strong defenses. The German command was using the same tactic as against Moskalenko: It had brought up reinforcements and concentrated troops mostly near the mountain roads and passes. But it could not stop our army's advance. Grechko took energetic measures. He himself was constantly to be found at the most critical sectors; he made all his unit commanders bring their command posts near to their forces; and things moved ahead.

After five days of vigorous actions, the enemy's defenses had been broken through over a sector of thirty kilometers and to a depth of ten to twelve kilometers. The most important thing, however, was not this result but the fact that the 1st Guards Army had become the key which might open up the way beyond the Carpathians. The enemy had expended his last efforts, and the time was near when his defenses would collapse. The pulse of the operation showed that this was most likely to happen in the battle zone of Grechko's forces. It was vital to take advantage of this most recent development.

Both the enemy and Petrov (commanding the 4th Ukrainian Front) grasped the essentials of the situation; but of course each reacted in his own way to the development of the situation. The German command had to take some of its forces from other sec-

315

tors of its defense line facing the 4th Ukrainian Front and hurriedly put them into the battle zone of the 1st Guards Army. This was noticed by Petrov, who then put in the 18th Army and the 17th Guards Rifle Corps. Now the front was using all its forces in its advance.

We at the General Staff carefully analyzed each decision made by the front commanders. This decision made by the commander of the 4th Ukrainian Front was no exception. We noted that Petrov, in trying to skirt the crests of the mountains, was diverting his forces from the line of advance toward Komanch that the Stavka had fixed. This fouled up interaction with the 38th Army, which was moving ahead under difficult conditions. It was not separation that the situation required but close mutual contact and mutual aid among those forces taking part in the operation.

On the basis of the General Staff's report, the Supreme Command called Petrov's attention to the necessity of adjusting his decision, and ordered that the front's main line of advance be toward Komanch, Humenné, and Michalovce.

The Supreme Commander, who was trying in all ways to speed up the advance of our forces in the Carpathians, ordered his deputy, Marshal Zhukov (who at the time was with Rokossovsky and his 1st Belorussian Front) to go and see Konev and Petrov, to look into the situation personally, and to find out if our offensive couldn't be speeded up. He authorized Zhukov to issue orders in his name, if necessary.

On September 19 Zhukov flew to the headquarters of the 1st Ukrainian Front, and satisfied himself that the very trying situation there coincided with the information Konev had reported to the Stavka. He saw how great the enemy's forces were and how hard it was—with our limited means—to break through the enemy's defenses in the mountains. He reported: "Maskalenko has only a few rifle divisions, and those in action are exhausted and understrength."

The next day Zhukov visited Petrov's 4th Ukrainian Front. He looked into the situation thoroughly, and reported to Stalin: "After having checked on the grouping of Petrov's forces and the resources of his armies, I consider that the forces and resources are being correctly utilized. Personally, Petrov understands the structure of the operation correctly, and he knows his own job quite well." At the same time, Zhukov noted certain oversights in the conduct of military operations. And in the name of the Supreme Commander he ordered that the 3rd Alpine Rifle Corps and the 11th Rifle Corps be committed immediately in General Grechko's sector, and that four divisions of the 18th Army go on the offensive immediately, in close interaction with the 1st Guards Army. In this case, the quantity of forces advancing along the right flank of the 4th Ukrainian Front would be such as to ensure speeding up the break-through to Prešov and Komanch. Similar measures for stepping up the action were proposed for the left flank, where Petrov's forces were operating jointly with the 2nd Ukrainian Front.

In conclusion Zhukov reported to the Stavka: "Petrov is working closely with Mekhlis,[2] and has no complaints to make about him."[3] This postscript by the marshal testified to the great integrity and patience of Ivan Efimovich Petrov, who had figured Mekhlis out, had understood his special character traits (if one may so express it), and had managed to co-operate with him, as was required by duty and the conscience of a Communist.

Zhukov's visit to the scene of action was an important factor in stepping up the Soviet forces' offensive in the Carpathians. The results were not long in appearing. On September 20 the 1st Guards Army crossed the Czechoslovak border; and on September 25 the 38th Army (of the 1st Ukrainian Front), after throwing the enemy back to the main range of the Carpathians, started fighting for the passes. Considerable successes were also achieved on other sectors of the 4th Ukrainian Front, where Gen. E. P. Zhuravlev's 18th Army and Gen. A. I. Gastilovich's 17th Guards Rifle Corps were operating. Zhuravlev's army drove toward Uzhgorod, while Gastilovich's corps moved on Mukachevo, and these two important administrative hubs of the Transcarpathia were soon cap-

[2] The front's commissar. (Translator's note.)
[3] Stalin had not forgotten that Mekhlis had previously told him a good many unfavorable things about Petrov, and he had instructed Zhukov to see how Petrov and Mekhlis were getting along at this time—S. Sh.

tured. Now the main mountain range was behind us! But it was still a long way to the area of the Slovak antifascist uprising. . . .

The fighting in the Carpathians continued, day and night, throughout the month of October 1944. While the Soviet forces and Svoboda's corps were breaking through the German defenses, the Soviet command devoted no less attention to supplying the insurgent Slovaks with weapons, ammunition, equipment, and medical supplies. When the weather was good, aircraft made drops of weapons every night. In 1944 we sent the insurgents a total of more than 10,000 rifles, machine carbines, carbines, and pistols, about 1,000 machine guns, hundreds of antitank weapons, and several million rounds of ammunition.

Among the units and individuals airlifted to Czechoslovakia to help the insurgents were the Czechoslovak Independent Airborne Brigade, the Czechoslovak 1st Fighter Regiment (both of these units having been formed in the USSR), and many instructors and partisan commanders. For the most part, the airborne brigade was made up of Slovaks who had come over to our side in the autumn of 1943 in the region of Melitopol. It included almost 3,000 men. Some of them had taken part in the battles near Kiev and Belaya Tserkov, and a number had been decorated for valor. On April 23, 1944, after basic combat training, the brigade was given its colors, and the troops swore the oath. Now the brigade had to perform difficult tasks behind the lines of the enemy against which it had fought with honor. The fighter pilots of the Czechoslovak 1st Fighter Regiment had also given a good account of themselves.

The uprising of the Slovak people continued until late in the autumn of 1944. It was the most important political and military event in the history of the Czechoslovak national liberation struggle, and holds an honorable place in the history of the European resistance movement. At the most trying moments the insurgents —especially the Communists—courageously looked danger in the eye and went on fighting hard. They knew that the Red Army was hurrying to relieve them, so they held out to the last.

But the days of the uprising were already numbered. Valuable time had been irretrievably lost because of the fascists' crushing of the Slovak Army. The Beneš government had once again demonstrated its infirmity—something for which the heroic insurgents had to pay in their own blood. The SS divisions squeezed the insurgents in a ring of iron and dealt out harsh reprisals to the antifascists. And thousands of Soviet soldiers who had hurried to help Slovakia and had stormed the Carpathians perished in bitter fighting. It was another six months before the Soviet troops and their comrades-in-arms of the Czechoslovak Corps wound up their victorious liberation campaign in a Prague that greeted them rapturously.

9

ON TO VIENNA

From the defensive to the offensive. Karl Renner offers his services. A declaration by the Soviet Government. Secret peace envoys from Vienna. Before the assault. The shadow of Allen Dulles. Karl Renner's letter to the Kremlin. The beginning of peaceful coexistence. The Austrian burgomeister and the Soviet commandant.

As a result of the defensive battle of Lake Balaton, the deployment of the Soviet forces along the line of advance to Vienna was such that the main grouping of forces was now in the zone of the 3rd Ukrainian Front. Consequently this front had to cope with the main tasks required for the enemy's defeat in the upcoming offensive operation. There was no time for any lengthy preparations: The front reported to us that the enemy was digging in, and that we must not wait but hit the enemy before he managed to dig in really well.

The 3rd Ukrainian Front had to advance its right flank, which from the north overhung (as it were) a deep salient formed by the enemy's defense line south and southwest of Székesfehérvár. Here, in this salient, were the remaining tanks of the SS 6th Panzer Army. To defeat that army would mean to remove the bronze shield of the German command and liquidate the basic force in his

The Karelian Front: a line of antitank stakes in the region of Obzha (the Finns Olonetsk fortified region).

Landing units of the North Fleet bound for Kirkenes, October 24, 1944.

The Petsamo-Kirkenes Operation.

Soviet troops cross the Norwegian border.

A control point on the Soviet-German border.

Col. Gen. A. A. Zhdanov signs the official report on the armistice with Finland.

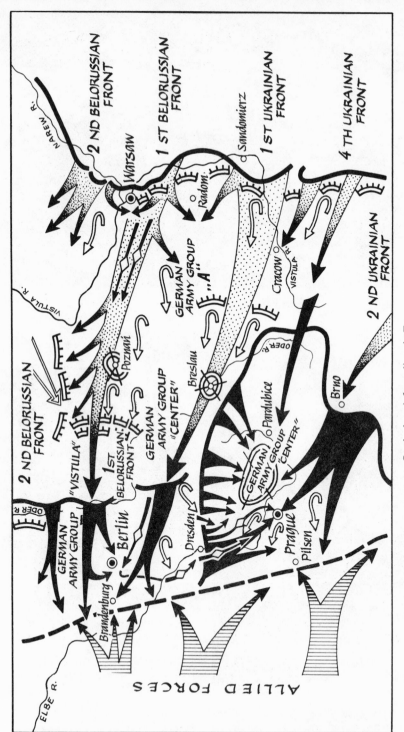

On the last defense lines in Europe.

Soviet soldiers reach Berlin.

''That's how we fought!'' says A. Ivashchenko, a Red Army soldier.

Col. L. I. Brezhnev, chief of the Political Division of the 18th Army.

Commanders of the Allied Forces in Berlin: B. Montgomery, D. Eisenhower, G. K. Zhukov, and J. de Lattre de Tassigny.

One minute left to victory. Marshal G. K. Zhukov of the Soviet Union makes a statement before signing the surrender of fascist Germany.

The end: surrender of the Nazi troops at one of the sectors of the Soviet-German front.

The first trainload of demobilized troops leaves Berlin. Lt. Gen. K. F. Telegin, member of the Military Council of the 1st Belorussian Front, sees the men off. The lettering on the train reads: ''We're from Berlin.''

Before the opening session at the Potsdam Conference.

The Soviet Military Delegation to the Potsdam Conference. From left to right: Adm. S. C Kucherov, Lt. Gen. N. V. Slavin, Marshal G. K. Zhukov of the Soviet Union, Maj. Gen. M. A Vavilov, Adm. N. G. Kuznetsov of the Soviet Navy, General of the Army A. I. Antonov, Marsh of the Air Force F. Ya. Falaleev.

Commanders of the fronts during the final stage of the Great Patriotic War. From left to right (fir row): Marshals of the Soviet Union I. S. Konev, A. M. Vasilevsky, G. K. Zhukov, K. F Rokossovsky, K. A. Meretskov; (second row): Marshals of the Soviet Union F. I. Tolbukhi R. Ya. Malinovsky, L. Govorov, General of the Army A. I. Eremenko, and I. Kh. Bagramya defenses. As a result, we would have cleared the way through western Hungary into Austria and on to Vienna.

Tolbukhin's plan was to break through the enemy's defenses, and surround and destroy his main armored forces, by striking with the 9th and 4th Guards armies (on Tolbukhin's right flank) from the area of Gant, and Lake Velencei in the direction of Veszprém. The terrain along the main line of advance was hilly and wooded; but Tolbukhin assured the General Staff and the Stavka that this was not an insurmountable obstacle to surrounding the enemy, especially since the latter would have to fight in a relatively narrow corridor between Lake Velencei and Lake Balaton.

What disturbed Tolbukhin was something else: There was not enough artillery to create a density of 180 guns per kilometer of front, and there was a shortage of strong armored forces. In particular, the 9th and 4th Guards armies between them had only 197 tanks and self-propelled guns. Along the line of the main advance, the correlation of forces as regards tanks was equal. . . . On the other hand, General V. A. Sudets's 17th Air Army would be able to supply more than 500 aircraft for use along the line of the main advance.

Meantime our reconnaissance parties reported that the German tank crews were working ceaselessly, digging in their tanks. A kind of fortified zone was being built right in front of our eyes; and from hour to hour, it was becoming harder to cope with. There was only one thing to do: immediately transfer from the 2nd Ukrainian Front, to Tolbukhin, Gen. A. G. Kravchenko's full-strength 6th Guards Tank Army (more than 400 tanks). This the General Staff proposed to the Stavka. But the Supreme Commander was not at that moment convinced that the enemy had given up plans for an offensive; and so he did not give permission for the transfer of the tanks, but rather ordered Tolbukhin to wait a bit.

In order to comply with the Stavka's directive to begin the offensive no later than March 15, Tolbukhin had to move his forces forward without a tank army. The artillery preparation and the support of infantry were effected strictly in accordance with the then-accepted rules. But the weak armored basis of our attacking formations, plus the inadequate density of artillery, predetermined the strength of the blow at the enemy's defenses and dictated a slow rate of advance for the 3rd Ukrainian Front.

The enemy's resistance was fierce. By the end of the day the Soviet forces had not managed to penetrate his defenses beyond a depth of three to seven kilometers. Now the element of surprise was lost. In order to carry out the plan to surround the SS panzer army, it was necessary to step up the rate of advance considerably —especially by putting in the 6th Guards Tank Army and intensifying artillery and air bombardment. Failure to do this would mean giving the German command the time and opportunity to organize resistance to our offensive, and to get their forces out of the dangerous area.

On the evening of March 16, after the first day of the offensive, Antonov, in my presence, gave the Supreme Commander a detailed report on the situation as regards the 3rd Ukrainian Front. When he had heard the report, the Supreme Commander agreed (this time) that it was urgent to put in the 6th Guards Tank Army, and to issue an order to that effect. He himself called Malinovsky, who at the time was at a forward command post, and explained to him why the tanks had to be transferred to Tolbukhin. He ordered that Malinovsky personally tell the tankers of their missions, and transfer the army to Tolbukhin in a hurry. Malinovsky was dismayed by the Stavka's decision; but he understood the necessity for it, and quickly carried out the order. Kravchenko's army was transferred to the 3rd Ukrainian Front in full strength, with all reserves for developing the right flank's attack and destroying the enemy's panzer grouping.

But Tolbukhin was not able to put in the tank army until March 19. It had taken two days to bring it up to the front and create the minimally necessary conditions for deployment and action. The fighting was continuing fiercely, and we couldn't risk the tanks. Unfortunately, each minute of our delay (now due to the circumstances) was utilized by the enemy to strengthen his defense lines and withdraw his forces.

In that battle we did not succeed in trapping the SS panzer army in a cauldron and destroying it, as had been planned. The enemy was able to set up strong armored shields on the north and east. And he took advantage of the canals and woods in this area to withdraw his forces. On the evening of March 23, they were lucky enough to slip out under heavy fire via the two-kilometer corridor to the northern shore of Lake Balaton.

On March 22 the Military Council of the 3rd Ukrainian Front reported to the Stavka its plan to crush the enemy north of Lake Balaton, advance to the Austrian border, and make preparations for pushing on to Vienna. The main thrust would be toward Szombathely, along the shortest (but mountainous) route to the Austrian frontier. In the opinion of the General Staff, a drive toward Szombathely was not the best plan. The mountainous terrain would hamper maneuvering (especially by tanks). Also, this route led away from the Viennese industrial region and from Vienna itself, which was very important in all respects. The General Staff proposed to the Supreme Commander that the main thrust of the 3rd Ukrainian Front be made toward Pápa and Sopron, along the shortest route to Vienna. (An added advantage was that here the terrain would make it possible to use all the strength of the 6th Guards Tank Army.) Stalin agreed, and the front advanced toward Vienna. On March 29 Soviet forces captured the towns of Szombathely and Köszeg in Hungary, and reached the Austrian border.

There was no dense enemy panzer grouping along the 2nd Ukrainian Front's line of advance, although the German defenses were also strong in this zone. Hence Malinovsky's forces could advance on a broad front, striking their main blow south of the Danube with the forces of Gen. A. V. Petrushevsky's 46th Army and Gen. K. V. Sviridov's 2nd Guards Mechanized Corps. The offensive was launched on March 17.

Success attended the forces of the 2nd Ukrainian Front. By noon on March 20 the 46th Army, having broken through the enemy's defenses, reached the Danube at Komárno, surrounded a force of some 20,000 in the region of Esztergom (the so-called Tovaros-Esztergom group), and acting jointly with units of the

Danube Flotilla, set about destroying it. A part of these forces developed the success in the direction of Győr.

The fact that the fronts were winning battles along their main lines of advance had a favorable effect on the situation along their flanks. The right-flank armies of the 2nd Ukrainian Front drove toward Bratislava and took it by storm (on April 4), along with sixty other inhabited localities. On April 2, on the left flank of the 3rd Ukrainian Front, the 57th Army and General Stoichev's Bulgarian 1st Army captured the town of Nagykanizsa, the center of the Hungarian oil industry, where the workers tried to protect the oil-producing equipment against destruction.

Meantime, the armies of our allies were advancing from the west to meet us. They had crossed the Rhine, and after moving east, had captured Frankfurt am Main and several towns in the Ruhr, Germany's chief industrial region.

One day during a briefing the Supreme Commander wondered aloud (as he often did), without addressing anyone in particular, "And where is he now, that Social Democrat Karl Renner who was a student of Kautsky's? For many years he was a leader of the Austrian Social Democrats, and if I mistake not was the chairman of Austria's last parliament."

No one said anything, the question being quite unexpected.

"Influential people should not be neglected," Stalin went on, "if they are antifascists. Probably Hitler's dictatorship taught something even to the Social Democrats."

And right then and there we were instructed to inquire about Renner and, if he was alive, to find out where he was living. So we forwarded the appropriate instructions via telephone to the 3rd Ukrainian Front.

We did not know much about the internal situation in Austria. We did know, however, that in June 1944 the Austrian Communist leaders had called upon the people to combat fascism. In October we had reports of local but serious skirmishes between Austrian partisans and Nazi forces. The following month witnessed the formation, in Yugoslavia, from among Austrian partisans and prisoners, of the 1st Freedom Battalion, which took part in heavy

324

fighting against the fascists. Early 1945 was marked by new partisan battles in the Alps and the creation of the 2nd and 3rd freedom battalions. But we had no information on any antifascist struggle by the Austrian bourgeois leaders. Nor was there any information on Karl Renner.

Then on April 4 we had a report from the Military Council of the 3rd Ukrainian Front stating that Karl Renner had shown up in person at the headquarters of the 103rd Guards Rifle Division. Later I was told that it happened as follows. A tall gray-haired man in a black suit was brought into the room where the staff officers were working, and introduced himself in German. At first no one paid any special attention to him. But then one of the political workers realized who he was, and promptly informed his superior.

Renner turned out to be a sociable fellow, and he quite willingly told the officers some of his lengthy life story. He had been a member of the Social Democratic Party since 1894, a deputy since 1907, and chairman of the Austrian Parliament from 1930 until almost ten years later. After the Anschluss he went off to lower Austria, having gotten out of official political activity.

Our officers asked Renner about his plans for the future. He said he was already old but was ready "in conscience and in deed" to help set up a democratic regime in Austria. "Today," he said, "the Communists and the Social Democrats have the same task: to destroy fascism." With his keen understanding of the situation in Austria, this perceptive old man, who was almost eighty, correctly evaluated his own importance as the last pre-Hitler leader of the Austrian Parliament. He offered his co-operation in forming a provisional wartime government for Austria, and warned in advance: "I shall exclude Nazis from the Parliament."

The talk lasted for rather a long time. It was important for us to learn the mood of the Viennese, since our intelligence service had reported large-scale preparations for fighting in the Austrian capital. Apparently the Nazi leaders were preparing the city for the same fate as Budapest. We had also received some very vague information about a supposed resistance movement within the Vienna garrison.

Renner figured that nine tenths of the Viennese were anti-Nazi, but that the Nazi repressions and the Anglo-American bombings had frightened them: They felt impotent and incapable of vigorous action. For their part, the Social Democrats had not taken any steps to mobilize the inhabitants for a struggle against the Nazis.

The report on the talk with Renner was received in Moscow on the evening of April 4. Antonov and I realized that some sort of decision would be taken on this occasion. Usually, if things were going well at the front, Stalin, the members of the Politburo, of the National Defense Committee, and of the government (who usually gathered for sessions in this room in the Kremlin) did not ask special questions. But on this occasion, during the briefing on the situation at the 3rd Ukrainian Front, Stalin, screwing up his eyes in a crafty manner, stopped pacing the floor and stared for some time at "the General Staff." Having made sure that we understood his thinking and his mood in connection with the telegram about Renner, he resumed pacing the carpeted floor with a satisfied expression on his face. Then, after talking with the members of the Politburo, he dictated to us a telegram from the Stavka to the Military Council of the 3rd Ukrainian Front. It read as follows:

> 1) Trust Karl Renner; 2) inform him that for the sake of restoring democratic government to Austria, the command of the Soviet forces would give him support; 3) explain to Renner that the Soviet forces were entering Austrian territory not in order to seize that territory but in order to drive out the fascist aggressors.

The telegram was signed by Stalin and Antonov. I immediately took it to the operations office for transmittal to Tolbukhin.

It was also decided that the commander of the 3rd Ukrainian Front should call upon the inhabitants of Vienna to resist the Nazis and not allow them to destroy the city. Further, that the Soviet Government should issue a declaration on Austria. We were instructed to put on paper our suggestions for expediting the capture of Vienna by the forces of the 2nd and 3rd Ukrainian fronts, and to report on this one day later.

The Soviet Government's declaration and the front commander's appeal were based on one and the same idea. The declaration was formulated as follows:

> The Soviet Government has no intention of acquiring any part of Austrian territory or of changing Austria's social system. The Soviet Government abides by the viewpoint of the Moscow Declaration of the Allies on the independence of Austria. It will implement that declaration. It will work toward the liquidation of the regime of the German fascist aggressors, and the restoration of democratic ways and institutions in Austria.[1]

Marshal Tolbukhin's appeal to the inhabitants of Vienna, dated April 6, 1945, stated *inter alia:*

> The Red Army has entered the territory of Austria not with the aim of seizing Austrian territory but solely with the aim of defeating the inimical German fascist forces and liberating Austria from dependence on Germany. . . .
> The Red Army is waging war on the German aggressors and not on the inhabitants of Austria, who may pursue their peaceful labor undisturbed.[2]

Tolbukhin went on to say that the hour of Vienna's liberation from the enemy had struck, but that the retreating enemy wanted to convert Austria into a field of battle, which meant that Vienna and its inhabitants were threatened with tremendous destruction and the horrors of war. For the sake of preserving the Austrian capital and its historic and cultural monuments, he proposed to the inhabitants that they stand their ground and not allow the enemy to destroy the city. "Citizens of Vienna!" the front commander wrote. "Help the Red Army to liberate the Austrian capital. Make your contribution to the cause of liberating Austria from the German fascist yoke!"[3]

Tolbukhin published his appeal to the inhabitants of Vienna on the same day that Soviet forces broke into the southwestern part of the city, and then the southeastern part, where they engaged in

[1] *Vneshnyaya politika Sovetskogo Soyuza v period Otechestvennoi voiny,* Vol. III, p. 171.
[2] Ibid., p. 172.
[3] Ibid., pp. 172–73.

heavy fighting. The most critical moment in the history of the Austrian capital's liberation was at hand.

At this point I shall take the liberty of making a slight digression. It has to do with the Austrian resistance movement. On the same day that we at the General Staff received the report from the Military Council of the 3rd Ukrainian Front concerning Karl Renner, we got another telegram reporting a talk on April 2, 1945, with peace envoys from the enemy's military units in Vienna.

By this time, the appearance of peace envoys was not in itself an extraordinary event. Whereas earlier, when the enemy was driving forward and winning victories, Hitler's commanders gave no thought to getting out of the war, now, as a result of the defeats, many of them were thinking about getting out. And in 1945 it was a fairly common thing for people from the other side to show up in front of our lines bearing a white flag. Such was now the case in the zone of the 9th Guards Army, where the front lines had been crossed by Sgt. Maj. F. Koez, a clerk, and Pfc. I. Raif, a driver. They identified themselves as representing the staff of the 17th "Mobilization Corps of Austrians," stationed in Vienna and engaged in training reserves for the front.

The peace envoys stated that an uprising against the Nazis was being prepared in Vienna. According to them, the insurgents consisted of antifascist military personnel and a part of the population of Vienna. In addition to two reserve infantry battalions and one artillery battery, there were supposedly 1,200 Austrian soldiers in other units who were ready to take part in the uprising. The peace envoys estimated that as many as 20,000 inhabitants of the city would join in the uprising.

The leader of the uprising was one of the corps staff officers, Maj. Karl Sokoll, chief of the Mobilization Department. It was he who had sent the peace envoys to the Soviet command.

All this was very important, and the top officers of the 9th Army and of the 3rd Ukrainian Front listened closely to what the peace envoys had to say. Then they assigned missions to the insurgents: to seize and guard the bridges over the Danube and its tributaries within the city limits of Vienna; to destroy the headquarters of the Nazi forces and institutions of the Nazi Party and the police located in the city; to seize key communications centers, means of communication, and other facilities of Vienna's municipal services system and the enemy's defense system.

With the help of the peace envoys, radio communications were established with the leaders of the uprising.

Soon Karl Sokoll himself crossed the front lines. He said that he was the head of an underground organization called "Austria, Awaken!" The staff of the front co-ordinated all necessary matters with him, including the signals to be given for the uprising.

The most opportune time to give the signal for the uprising would be on the eve of the assault on Vienna by the Soviet forces, when at the headquarters of the 3rd Ukrainian Front preparations were being completed to issue the commander's appeal to the Viennese. The uprising would disorganize the enemy's defense and substantially lighten the tasks of Tolbukhin's troops.

So the signal was given at that time—both on the radio and from aircraft, as had been agreed with the Austrian patriots of the 17th "Mobilization Corps." The time for the uprising was set at 1230 on April 6. The signal was acknowledged. . . .

On April 6 the Soviet forces launched their assault on Vienna. They had to fight for each building, for each district of the city, where the Nazis had built strong defenses. The crack troops of the 4th, 9th, and 6th tank armies, the pilots of the 17th Air Army, the sailors of the Danube Flotilla, and the soldiers of other units drove the enemy out of his fortifications step by step. Each encounter with the enemy demanded unparalleled courage and great skill.

But what of the uprising? As we found out later, the Nazis had managed to pick up the tracks of Karl Sokoll's organization. Actually, traitors had fingered the leaders planning the uprising. On the morning of April 6 many of them were seized and promptly executed. Since the uprising was thus bereft of leaders, it did not take place.

By driving into the city and enveloping it from the south and west, the Soviet tankmen and infantrymen had cut the enemy off from all communication with Germany in those two directions.

But for a long time Vienna was not isolated from the north; and it was from there that reserves might come to reinforce the fascist forces. This circumstance was borne in upon us at the General Staff as we were working on how to implement Stalin's order to speed up the capture of Vienna. Obviously, we said to ourselves, the enemy would not opt for defending a city that was completely surrounded: At the slightest threat to his withdrawal routes to the north, he would try to pull his troops out. So we had to put pressure on Vienna not only from south of the Danube but from north of it, where the enemy had not yet been hit by our blows. It was practicable to exert this pressure by putting the 46th Army of the 2nd Ukrainian Front (and the units reinforcing that army) across the Danube from the south bank, so that they could envelop Vienna on the north.

And there was another reason why a thrust by the 2nd Ukrainian Front was especially necessary—a reason having to do with the economics of Nazi Germany. I refer to the fact that in the spring of 1945 it had become evident that the aggressor was collapsing not only politically but economically. His forces were short on fuel. The stocks of fuel had been virtually exhausted; Germany had no reserves of crude oil; and we had already seized its main sources of crude. But the enemy still controlled the big Austrian oil-producing region of Zistersdorf, located northeast of Vienna.

It was in this direction that the blow by the 2nd Ukrainian Front should be struck. (As the documents now show, we judged correctly at that time. Hitler was very much disturbed by the situation with regard to the oil region, and ordered reinforcements sent there—including a panzer division from Army Group Vistula.) Stalin approved the proposal of the General Staff.

On the very next day, Stalin began asking how things were going with the maneuver by the 2nd Ukrainian Front. But putting that many troops across the Danube was no easy matter. The effort involved not only engineering resources but the Danube Flotilla, which was playing an important role in forcing the river. Things were hardest for the 2nd Guards Mechanized Corps and the 23rd Tank Corps, with their heavy machines.

Two days later the Supreme Commander showed great dissatisfaction, since he figured that the enemy might dodge the blow by Malinovsky's forces, and that it would be hard for Tolbukhin's front to take Vienna alone. His orders were to get moving and "cut off all of the enemy's escape routes from Vienna to the north" no later than April 10. Soon the enemy wavered, and was driven out of Vienna. In order to avoid being surrounded, he had rapidly retreated via the remaining routes to the north. By April 13 Vienna was completely in our hands.

After the capture of Vienna, the forces of the 3rd Ukrainian Front moved some distance westward to the defense line of St. Polten, where they were ordered to dig in. The armies of our allies were on their way to link up with us, and the remaining troops from the enemy's defeated units, who had retreated under our blows, were already surrendering to those armies. In Austria the problems of peaceful political regulation now emerged to the fore.

While the fighting for Vienna was going on, there was no time to look into why the antifascist uprising had failed; but after the liberation of the city the question was raised again. It was learned that on April 15 (two days after the liberation of Vienna), two persons had shown up at the office of the Soviet commandant, one of whom identified himself as chairman of the Central Committee of the resistance movement in Austria, the organization Austria, Awaken! and the other as a member of that committee. They stated that they had formerly been officers in the Austro-Hungarian Army; that they had been incarcerated for a long time in the concentration camps of Dachau and Buchenwald, but that the Nazis themselves had released them. According to them, their organization had made great contributions to the struggle against the Nazis.

The appearance of these persons was a reminder that it was necessary to check into the activity of the organization in question. It developed that the organization occupied a large house in Vienna, with a sign on the front saying it was the headquarters of the Austrian resistance forces. The organization provided its members with identification papers stamped with a seal.

331

The owner of the house in which the headquarters was located turned out to be a member of the headquarters staff. He had the title of baron. He had served in Hitler's army but, according to him, he had been imprisoned by the Gestapo five times and had escaped an equal number of times. Another man who turned out to be a member of the staff was a certain prince who had likewise served in the German Army as a first lieutenant. And several other persons there had pasts that were equally ambiguous. It was ascertained that none of them had been in contact with the resistance groups at plants and factories or with the insurgent movement. It became evident that the leaders of the organization did not enjoy the support of the people; yet they had obviously schemed to seize power when the day of liberation came. It was also ascertained that certain members of the group had been spreading false rumors about the Soviet troops with the aim of undermining the Red Army's prestige in the eyes of the inhabitants.

Then an even more serious circumstance came to light: The organization had been formed with the knowledge and support of Allen Dulles, the American intelligence agent. The organization's leaders had enlisted the support of the power represented by Dulles with a view to assuming the leadership of democratic circles in Vienna when the city had been liberated by the Red Army, and to taking over the control of the resistance movement. Next, in accordance with American interests, they would strengthen the position of conservative groups in Austria, and ensure their own accession to the rule of that country. The plotters also intended to remove the Communists from the resistance movement.

Leaders of this organization had established contact with French and British government circles. They had everywhere demanded that it be recognized as "the sole representative of all Austrian parties, resistance groups, and the Austrian people in general."[4]

The visit that the two leaders from this group paid to the Soviet commandant in Vienna was necessary (in accordance with the

[4] Quoted in S. I. Voroshilov, *Rozhdeniye vtoroi respubliki v Avstrii* (Leningrad University Press, 1968), p. 41.

principle of striking while the iron is hot) so as to secure our recognition of the group's contributions and the legitimacy (so to
speak) of its claims to leadership in the Austrian capital and in
the country as a whole. For that purpose the group was given the
name of the Central Committee of the Austrian Resistance Movement. But the Soviet commandant, although up to his ears in
work, got to the bottom of the business.

The visitors had mentioned that their organization included a
military group headed by Maj. Karl Sokoll. They also mentioned
the matter of the uprising, which in their words had "collapsed."

After this talk it became clear why those antifascists who had
risked their lives in crossing the front lines to make contact with
the Soviet command had failed to foment an uprising in Vienna.
They had become the victims of their trust in the leaders of that
organization, who were pursuing aims far different from those of
the resistance fighters.

In the second half of April 1945, when the time was drawing
near for the decisive assault on Berlin to begin, events in Austria
were characterized by a normalization of life in that country. By
that time we at the General Staff were receiving not only military
documents but political ones. The liberation of Vienna had
created firmer foundations for the activity of democratic organizations. Karl Renner had instituted practical steps toward the
forming of a provisional government. With great political skill, he
took advantage of the military situation's special aspects; and he
was unsparing in his promises and solemn pledges for the future.
His letter to Stalin dated April 15 is significant in this respect.

As we read the first lines of that letter, we at the General Staff
could not help smiling. Renner, striving to emphasize his solidarity with the revolutionary movement, began by telling of his personal contacts with (as he expressed it) "many leading Russian
revolutionary fighters." Those contacts were very much in character. Although he had met Lenin only once (at a conference), he
had had a long acquaintanceship with Leon Trotsky and Rya-
zanov. "However, I have not yet had the good fortune to meet
you personally, dear comrade," Renner wrote, employing our
favorite word "comrade" and thereby hinting at his ideological

"closeness" (so to speak) to Stalin, although back when the latter had written his *Marxism and the National Minorities Question* he had completely demolished Renner's ideas on the national minorities issue.

For that matter, in Renner's letter it was not so easy to draw a line between his sincere enthusiasm about the liberating mission of the Red Army and his patently self-serving flattery. Here is what he wrote at the time:

> In the course of its advance, the Red Army found me and my family at my residence of Glogniz (near Wiener Heimstadt), where I and my party colleagues, full of confidence, were awaiting its arrival. The local command treated me with great respect, immediately taking me under its protection and allowing me that complete freedom of action I had had to give up, much to my distress, during the fascism of Dolfuss and Hitler. For all this, I most sincerely and humbly thank the Red Army and you, its glorious Supreme Commander, in my own name and in that of the Austrian working class.

Renner next proposed quite frankly that the leadership of the country be handed over to him.

> It was the will of Fate [he wrote] that of those members of the Central Committee who remained in the country, I should be the first to be given freedom of action again. And it is a happy circumstance that I, as the last president of the former free people's body of representatives, can regard myself as entitled to speak and act in the name of the Austrian people. And I have one further advantage in that as Chancellor of the first Austrian Republic I was entrusted with the job of transforming the foundations of the State in organizing a government by the people, so that now I am worthy of trust in initiating and taking charge of the job of awakening Austria.

Noting that he had received the necessary assistance from Tolbukhin's forces, Renner wrote:

> Without the help of the Red Army, not a single step forward could have been taken. Therefore not only I but the entirety of the future "Second Republic of Austria" and its working class will be beholden for many long years to you, *Herr Marschall,* and to your victorious army.

The last part of Renner's letter of April 15, 1945, consisted of various requests. *Inter alia,* he wrote the following:

> The Nazi regime doomed us to complete helplessness here. And when the transformation of Europe is effected, we shall be standing helpless at the gates outside. Early as it is, I ask that you look kindly upon Austria at the conference of the Great Powers; and insofar as the tragic circumstances permit, I ask that you take us under your powerful protection. Right now we are threatened by famine and epidemics; and in talks with our neighbors, we are threatened with loss of territory. Already, in our rocky Alps, we have very little arable land: It yields us only a skimpy day-to-day nourishment. If under these circumstances we are deprived of any part of our territory, we shall not be able to live.

Continuing with this thought, Renner took a crack at our allies:

> The victors simply cannot intend to doom us to an impotent existence. The West, however—as was demonstrated in 1919—shows too little interest to assure the prerequisites of independence for us.

At the end of his letter, Renner made a political declaration:

> . . . Thanks to the amazing flourishing of Russia's might, the Austrians have completely realized the falsehood of twenty years of Nazi propaganda, and are astounded at the great successes of the Soviet Union. In particular, the Austrian working class has boundless trust in the Soviet republics. The Austrian Social Democrats are reaching agreements with the Communist Party in a brotherly way, and they will work together as equals in the restoration of the republic.

Renner's remarks about the attitude of the Austrian working class and the great majority of the Austrian people toward the Soviet Union certainly reflected most accurately the moods prevalent in Austria at that time.

Stalin replied to Renner:

> Thank you, esteemed comrade, for your letter of April 15. Rest assured that your concern for the independence, integrity, and prosperity of Austria is also my concern.

Stalin also stated that he was ready to give Austria whatever assistance was possible.

Late April witnessed the formation of a provisional government headed by Karl Renner—a government that included Communists. On May 15, 1945, with the co-operation of the USSR, a state treaty guaranteeing the neutrality and independence of Austria was signed.

Immediately after the liberation of Vienna, we had to deal with the problem of administering the city. It might seem that such a problem was far removed from the General Staff; but at that particular time the General Staff dealt with just such problems. We knew that out of Austria's population of seven million, about a million and a half lived in Vienna. And at first it was up to our military authorities to see that they were fed and that their other needs were taken care of.

We at the General Staff felt that the problems of running Vienna could be handled by military authorities; in particular, by the commandant. We recommended Gen. A. V. Blagodatov, deputy commander of the 57th Army, for the job. We got in touch by telephone with Tolbukhin, who shared our opinion; and then we spelled it out in a document for the Stavka. But the Supreme Commander did not agree with the views of the General Staff and Tolbukhin. He explained to us that our proposal did not take into account one vital necessity: that the domestic problems of Austria, including Vienna, be solved by the Austrians themselves. If the sole authority in the capital were a Soviet military authority, this would contravene both our policy and the Soviet Government's declaration on Austria. Moreover, a military authority would not be able to develop the inhabitants' initiative in restoring normal living conditions to the same degree as could be done by a prestigious Austrian magistrature intimately familiar with local conditions. And the essence of Soviet policy in liberated Austria consisted in just those two things: initiative and the normalization of life for the people.

It was for precisely those reasons that the members of the Soviet Government and the Stavka, when they gathered for a regular session at the Kremlin, categorically came out in favor of having the city run by an Austrian civilian. But since neither Tolbukhin nor Renner (who had begun to form Austria's provisional government) had come up with any specific candidate for the position of burgomeister of Vienna, the Stavka sent Tolbukhin the following instructions: "Vienna cannot be left without a burgomeister. Let the Austrians of good repute agree on a candidate, and then clear him with you."

Such was the solution found for the problem of Vienna's self-government, and the participation of the Austrian authorities in the election of a burgomeister. In due time that post was occupied by the former general Theodor Koerner. His candidacy was approved by Austrians from all walks of life. Koerner was a Social Democrat; and he had protested against the Nazi dictatorship. He had done this openly and was arrested by the Nazis. He remained in incarceration until the liberation of Vienna by the Soviet forces. In prison, he had behaved as an Austrian patriot and an anti-fascist. He was a very competent man, highly informed not only on military matters but on complex political questions. In Vienna he enjoyed great respect. "He is known as an honest man," was the report we had from General Blagodatov, the military commandant in Vienna, who later worked closely with the burgomeister.

But the one who had occasion to work especially long and hard with the burgomeister was Col. Gen. A. I. Shebunin, Tolbukhin's deputy for administrative installations. An old Communist with long experience in the school of life and in the Army, he was good at organizing rear-area services, and in Vienna this came in handy. Shebunin organized the supplying of foodstuffs to the Viennese; and Koerner, who also proved to be a good manager, helped his Soviet colleagues in every way.

In the days immediately following the liberation of Vienna a procedure was set up whereby the ministers of the Austrian Provisional Government rather frequently consulted with our command and the front's military council as to the best way of solving urgent problems. Of course the Austrians asked for many things; but usually their requests were well founded and were granted. In Vienna, and throughout the country, restoration projects were in progress. Construction workers who had thrown away their tools during the war were again at work. In Vienna the Soviet commandant often visited construction projects. He talked with the workers, and helped the local authorities out with trucks and sometimes with man power.

General Shebunin also had to settle very ticklish questions (something at which he was a great expert), and he seldom made a blunder. Yet on one occasion the meticulous Koerner discovered that even Shebunin had made a mistake. It had to do with supplying salt to the inhabitants of Vienna. Shebunin had calculated how much salt the Viennese needed, and had ordered that it be delivered to the city. But shortly afterward Koerner asked for more salt. Shebunin was puzzled, and queried the burgomeister in an attempt to find out what was going on. But he had to acknowledge his own mistake: It turned out that he had not allowed for the salt needed for baking bread—something that the new burgomeister of Vienna had not forgotten.

The incident is a slight one, but it testifies to the good relations between the Austrian authorities and officers of the Soviet command in a Vienna only just liberated from the Nazis.

The Soviet command did a good deal toward restoring a normal life to the Austrian people liberated from Nazi rule. In conclusion I want to emphasize that all this was done at a time when the people of the Soviet Union were living on semi-starvation rations amid the ruins of an economy (in the western regions) destroyed by the enemy.

It was not easy to work at normalizing life in the countries liberated from the Nazis while at the same time commanding military forces in action. This demanded constant and extreme efforts from the people involved. Tolbukhin, A. S. Zheltov, and other top officers of the front had to have iron nerves and threefold attention to get to the bottom of the intricate local problems. It was especially hard on Tolbukhin, whose health was in any case not really good. Almost every time when Antonov and I were briefing the Stavka on the situation at the front and we got to the subject of the 3rd Ukrainian Front, Stalin or some other member of the Stavka would ask about Tolbukhin's health. For that matter, many of our marshals and generals who regularly carried tremendous work loads were not the healthiest of men. But during the war years they gave little thought to their own health.

Until the very end of the war the soldiers of the 3rd Ukrainian Front fought on Austrian territory against Nazi forces holed up in the mountains in the western part of the country. The enemy's second largest concentration of forces after Army Group Center —a concentration numbering almost 450,000 men—was positioned here. And it was in this area that the long-awaited victory came to the Soviet soldier. But more than 26,000 officers and soldiers did not live to see that great day: They had hastened the liberation of Austria at the cost of their own lives.

10

THE SECONDARY THEATER
OF OPERATIONS

**What a secondary theater is. The Finns request and
reject an armistice. K. A. Meretskov at the Karelian
Front. Unofficial talks in Moscow. We prepare for
an offensive. Defeat. Official talks. The liberation
of the Soviet Arctic and the northern part of Norway.
Bornholm Island.**

Military men employ the concept of "the main theater." This is
the area where the basic tasks of the war, the operation, or the engagement are accomplished; the area to which the most—and the
best—troops and matériel are sent. Special attention is devoted to
it. Any soldier, officer, or commander wants to be in the main theater. In a secondary theater, the tasks are more modest. There are
fewer troops and less matériel, and there is also less attention
paid. Yet the fighting here is no easier, and it may well be harder.

Such was the case on the northern flank of the Soviet-German
front, which extended for almost 1,600 kilometers. The Arctic
Circle invisibly divided it into two unequal and dissimilar parts.
Karelia is a land of quiet dawns, age-old forests, and pure, spar-
kling lakes. The Arctic region consists of tundra, rocky, barren
plateaus with inhospitable hillocks, lakes that reach out toward

340

the sea, and turbulent rivers. After the long nights comes a season of constant daylight. Nature is harsh: Even the sun is powerless to melt the patches of permafrost. But at Murmansk the shore is washed by a warm current, and is a scene of activity the year round, with ships coming and going.

These two dissimilar regions are neighbors, and each is rich in its own way: in timber, fish, and metals.

In its war plans, the German High Command took into account the economic importance of this theater of war, and its great strategic importance to our country. The Germans correctly evaluated the role of our sea communications and of the railroad to Murmansk. Hence at the very outset of the war, in July 1941, on the northern flank of the Soviet-German front they launched an offensive of great breadth—one extending over all sectors accessible to them.

The German 20th Army (the so-called Lapland Army), specially trained for operating under the harsh conditions of the North, drove toward the ice-free shores of the Barents Sea: toward Murmansk and the White Sea. And Finnish forces advanced along the narrow, difficult roads of Karelia. The enemy was rushing ahead, hoping to capture the Soviet Arctic and the railroads leading to it.

At that time, the ratio of forces on that part of the northern front that was land was in favor of the enemy. As a result of some hard-fought battles and at the price of great losses, the German forces had managed to move forward, to seize Pechenga (Petsamo), to advance right up to Kovdozero, Ukhta, and Rugozero, to seize Medvezhyegorsk and Petrozavodsk, to force the Svir, and to establish a bridgehead on its southern bank. Along this line of defense the enemy was stopped. Every day from then until June 1944, Gen. M. A. Kraskvets, in command in this sector of the front, confirmed the almost invariable line running along the forward positions of the Soviet forces.

The stabilization of the front by no means meant that life was quiet and serene. Both on the Karelian Front, in the 7th Independent Army's sector between Lake Onega and Lake Ladoga, and on the Karelian Isthmus, where the forces of the Leningrad

Front were defending the city on the Neva, there was constant fighting on a local scale which kept the enemy in a state of tension and prevented him from withdrawing his forces for use in the main sector.

Day and night the vessels of our Northern Fleet plowed the unquiet Barents Sea, convoying allied merchant ships, securing the defense of our country's northern frontiers from the sea and (with the fleet's aircraft) from the air. And on Lake Ladoga and Lake Onega our lake flotillas were operating.

In this part of the world, the vast expanses—so inconvenient for human beings—seemed to absorb both people and equipment. As we know, the ordinary operational concept as to the density of forces on a front is usually expressed in the number of kilometers per division and the number of tanks, guns, and mortars per kilometer of front. But in this theater of operations it was expressed by a formula in which the first figure often exceeded 100, while the quantity of tanks and guns per kilometer was given with a single-digit number. Thus at the very best times, there were only twenty (estimated) divisions for the 1,600 kilometers of the front; i.e., a ratio of 73 kilometers per division. The many uninhabited areas were observed only by individual detachments and patrols.

Tanks could not be deployed here, and they were used very little, except for certain sectors where the terrain made it possible to use them on a limited scale (though only after complex technical and engineering preparation).

On the northern flank, defense was effected in accordance with the principle of actions over a broad front. The Karelian Front was short on both troops and matériel. The commander had to improvise, and often appealed to the Stavka for help. The Supreme Commander called this front "the eternal beggar." He realized the conditions under which it was fighting, and sympathized; but he would not give it any troops, since he always had the other, main theaters in mind.

In this theater the troop disposition took the form of "centers" in individual sectors, usually with no direct communication among them. Often a battalion, a company, or even a platoon, cut off from the other troops, would defend a long time a hill, a road through the woods, swamps, and mountains, or another important objective. They did this under conditions of winter cold and the Arctic night, the snows and barren northern cliffs of Karelia, the impassable swamps and unbearable summer insects, clinging (as if they owned it) to a patch of dry land among the swamps or the rapids, digging themselves in so they were better positioned for shooting or for hand-to-hand combat. To supply troops under such conditions was a terribly complicated job.

After the enemy's 1941 offensive on the northern flank of the Soviet-German front had been really stopped, the Stavka and the General Staff did not give any special attention to that theater of operations. All their thinking was directed toward defeating the German forces in the main strategic theaters: It was there that the outcome of World War II was being decided, and it was there that the key to the lair of the fascist beast was to be found. It was essential to crush the Wehrmacht—the main force of fascism. And then (such was the thinking at the Stavka) the same thing would happen to Germany's satellites (including Finland) as happens to the branches of a tree when it has been felled.

By the end of 1943 the turning point in the war had been passed beyond any doubt. The German command's schemes to regain the initiative were demolished for good at the battle of Kursk. The Nazi offensive strategy had collapsed completely.

The victories of the Soviet Armed Forces opened the eyes of politicians and generals in many countries to the immediate prospects in the war. Our allies stepped up their activities. They landed troops on the Apennine Peninsula. Italy ceased to wage war on Germany's side. In many European countries occupied by the German aggressors, the resistance movement broadened. Now, for the most part, it was the forces of the anti-Nazi coalition that were advancing, both on land and at sea.

The Teheran Conference of the Big Three (the name commonly used at the time for Franklin Roosevelt, Joseph Stalin, and Winston Churchill, representing the three great allied powers) resulted in the making of very important decisions on the second front and subsequent operations.

Early 1944 was a favorable time for the Red Army. In the winter campaign it had broken through the Nazi defenses near Leningrad, in the western Ukraine, and in the Crimea. The glorious victories of the Red Star troops were important not only in themselves: They now meant the collapse of the Wehrmacht's *defensive* strategy on the Soviet-German front; and they marked a new phase of the war. By this time it was plain to all thinking people that the Soviet Union was able, using only its own forces, to defeat the enemy on his own territory, to liberate the occupied nations of Europe, and to crush Germany utterly.

Yet this prospect, which gladdened the nations of the whole world, frightened both our enemies and our allies, each in a different way. The fear of losing moral and political prestige compelled the ruling circles in the United States and Great Britain to expand in a businesslike way their preparations for opening a second front.

Meantime, in the camp of Nazi Germany a serious process of weakening had taken place: Finland was wavering.

The General Staff had sensed dismay among Hitler's Finnish myrmidons in mid-February 1944, when the Leningrad Front and the Vokkhovsky Front dealt a jolting defeat to the German 18th Army, which had been besieging Leningrad since 1941. Soviet forces liberated Novgorod and Luga. Troops of the Leningrad Front advanced to the Narva River, beyond which loomed the city of the same name, which the Germans had transformed into a strong defense position. And troops of the Volkhov (later of the 3rd Baltic) Front moved on Pskov and Ostrov.

The Finnish Government realized that the defeat of the German forces near Leningrad and Novgorod would be promptly followed by a Red Army offensive against Finland. The Finns did not have enough troops to counter it; and the Germans, who themselves had suffered serious defeats in the main sectors, could not provide much assistance. So in mid-February the Finns began to seek out contacts with Mme. A. M. Kollontai, our ambassador in Sweden. What they were looking for in these contacts was a way out of the war—out of the coalition with Hitler. The man the Finnish Government sent to Sweden was Yu. K. Paasikivi, an outstanding figure known for his progressive views. As a Finnish envoy he was to ascertain the Soviet Government's conditions for an armistice.

The Finnish leaders, however, had not stopped hoping that the fortunes of war would smile on them; and in sending Paasikivi to Sweden, they were trying to postpone the date of the inevitable surrender.

By that time (in early February) the Stavka had already decided that when the Volkhov Front reached the approaches to Pskov and Ostrov, its forces would be transferred to the Leningrad Front and the 2nd Baltic Front, while the staff and other command personnel would be shifted to the Karelian Front, where they would take over command of the forces. This step was very necessary. The staff of the former Volkhov Front was a well-knit team very familiar with combat conditions in the north, with experience in handling large-scale offensive operations. The staff that the Karelian Front then had was lacking in such experience.

On February 13 the Volkhov Front was disbanded, and its commander, Gen. K. A. Meretskov, was summoned to the Stavka, where Stalin offered him the command of the Karelian Front. Like everyone else, Meretskov wanted to serve in the main theater; but after a brief talk he accepted. The Supreme Commander quickly spelled out Finland's political situation, and noted that personally he did not believe Finland would withdraw from the war promptly. He ordered Meretskov to get to the front in a hurry, and to pay special attention to reconnaissance. And he had one more piece of advice to offer: Since Finland had put out feelers for armistice talks, he recommended that the German forces (in the north) be given priority in matters of defeat.

Along with these organizational measures, we took certain steps by way of (so to speak) putting psychological pressure on the Finns and nudging them into armistice talks.

On February 14, about midnight, Stalin instructed the General Staff to inform L. A. Govorov, commander of the Leningrad Front, that it was essential to capture the city of Narva no later than February 17. "This is demanded by both the military and the political situations," Stalin emphasized. "It's the most important thing right now. I insist that you take all necessary steps to liberate Narva no later than at the time indicated."

The meaning of the dispatch was clear, since liberating the southern shore of the Gulf of Finland from Nazi troops would mean creating yet one more factor negatively influencing the military situation of Finland. It should be noted that the Germans fully realized the importance of Narva, and defended it stubbornly.

The armistice conditions that the Soviet Union offered to the Finns were minimal. They called for a rupture of relations with Germany and the interning of German troops in Finland. (The USSR offered its help, in the event that Finland could not cope with the job of interning the Nazi troops.) Another of the USSR's conditions was that the Finnish forces be withdrawn to the 1940 border, and that the latter be restored. Soviet and allied POWs were to be immediately returned. Settlement of all other questions was deferred until there should be talks in Moscow.

While these complex diplomatic talks were going on, General Meretskov (shortly followed by his staff) reached Belomorsk, where the command post of the Karelian Front was located. Meretskov was a sociable, practical man, and he quickly got the lay of the land. Col. Gen. V. A. Frolov, who had previously commanded the front, did not consider it demeaning to become Meretskov's deputy; and he quickly acquainted the latter with the disposition of the troops and the special features of the actions they were engaged in.

Lt. Gen. T. F. Shtykov, one of the most experienced political workers, who had been with this front for only six weeks, was (first) member of the front's military council. While getting the lay of the land, he too gladly accompanied the front commander on his visits to the different forces. The front's chief of staff was Lt. Gen. B. A. Pigarevich, already a rather old man, who knew staff work very well but unfortunately did not have experience in organizing and exercising command control over large-scale offensive operations—especially under such difficult conditions as those in Karelia. Later he had to yield his post as chief of staff to Gen. A. N. Krutikov, a younger man who was more vigorous and better trained in all respects. Up until that time General Krutikov had successfully commanded the 7th Independent Army, which in the spring of 1944 was transferred to the Karelian Front.

Meretskov also struck up good relations with the generals commanding his armies. Lt. Gen. V. I. Shcherbakov commanded the 14th Army in the north, Lt. Gen. G. K. Kozlov the 19th, Maj. Gen. L. S. Skvirsky the 26th, Lt. Gen. F. D. Gorelenko the 32nd, and Lt. Gen. V. A. Gluzdovsky the 7th (beginning in September 1944).

Meretskov also visited the Northern Fleet, which in co-ordination with the Karelian Front was operating over an extensive maritime zone. At that time the Northern Fleet was commanded by Rear Adm. Arseny Grigoryevich Golovko, an amazing man with a variety of talents who was responsive to people, to intelligence, and to warmth of heart. He had taken over command of the Northern Fleet in July 1940, and in his thirty-fourth year had become an outstanding fleet commander, able to evaluate the situation and make basic decisions in a matter of minutes. Everyone who had fought alongside him or worked with him liked him and respected him for his good sense and his warm and generous heart.

While studying the front, Meretskov remembered the Supreme Commander's personal instructions about reconnaissance. Stalin did not like belated reports or the delays he often had to allow for. (Things were made especially difficult by the unexpected questions the Supreme Commander often asked.) In March the reconnaissance carried out by forces of the Karelian Front yielded important results. The prisoners that had been captured stated that the German 20th or "Lapland" Army, consisting of the "Norway" Corps, the 36th Army Corps, and the 18th Alpine Corps, had taken over a new sector near Ukhta by way of expanding the defense zone of the 18th Alpine Corps. It was ascertained that some Finnish divisions had been pulled back to the rear area. Apparently, reserves were being built up.

The intensified reconnaissance made it possible to spot the weak points in the enemy's defenses and to deal him painful blows. For example, on March 20 the commander of the 94th Rifle Regiment of the 21st Rifle Division, being in the Kandalaksha sector, found out that he was faced with less than a battalion of Germans, who had managed to dig only snow entrenchments. He decided to crush the enemy before he could dig in well, and the divisional commander approved. That same day the regiment rushed the German battalion, surrounded it, and defeated it. The POWs stated that the battalion had been brought up from the reserve to stop the Russians from building a road toward Alakurtti.

The information obtained via reconnaissance provided food for thought. Obviously, the enemy was expecting us to attack and was preparing to ward off the blow. Apparently the German patrons of the Finnish politicians did not trust them as boundlessly as before, as was shown by the incident with the German battalion destroyed by the 94th Regiment. On the other hand it might be assumed that the Finns were not intending to stop fighting if they were pulling divisions back into the deep reserve.

And yet they sent a delegation to Moscow (it consisted of Yu. Paasikivi, K. Enckel, and O. Enckel) to get from us a more detailed interpretation of the Soviet armistice conditions. The talks were to be conducted by Molotov. The day before, he called me in to see him. He said that I was to take part in the talks; that I should be ready, and should show up at his office the next day in civilian clothes.

Everything seemed to be in order: I knew by heart the troop dispositions (both enemy and friendly) on the front, and I had a good notion of the various military problems that might come up in the course of the talks. But—I didn't have a civilian suit! That may seem strange today. But before the war we somehow never gave a thought to civilian clothes; and for that matter it wasn't the custom to wear them when off duty. When I was a boy we used to wear a pistol and sword when we put on plays, and we were proud to do it. But in wartime it would of course have been sacrilege to even think of wearing civilian clothes. Yet now I had to have a suit. . . . Molotov saved me. He gave orders that a black suit, complete with vest, be tailored for me immediately. A grave old man with the comportment of a magician showed up. He measured me from head to foot, and the suit was made overnight (with no fitting). . . .

Our armistice conditions were explained to the Finnish delegation in detail. In late March they went back to Finland. But after that, days and weeks went by without our getting any reply from them.

What Meretskov found out from visiting the troops and staffs of the Karelian Front was that both needed to learn modern methods of conducting offensive operations and battles.

The General Staff had been especially anxious about the command organs of the forces, since it is no easy matter firmly and constantly to exercise command control over an offensive on a broad front under the kind of conditions found in the Arctic and Karelia. When Meretskov was in Moscow, this had been put to him directly. He had not forgotten it; and in April and May of 1944 he put into operation a very broad and fundamental program to teach the troops offensive tactics. Everyone learned, both privates and chiefs of staff, from the platoon level to that of the front.

There are many good things one could say about Meretskov and his comrades-in-arms, who showed great persistence in training their forces. That training, difficult and anxiously conducted, saved us many lives in later battles.

On April 19 the Finnish Government replied that it could not accept the armistice conditions offered by the Soviet Government. In Finland the reactionary element of the Cabinet—Rysto Ryti, Tanner, and others—had got the upper hand, and these people were calling upon German envoys for help.

The Finnish Government's rejection of our terms compelled the Stavka and the General Staff to reconsider the question as to which forces to crush first—the Finns or the Germans. In the course of a routine briefing on the situation at the front, Antonov made a casual mention of the question, putting it in rather neatly. He said that now that the Finns had rejected our armistice conditions, we should perhaps not begin with the German forces but with those of the Finns, who were weaker.

The Supreme Commander agreed. But he ordered that we should create for the enemy (and subsequently maintain) the illusion that the Soviet command intended to capture Petsamo. In Stalin's opinion, this would relax the vigilance of the Finns and lessen their readiness to ward off a blow by Soviet forces in the region of Petrozavodsk and near Leningrad.

The General Staff worked up a rather simple "disinformation" plan for misleading the enemy. This plan called for feigned preparations for a Soviet offensive in the region of Petsamo, which would involve the Northern Fleet's putting troops ashore on the adjacent stretch of the Norwegian coast. On April 20 the commander of the Karelian Front and the admiral commanding the Northern Fleet issued all of the orders called for in the disinformation plan. Actually, however, all our designs concerned that part of the front where the Finnish forces were positioned.

The guilt for the thousands of Finnish and Soviet lives lost in the battles of the summer of 1944 rests with the reactionary politicians of Finland—Ryti, Tanner, and their ilk—who were unwilling to accept the humane armistice conditions offered by the USSR.

The plans for the operations on the northern flank of the Soviet-German front were based on the idea of defeating the enemy step by step. Now, after April 20, the first blows of the Soviet forces were to be rained down on the Finnish Army. We at the General Staff figured that the Finns, less well armed and trained than the Germans, would be defeated in a relatively short time.

According to our calculations the defeat of the Finnish forces would seriously weaken the position of the German 20th (Alpine) Army, occupying the sector above the Arctic Circle. The southern flank of the German defense line would inevitably be exposed, and this would open up broad possibilities for our succeeding thrusts. We could see the prospect of isolating the enemy's main forces from their escape routes to the western ports of Finland and into Norway.

This sequence of operations was based on the existing situation. In the Finnish sector of the front we could more rapidly come within striking range of Finland's main population centers, since here they were closest. And the main Finnish forces were stationed here. With their defeat the Finns' entire system of defenses would collapse. And for this offensive we had available the Leningrad Front, the Karelian Front, the Baltic Fleet, the lake flotillas, and a large number of aircraft.

True, the enemy's defenses in this area were very strong. On the Karelian Isthmus they consisted of the permanent structures making up the notorious Mannerheim Line, which had been restored by the enemy, and many other obstacles of various kinds that had been skillfully erected. There were also strong fortifications in that sector of the front along the Svir River. We would have to break through all this, but the Soviet command had the troops and resources to do it.

It was finally decided that the operation on the Karelian Isthmus would be carried out by the Leningrad Front, acting jointly with the Baltic Fleet and long-range aircraft. The offensive on the Svir-Petrozavodsk sector would be mounted by the Karelian Front, supported by the lake flotillas under its command.

The Leningrad Front was to strike the first blow at the enemy's main forces. Its mission was to break through the Finnish defenses in the direction of Vyborg and pose the threat of the Soviet forces' driving deep into Finland toward the main political and economic centers, including Helsinki. In its secondary sector the Leningrad Front was to move part of its forces forward to Sortavala and along the northern shore of Lake Ladoga, so that they could strike behind the enemy's defense lines in Karelia. The 21st Army, which since late August had been under the command of Col. Gen. D. N. Gusev, former chief of staff of the Leningrad Front, was brought up from the Stavka reserve and attached to the Leningrad Front for this operation.

With Soviet forces in their rear, the Finns facing the Karelian Front could hardly feel calm and collected. At that moment, the offensive by Meretskov's forces was to be launched.

The operations plan of the Karelian Front called for its main blow to be delivered in the sector along the Svir River. The 7th Army was positioned here, along with enough reinforcements (in our estimate) to force the deep Svir River without losing its stride. A break-through to the north along the eastern shore of Lake

Ladoga would provide the advancing Soviet forces with a favorable flanking position vis-à-vis the Finnish defense line in the region of Petrozavodsk, with the prospect of breaking into his rear area. These considerations were carefully thought out. Work on the plans continued throughout April and (with the front commanders now participating) May.

In late March 1944, when the General Staff was working on the plans for the operations on the northern flank of the Soviet-German front, Moscow was enjoying fine spring weather. But we at the General Staff were, to put it bluntly, sweating. Those were the days when the 1st and 2nd Ukrainian fronts were battering Army Group Ukraine and Army Group South on the right bank of the Dnieper and chasing them beyond the Prut and the Seret. And the 3rd Ukrainian Front was driving toward Odessa. Naturally, we were in work up to our ears, and couldn't even manage to gulp in a chestful of that refreshing spring air. But I was better off than my colleagues, since every day Antonov and I took those short car trips to the Kremlin, or longer ones to Near House, Stalin's dacha in Kuntsevo.

Also, I sometimes had occasion to report alone to the Supreme Commander, since he often wanted to know how work was progressing on one operation or another, or would demand that the maps on his desk be replaced with more recent ones. This happened once in late March. Antonov passed on to me Stalin's instructions that I should come to Near House in three hours.

"The boss wants to have another look at the maps for the operations on the northern flank," he said. "Take them to him."

I collected the necessary materials and looked them over carefully. Then, at the appointed hour, I set out for Kuntsevo. On the way I once again went over the General Staff's proposals, which the Supreme Commander had already approved in general.

The rather narrow asphalt road to the dacha branched off to the left from the Minsk Highway, crowded with cars and other vehicles. It zigzagged along the edge of a woodland, and then through the woods themselves (a mixed stand of conifers and deciduous trees), fetching up at a green board fence with a wide gate, also made of wood. Beyond the gate were more woods: to the right, tall pines; to the left, a "round dance" of slender birches, and beyond them more pines. Here and there, fir trees loomed sullenly. Usually, not a single guard could be seen along the winding road through the woods, all the way from the gate to the dacha. There were guards at the gate; and there were also guards in the woods around the dacha, but they did their job skillfully and kept out of sight.

Coming into the grounds of the dacha, I found myself admiring the serene beauty of the landscape near Moscow. But the road was short, and the enchantment didn't last long.

The low two-story dacha with a gable roof was scarcely noticeable in the woods. It, too, was green; and it loomed up suddenly as soon as the car made a sharp turn from the woodland realm into the circular driveway in front of the main entrance to the dacha. Here, in the summer, a fountain gushed from a small stone basin. And the whole was walled around by pines. . . .

I got out of the car and, carrying a briefcase bulging with maps, went up to the house. The sergeant of the guard met me at the threshold. Since he knew me personally, he asked me to go in and take off my coat.

After crossing the threshold, the visitor to Near House went through a small vestibule into the entrance hall proper. Here he could take off his coat, and if necessary tidy himself up for the impending interview. Along the wall on the right was an unpretentious coat rack with solid nickel-plated hooks and hangers for a dozen coats. A full-length mirror and brushes for clothes and footwear were provided for the convenience of the visitor. On the floor was a wall-to-wall woolen carpet with an intriguing varicolored design. But the first thing that struck anyone entering the room was the two big maps on the wall: one showing the front lines, and the other showing (with symbols) the great construction projects of socialism. From the entrance hall one went into see Stalin without being announced.

There were three doorways through which one could go from the entrance hall into the inner rooms of the dacha. Straight ahead into the dining room and through it into Stalin's bedroom on the left. To the left, along a long narrow hallway off of which, to the right, were two living rooms. One had served as a nursery, and then been converted into a study. The other was of the same size and shape, but a bit darker, and was used for guests. Along the other side of the hallway ran a long open veranda. There was no furniture on it except for a low broad sofa and a portable coat rack that was taken into the entrance hall when the one already there did not suffice.

As a rule, Stalin worked in a spacious bright room to the left of the entrance hall. It was furnished with a big broad desk with plenty of room for military maps, and a sofa—something found in all the other rooms.

Along the back of the dacha was an open veranda with a big rug on the floor and a deep sofa of the same pleasant gray-green color. In one corner of the veranda, to the left of the door, stood a shovel whose handle was polished from use. The rest of Stalin's gardening tools were stored in a large closet. He liked to take care of the roses and the apple trees planted along the shore of the pond; and along with some hothouse lemons, he was even growing watermelons.

The big dining room was used for receptions and on other formal occasions. It was devoid of ornamentation except for two huge portraits between the windows on the right: one of Lenin and one of Gorky.

In the middle of the room, taking up almost three quarters of its length, stood a broad highly polished table. Near the doorway stood a mahogany baby grand piano. (In 1945, the gift from the Americans that the reader has already heard about—an automatic record player—was placed next to the piano.) This room also had two sofas: a small one with a mirrored back, and a large one of the same type and color of those to be found in virtually all of the other rooms in the house. It was on this sofa in the dining room that Stalin died on March 5, 1953.

The master of the house seldom visited the second floor. It had two large bright rooms. The first served as a drawing room and reception room, the second as a bedroom. These rooms were occupied by Winston Churchill in August 1942, on the occasion of his first visit to Moscow. In his memoirs he refers to this house as State Dacha Number 7, and recalls his stay there with pleasure.

This dacha also had a big kitchen. Perhaps one should not talk about the kitchen, except for the fact that it too reflected the master's tastes and habits. In addition to the ordinary gas ranges on which simple, healthful meals were prepared, the kitchen had a special stove for shashlik. And—most worthy of note—beyond a wooden partition was a big Russian stove of the oven-type in which the bread was baked. Also, according to the people who worked in this kitchen, when Stalin's radiculitis was bothering him, he would come to the kitchen, undress, put a broad plank on the hot bricks and, groaning, crawl up on it to give himself a "treatment."

The entrance hall was empty. Now everything was very quiet. I opened the door leading into the dining room. Nobody! . . . I dallied there for a bit, coughing to attract attention. Again, nobody! . . . What kind of a summons for a briefing was this? Stalin had never yet failed to be on hand to receive anyone when he had summoned him.

Suddenly a door opened (it was the one on the left, leading to the hallway), and a figure in a very long sheepskin coat appeared. The collar of the coat was turned up high, and beneath its skirt one could glimpse the turned-up toes of big black boots with thick felt soles.

The figure, from which emanated a strong scent of the woodland, flapped the sleeves of the sheepskin coat and said in the voice of Stalin, "I'll be right with you, Comrade Shtemenko. Go into the study, and I'll be there in a moment."

Now everything was clear to me. It was Stalin's habit on winter days to rest on the veranda, lying there in his felt boots and his fur cap with the ear flaps, bundled up in his long sheepskin coat. It turned out that I had come at just such a time.

Soon the Supreme Commander—wearing his usual gray attire of military cut and his soft shoes, with his pipe in his hand as always—was listening to my report. After looking over the maps, he asked a few questions about the maneuvering conditions for the forces and matériel available on the northern flank of the Soviet-

German front. As I answered, I did not forget that Stalin had a good knowledge of this theater of operations, dating back to the Soviet-Finnish War.

The Supreme Commander did not interrupt me. When I had finished, he started pacing back and forth in the study, thinking aloud about the sequence of operations by the Soviet forces. In my notebook, I jotted down the gist of his observations, which was pretty much as follows. Whereas the Leningrad Front had to carry out several simultaneous operations on the Karelian Isthmus, the Karelian Front had to carry out two similar operations over the vast expanses of the North, but in sequence: the first against the Finns and the second against the Germans.

Stalin went to the fireplace and threw a few chunks of wood on the fire, which had already died down. Then he said that despite all this, we must not weaken the Karelian Front's northern sector, where it was opposed by the German 20th (Lapland) Army. The forces there must be kept in full readiness for immediate attack, not allowing the enemy any chance of maneuvering toward the south. At this stage of the war the Soviet Supreme Command could allow itself such a reserving of forces. We were in a position to build up by other means the troops and matériel needed for the operation against the Finns, especially since any maneuvering would be far from easy under the bad road conditions in the north. Besides, the Finns were no longer what they used to be: They were exhausted in all respects, and seeking peace.

I remembered this brief incident because the Supreme Commander's remarks were taken into account in the subsequent work-up of the plans for the Karelian Front. Stalin repeated those remarks to Meretskov when the latter was summoned to the Stavka in late May 1944. He ordered Meretskov in no case to weaken the forces facing the German forces, bearing in mind that they might at any time be needed to crush the enemy across the lines from them.

"And the General Staff," Stalin said at that point, "must remind Comrade Meretskov of my order, and see that it is carried out."

At the same time work was going ahead on planning the operations of the Leningrad Front, which, as we know, was to launch its offensive first. By the time actions against the Finns were begun, great changes had been made in the Leningrad Front. As I have already mentioned, after the disbanding of the Volkhov Front, several of its armies were transferred to General Govorov (commanding the Leningrad Front). As a result the Leningrad Front's battle zone expanded considerably. The armies of the left flank (in the Pskov-Ostrov sector) had tried to break through the enemy's defenses, but had failed. On April 15 Govorov reported this to the Stavka with his usual frankness, pointing out that the operation had failed for lack of troops and matériel.

The Stavka felt it necessary to break up the Leningrad Front, using the 42nd, 67th, and 54th armies to form the 3rd Baltic Front under the command of Col. Gen. I. I. Maslennikov. In this way Govorov and his staff (which since April 28 had been headed up by General M. M. Popov) were able fully to concentrate on the operations against the Finns. (Incidentally, our attacks at Narva did not at this time result in the liberation of the city.)

The staff of the Leningrad Front spent the month of May working hard at getting the operations plans in shape, co-ordinating operations with the fleet, and concentrating troops and matériel. Govorov came to Moscow, and the operations plan was reviewed and approved by the Stavka. The front's work went very systematically, thanks to the firmness and punctuality of Govorov, and to the initiative of the new chief of staff, Popov, who knew the zone of operations very well.

In early June the Stavka also approved the Karelian Front's operations plan. (I did not take part in that, since I had had to visit the 2nd Belorussian Front to follow up on preparations for the main battle of 1944 in Belorussia.) And on June 10 the thunder of artillery on the Karelian Isthmus announced the beginning of the Leningrad Front's offensive.

The Leningrad Front's possibilities for maneuvering both troops and weapons in the course of the offensive were seriously limited by the complex physical and geographical conditions on the Karelian Isthmus and by the three strong defense lines (with their many pillboxes) that the enemy had built. Hence the plan for the operation called for a head-on assault aimed at breaking through the enemy's defenses on our left flank, where the land forces would work closely with the Baltic Fleet throughout the offensive. It was planned to develop the operation by distributing in depth the troops of the armies and the large reserves at the front level. It was proposed to capture Vyborg on the fifth or sixth day of the operation.

In this operation by the Leningrad Front, the attacking forces had decisive superiority in troops and matériel. The ratio of forces was in our favor as regards infantry (2:1), artillery and tanks (almost 6:1), and aircraft (3:1). Most of the troops and matériel on the Karelian Isthmus were concentrated in the battle zone of the 21st Army, which delivered the main blow. The 23rd Army also attacked in this sector. In the break-through sector of 12.5 kilometers the ratio of forces was even more impressive, especially as regards artillery.

The offensive by the Leningrad Front proceeded systematically, although it demanded great efforts by both the troops and the staffs. The soldiers showed both great heroism and great resourcefulness; and on June 20 at 1900, as planned, the old Russian city of Vyborg was taken by storm. That same day the forces of the Leningrad Front's 23rd Army, moving forward through the eastern part of the Karelian Isthmus, reached the Vuoksa reservoir system. The time was ripe for our armies to move into Finland beyond Vyborg, and to advance along the western shore of Lake Ladoga and into the rear of the enemy's defenses in Karelia.

The enemy tried to stop the forces of the Leningrad Front by stubbornly defending every fire point and fortification. But his defenses had crumbled. On the ninth day of the offensive the Finnish command had to inform the Finnish Government that the nation was threatened with a military catastrophe. The government empowered Gen. E. Heinrichs, chief of the General Staff, to appeal to Hitler for emergency aid in the form of six German divisions. Hitler promised he would help, requiring in return that resistance at Vuoksa be strengthened. The Finns started scraping up reserves from just about anyplace, and decided to shift several divisions from southern Karelia to the Vyborg sector, which considerably weakened their defenses across the lines from the Karelian Front. But Hitler's assistance turned out to consist of a single infantry division, reinforced by a few other units. It had become clear that henceforth Finland could count only on its own resources.

The Stavka and the General Staff closely followed the development of events. On the evening of June 18, in the course of the briefing on the situation at the front, Stalin remarked that it would soon be time for Meretskov's forces to jump off. He instructed Antonov to again call the attention of the Karelian Front's Military Council to the necessity of preserving intact the forces and matériel across the lines from the German 20th (Lapland) Army.

At 1845 Antonov sent the Karelian Front a special dispatch, saying:

> The Supreme Commander has ordered that you be reminded of his insistence that you not weaken the front's right wing and center, and that in the absence of the Stavka's authorization you not shift from that sector any forces and matériel other than those previously authorized for transfer by the Stavka.

As best I can recall, Stalin again asked about the matter on the following day, when the battle for Vyborg had already begun. In his mind's eye he saw the totality of the operations: the shifting of the enemy's forces to the Karelian Isthmus, the consequent weakening of the Finnish forces facing the Karelian Front, the latter's advance to the flank of the main concentration of Finnish forces, and the consequent operations aimed at the final defeat of the Finnish Army, and then of the German forces, which by this time would have been virtually isolated.

There was growing dismay in the enemy camp. The Finns were calling up reservists of the oldest age category, and bringing up reinforcements (including troops from other sectors) to the Karelian Isthmus.

On June 21, when this kind of enemy activity was at its height, the armies of Meretskov's front jumped off. The defeat of the invaders in Karelia had begun.

In accordance with the operations plan, in this offensive too we had superiority over the enemy in both troops and weapons. In the case of the 7th Army, which made the main thrust in the direction of Pitkyaranta, the ratios were 2:1 for infantry, almost 6:1 for tanks and artillery, and 4.5:1 for aircraft. When the enemy was compelled to shift some of his forces to the Karelian Isthmus, this superiority was considerably increased.

Although they realized defeat was inevitable, the Finns did everything possible to hang on to their positions and beat off our attack. Before the operation began, the Finnish forces holding a bridgehead across the Svir had been pulled back to the other side of the river. In this way the Finns shortened their front and took cover behind a big water barrier. They stubbornly defended each fortified position and the entire Olonets region, which was stuffed with all kinds of engineering structures and covered by intense fire. The enemy's positions in the regions of Medvezhyegorsk and Petrozavodsk, where the 32nd Army was advancing, were not so strong as this.

The actions by the Karelian Front brought tangible results. On June 23 Medvezhyegorsk was liberated. The next day the troops of Gen. A. N. Krutikov's 7th Army had put the Svir River behind them for the entirety of its length. Breaking through the enemy's resistance, the Soviet forces drove into the Olonets fortified zone and liberated the town of Olonets.

The naval vessels of the Ladoga and Onega flotillas greatly assisted the attacking troops. On June 28 the troops of the 32nd Army returned Petrozavodsk, the capital of Karelia, to the motherland. Moscow fired off a salute in honor of this feat.

Nonetheless, the Stavka and the General Staff repeatedly expressed dissatisfaction with the actions of the Karelian Front. Many mistakes were made in the command control of the forces. Thus the staff officers at the auxiliary command post in the battle zone of the 7th Army did not cope with their tasks. These officers, who were lacking in experience, failed to assure the proper continuity, firmness, and efficiency in controlling the actions of the two armies, the aircraft, and the vessels of the flotillas. As a result, the enemy was able to pull back and avoid the blows threatening him. It turned out that we had not destroyed the enemy but merely pushed him out, enabling him to slip away and preserve his force.

As early as the first days of the offensive the General Staff had noticed mistakes in the command control of the forces, and had so informed the front; but things were not improved. Not only that, but when our troops approached the national boundary in the vicinity of Kuolisma, two divisions found themselves in a critical position. In that rugged terrain the Finns had enveloped them in small groups, in some areas infiltrating the positions. One division was cut off from its supply route, and for a time, stores and ammunition had to be air-dropped.

These failures were all the more vexing in that as a whole the operation intended to defeat Hitler's Finnish accomplices had gone off successfully. The Stavka pointed out to the military council that "it was largely due to poor organization of command control that the last operation of the Karelian Front's left flank was a failure. The Stavka also notes that the staff of the front is cluttered up with unproductive and incapable personnel." The Stavka ordered the Military Council of the Karelian Front to correct the shortcomings it had noted. Certain high officers were transferred. In particular, on September 2, 1944, Lt. Gen. A. N. Krutikov became chief of staff of the Karelian Front (as I mentioned earlier).

The catastrophic trend of events on the front compelled the Finnish Government to change its policy. Finland, faced with an imminent military defeat, had to look for a way out of the war. Under the pressure of circumstances, President Ryti and his Cabinet resigned. Carl Gustaf Mannerheim became the new President.

Now it was Hitler's turn to sound the alarm, since the prospects for the German forces in Finland were bleak. Gen. Wilhelm Keitel came to Helsinki to look into things on the spot and put pressure on the Finns. On August 17 the new President told him that he did not consider himself bound by the agreement with the German Government that had been signed by the former President, Ryti.

Within a week the Soviet ambassador in Sweden, Mme. Alexandra M. Kollontai (a remarkable Soviet woman), got a request from the Finnish Government that the Soviet Government receive a delegation, agree on an armistice, and conclude a peace. The answer was as follows: The USSR would accept the Finnish delegation if the Finns agreed to meet the following preliminary conditions: make a public announcement of a rupture of relations with Germany; demand that Germany withdraw its armed forces from Finland in two weeks, and in any case no later than September 15; if Germany does not comply with the demand to evacuate its forces, disarm the German troops and turn them over to the allies as prisoners of war. (The Soviet Government had previously cleared these preliminary conditions with the governments of the United States and Great Britain.)

While awaiting an answer from the Finnish Government, the Stavka ordered that the forces of the 7th and 32nd armies of the Karelian Front break off their offensive and go on the defensive at the farthest point of their advance. This directive strongly emphasized that "you will not carry out offensive actions without authorization from the Stavka."

In late August 1944 the weather was splendid. Stalin, who like the rest of us was weary from the incredible tensions of day-to-day military tasks, had chosen to work at Near House, his dacha at Kuntsevo. It was there that we briefed him on the situation and got his signature on documents. And it was there that, from time to time, the members of the government assembled.

During his brief moments of relaxation, the master of the house was very hospitable, and liked to show his guests around the grounds. On one occasion, pointing to a small plot of high ground that had been cleared of trees, Stalin said that after the war he was going to grow watermelons there. Antonov and I exchanged glances as if to say, "This is Kuntsevo and not the Kuban." But shortly after the war we were reminded of those watermelons. Following a fly-past at Tushino (one that had finally taken place after many postponements due to the bad weather), Stalin invited the members of the Politburo and the top officials of the War Ministry (as it was then called) to have lunch at Near House. The tables had been laid beneath the birches. The weather was marvelous, and everyone was in a good mood. After lunch Stalin took us to that same small rise of ground, where a few dozen watermelons were actually growing! In leisurely fashion, he chose a rather large melon, brought it to the table, and sliced it in half with one stroke of a long knife. It turned out to be a beautiful red and rather sweet. One could only be amazed that such melons could have been grown out in the open in the climate of the Moscow region.

On September 2, 1944, two different messages were sent out from the presidential residence in Helsinki: one to Hitler in Berlin, and the other to the Soviet ambassador in Stockholm for forwarding to the Soviet Government. The first message stated that Finland was compelled to get out of the war, and that it was deeply grateful to its ally, the German Army. The second message contained a reply to the preliminary conditions laid down by the USSR, the United States, and Great Britain, and stated that Finland itself would voluntarily evacuate or intern the German troops in the southern part of Finland. It also contained a proposal to cease hostilities and pull back the Finnish forces to the Soviet-Finnish border of 1940.

The President further stated that the Finns were also ready to take part in an operation to disarm the German forces in the northern part of Finland, but that they would like to reach agreement in Moscow on co-ordination and help from the Soviet command in this matter.

On the night of September 3 the Finnish Prime Minister, Kaksel, made a speech on the Finnish radio. He talked about the state of affairs, about Finland's "honorable" alliance with Nazi Germany, and about Finland's leaving the war under the pressure of circumstances; but he made no mention of the Soviet Government's demand that the German troops be disarmed and relations with Germany be broken off: He did not say that Finland was breaking off those relations.

The Soviet Government had to make a strong statement. It insisted that Finland accept the preliminary conditions, and warned that until that was done, there would be no talks about a truce and peace.

This statement produced an effect; and the next night the Finnish radio announced that the government was accepting all the preliminary conditions. It was also announced that the Finnish forces were ceasing hostilities. Immediately thereafter, the General Staff received an order from the Stavka to cease firing on the Finnish Army.

Upon cessation of hostilities against the Finns, the command of the Karelian Front ordered its forces to make ready for an offensive against the German 20th (Lapland) Army. The mission was to crush the enemy, take Petsamo and Salmijärvi, and cut off the Nazis' escape routes to the Finnish and Norwegian ports.

On September 8 the Military Council of the Karelian Front reported to Moscow that the enemy had initiated a partial withdrawal of forces in the Kandalaksha, Kestenga, and Ukhta sectors toward the Finnish port of Oulu and northern Norway. Just at this time the front was transferring several units by rail from the southern flank to the Arctic region for the next offensive.

The General Staff carefully analyzed the situation on the northern flank of the Soviet-German front. There were many items to weigh, and just as many contradictions. Hostilities had ceased on the Finnish front, but it was not entirely clear what the Finnish Army was doing. The German troops were supposed to be either evacuated or interned; yet they had begun a partial withdrawal on their right flank, and were effecting it without interference.

The Finns had expressed their readiness to take part in disarming the German forces in the northern part of Finland; yet the actions of the Soviet and Finnish forces in that respect had not yet been co-ordinated. The Finns wanted to talk about all these things in Moscow. But when?

According to Soviet military doctrine and practice, if the enemy begins to withdraw his troops from the positions they have been occupying, our troops are to go in hot pursuit. But how should the Soviet forces proceed in this situation, since pursuit would inevitably involve violating the USSR's border with Finland, which was not supposed to be crossed? And if we did go in pursuit, what was the best way to do it, since we did not yet have the shock groups that would be needed for complete success? Although the front had preserved intact the forces in the German sector, it had only

just begun regrouping the troops and ordnance calculated to be
necessary for the offensive, and it must be admitted that it was not
doing this very rapidly.

Likewise unclear was the plan the command of the Karelian
Front was supposed to follow in the immediate future.

I reported our doubts to Antonov. He told me that a delegation
from the Finnish Government had already arrived in Moscow to
hold peace talks; but he agreed to send Meretskov a brief dispatch
instructing him to respond to all the unsettled questions, so that
we could know where we stood with respect to the future.

I quote from that dispatch, sent on September 10 at 1330:

> The front's actions and regrouping are being effected very
> slowly. In no sector have you formed a shock group to de-
> stroy the German forces, which in several sectors have al-
> ready begun to withdraw.
>
> In the Kandalaksha and Kestenga sectors our forces have
> been sucked into head-on engagements with the enemy's cov-
> ering units and are letting him make an orderly withdrawal
> rather than cutting off his escape routes and crushing him.
>
> For purposes of briefing the Stavka, I ask you to send me a
> detailed plan for the operations of the front's right wing, in-
> dicating the groups, the sequence of the actions, the objec-
> tives, and the ETAs for each sector in particular. Antonov.

From the reply to this dispatch it was plain that the front command was preparing to carry out a decisive operation against the
German forces withdrawing from Finland—an operation that involved extensive and difficult turning movements. The General
Staff reported this to the Stavka.

The Supreme Commander sympathized with the intentions of
the Military Council, but he did not agree with them. He was supported by Molotov, who had already begun preliminary armistice
talks with the envoys of the Finnish Government. In those talks,
great respect was shown for the sovereignty of Finland. The main
idea was that the fate of the Nazi troops in Finnish territory
should not be decided by us but by the Finns, the masters of the
country. If they needed help and asked for it, we would supply it.
But under any circumstances we had to preserve our own forces
so as to smash the units of the German 20th (Lapland) Army,

which were still on Soviet territory, and clear the invaders out of the Arctic region.

After a brief exchange of opinions, the Stavka sent the Karelian Front an order canceling the front command's orders as incorrect. "In accordance with our talks with the Finns," the Stavka said, "the Finns themselves are to be responsible for evacuating the German forces from Finland, while our forces will merely aid them in this matter."

On this basis the Stavka forbade the front to initiate attacks against the German forces: "In case the Germans withdraw, follow them without engaging them in any big battles and without exhausting our forces by combat and extensive turning movement, so that our forces may be better preserved."

This decision was of course very unusual; but it conformed fully to the demands of the situation and of high-level policy.

Another question arose at this session of the Stavka: Would not the energetic General Meretskov rush in pursuit of the enemy despite such clear and definite orders from the Supreme Command? It was decided that that, too, should be prevented. So the order included the following: "The Stavka demands that you carry out its orders to the letter, and again warns you that your failure to carry out its orders or your attempts to rush on ahead will result in your removal from command of the front."

The order ended with the routine sentence: "Report what orders you have issued." This time it had a special ring to it.

It must be admitted that the General Staff, too, wanted to defeat the German forces as soon as possible. And—let's face it—with our verbal and written demands we had been nudging Meretskov on. So that the order sent to him was an explanation not only for Meretskov but for the General Staff, although written up by the latter.

The peace talks with Finland began in Moscow on September 14. Shortly before, I was told that I had been appointed to the Soviet delegation, which was headed by Molotov. It also included Voroshilov, Zhdanov, Litvinov, and Rear Admiral Aleksandrov. Great Britain was represented by Ambassador Kerr and Counselor Balfour. (The Soviet and British delegations were acting in the name of all nations in the anti-Nazi coalition.) The Finns had sent K. Engkel, their Minister of Foreign Affairs, Gen. R. Valden, their Minister of War, Gen. E. Heinrichs, chief of the Finnish General Staff, and Gen. O. Enckel.

At some points the enemy's defense line in Karelia extended a considerable distance into Soviet territory. The Finnish forces had created an in-depth defense, fortifying all approaches to outposts, positions, and pillboxes with a great many obstacles of complex configuration and varied technical design and function. In addition to antitank ditches and stakes there were mine fields, booby traps, wire entanglements (both electrified and ordinary), and all kinds of traps, pitfalls, and other obstacles. They had been placed everywhere in those parts of the terrain that were not impassable: on the roads (and even the paths) that could be used by troops on foot or by transport. The rivers, the lakes, and the Gulf of Finland were full of mines and other obstacles. Finally, all the inhabited localities, the facilities of the railroad and communications systems, of industry, and municipal utilities systems, had been made ready to blow up, while the reserves of matériel were to be destroyed.

We military men were to formulate such demands on the Finnish side as would ensure the security of our forces as they moved up to the border, and the preservation of stores and installations. Also, we had to work out the procedure for removing obstacles in the water and on land, for objectives in the area, and for preserving commercial and other installations. We had to give thought to guarantees of the personal inviolability of people living on Soviet territory who had temporarily been under the control of the Finns, and to seeing that they were not driven over the border.

Such work was not easy, but we gained strength from knowing how important the task was. The tension was very great, and the tempo of the work extraordinarily fast. Both prior to the sessions and during them, Molotov communicated with us via short notes handed across the table. In those notes he would express a viewpoint or ask a question in two words. And we had to answer immediately so as not to interrupt the businesslike flow of the talks.

The talks lasted for several hours each day, with some time left to prepare for the next session. For me this was especially important, since no one had been relieved of his regular work. We had to snatch moments to write up and transmit to the front the necessary instructions based on our questions. (The pull-back of the Finnish forces was set for 0900 on September 21, 1944.)

The problem of disarming those German forces—land, sea, and air—which had remained in Finland after September 15 was accorded special attention during the talks. The Finns had committed themselves to disarming those forces and handing the personnel over to the Soviet command as prisoners of war, while the Soviet Government was to help the Finnish Army. Also, an annex to Article 2 of the armistice agreement stipulated that the Finnish military command would give us all the information they had on the German armed forces and their plans for operations against the USSR and other countries in the anti-Nazi coalition.

No great difficulties arose when the problem of disarming the Germans was discussed. As the reader will recall, this problem had arisen before the beginning of the official talks; and the Finns had come to Moscow already realizing that that job would have to be done simultaneously with other most urgent ones. The USSR and our allies insisted on unconditional compliance with this article, since they figured that to leave German forces intact in Finland for a long period of time would mean the likelihood of new warfare on Finnish soil.

The third article of the agreement was chiefly concerned with air force matters. At the demand of the Soviet command (as the reader will recall, we were speaking in the name of all the allies), Finland made available several airfields along its south and southwest coasts. These airfields were needed by the aircraft supporting the operations of Soviet forces in Estonia and against the German Navy in the northern part of the Baltic. An annex to this article also stipulated that allied naval vessels were entitled to use Finland's territorial waters, ports, docks, and anchorages.

Provision was also made for the use of railroad and other means of communication serving the regions of the airfields, for transmitting meteorological information, and for other things essential in assuring the functioning of aircraft, ships, and other military equipment in Finland.

Finally, a procedure was spelled out for putting the Finnish Army on a peacetime footing within ten weeks after the signing of the agreement, since we could not count on that Army's taking part in the subsequent operations to liquidate the German forces in the Arctic. (And such proved to be the case. The Stavka and the General Staff depended entirely upon the Red Army and the Soviet Navy, which performed brilliantly their task of defeating the invaders in the North.)

These articles comprised most of the technical military aspect of the talks. But there were other matters that required consultation with military men. For example, we relinquished our right to lease Hangö Peninsula but got territory and maritime rights in the region of Porkkala-Udd. Thus in one way or another, we representatives of the General Staff participated rather extensively in the talks.

On September 19 at 1200 hours, A. A. Zhdanov—first member of the Leningrad Front's Military Council and future chairman of the control commission in Finland—signed the armistice with Finland and the necessary annexes, in the name of the allies.

The prohibitions against wearing out our forces and not provoking engagements for the time being were strictly observed: Meretskov issued the appropriate orders to his armies. Soon, however, new complications arose. As stipulated in the armistice, the Finns withdrew to the border. But our forces had been operating in various ways: Where they were faced with Finns, they had advanced only as far as the border; but where they were faced with Germans, they had pursued them into Finnish territory.

The 19th Army was given the mission of taking Kuolajärvi and advancing as far as the very important industrial region of Rovaniemi, a communications hub in northern Finland. This would enable the Army, if necessary, to give the Finns real help in driving the Germans out of the country.

The units of the German 20th (Lapland) Army proved incapable of creating a new front on the territory of Finland. They were obliged to effect a slow withdrawal, which they did in two directions: to the west, toward ports on the Baltic, for subsequent evacuation by sea; and to the north, toward the region of Petsamo, where they intended to dig in with strong defenses.

The enemy's rear-guard units began their withdrawal on September 25, and Meretskov duly reported this to the General Staff. The 19th and 26th armies moved forward.

The Finnish forces were also withdrawing after the Germans, but very slowly and lagging far behind them. The Karelian Front's intelligence reported that the Finns had no contact with the Germans, and there letting them withdraw unhampered from the regions of Kuolajärvi and Rovaniemi.

At that moment a complex situation fraught with unexpected consequences developed in the Karelian Front's battle zone—a situation that Meretskov noticed: In pursuing the Germans, G. K. Kozlov's 19th Army might find itself between them and the Finnish forces, who were lagging far behind them. "What should we do," Meretskov asked the General Staff, "if the Finns are in fact separated from the Germans, and we follow on the Germans' heels with the result that the Finns are behind the 19th Army's lines?" He asked us to inform him as to the position of the Finnish forces assigned to disarm the Germans so that he could regulate the actions of his own units.

At the General Staff we carefully checked on the possibility of that undesirable situation's arising. It turned out that Meretskov was right. On September 26 we reported on the situation to the Stavka, noting that our forces could be sucked into an engagement first. This would contravene the spirit of the armistice, and the Finns would remain on the sidelines. Also, they would be entitled to protest, since the agreement provided for operations by Soviet forces on Finnish territory only if the Finns requested them.

After carefully studying the situation on the northern flank of the Soviet-German front, the Stavka agreed with the opinion of the General Staff and the front command: It would be extremely undesirable to be sucked into an engagement with the Germans while a Finnish army was behind the lines of our forces.

The decision taken by the Stavka was as follows. The 19th Army would not move deep into Finland but would seize the border region to the west of Kuolajärvi, where it would pull up and let the Finnish forces move toward the north. The possession of this region would also make it possible to operate toward the northwest to help the Finns in case of need. General Kozlov's forces were to proceed farther only with the permission of the Stavka. At the same time the Stavka ordered the Karelian Front to plan an offensive operation using the forces of the 14th Army and the front's reinforcement capacity to clear the enemy out of the Petsamo region. Thus the final phase in the struggle against the invaders of the Soviet Arctic had begun.

I have already remarked that combat conditions in the Arctic were unique and very difficult. Some bitter fighting had been going on in this harsh region. In 1941 the Soviet forces had courageously beaten off a powerful enemy offensive, and since then had not let him advance a single step. The defense of the Soviet Arctic contributed a splendid page to the chronicle of the war, along with other glorious battles for the honor and independence of the Soviet Land. In commemoration of the Soviet soldiers' valor and courage, a special medal, "For the Defense of the Soviet Arctic," was struck as a token of socialist fatherland's gratitude toward the heroes of the northern latitudes.

Meretskov had long been awaiting the Stavka's orders to prepare and carry out an operation in the Arctic; and as soon as he received that order, he submitted for Moscow's approval his plan for operations in the Petsamo region.

The Karelian Front's 14th Army was opposed by the German 19th (Norway) Corps and the 20th (Lapland) Army, reinforced by chasseurs and other units. The·enemy had occupied these defenses for three years, and had built strong, deep positions with reinforced concrete bunkers at intervals. Hitler's High Command had ordered that the troops not retreat one step: that they hang on to this nickel-mining region. Because of the vast, uninhabited expanses, the Germans could not organize solid defenses on every side. Thus the southern flank of their fortified positions dwindled away along the Finnish border west of Mt. Matert. Their defenses were especially strong on the approaches to Petsamo, Luostari, and Nikel. In this region the German command had taken advantage of the impassable rivers—the Bolshaya Lits, the Titovka, and the Pechenga—and the many lakes, and had fortified the steep slopes of the hills.

The German 2nd Alpine Division occupied the strongest fortified positions, in the middle of the defense line. Its forces held the sectors of Luostari and Petsamo. If this division (on which the other German forces seemed to be depending) were defeated, the way would be cleared to the inhabited localities.

Meretskov, who had correctly grasped the role of the enemy's 2nd Alpine Division, decided to strike his main blow against it, to break through the German defenses on a narrow sector of the front south of Lake Chapr, and to develop the success throughout the depth of the enemy's operational structure, and take Petsamo. Elsewhere on the front the weak forces of the 45th Rifle Division and the 3rd Motorized Rifle Brigade were to be on the defensive during the break-through. At the same time Meretskov planned to use the 126th and 127th light rifle corps to turn the southern flank of the enemy's defense line. One of them, the 127th, was given the mission of advancing to the region of Salmijärvi (at a great distance from the main forces) to isolate the German garrison in the town of Nikel from the escape routes to Norway. Then Meretskov planned to secure cover in the direction of Salmijärvi (from where he expected the enemy's possible counterattack), while his main forces wheeled north to smash the enemy's defenses along the Titovka River. At that moment the 45th Rifle Division and the 3rd Motorized Rifle Brigade, which had been on the defensive, would go over to the offensive and strike the enemy's defense line from the front. On the break-through sector the density of artillery and mortars was 160–170 per meter, and we had considerable air superiority.

The Stavka looked over the proposals of the Karelian Front's Military Council, and in general agreed with them. But it made several substantial corrections that had to do above all with the interaction between the 14th Army and the Northern Fleet. During the break-through of the enemy's defenses, the Northern Fleet would be able to ashore sizable (under the circumstances) quantities of troops and matériel along the Srednyi Peninsula. And in the course of the operation it could do the same at various points along the seacoast. This opportunity had to be utilized.

Admiral Golovko, commanding the Northern Fleet, was instructed to organize an attack by a brigade of marines, who would advance southward from Srednyi Peninsula. Their blows would be aimed directly toward the rear of the Nazis' defenses along the Titovka River, and if vigorously delivered would disorganize those defenses interaction with the frontal blows of those small forces of, the 14th Army assigned to deliver them.

The maneuver along the Titovka River that was called for in Meretskov's plan was complex. Moreover, with the marines attacking from Srednyi Peninsula, it would not be at all necessary.

The Stavka ordered the front: "Do not scatter your forces for a thrust to the northeast along the Titovka River." And it insisted that the main forces be sent toward Petsamo, so they could take it as quickly as possible. As for the 127th Light Rifle Corps, the Stavka ordered that it not be sent far ahead to Salmijärvi with a risk of being cut off from the main forces but that it be echeloned along the left flank of the attacking group of forces.

By early October 1944 the 131st and 99th Rifle corps had been concentrated in the break-through area south of Lake Chapr, and all the matériel had been brought up. The Northern Fleet was also ready. On October 7 Gen. V. I. Shcherbakov's 14th Army jumped off. It had great success: The enemy's defenses were smashed, while the 126th Light Rifle Corps skillfully turned the Germans' open flank on the south, and by the end of the third day was west of Luostari. The frontal break-through, in combination with our turning movement, compelled the enemy to reduce resistance at the positions east of Petsamo. This was also facilitated by the marine brigade's lightning attack from Srednyi Peninsula on the night of October 10–11. The marines broke the enemy's resistance on the crest of Musta-Tunturi, and wheeled toward the west.

On October 12 our forces took Luostari, and the next day they reached the approaches to Petsamo. The fighting was very bitter. The 368th Rifle Division, under the command of Maj. Gen. V. K. Sopenko, beat off sixteen counterattacks in only twenty-four hours. In the air, the front's aircraft shot down sixty-six planes.

On October 15, units of the Karelian Front's assault group, operating jointly with units of the Northern Fleet, forced the Pechenga River and took the town of Petsamo. In an intrepid thrust the heroic marines seized the port of Linakhamari, covering Petsamo from the north.

The defeat of the German forces in the Soviet Arctic had become a fact. In its operational summary as of 0700 on October 16, the headquarters of the Karelian Front reported to the General Staff: "The remnants of the enemy's battered units in the Petsamo region are retreating along a road running northwest toward Norwegian territory. . . ."

The Military Council of the Karelian Front had already planned the next operations with a view to clearing the enemy out of the entire region from Petsamo northwest to the Barents Sea and to the west as far as the Norwegian border, and seizing the nickel-mining region. Meretskov now asked that the front be authorized to pursue the enemy's defeated forces across the border into Norwegian territory.

The Stavka authorized the crossing of the Norwegian border and the development of our offensive toward Kirkenes, which was the enemy's main base in that region. On Finnish territory the blows of the Karelian Front were to be struck toward the southwest along the Finnish-Norwegian border in the direction of Nikel and Nautsi. These two places were in the center of the nickel-mining region and lay along the main route from Lapland into the interior of Norway and Finland. The task of defeating the German forces in this region was assigned to the troops of the 31st Rifle Corps and the 127th Light Rifle Corps. Since the start of the offensive, both formations had been in the second wave (of the 14th Army) and had advanced right behind the first wave. But on October 18, from the region of Luostari, they drove toward Nikel along the only road then existent, branching off to the left from the main advance of the Soviet forces.

As we know, the military art has since the days of Epaminondas required that one's main forces be concentrated in the sector of the main thrust. But at this stage in the battle to liberate the Arctic region from the Nazi invaders, such a tactic was by no means required. The enemy's main forces had been crushed, and no compact group of them existed any longer. So that the front commander could, without running any particular risk, divide his forces for operations in divergent directions. It was a measure justified by the conditions of the battle. On October 22 Nikel was taken, and not long afterward troops of the 31st Rifle Corps and the 127th Light Rifle Corps entered Nautsi.

On October 25 the main forces of the 14th Army liberated Kirkenes. At the same time the 126th Light Rifle Corps advanced from the region of Akhmalakhti across Norwegian territory toward Neiden. The scattered and disorganized units of the battered enemy forces were on the run into the Norwegian interior. Here they came up against the gunfire of the Norwegian resistance fighters.

On the night of October 29, 1944, by which time the Soviet forces had left behind them the small Norwegian town of Neiden, the Military Council of the Karelian Front reported to Stalin that there was no more enemy opposing the front. The mission of clearing the Nazi invaders out of the Soviet North had been accomplished.

On October 25 two victory salutes were fired in Moscow, one of them in honor of the Karelian Front which, operating jointly with the Northern Fleet, had liberated Kirkenes. That day our soldiers had crossed the border of a country which had been one of the first to fall under the yoke of the Nazi invaders. Also liberated along with Kirkenes were the inhabited localities of Sturbugt, Yakobsnes, Elvenes, Berkkheim, Sandnes, Bernevand, Longfordbotn, Nigord, Fossgord, Langli, and Svanvik.

The Norwegian Government had sent Moscow a message saying that the people of Northern Norway would greet the Soviet troops as their liberators. And in fact these Norwegians became not only our friends but fighters for victory over our hated, common enemy.

. . . The cold waters of Jarfjord had blocked the approach to Kirkenes from the east. The suspension bridge has been destroyed. It was extremely difficult to cross that deep wide fjord with its steep rocky cliffs, and with a strong and crafty enemy behind his defenses on the other side. At this point Meretskov brought into play the amphibious "ducks" with which the forces had been endowed. What with the explosions of enemy shells and the choppy water, the ducks did not always reach their destination: They would capsize, and the soldiers with their heavy equipment would sink to the bottom. When the battle had reached its critical point, low-slung, sturdy fishing boats made their appearance in the fjord. They were being operated by their owners— local fishermen who knew each stone of the fjord's rigged shores. Working under enemy artillery and machine-gun fire, the Norwegians saved Soviet soldiers who had fallen into the water; and on instructions from our officers, they ferried troops to the other side. One of these Norwegian patriots, M. Hansen, ferried an entire rifle battalion across in his boat. And T. Ballo, S. Martensen, O. Hansen, and P. Hanse also took many troops across. These valiant Norwegians also found plenty to do on shore: They put out the fires that had broken out in the town, and repaired the bridges so that Soviet troops and equipment could come across. A. Martensen and U. Holstensen distinguished themselves in this respect. The latter disarmed some bombs that had been placed in an electric power station, so that it was intact when the Soviet troops arrived.

The same kind of thing happened inland, when forces of the Karelian Front were crossing the Neiden River. Once again the bearded taciturn Norwegians ferried our troops across in their own boats, making more than one trip under heavy fire from the enemy. E. Kaikunen took 135 Soviet soldiers across. A. Labakhu took 115, L. Sirin 95, U. Ladago 95, and P. Hendriksen 76. And there were still other heroes whose names, unfortunately, have not been preserved. Our common goal and the actions of those Soviet troops who lent the Norwegians a hand in a difficult year of the war made the traditional friendship between our two nations even stronger.

The fact that forces of the Karelian Front had entered Norwegian territory created favorable conditions for the systematic activity of the Norwegian Resistance. In the Soviet Union we had understood and appreciated the difficulty of the struggle that the

Norwegian patriots had waged unremittingly during the worst years of the Nazi occupation. The Soviet Government and the Soviet Command had done everything possible to help in that struggle. In Moscow there was a Norwegian Military Mission headed by Colonel Dahl which performed tasks similar to those of the military missions of other nations. In particular, it was via that mission that the Soviet Supreme Command maintained liaison with the armed forces of Norway. Before the time the Karelian Front reached the Norwegian border, the General Staff knew that outside of Norway the Norwegian Government was training special detachments of a few hundred men each to carry out military missions in their native land. Also, those detachments were to become the nucleus of the Norwegian armed forces. The time had now come when the Norwegian detachments could go to northern Norway. Talks had already been held on the subject, and Murmansk had been named as the destination of the transport ships carrying the troops.

But events were moving fast, and it became necessary even before the Norwegian troops reached the liberated part of their country to get to work liquidating the consequences of the occupation. Through its military mission in the USSR the Royal Norwegian Government gave us to understand that it would be appreciative if the Red Army, having entered Norwegian territory, would do what it could to help local administrations and the forces of the Norwegian Resistance.

But the arrival of the Norwegian forces was delayed, the "Murmansk run" being difficult and dangerous, so the command of the 14th Army had to take on the initial organizational work paving the way for collaboration between Soviet and Norwegian forces on the territory liberated by the Karelian Front. The command's authority for this was the Norwegian Government's message to the Soviet Government, King Haakon's address to the Norwegian people, and the agreement on civil administration on Norwegian territory concluded on March 17, 1944, between the governments of the USSR, the United States, and Great Britain on the one hand and the Norwegian Government on the other. (According to this agreement, during time of hostilities the allied commanders

377

were invested with supreme authority vis-à-vis the civil administration.)

On November 3, 1944, exercising that authority, Maj. Gen. A.
Ya. Sergeyev, a member of the 14th Army's Military Council,
summoned members of the local (Norwegian) government and
proposed organized detachments to combat the German fascists.
There were some 20,000 to 22,000 inhabitants in the liberated
part of the country, according to the estimate of the Norwegian
Military Mission. The proposal was to organize two detachments
of about 400 men each.

The leaders of the local government promised to bend every
effort to form the detachments. It was decided to train them in a
tunnel at the iron mine near the settlement of Bernvad, since there
was no other building available for this kind of work in a region
laid waste by the enemy. Time was pressing. The sooner the Norwegians started defending their own country against the enemy,
the better. The representatives of the local government declared
they would work day and night. But the difficulties were great.
The local inhabitants lived on farms or in settlements up to a hundred kilometers apart. There were no roads, no transport, and no
communications. The situation with regard to provisions was very
bad. The necessary uniforms were lacking, and there was no footwear at all. Also, none of the inhabitants had had any previous
military training, and it was simply impossible to find any officers.

But the local government people did not lose their presence of
mind or their belief that the problems of training the detachments
could be licked. They asked the Soviet general to do what he
could toward getting the Norwegian Government to send them in
short order a representative to settle urgent questions concerning
them as Norwegians. (They openly stated that the inhabitants of
northern Norway were organizing detachments to combat the German fascists, and that those units were an integral part of the Norwegian Army.) And they asked something else of the Soviet command: to help them by supplying matériel, to issue provisions and
uniforms to the troops, and to supply vehicles for the purpose of
carrying the word to the inhabitants.

The 14th Army's Military Council complied with these requests by the Norwegian patriots. The provisions and uniforms were issued. And motor vehicles were allocated to that notice that the self-defense detachments were being formed could be conveyed to the inhabitants.

But our aid to the local population didn't stop there. On the liberated territory of Norway we built a hospital base (vital to that part of the country), combated infectious diseases among the population, and set up communications systems. Soviet soldiers helped to put installations of economic value into operation; and sometimes they shared with the Norwegians things that they themselves had plainly been short of.

After the holiday of the Great October Revolution, representatives of the Norwegian Military Mission in Moscow and the first combat brigade arrived in Norway.

Obviously, the self-defense forces were not adequate to provide full security for the liberated territory. Hence the Stavka instructed the Karelian Front (on November 9, 1944) to go on the defensive and dig in along the Norwegian border, with covering and reconnaissance units positioned along the Neiden-Vortaniemi line, which marked the limit of the front's advance. The troops set about regular exercises to keep them in combat-readiness.

On November 15 the Karelian Front was disbanded. The 14th Army became a detached formation, under direct command of the Stavka. In January 1945 Meretskov came to Yaroslavl. He was scheduled for transfer to the Far East to discharge new responsibilities.

The defeat of the enemy on the northern flank of the Soviet-German front was of great political and military significance. The German forces were now short of many thousands of crack troops who had vanished under the blows of the Soviet armies in the forests of Karelia and the tundra of the Soviet Arctic. The enemy lost an extensive bridgehead from which he had threatened important regions of the USSR. The Soviet front was firmly consolidated along the national boundary line. Operating conditions had considerably improved for the Northern Fleet and the Baltic Fleet, as well as for our fronts in the Baltic area. And the threat to Leningrad had been considerably lessened.

Bornholm Island is situated in the gray waters of the Baltic 135 kilometers east of Denmark. The encyclopedias give us some scant information on it: The island has an area of 587 square kilometers, and 47,000 inhabitants.

It was not by chance that the Germans were there. In 1940, after seizing Denmark, they hastened to put a garrison on Bornholm, which controlled the southern part of the Baltic. The islanders were cut off from their motherland, and the German commandant became the master of their fate.

Toward the end of the war, the island began to fill up with German soldiers who had fled from the mainland and the Soviet and Polish troops' retribution. The Nazis (who had not laid down their arms) soon began to gobble the island up, quite literally. Not a grain of wheat or a drop of milk was left: The meat of the islanders' dairy herds had gone into the German soldiers' stomachs. The inhabitants were dying of starvation. And even the Nazis were faced with the specter of famine.

A humanitarian desire to save the inhabitants of Bornholm from death and the dominance of the German invaders prompted the Stavka to decide that the island should be occupied and the armed Nazis taken prisoner. On instructions from the Supreme Commander, our allies were informed of this decision. And on May 11, 1945, the 19th Army's 132nd Rifle Corps, under the command of Maj. Gen. F. F. Korotkov, was landed on the island from ships of the Baltic Fleet. The 12,000 enemy troops had to lay down their arms.

Life on the island had to be put into some kind of order. The Soviet soldiers worked alongside the islanders in the fields, and helped restore communications and the fishing industry. Gradually the inhabitants came back to normal, after the tortures of the fascist occupation. Agriculture and crafts were revived. Soon the number of Soviet troops on the island was reduced to division strength. And one year after the landing—in April 1946—

Bornholm Island was formally handed back to the Danish authorities, and the Soviet troops left for home.

Since time immemorial the people of our country, of Norway, and of Denmark have been living in friendship and mutual respect. There are no military conflicts—there is no bloody strife—in their past. But there is something else: our joint struggle against the oppressor—the German fascist invaders. That struggle has bound us together in brotherhood, and remains a glorious and perduring page of history.

The liberation struggle in Norway took a great toll of victims: Almost 2,900 Soviet soldiers laid down their lives along with the heroes of the Norwegian Resistance. The feat of those who fell in battle serves to remind us of the hardships and lessons of the war against the Nazi aggressors—as a call for new efforts and feats for the sake of peace and progress.

11

ON THE LAST DEFENSE
LINES IN EUROPE

Disorder in the enemy camp. Intrigues behind our back. A démarche by the Soviet Government. Forecasts by the General Staff. The talks in Reims. Should one sign? "We must cut through the spider web." The fall of Berlin. Where is Hitler? The rats leave the sinking ship. Onward to Prague! Events in the capital of Czechoslovakia. Unconditional surrender. Schörner "washes his hands." The traitors' end.

The Nazi ringleaders had long ago thought about withdrawing forces from the western front and shifting them to the east, so that all their strength could be pitted against the Red Army. But this could be done only if they surrendered to our allies and made a separate peace with them, or if they reached an agreement with them. Incidentally, as I have said earlier, Hitler's Rumanian and Hungarian minions had already tried to do that behind our back. Now, with the beginning of large-scale operations on the western front, we could expect new attempts to impair the unity of the three Great Powers.

Our predictions proved correct. In this connection it would not be out of place to recall certain events of those days that the General Staff had to cope with. For example, in his *History of the Second World War,* Kurt von Tippelskirch testifies that in planning the Ardennes operation (the Battle of the Bulge) the German command was not pursuing an exclusively military aim. It was hoping in case of success to sow serious dissension between Roosevelt and Churchill.[1] On that occasion we helped our allies out of trouble by launching our Vistula-Oder operation ahead of schedule. Our swift advance (in January 1945) from the Vistula to the Oder prompted certain leaders of the German fascist state (in particular, Gen. Heinz Guderian) to sound the alarm and try to lay the groundwork for Germany's withdrawal from the war. Their view was shared by certain influential officials in Joachim von Ribbentrop's ministry. Attempts to save the sinking ship of the Nazi state were dressed up as "acts of humanitarianism" whose purpose it was to save the people of Germany and Europe from the "threat of Bolshevism." Guderian, recalling a talk he had on January 23, 1945, with the official of the Ministry of Foreign Affairs who served as liaison officer with the OKH (Army High Command), of which Guderian was then chief, wrote that both wanted to conclude "a separate peace if nothing better." Moreover, the Nazis were already regarding an opening up of the front to the Anglo-American forces as a practical problem. The German Minister of Foreign Affairs (Ribbentrop) also felt that the British and Americans should become the Nazis' allies against the USSR, but at that particular moment he couldn't bring himself to support the army chief of staff's (Guderian's) viewpoint. Guderian, who had not yet given up hope of finding support at the very summit of the Nazi elite, next turned to Heinrich Himmler. But the latter replied, "My dear General, it is still too early!" And on the evening of that same day, Hitler gave Guderian a four weeks' leave of absence "to improve his health."

There were also direct attempts, on neutral soil, to sound out the possibilities for concluding a separate peace with our allies. Gen. K. Wolf, who commanded the SS and the police on the

[1] See K. Tippelskirch, *Istoriya vtoroi mirovoi voiny* (Moscow: Foreign Literature Publishers, 1956), p. 495.

Italian front, met with Allen Dulles in Switzerland on March 8. It was hardly likely that Wolf had decided on his own to take such a step; obviously, it had been thought up by his superior or superiors. Just who did it, we did not know, nor did it particularly matter. At the General Staff we received information from intelligence as to the fact of the meeting; and it was not hard to surmise what was discussed. We also had some reports (not very precise, to be sure) of a power struggle among the leaders of Nazi Germany.

It should be noted that the notion of "surrender" entertained by our allies very much served the purposes of the German generals. Although our allies wanted and demanded Germany's unconditional surrender to the United Nations on a "war-wide" scale, they did make a very substantial exception to that principle in authorizing their commanders to accept the enemy's surrender on the field of battle—something that was very widely interpreted, even to the point where it meant the cessation of hostilities on individual fronts.

Having got wind of this "exception," the Germans were quick to realize that many convenient loopholes were available to them. After having surrendered "on the field of battle," they could (as it were) invite our allies into Germany, and let their forces go deep into the country and occupy its territory, thereby making it unnecessary for the Red Army to advance that far. Also, with this kind of surrender, provision would not be made for its being unconditional; and one could legally (so to speak) reserve several advantages for oneself, up to and including the withdrawal of the German forces to their own country, to spare them from defeat. Naturally, when the Anglo-American forces entered Germany, the Reich's industrial base and the forces of the Nazi Army would be preserved, along with the territory needed to prolong the war against the Soviet Union. It was known that our allies had a tolerant attitude toward the institutions of the fascist state, which at the time gave the Nazis hopes for the future.

The second meeting between General Wolf and Allen Dulles (the second one that we learned about) took place on March 19.

But this time the chiefs of staff of the British and American forces in the Italian theater of war also came to Switzerland—secretly.

The talks in Switzerland had been going on for almost two weeks, yet the Soviet Government had had no notice from our allies. It was not until March 21 that the British Minister of Foreign Affairs, Anthony Eden, saw to it that the Soviet Government was informed.

The Soviet Government, fighting for the unity of the Allies and unwilling to let the enemy save his Army and state from defeat, reacted very sharply to these talks that had been started behind the back of the USSR. Churchill, as he wrote in his memoirs, was "exasperated" by the Soviet *démarche,* but did not risk an aggravation of relations.

The parties to the talks in Switzerland did not reach agreement on anything at that time. The Nazi generals' demands were too great. Also, the Soviet Government's sharp protest had yielded the requisite result: The British and Americans began regularly to inform us of the course of the talks on the Italian front. On April 22, 1945, the chief of staff of the Red Army received a letter from chiefs of the British and American missions in the USSR. We were informed that the commander in chief of the German forces in Italy had no intention at that time of surrendering with his forces *"under conditions acceptable to us"* (italics mine—S. Sh.), and that therefore, in accordance with instructions from the chiefs of the joint staff, all talks had been called off and the question was considered closed. True, the talks were resumed five days later; but this time the German generals were not allowed to pose any conditions, and the talks were held not in Switzerland but at the headquarters of General Alexander, commanding the British forces in Italy.

In another letter that same day the chief of the military missions informed the General Staff that there was a possibility of a surrender by the German forces in Denmark. In that country the Nazis had got in touch with the Danish Freedom Council through intermediaries; but they had "forgotten" to include, among the forces that were to surrender, the SS and the police—both of which, as we know, had distinguished themselves by their special qualities as punitive forces. We were delighted both by the fact that the fascist beasts' occupation of Denmark was coming to an end, and by the promptness with which our allies had informed our General Staff of the likelihood of talks with the enemy's envoys. Shortly thereafter, on April 27, we had still another letter: It had to do with the possibility of a surrender by the enemy on the territory of Holland.

The General Staff took careful account of all these circumstances and of the situation on the front that had arisen owing to such events, and demanded of our allies that they not permit any strengthening of Nazi resistance in the east by means of forces from the western front. Eisenhower, Supreme Commander of the Allied Forces, assured us that he was strictly complying with our legitimate request.

Still, we did not rule out the possibility that German forces would appear on our front after having been withdrawn from the western front. And this posed new problems for the Soviet intelligence system and the operations officers: The intelligence agents had to inform the Supreme Command promptly of any enemy troop movements; and the operations officers had to propose measures for taking care of the enemy forces approaching our front.

One other thing was obvious: The Nazis were trying to preserve their forces from total defeat on the eastern front, depending on the virtually inaccessible defense lines in the southern and southwestern parts of Germany. Those defense lines comprised the mountain ranges north and northwest of Czechoslovakia, and the Alps on the territory of Austria. If necessary, the Nazis could withdraw here beyond the front line of the Americans and British rushing in from the west. Hence our task consisted in preventing the enemy from occupying such a strong defense line, or from crossing over to our allies' positions.

The correctness of our conclusions was soon borne out by the facts. In late March we learned from the British that a good many of the German governmental departments had already been transferred to some place in the south. Then the Americans informed us that on April 7 Ribbentrop had called in the Japanese ambassador, Osimu, and told him that changes in the military situation might "Necessitate the temporary transfer of the German Government to south Germany." We began to get reliable reports that Hitler was building an "Alpine Redoubt." From late March on General Pika, chief of the Czechoslovak Military Mission, who sent us brief daily summaries of the situation in Czechoslovakia, invariably reported concentrations of German troops and matériel in the mountains. Trains and trucks with cement and other building materials were going there; and entire repair shops, staff equipment, and crews of workmen were being sent there. It was plain that the enemy was not wasting either time or resources in outfitting command posts and building warehouses, systems of fire points for various kinds of weapons, places to accommodate troops, and defenses for them. All of the measures being taken were carefully camouflaged.

The location of the "Alpine Redoubt"—on the boundary between Germany and Austria (the region of Munich, Innsbruck, and Salzburg)—corresponded perfectly to our conclusions. This was alarming—especially since Churchill, addressing himself to the joint Anglo-American command, had bluntly insisted that Berlin be taken by their forces and not be left to the Russians, for purely political reasons. In a letter to Eisenhower dated March 31, 1945, he recommended forcing the Elbe and moving on to the German capital.

At this point the Soviet Government managed to prevent possibly serious complications in inter-allied relations. From one day to the next, our forces were decisively beating the enemy—the best way of bringing the hour of victory closer. The forces of the 1st and 2nd Belorussian fronts had quickly liquidated the enemy in Pomerania. Here a large group of German forces had simply ceased to exist. Now our operations on the Berlin sector were soundly secured in all respects.

In April 1945 the Nazis started casting their political nets even farther. After the Berlin offensive had been launched by three Soviet fronts on April 16, Marshal Zhukov, commanding the 1st Belorussian Front, was shown a deposition from a prisoner of war to the effect that the enemy had been ordered by no means to yield to the Russians, and to fight to the last man, even if the American forces got behind the lines of the German units. Zhukov forwarded this unusual information via dispatch to Stalin, and of course the General Staff learned of it immediately.

At that time we had to give several briefings daily at the Kremlin on the status of the Berlin operation. Such was the case on April 17, when Antonov and I arrived at the Stavka with the good news that the Seelow Heights had been seized. In the course of the briefing, Zhukov's dispatch was mentioned.

"Comrade Zhukov should be told," said Stalin, "that he may still not know all there is to know about talks between Hitler and our allies."

He paused. Then having noticed that Antonov and I were getting ready to take notes, he dictated a brief wire to the 1st Belorussian Front. After acknowledging receipt of Zhukov's message, he went on:

> Pay no attention to the statements made by the German prisoner. Hitler is spinning a spider web around Berlin so as to cause dissension among the Russians and their allies. We must cut through that spider web by taking Berlin—taking it with Soviet forces. We can do it and we must do it.

On April 20 our artillery opened fire on Berlin; and on the next day Soviet troops broke into the city. The bombardment not only spoiled Hitler's birthday for him (it had been a sad enough day as it was) but it compelled him to issue orders that an advance detachment be sent off to Salzburg to the Alpine Redoubt, since time was pressing.

As we know, Hitler did not manage to get to the new place. There were many reasons why: *Inter alia,* the "redoubt" was not yet ready, and the Americans had already moved up close to it. But the main reason, apparently, was that until the last moment Hitler was hoping that the Allies would quarrel before Berlin fell.

The Red Army's actions in the region of Berlin threatened the enemy with something more than the loss of the city (with whose status most Germans associated their notions of the solidity of the Nazi state). They also posed the threat that the Soviet forces would execute a turning movement around the city and then reach the Elbe. Here they were to link up with the forces of our allies, which would mean the enemy's entire front was split—with resultantly great difficulties for him.

The threatening circumstances spurred the Nazis on. On April 19 and April 21, Himmler approached England and the United States with a proposal for a surrender of the German forces in the west. The proposal was made *viva voce* in Stockholm to Count Folke Bernadotte, deputy chairman of the Swedish Red Cross Society. Our allies did not reject the proposal; but they made it plain that they would accept such a surrender jointly with the USSR or not at all.

On that same day (April 21) the British and American military missions informed the Soviet General Staff that an unconditional surrender of large enemy forces on any sector of the main fronts was possible in the near future.

They wrote:

> The Chiefs of the Joint Staff consider that each of the main Allied Powers should be able, if it wants to, to send representatives to take part in the talks on any such surrenders. However, no offer of surrender must be refused simply because representatives of one of the three Allies would not be present. . . .

We agreed to this, although the tone of the letter was not very respectful, and the implications of the text seemed to be: Whether you like it or not, we will accept a surrender under any circumstances, even if it is essentially aimed against you, our ally.

On the evening of April 21, obviously prompted by the benevolent tone of the talks with the Anglo-Americans, the German command ordered its forces in the west to withdraw all troops from those sectors where the Americans were operating, and transfer them to the eastern front. In this way did the results of the talks between the Nazis and our allies begin to appear, and to militate against us.

On April 22, when the last operations conference was held in the bunker of the Reichskanzlei, Alfred Jodl proposed something that, as yet, no one had risked proposing officially: that all troops be withdrawn from the front facing the Anglo-Saxons and thrown into the battle for Berlin. Hitler accepted the proposal, and assumed responsibility for the operation. On April 24 he issued a special directive ordering all army group commanders to send all available troops "against the deadly enemy—against Bolshevism." (The commanders were further ordered to ignore the fact that the Anglo-American forces could conquer considerable territory.) This directive was sent to all army group commanders of the German forces in Europe. On that same day, near Berlin, General Wenck's 12th Germany Army was sent against the Soviet forces.

Meantime the Soviet forces had encircled Berlin and, storming districts and fortified buildings one after another, were driving in toward the Reichstag from all directions. West of Berlin our units reached to the Elbe; and on April 25, in the region of Strehla and Torgau, they linked up with the Americans.

And now Göring—who was closest of all to the American forces—also pricked up his courage. On April 25 he sent Hitler a message reminding him that in accordance with the Führer's own will, he (Göring) was his successor. The time had come (he said) when the succession should be effected on the practical plane. Göring said he was taking over the leadership of the Reich, since Hitler, in encircled Berlin, was not able to act efficaciously. But he (Göring), being duly empowered to do so, could enter into direct talks with the Anglo-Americans.

Hitler was enraged that someone who had previously been close to him could already regard him as a political corpse. He condemned his "successor" as a coward and traitor, and removed him from command of the Air Force.

Two days after the tizzy of Göring's telegram a highly placed press official informed Hitler of a Reuters dispatch saying that Himmler had approached the governments of the United States and Britain with a proposal for concluding a separate peace. This official also reported to Hitler that Himmler had informed both governments about Hitler's illness, alleging that he was near death and would not live long.

Hitler was furious. He had to demonstrate his exclusive right to influence the course of events. He placed his last hopes in Wenck's

12th Army, which might prove a strong argument on the field of battle. At this point a letter to the commander of the 12th Army made its appearance (apparently not without pressure from Hitler)—one that was signed by Martin Bormann and Lt. Gen. Hans Krebs on April 29. They wrote:

> Dear General Wenck:
> As is evident from the enclosed messages, Reichsführer SS Himmler has made a proposal to the Anglo-Americans which will unquestionably betray our city to the plutocrats. A change of policy can be effected only by the Führer personally—only by him! A condition precedent to this is the immediate establishment of contact between your army and us, so as to give the Führer intra- and extra-political freedom for conducting talks. . . .

But events did not develop in favor of Hitler and his minions. In Berlin, there was fighting close to the Reichstag and the Reichskanzlei, which for several days had been under constant and accurate fire from the Soviet infantry and artillery. Realizing that the end had come, and having gone through the comedy of marrying Eva Braun, Hitler committed suicide (along with his wife) on April 30.

After the death of the ringleader his successors continued to issue urgent orders to the German forces to bring all of the fronts into a close order and hang on to their positions at any cost, stopping the Soviet forces from seizing extensive German territory. And they continued to hope for "a political windfall"—dissension between the USSR and its allies. Adm. Karl Doenitz, the new head of the Nazi "government," called Hitler's suicide a "heroic death," and all those who wanted to stop the war, cowards and traitors. Under the threat of harsh punitive measures, the German soldiers on the eastern front went on fighting stubbornly.

I have brought up these (by now) well-known facts to show once again how the Nazi leaders—even when resistance was senseless—continued to spill German blood for the sake of unrealizable and criminal aims.

The fall of Berlin on May 2, 1945, coincided with new attempts by the Nazis to get out of the war in the west. On that same day, hostilities ceased in Italy. At the time, the following entry was made in the OKW (Armed Forces High Command—German) diary:

> For the High Command, from this day forward, the following principle has become the basis of policy: saving as many Germans as possible from being taken prisoner by the Soviet forces; and talks with the western allies.

The day after the surrender of the German armies in Italy, Doenitz empowered Field Marshal Albert Kesselring, commanding the forces of the Reich in the west, to conclude an armistice with the Americans. Kesselring was instructed not only to ascertain intentions of the Anglo-Americans with respect to moving toward the east but to lay the groundwork for talks about saving the forces of Ferdinand Schörner's Army Group Center, Lothar Rendulic's Army Group Austria, and Löhr's Army Group Southeast. These forces were still in Czechoslovakia, southern Austria, and Yugoslavia. On May 4 the three army groups were put under Kesselring's command so that if a general armistice plan for the German forces in the west were drawn up, all the other troops could be slipped into it—just so long as they were spared our blows.

At the same time the problem of moving Germany's high government offices was taken up. Orders were even issued to prepare accommodations for two hundred persons in Prague. But the Soviet forces did not allow the Nazis either to solve this political problem or to settle the fate of the army groups under Schörner, Rendulic, and Löhr.

For us General Staff officers the last week of April and the first days of May 1945 was a time of great and intense but joyful work. Everyone was striving to help find the quickest solution to the innumerable staff problems that were arising. The Soviet forces were fighting very successfully. As for the Germans, although their general headquarters set up separate commands— one for the northern part of the country, headed by Keitel, and one for the southern part, headed by Kesselring—it could not keep command control of its own forces. The hour of victory was near.

When he learned that our forces had reached the Elbe, the Supreme Commander said it was time to strike a blow at Prague.

And about a day after the link-up with the Americans, he himself called Marshal Konev, commander of the 1st Ukrainian Front. Without any preliminary remarks, he asked: "Who's going to take Prague?"

For Konev the answer didn't involve any difficulties. The current situation was such that it was more convenient for the 1st Ukrainian Front than for any of the others to strike a blow at Prague along the shortest line, from the north and northwest, thereby cutting off escape routes to the west for the German forces. So Konev was instructed to submit his ideas on the Prague operation, and the General Staff was told to work up its own proposals on the subject.

The capital of friendly Czechoslovakia held a very special place in the plans of the Soviet Supreme Command. Our strategic commanders had tried in every way to preserve from destruction that marvelous old city with its many monuments of culture. Above all they had to protect Prague from American bombs, since our allies regularly put it on the list of bombing targets. Since the Prague region was within the theater of the Soviet forces, and since bombing targets had to be cleared with us, the General Staff just as regularly took Prague off the list.

By sunset on April 30 the enemy's resistance in Berlin was basically broken, and the capital of the Nazi Reich was on the eve of surrender. The situation permitted the hope that the forces of the 1st Belorussian Front would suffice for the enemy's complete defeat in Berlin. That front's 31st Army had already been transferred to the 1st Ukrainian Front, which could now drive toward Dresden and then against the Army Group Center. In the battle zone of the 4th Ukrainian Front, Soviet forces stormed (Moravská) Ostrava, a great industrial center and a strong link in the German defenses in Czechoslovakia. At the same time, other forces of the same front took the town of Žilina, an important communications hub in the western Carpathians. Among those who distinguished themselves in the battles in this sector were the troops under Colonel General Grechko, Colonel General Moskalenko, Colonel General Kurochkin, and Lieutenant General Gastilovich.

As before, the Czechoslovak 1st Army Corps, now commanded by Brig. Gen. Karl Klapalek, was our adoptive brother-in-arms during the battles on the steep slopes of the Carpathians.

Ludvík Svoboda had been named Minister of National Defense of the Czechoslovak Republic. When he left to take up his new post, he wrote a touching letter to the Military Council of the 4th Ukrainian Front:

> It was a great honor for me to command a Czech unit, formed and trained in the USSR, which jointly with the heroic Red Army fought at the front against our common enemy, and side by side with the brave troops of the 4th Ukrainian Front helped to liberate our dear country.
>
> I ask you to accept my expression of most sincere gratitude for the brotherly, effective aid that the command of the 4th Ukrainian Front and its Military Council constantly gave us during the period of our joint struggle.
>
> Today the main task of all the Czechoslovak people is to step up all-around assistance to the Red Army, our liberator; to increase our military efforts to the maximum; and to continue building a democratic Czechoslovak Army at a quick tempo.

The Czechoslovak Corps, along with other units, was thanked by the Supreme Commander for the capture of Ostrava and Žilina. Moscow gave the front's forces a twenty-round salute.

After losing Ostrava, the enemy no longer had such advantageous terrain for organizing a defense line in the near hinterland. Moreover, the Soviet forces had effected turning movements in depth around his flanks on the northern and southern borders of Czechoslovakia. The enemy's only recourse was to retreat to Olomouc. This retreat very much changed the situation in the battle zone of Malinovsky's 2nd Ukrainian Front. Now the most important thing for that front was rapidly to move its main forces toward Prague, thereby forming a southern segment for the future encirclement of Army Group Center. In this case Tolbukhin's 3rd Ukrainian Front would reliably secure a strategic operation from the direction of western Austria, where there were still almost a half-million German troops under the command of General Rendulic.

When we went to give our evening situation report to the Stavka (on April 30), Stalin instructed us, in view of the enemy's retreat before the 4th Ukrainian Front, to issue a directive to Malinovsky and Marshal Timoshenko, the Stavka representative.

"The main forces of the front will be deployed toward the west [the directive stated], and will strike a blow in the general direction of Jihlava and Prague, with the mission of reaching, no later than May 12–14, a line running Jihlava-Ulabinch-Horní, and then advancing to the Vltava River and taking Prague." Only a part of the 2nd Ukrainian Front's forces were to move on Olomouc, where the enemy was continuing to resist.

As the reader can see from the excerpt from the directive, we figured at the time that the operation would take at least two weeks, since our fronts were opposed by the very strong Army Group Center.

The events on the front had immediate repercussions behind the German lines on the territory of Bohemia. There the flames of the antifascist struggle burned ever higher. The patriots had taken up arms, and in some places had seized power. The events that would decide the future of the Czechoslovak people were about to begin. At the General Staff we kept Prague constantly within our field of vision. Large contingents of German troops were retreating to Prague. And the defense system of Schörner's armies was set up east of the city, in the mountains. In the opinion of the General Staff, it was there that the main events would take place.

On the night of May 1, 1945, the Stavka ordered that the forces of the 1st Ukrainian Front that were in Berlin (its right-flank forces) be replaced, no later than May 4, by the forces of the 1st Belorussian Front's left wing. Konev was ordered to finish mopping up the German forces surrounded east of Luckenwalde no later than May 3 and, after the aforementioned replacement, to employ his right-flank forces in a rapid thrust in the general direction of Prague. As of May 6 the demarcation line between the fronts was designated as follows: as far as Lübben, the former line; then Wittenberg, for the 1st Ukrainian Front inclusive.

Such was the origin of the basic idea of the Prague operation. The 1st Ukrainian Front was to serve as the main force. It was to cut off the enemy's escape routes to the west and southwest, and form the northern and western segments of the ring to be closed around Schörner's forces in the Ore Mountains and the Sudetes. Eremenko's 4th Ukrainian Front was to move in from the east, zeroing in toward Olomouc. And Malinovsky's 2nd Ukrainian Front would strike from the south. Having encircled the enemy, these fronts were to dismember and annihilate his forces with both simultaneous and consecutive air and ground attacks. Meantime, the forces of our allies would be entering western Czechoslovakia.

Plans for the Prague operations—the last major offensive by Soviet forces in Europe—were ready by May 4. The operational directive was issued on that same day at 1310. It stated:

> The armies of the right flank will mount a swift advance along both banks of the Elbe in the general direction of Prague, with the aim of crushing the enemy concentration between Dresden and Görlitz, and on the sixth day of the operation the tank armies will take the capital of Czechoslovakia, Prague.

General Nikolai Pavlovich Pukhov, commanding the 13th Army, was ordered to break through the passes in the Ore Mountains and, on the seventh day of the operation, to reach Beroun, thirty kilometers southwest of Prague. His army's forces would secure the front's operation in case the enemy struck from the west, would cut off the escape routes for Schörner's forces from the Prague region toward the west, and would establish direct contact with our allies along the Mulde River and the rest of the demarcation line. This army was given Gen. E. I. Fominy's 25th Tank Corps, which was to advance at the head of the army's main forces.

Gen. D. D. Lelyushenko's 4th Guards Tank Army went over to the attack in the 13th Army's sector. It had the mission of breaking through to Prague via the mountain passes and (as has been said) of taking the capital on the sixth day of the operation by striking from the northeast and the west. It was operating jointly with P. S. Rybalko's 3rd Guards Tank Army, which was to advance from the Dresden region along a parallel with Lelyushenko's line of advance, and break into Prague from the northeast and the east. Since it was expected that Schörner's forces would try to retreat toward the west, Rybalko's army had a twofold mission: to crush the enemy opposite it and liberate Prague; and to form an impenetrable barrier between the city and the main mass of Army Group Center's forces. Gen. V. N. Gordov's 3rd Guards Army and Gen. A. S. Zhadov's 5th Guards Army were to enter Prague immediately after the tanks. (These two forces, like all those listed above, formed part of the 1st Ukrainian Front's main group of forces.)

The Polish 2nd Army, commanded by Gen. Karol Sweszczewski, positioned to the east of the front's main forces, with its own main group adjacent to them, would advance toward Pirna. Behind it were the remaining armies of the front, Gen. A. A. Luchinsky's 28th Army and Gen. K. A. Koroteyev's 52nd Army, deployed fan-wise toward the south. Two divisions of Gen. P. G. Shafranov's 31st Army were to jump off on May 6.

The assault group of the 2nd Ukrainian Front—Gen. I. M. Managarov's 53rd Army, Gen. M. S. Shumilov's 7th Guards Army, followed by Gen. A. G. Kravchenko's 6th Guards Tank Army—was to advance on Prague from the southeast. The front's right flank—Gen. F. F. Zhmachenko's 40th Army under the command of General Descelescu—would continue to strike in the direction of Olomouc.

The 4th Ukrainian Front was to take Olomouc and, as I have said, strike from the east.

On the day before our forces were to jump off for Prague, Marshal Konev met with Gen. Omar Bradley, commanding the American 12th Army Group, and with the officers accompanying him. As Konev later reported to the Stavka, operational matters were not touched upon. But the Americans did offer us their help in crushing the German forces in Czechoslovakia.

I should note that by that time Eisenhower's staff and the Soviet General Staff had reached agreement on a line of demarcation which, once one had reached it, was not to be violated by either the Soviet or the American forces. This line ran as follows: Mulde River-Chemnitz-Karlovy Vary-Plzeň-Klatovy. Bradley's proposal meant a violation of an arbitrary but important boundary and, consequently, of an agreement between the highest organs of strategic leadership. Also, Konev knew that the Germans would play tricks, and would undoubtedly take advantage of the American advance to see that their rear areas and forces escaped the blows of the Red Army and ended up under American control. So Konev, after thanking the Americans, cited the fact of the demarcation line, had assured Bradley that the Nazi forces would be crushed by the Soviet forces—which soon happened.

At noon on May 5, 1945, the people of Prague had their say, rising up against the German fascist tyranny. We learned of this the next day at 0400, when we had a telephone call from the Czechoslovak Military Mission. General Pika briefly informed us that an uprising against the German occupying forces in Prague had begun on May 5 at noon. The patriots had seized radio stations and called upon Czechoslovak soldiers and police, along with the inhabitants of the city, to take up arms. At 1230 Czechoslovak, Soviet, and allied flags were flown in Prague. German signs and inscriptions were ripped off walls or covered up. The patriots seized German equipment, machine guns, and several pieces of artillery. The escape routes from Prague were blocked off.

Pika also stated that the Czech National Council (Rada) was directing the uprising. It had broadcast an appeal to the Czech people, and then an ultimatum to the German forces, proposing that they surrender. The ultimatum stated that the "protectorate" had ceased to exist, and that most of Bohemia was in the hands of Czech troops and patriots. The German units were to surrender. The council promised they would be treated in accordance with international law. Pika said the German garrison in Prague was isolated in various parts of the city, and was combating the insurgents.

On the night of May 6 the Prague radio continued to call upon people to fight, and listed places where specialists—gunsmiths, tankmen, etc.—should report. Barricades were still going up in the city. That same night the radio broadcast the council's appeal to the Allies for help:

398

A request from the city of Prague to all Allied armies. The Germans are advancing on Prague from all directions with tanks, artillery, and infantry. Prague urgently needs help. Send aircraft, tanks, and artillery. Help! Help us quickly!

At 0500 on May 6 one more request was broadcast, this time in Russian:

> To the Soviet Union, the 4th Ukrainian Front . . . Send paratrooper support immediately. Drop zone in Prague, 12 Vinogrady—Olsansky Cemetery. Signal: a triangle. Send arms and aircraft.

Then for a long time we could not hear the Prague radio because of atmospheric interference. For his part, the chief of the Czechoslovak Military Mission also asked that the Soviet Supreme Command help the uprising and provide weapons for the insurgents. He gave us the frequency of the radio station in Prague seized by the insurgents, and said that there had been reports from London of the beginning of talks between the German command and the Czech National Council.

That was the news we had on the morning of May 6. We immediately reported it via telephone to Stalin. He asked Antonov whether Konev could launch his offensive on Prague immediately rather than on May 7, as planned. Antonov replied in the affirmative, since May 6 had been set as the readiness date for the front's assault group. Next, Stalin formally ordered Konev to launch his offensive on May 6. The advance detachments jumped off at 1200 on that day, and the main forces of the assault group at 1400.

By that time, German forces had surrounded Prague with tanks. Heavy fighting was going on. The insurgents suffered heavy losses, but they fought on stubbornly. . . .

In order to get a better understanding of these events, let us have another look inside the enemy camp. No major changes had taken place there. After Hitler's suicide and the surrender of Berlin, the fascists had mobilized all their internal resources for resistance in the south. Schörner was named commander in chief of land forces in the Third Reich, which was already in its last few days. We knew more than enough about this general of the fascist Reich. He was devoted to Hitler, and had earned the latter's trust by his efficiency and unusual harshness in dealing with German soldiers, and especially with POWs and the populations of occupied countries. There had been a time when Hitler had even named Schörner chief of a staff for the Nazi training of the troops. But the growing successes of the Red Army had compelled the German High Command to again assign Schörner to the most important sector of the eastern front. And he was given the rank of General Field Marshal. In the last days of his life, Hitler had also awarded this highest military rank to another dyed-in-the-wool fascist, Ritter von Greim, named to replace the "traitor" Göring as commander of the Luftwaffe. But what could that change? When people are throwing life belts into the sea from a sinking ship, it is hardly likely that even the most experienced admiral can save the ship.

From May 2 through May 4 the top military leaders of fascist Germany conferred at Doenitz's headquarters. Those present included Doenitz, Keitel, Jodl, and others. They discussed surrendering to the Anglo-Americans and continued resistance to the Red Army. This conference of the German command in the west regarding an armistice on several fronts was over on May 5. Doenitz extended the scope of several agreements to include the northern regions. From our missions abroad—and especially from Gen. I. A. Susloparov—we received regular bulletins on all talks and their results.

Col. Gen. Alfred Jodl was soon hurrying off to Eisenhower's headquarters at Reims. This major war criminal had not been empowered to sign a surrender for all the German forces on all fronts. He had only been given instructions to conclude an armistice, but in such a way as to gain as much time as possible to save the Germans retreating from the east. On the Soviet front, hard fighting was still going on; and the enemy troops had had no indication from higher authority as to a cessation of hostilities.

The Jodl talks began on May 6, in the afternoon. He openly told our allies of the intention "to save as many Germans as possible for the German nation, and save them from Bolshevism." Not only that, but he said that nothing could compel the troops under Generals Löhr and Rendulic and Field Marshal Schörner to surrender so long as they had an opportunity to make their way to regions occupied by American forces. In other words, Jodl was refusing surrender for the German forces in the east. But all his proposals were rejected. And since he was not empowered to sign a capitulation for all the German forces, he was told that the talks would be broken off. So he had to ask for the appropriate powers.

On the evening of May 6, an Eisenhower aide flew to Paris to see General Susloparov, chief of the Soviet Military Mission, and conveyed to him an invitation from the Supreme Allied Commander to visit him at his headquarters. Eisenhower received Susloparov in his quarters. Smiling, he said that a Nazi general, Jodl, had come with an offer to surrender to the Anglo-American forces and fight against the USSR.

"What do you say to that, General?" Eisenhower asked.

Susloparov also smiled. So the end of the war with Germany was near, although the enemy was still playing tricks in order to mislead the Allies. Susloparov also knew that a German general, Friedeburg,[2] had been at SHAEF for several days, but had not managed to talk Eisenhower into a separate peace. The chief of the Soviet Military Mission's reply to the Supreme Allied Commander was that there were certain obligations jointly undertaken by the members of the anti-Nazi coalition regarding the enemy's unconditional surrender on all fronts, of course including the eastern front.

Eisenhower hastened to assure Susloparov that he had demanded of Jodl the complete surrender of Germany, and would not accept any other. The Germans had to agree. Then Eisenhower asked Susloparov to communicate the text of the surrender to Moscow, get it approved, and then sign it in the name of the Soviet Union. He said the signing would take place at 0230 on May 7, 1945, in the Operations Room of SHAEF.

The text of the agreement (of which Susloparov was given a copy immediately) stipulated the unconditional surrender of all land, sea, and air forces under German control at the given moment. The German command pledged itself to order the cessation of hostilities on May 9 at 0001 (Moscow time). All German

[2] Gen. Adm. Wilhelm von Friedeburg. (Translator's note.)

troops were to remain in the positions they occupied at that time. It was forbidden to damage weapons or other means of armed struggle. The German command guaranteed the execution of all orders from the Supreme Commander of the Allied Expeditionary Forces and the Soviet Supreme Commander.

Susloparov had been given very little time to get instructions from his government. Acting promptly, he cabled Moscow about the impending signing of the surrender, sending along the text of the agreement, and asked for instructions. It took several hours for his cable to reach its addressee. In Reims it was after midnight, and getting close to the time for the signing, but still no instructions had come from Moscow. Susloparov's position was very complex. Now everything depended on him. Should he sign in the name of the Soviet Government, or should he refuse to?

He realized that in case of an oversight by him, the maneuvering by Hitler's successors so as to surrender only to our allies could result in a catastrophe. He read and reread the text, but could find no camouflaged malicious intent in it. At the same time he mentally reviewed scenes from the war—a war in which every minute meant the loss of many human lives.

The chief of the Soviet Military Mission decided to sign the surrender. But when he did sign it, he made a marginal note securing for the Soviet Government the possibility, if necessary, of influencing the subsequent course of events. His notation said that the present text of the armistice agreement did not rule out the subsequent signing of another, more complete document on the surrender of Germany, if any allied government should demand it.

Eisenhower and those representatives of other powers who were at his headquarters, agreed to Susloparov's notation. The agreement on the surrender of Germany was signed on May 7, 1945, at 0241 in the SHAEF Operations Room.

Eisenhower congratulated Susloparov on the signing of the document. Then the latter sent his report to Moscow. It crossed with a dispatch from Moscow saying, "Don't sign any documents!"

Meantime, on the eastern front the fighting continued. By way of "aligning the front," Army Group Center had reached a defense line running from the Ore Mountains to the Sudetes; and here, in well-engineered positions, they dug in for prolonged fighting. And the German forces in southern Czechoslovakia, Austria, and Croatia went on fighting too.

Schörner figured it was possible to stop the Red Army at his defense line, and to hold on for no fewer than three weeks—time for the Americans to show up. But Doenitz thought otherwise. He had already had some information about the crisis in Prague, and was allowing for the possibility of an imminent uprising of all the Czechs. He did not think the Germans could hold on in the Sudetes under such conditions. And so on May 3, after getting the opinions of the members of his "government" and the military leaders, he decided to move the forces closer to the American front, and to do it fast. But he did not manage to carry out this decision: For Army Group Center, the road west was blocked— first by the Czechoslovak insurgents, and then by Red Army troops.

Meantime the situation in Prague was growing ever more tense. General Tussen, the German commandant of the city, reported to Wehrmacht operations staff: "The general situation has sharply deteriorated. . . ." As he stated further on, everyone was expecting an immediate political settlement. But he did not lose his presence of mind and figured that in twenty-four hours he could restore order. The insurgents, however, were doing things their own way; they expanded the uprising to the fullest, and in a suburb of Prague they wrecked the railroad to the west. This would compel the German forces trying to get across the demarcation line to move in march formation, which considerably complicated the situation of Army Group Center.

With their first shots the Prague insurgents forced the Nazis to give up their notion of switching their government offices to the Prague region, although Jodl had already ordered the preparation of accommodations for the OKW here. Some 1,600 barricades and 30,000 people behind them are worth something, even if the people are not fully armed. Several of Army Group Center's divisions with tanks moved against the insurgents, and they raised up the entire German garrison. There were many SS units among the German formations. The fighting in Prague grew fierce.

May 6 was a hot day at the Nazi GHQ as well as at our own. At 1412 Keitel ordered that Army Groups Center, Austria, and Southeast immediately withdraw to the American zone of operations. This had been prompted by reports from the front saying that the Red Army was launching an offensive toward Prague. Kesselring was ordered not to oppose any eastward movement of the Americans into the protectorate (as the Germans called Czechoslovakia).

As the reader will recall, the talks with Jodl about the surrender of the German forces on the western front were begun in Reims that day. So long as it was not clear how the British and Americans would respond to the Nazi proposals, the German command in Prague was trying to put down the uprising with force. But when word came that the surrender would be made in the west to the Anglo-Americans, the Nazis in Prague changed their tactics. On May 7 Doenitz ordered that the German forces withdraw from the eastern front with the aim of surrendering to our allies.

Now, in the interests of accomplishing their new mission, the Nazis were barred from expanding the fighting in the streets of Prague: It would be more useful to somehow weaken the uprising, and if possible to reach agreement with the insurgents. General Tussen undertook to do this. He managed to arrange for talks with the Czech National Council beginning on May 7 at 1000, when the surrender had already been signed at Reims and the Red Army was advancing all along the front. The course of the talks revealed that a majority of those on the council were bourgeois who took a very limited view of what the uprising meant. The chairman of the council, Professor Albert Prazhak of Prague University, later said about this: "The uprising was intended to save the city from threatened destruction, since the Germans did not intend to give it up without fighting. We were expecting the Allied forces to arrive from one hour to the next." Josef Smrkovsky, who at the time was in the Communist Party, did not exert any influence on the conciliatory attitude of the bourgeois majority on the Czech National Council.

Because of this situation, Tussen quickly found the weak point in the leadership of the insurgents. And on May 8 at 1600, when according to the document signed at Reims the time was approaching for the surrender of all the German forces, he was able in his turn to sign an agreement with the Czech National Council that was very advantageous for the German command. The latter got a guarantee that the German troops would withdraw unhampered to the American lines. And on May 8 at 1915 the International Red Cross broadcast the following message over the Czech Radio in Czech and German:

> By the terms of an agreement with the Czech National Council, hostilities are to cease in Prague and its environs. A similar order has been issued to the Czech units and to citizens. Anyone failing to comply with this order will be brought to trial. Signed by the commander of the German forces in Bohemia and Moravia. Prague. The Czech Radio.

The agreement contained items like the following:

> 5. Arms will be handed over in the following manner: Artillery and mortars will be handed over to units of the Czech Army on the outskirts of the city; aircraft will remain on the airfields at Ruzin and Gbely.
> 6. The remaining weapons will be turned over to forces of the Czechoslovak People's Army at the American line of demarcation. All weapons will be turned over in good condition and with ammunition.[3]

So the German troops would keep their light infantry weapons until they had passed through the danger zone where they might be attacked by Soviet forces and the Czechoslovak insurgents. Also, the agreement provided that the personnel of Army Group Center could draw from the warehouses whatever provisions they needed for the time they would be on the march.

Actually, there had been no surrender of the German troops in Prague and its environs. Prazhak himself, after the Soviet forces had entered the city and crushed the Nazis, characterized the document that had been signed as a "German trap."

[3] Arkhiv MO SSSR, f. 296, op. 2675, d. 354, ll. 221–24 [Archives of the USSR Ministry of Defense, fund 296, inventory 2675, file 354, sheets 221–24].

Thus the council's bourgeois majority had been tricked by the enemy. It should be noted in this connection that the Prague insurgents paid heavily for the road to freedom. Prazhak himself said of the fighters in the Prague "brigades": "The underground Communists played the leading role in the uprising. The people showed great courage. They hated the Germans, and did not spare them. . . . During the uprising we had 13,000 casualties: 3,000 killed and 10,000 wounded."

The surrender of the Berlin garrison brought us not only joy but new concerns. The latter were associated with the hunt for the main war criminals. We knew that many of the ringleaders of the fascist state and the Nazi Party, including Hitler himself, had remained in the besieged city, and we were looking for all of them. To help in this search, we had assigned special groups of intelligence agents to literally all of the corps of Soviet forces moving in on Berlin. The groups were led by experienced men. Each group had a list of Nazi criminals, and the agents had a good idea of where they might be holed up. Naturally, most attention was focused on the district where the government buildings were and, within that district, on the gloomy building of the Reichskanzlei. Several units had been directed toward it: They all wanted to storm fascism's last fortress in Berlin! On April 30—along with other assault teams—a search group headed by Lt. Col. Ivan I. Klimenko, an officer from the 79th Rifle Corps of the 3rd Shock Army, reached Hitler's bunker. The results of its work will be taken up later.

So long as the fighting was far from the center of the city, we had not expected any special news. But now that there was fighting within the district where the government buildings were, anything could happen. Even Antonov, ordinarily cool and reserved, began to show impatience.

We first heard of Hitler's death on May 1, after Gen. V. D. Sokolovsky and Gen. V. I. Chuikov had met with Gen. Hans Krebs. (Soviet readers know quite a bit about these talks from the memoirs of Zhukov and Chuikov.) But it was hard to believe this report, since Hitler's remains had not been found. Nor was there any information on what had happened to Goebbels, who according to Krebs had remained the number one man in the bunker under the Reichskanzlei. The days passed. Berlin fell, and the surrender of the German forces began, but the General Staff received no new information on the ringleaders of the Nazi state. The reply to our telephoned inquiries was always the same: We're looking. . . . True, on the morning of May 4 the answer was a bit different, being to the effect that something had been found that resembled Hitler.

On the night of May 4, when Antonov and I went into the Supreme Commander's office to give him our regular report on the situation for the past twenty-four hours, Stalin showed us a telegram from Zhukov and K. F. Telegin. It stated:

> On May 2, 1945, in Berlin, on the grounds of the Reichskanzlei of the Reichstag on the Wilhelmstrasse, where Hitler's GHQ had been located most recently, two charred corpses were found and were identified as those of Reich Minister of Propaganda Goebbels and his wife.
>
> On May 3, on that same territory, in Goebbels' quarters, . . . the corpses of three of the six Goebbels children were found and removed. According to all the signs on the corpses of the children, it may be concluded that they were killed by a virulent poison.
>
> Comrade Lieutenant General Vadis, Chief of the Counterintelligence Department of the 1st Belorussian Front, personally showed the corpses to: Rear Admiral Voss (under arrest), Grand Admiral Doenitz's personal liaison officer at Hitler's GHQ; Schneider, superintendent of the Reichskanzlei garage; Lange, the chef[4]; and Ziehn, superintendent of technical installations at the Reichskanzlei. They identified Goebbels, his wife, and their children.

The message from Zhukov and Telegin went on to list the items found in the course of examining the remains of the family of the former Nazi Reich Minister, and stated that one other corpse had been found on the territory of the Reichskanzlei. It had been identified by Voss as that of Lieutenant General Krebs, chief of

---

[4] One Heinz Linge, Hitler's valet, was among the survivors from the bunker. (Translator's note.)

the Army General Staff, who had recently had a fruitless meeting with Sokolovsky and Chuikov regarding the surrender of Berlin.

The telegram said nothing about any Hitler—either a living one or a dead one.

"Comrade Zhukov also has doubts about Hitler's death," said Stalin, going over to his desk to get some tobacco for his pipe. "You can never believe those fascist scoundrels. We have to find out whether the ringleaders of the Nazi state have really departed this life. We have to check everything. . . ."

Then, picking up the telephone, he called one of the commissars of State Security and told him to send to Berlin an experienced top-level official whose mission, among others, was to include the verification of Hitler's death.

Meantime, in Berlin Telegin and the front's counterintelligence department had already got started on the necessary work. Physicians had already made a thorough patho-anatomical examination of the corpses of the Goebbels family and Krebs. It was established with absolute certainty that the cause of death was poisoning by virulent cyanide compounds.

It soon became necessary to do autopsies on other corpses as well—one a man's, one a woman's, and two canines—that had been found by Klimenko's team (again) in a shell hole in the Reichskanzlei garden near the emergency exit from the Führerbunker. The human corpses, covered with a thin layer of soil, were badly charred. It was impossible to identify them, so that the especially precise procedures of forensic expertise were required. Help was forthcoming from dental specialists who had provided Hitler and his mistress with dentures. They identified features of the dentures that were found only in their own work, and pointed out anatomical peculiarities in the oral cavities of their former patients. In their turn, the pathologists confirmed the accuracy of the testimony given by the specialists. After this there were no more doubts: The two corpses, charred beyond recognition, were all that was left of Hitler and Eva Braun, who had shared his fate. And examination confirmed that the cause of death was the same as for the Goebbels family: poisoning by virulent cyanide compounds.

The experts' examinations were concluded after the signing of Germany's unconditional surrender. They were paralleled by the process of interrogating prisoners who had had something to do with the Reichskanzlei and German citizens who, in one way or another, might throw some light on the last days of certain Nazi criminals. I must admit that at the time, we of the General Staff—like many other people—had no leisure for reading even such curious documents as the recorded interrogations of those who had witnessed the collapse of the Third Reich. We were snowed under with urgent matters that had to be dealt with for the sake of life on earth. It was only later that I read, *inter alia,* the testimony of Helmut Kunz, a doctor[5] at the Reichskanzlei. It was to him that Magda Goebbels appealed on April 27. In the name of her husband and herself, she asked Kunz to help her kill her children. The doctor agreed. On the evening of May 1, he took a syringe of morphine from Magda's hands and injected the children so they would sleep. But Kunz lacked the fortitude to carry the crime through. The children's mother then appealed for help to Hitler's personal physician, and together they put a capsule of poison into the mouth of each child. . . .

Such were the people the Soviet soldiers had been fighting. They loved everything wolfish. They built a *Wolfsschanze,* or "wolf's entrenchment," where Hitler's secret headquarters was located. They tried to launch a movement of "werewolves," or "wolf pack" [*sic*], to draw the people into armed struggle against the Soviet forces. And they even behaved like wolves with their young children!

When we got the news of the events in Reims (the surrender), Antonov asked me into his office and told me to draft a Stavka directive on the surrender. And he pushed a document toward me, saying only, "Read it." It was a letter that Antonov had just received from Gen. John R. Deane, chief of the United States military mission in Moscow. I gave it a quick look-over; and I must admit I did not immediately grasp its hidden meaning.

The letter stated:

[5] *Vrach: zubnoi vrach* means "dentist," which Helmut Kunz presumably was, but *vrach* alone means "doctor." (Translator's note.)

> . . . This afternoon I received from the President an urgent message in which he asked that Marshal Stalin agree to announce the surrender of Germany today at 1900 Moscow time.
>
> We have received a reply, via the Soviet Ministry of Foreign Affairs, saying that this cannot be done, since the Soviet Government has not yet received information on the German surrender from its liaison officers at Eisenhower's headquarters.
>
> I informed President Truman of this, and received a reply saying that he would not make an official announcement until May 8 at 0900 (or 1600 Moscow time), if Marshal Stalin had not agreed to an earlier hour. . . .

Then came a request to inform him, Deane, of the time when information was received from our liaison officers. I threw a questioning look at Antonov. "Our allies are pressuring us," he said. "They want the whole world to hear about the German forces' surrendering to them and not to the USSR."

Soon we were summoned to the Kremlin. In Stalin's office we found not only him but members of the government. As usual, the Supreme Commander was pacing back and forth on the carpeted floor. Everything about him expressed great dissatisfaction, and we noticed the same thing in the faces of the others who were there. They were discussing the surrender in Reims. The Supreme Commander was thinking aloud as he summarized the situation. He noted that our allies had set up a separate agreement with Doenitz's government. That agreement resembled a shady deal. Except for General Susloparov, no governmental representative of the USSR had been present at Reims. This meant there had been no surrender to our government, although we had suffered the most from Nazi aggression and had contributed the most to the victory, breaking the back of the fascist beast. Bad consequences could be expected from such a "surrender."

Now the meaning of Deane's letter was becoming clearer: It was turning out that even in such a matter as an unconditional surrender, one could reap political capital!

"The agreement signed in Reims," Stalin continued, "must not be abrogated. But on the other hand it must not be recognized.

The surrender must be arranged as a most important historical fact and accepted not on the territory of the conquerors but at the place where the fascist aggression sprang from: in Berlin. And it must be accepted not separately but by the senior commands of all the nations in the anti-Nazi coalition. Also, it must be signed by one of the ringleaders of the former fascist state or by a whole group of Nazis responsible for all their crimes against humanity."

Stalin then turned to us and asked if Comrade Zhukov could find a suitable building for the formal signing of the unconditional surrender of fascist Germany in Berlin.

Antonov said that the city itself was mostly in ruins but that the suburbs were in fairly good shape and that the kind of building needed could be found there with no great difficulty.

Then followed a discussion of questions relating to talks with our allies. In the course of the conversation Antonov and I gathered that Stalin and Molotov had already reached agreement with Allied representatives that the proceedings in Reims should be regarded as a preliminary surrender. Our allies also agreed that the matter should not be put off; and the formal signing of the surrender was scheduled for May 8 in Berlin.

In the course of all this it was decided to empower Zhukov, as Deputy Supreme Commander, to sign the text of Germany's unconditional surrender in the name of the USSR, and to name him Commander in Chief of the Soviet Zone of Occupation for the subsequent phase. Andrei Vyshinsky, who was present at the time, was named Zhukov's deputy for political affairs, and was instructed to fly to Berlin on the morning of May 8 with all necessary documents for the surrender.

Then the Supreme Commander ordered that he be put in telephone contact with Berlin; and himself informed Zhukov that he (Zhukov) was empowered to accept the surrender of fascist Germany in the name of the USSR. Next a brief note to Berlin on the same subject was drawn up and immediately dispatched by the Stavka's message center.

"The war is not yet over," the Supreme Commander said; and he ordered that an appropriate directive be drawn up for the fronts.

411

We showed him the draft we had already drawn up, and after some slight changes he signed it. This directive mentioned the surrender at Reims, and then ordered:

> 1. You will publish an appeal from the front to the German forces and their command stating that the Germans have signed a surrender, and will disseminate it by the evening of May 8, both in the form of leaflets and by radio, with a proposal that arms be laid down.
> 2. After 2300 hours on May 8 (i.e., on the morning of May 9) you will instruct the command of the German forces opposing you to cease hostilities, lay down their arms, and surrender.
> 3. If the German troops do not follow your instructions, do not lay down their arms, and do not surrender, you will strike a decisive blow of maximum strength at the German forces opposing you, and will carry out the missions assigned by the Stavka to each front. . . .

This document was signed on May 7 at 2235.

Before midnight a message came in from Eisenhower's headquarters saying that a German plane was to take off from Flensburg (where the High Command of the now-defeated enemy was working on the surrender of the German forces) for Courland with orders for the surrender of the forces blockaded there. No other communications link was working. We had to clear the aircraft so it would not be shot down.

Next the Special Missions Department reported that Eisenhower was sending Air Marshal Arthur W. Tedder, deputy commander of the Allied Expeditionary Forces, and ten staff officers to Berlin for the acceptance of the German surrender. Eleven correspondents and photographers were coming with them. Keitel, Hans Friedeburg, Paul Stumpff, and three other German officers were coming to Berlin on the same planes for the signing of the unconditional surrender.

We had to issue instructions to clear these planes, too.

Of course the operations work that is typical of wartime was still going on. And as before, there was a lot of it. But what a joy it all was!

That night seemed amazingly short, and not like any other.

Sleeping was out of the question. Everyone was waiting. And in thought, everyone was there in Karlshorst, where the final preparations were being made for Germany's surrender.

Promptly at midnight, the following people filed into the auditorium of a former military school: Marshal Zhukov, Andrei Vyshinsky, V. D. Sokolovsky, K. F. Telegin, other Soviet generals and other officers, and (representing the Allied command) Air Marshal (Sir) Arthur Tedder of the British Armed Forces, Gen. Carl Spaatz, commander of the U. S. Strategic Air Force, and Gen. Jean de Lattre de Tassigny, Commander in Chief of the French Army. They all sat down at a table.

Marshal Zhukov opened the proceedings and ordered that the representatives of the German High Command—Field Marshal Keitel, Colonel General Stumpff, and Fleet Admiral Friedeburg—be summoned to the room. In the first few minutes of the new day of May 9, 1945, after a brief check of credentials, the German delegation signed the document of fascist Germany's surrender. This was a document that juridically recognized the total military defeat of Hitler's Reich. . . .

General Susloparov was among those present at the signing. It was not until this time that he learned that Stalin had personally told Vyshinsky on the telephone that he did not hold any grudge against Susloparov for what the latter had done at Reims.

The surrender of the German forces also began to take effect at the front. But there were more than a million troops—in Schörner's Army Group Center and Rendulic's Army Group Austria—who had no intention of surrendering to the Red Army. And Doenitz was in fact conniving at this, taking no steps to punish those who violated the conditions of the surrender. Schörner, who considered himself a master of mountain warfare, covered up his sabotage of the surrender terms by claiming that the Czech insurgents were hampering him. He said they were constantly destroying telephone lines and seizing couriers carrying orders to his forces, thereby making it impossible to effect any systematic capitulation. Schörner asked Doenitz to exert urgent pressure on the Allies to have the insurgents promptly cease their attacks on the German forces, immediately give up control of the radio station, and thereby enable him, Schörner, to carry out the order to surrender.

The idea of pressuring our western allies so as to facilitate the withdrawal of German forces beyond the Allied lines was immediately seized upon by Doenitz's government. As early as the morning of May 8, Jodl sent Eisenhower a telegram reporting that the effectuation of the surrender in Czechoslovakia had been made difficult, since the insurgents were hampering it by cutting telephone lines and seizing couriers. Jodl asked the Allies to see that the radio station held by the insurgents was used to transmit orders to the German forces.

Meantime, Schörner himself had worked out a plan for Army Group Center to break through to the American zone and lay down their arms there. He shared his thoughts on this plan with Field Marshal Kesselring, and the latter reported this to Keitel, asking him to give him (Kesselring) his opinion. We do not know whether Keitel communicated his views on the Schörner plan; but in any case the latter never succeeded in carrying out that plan. He was prevented from so doing by the Soviet forces.

It is interesting that on the morning of May 8, Schörner was ordered to go personally to the Ore Mountains region to see about an organized effectuation of the surrender there. But he declared he saw no possibility of firmly controlling the troops and complying with the conditions of the surrender. He washed his hands of the whole thing and left his troops without the permission of his superiors. Army Group Center, which had had no order from Schörner to surrender to the Red Army, was still hoping for a relatively easy withdrawal beyond the American lines. And since in Prague it had got the Czech National Council's approval of such a withdrawal, it did not lay down its arms.

During the early hours of May 9 we awaited reports from the front with mixed feelings of hope and anxiety. The situation there had not changed. Fighting was going on in the region of Prague, toward which D. D. Lelyushenko's 4th Guards Tank Army and P. S. Rybalko's Third Guards Tank Army were driving. Ivan Efimovich Petrov, chief of staff of the 1st Ukrainian Front, in reporting on the tankers' drive on Prague, noted that on other sectors of the front the enemy was staying in the defense line it had been occupying previously. Such was the case up to 0300; then the German forces began to withdraw swiftly to the south. But they had not surrendered. . . .

We called the 4th Ukrainian Front. The situation there was the same. L. M. Sandalov, the front's chief of staff, reported that the enemy had not laid down his arms and had not stayed where he was but had begun a rapid withdrawal in the general direction of Prague, blowing up bridges and roads as he went. According to the POWs, the German command was withdrawing its forces "so that they could surrender to the English or the Americans."[6]

At the 2nd Ukrainian Front the situation was likewise the same. M. V. Zakharov reported that the enemy was withdrawing but not surrendering. Our forces were pursuing him in all sectors. In certain areas, fighting was still going on. Getting a bit ahead of the story, I note that even on May 10 in the region of Čáslav the 2nd Guards Mechanized Corps of Kravchenko's 6th Guards Army was encountering serious resistance from the enemy. Once again the tanks' cannon began to roar out and the machine guns to chatter. But the enemy was beaten, and more than seven hundred German soldiers taken prisoner. The corps continued on its way to Prague.

At that particular time it was especially painful to be aware that the reality behind the usual reports from the front was a continuing loss of life. More than 140,000 of our soldiers and officers had given their lives to liberate Czechoslovakia. Why did the enemy have to go on fighting when his position was plainly hopeless and when a surrender had already been signed? Only fascists—people who have lost any resemblance to humans—could have behaved like that, continuing to nudge soldiers over the edge of the grave.

Such were the facts. But almost a quarter century after the war, a strange opinion surfaced; namely, that the battle for Czechoslovakia was unnecessary.[7] This opinion contravenes the factual situation and the requirement of a law of war—"If the enemy does not surrender, destroy him"—which functioned with objective im-

[6] Arkhiv MO SSSR, f. 244, op. 3000, d. 1179, l. 333.
[7] Cf. E. Ziemke, *From Stalingrad to Berlin: Germany's Defeat in the East* (Washington, 1968), p. 504.

mutability. The forces under Schörner and Rendulic, which as I have said included more than a million Nazi cutthroats, did not merely pose a threat of new crimes: They were in action, dragging out the war and spilling blood.

The blame for those crimes can be placed squarely on Doenitz's "government," and especially on Field Marshal Schörner, who had left his troops and sabotaged everything that should have been undertaken there to organize the surrender and prevent useless bloodshed.

The Nazi Reich was in its death throes. . . . Those ringleaders of the Reich who were still alive were fleeing like rats from a sinking ship. And those traitors to the Soviet state, the Vlasovites—those of them who had not been killed on the field of battle—were hurrying along the roads of Bohemia toward the demarcation line. Farther south, along Austria's Alpine paths, the remnants of detachments of former White Guards and traitors to the motherland who had previously found shelter in the Balkans and Italy were heading for the same destination. There was something symbolic in that tragic picture of the flight and death of our enemies: History was not leaving unpunished their crimes against mankind.

For these dregs of society, the last chance of justifying themselves before the motherland was fading in different ways. Some furiously returned our fire and were killed in battle. Others waited in stupid passivity for what fate would bring. Still others conceived a hatred for the anti-Soviet propagandists who had deceived them, and sought at any price to redeem their crimes. Not all of them had lost the hope of being forgiven. It may be that this was what prompted (for example) some Vlasovites in Prague to take action when the time had come for a decisive uprising against the German occupying troops. These Vlasovites twice approached the Czech National Council and asked that they be allowed to help in defending the city against Schörner's forces. But their request was rejected. Such "allies" were simply too unreliable, and no one could say for sure against whom they would use their weapons. In desperation, some Vlasovites voluntarily started skirmishing with the Germans here and there, and some made ready to go over to the Red Army.

On the morning of May 10 we heard from M. V. Zakharov at the 2nd Ukrainian Front that many Vlasovites had been surrounded and taken prisoner in the woods northwest of Lutov. Obviously, they were heading for the border. And the ringleader of the traitors, Andrei Vlasov, was also fleeing toward the west. The forces of the so-called ROA (Russian Liberation Army) were acting in accordance with a plan drawn up on the basis of a conference of their ringleaders in Karlovy Vary. They had no intention of abandoning the struggle against the Soviet Union—even at a time when Nazi Germany was surrendering unconditionally. They had decided that in that case they would preserve their cadres and concentrate troops in southern Germany in the foothills of the Alps. There they intended to take advantage of the rugged terrain to sit it out until the beginning of a new war, this time with England and the United States fighting the Soviet Union! That would be the time for them to go into action on the side of the Western powers.

The traitors began to put their plan into action. In the west they sent people to make contact with the British and Americans; and on the eastern front they began to transfer troops to the southwest. A considerable part of the troops and ringleaders of these traitors to the motherland had already managed to reach the American lines. But Vlasov himself was still on his way through Czechoslovakia under the reliable (or so he thought) protection of the ROA's 1st Division. The nucleus of the division was the brigade that had been commanded by the notorious bandit Kaminsky, whose troops were soaked in the blood of Soviet partisans and Warsaw insurgents. It was said that Kaminsky himself had been shot by the Germans for outrages that were beyond belief, even using the criteria of the Nazi criminals. Bunyachenko, the divisional commander, likewise a traitor and ringleader of the ROA, had the rank of a fascist major general.

On May 12 the traitors' forces were only forty kilometers southeast of Plzeň. This city was one of the points on the demarcation line between the Red Army and the American forces that had been established by agreement among the Allied armies. Marshal Konev had agreed to it when General Bradley and his staff officers had offered to help us in crushing Schörner's forces. Had it not been for that agreement, Vlasov would no doubt have been able right then to run away to our allies, who would have advanced a long way, since they would have had no enemy in front of them.

But on that May day our forces were already moving toward Plzeň; and reconnaissance troops from Maj. Gen. E. I. Fominy's 25th Armored Corps found the Vlasovite unit. When the corps commander had got the recce report, he ordered Col. I. P. Mishchenko, commanding the 162nd Armored Brigade, to overtake the traitors. The brigade took after them. The most important thing it had to do was to hold up the units of the Vlasovite division and disorganize its action so that the brigade could overwhelm the enemy with its mass of formidable tanks and destroy him. The mission of holding up the enemy fell to the lot of a motorized rifle battalion in the advance guard under the command of Cap. M. I. Yakushov.

The battalion was in a difficult situation. However you looked at it, up ahead was an entire division of cutthroats ready for anything. And the fact that salvation was so near might give them extra courage. But quick wits, common sense, and an understanding of psychology did the trick. In carrying out his mission, Capt. Yakushov (with the help of two counterintelligence officers, 1st Lt. N. P. Ignashkin and Maj. P. T. Vinogradov) managed to win over the commanding officer of one of the Vlasovite battalions, Capt. P. N. Kuchinsky. The latter, although he had overstepped the line, realized the seriousness of his crime before the Soviet people and at what was perhaps the last hour wanted to redeem himself at any price. Kuchinsky pointed out the location of the divisional headquarters, and said that Vlasov himself was there.

Yakushov made a bold decision. With Kuchinsky in his vehicle with him, he overtook the column of Bunyachenko's headquarters company, stopped his vehicle so that it blocked the road and held up traffic. Then he quickly located the staff car in which Vlasov was riding. With the help of Kuchinksy and Vlasov's driver, the traitor was pushed into Yakushov's vehicle.

This took place under the very cannons of the corps' tanks, which by that time had driven up. The ringleader of the traitors was taken out of the general column and delivered to a Soviet unit. None of the troops accompanying Vlasov fired a shot. Later the entire division of Vlasovites, including their commander, was taken prisoner without their resisting.

The band of enemies of our motherland who had finally fallen into the hands of the law was soon swollen by new members. In the foothills of the Alps some ancient enemies of the Soviet regime were discovered: Gens. P. N. Krasnov, A. G. Shkuro, K. Sultan-Girei, and others. We had long since ceased even to think about these almost archaeological antiquities. But in 1944 when Soviet troops entered Yugoslavia, they found themselves engaged with units of a Russian White Guard corps. It turned out that all manner of *ci-devants* were still cherishing a dream of restoring the "one and indivisible" Russian Empire—along with their country estates and the monarchy. In the souls of these people, greedy calculations lived side by side with a violent hatred of everything Soviet.

Such, for example, was Krasnov, former commander in chief of all the armed forces of Kerensky's provisional government and ataman of the "Don Host." Such, too, was Shkuro, former commander of the 3rd Cavalry Corps of Denikin's army. And such was Sultan-Girei, former prince, strangler of the 1905 Revolution, and commander of the "Savage Division," which was given to bloody orgies. During the war years they had all returned to military pursuits and entered the service of German fascism. Acting under instructions from Nazi officials, these generals had formed Russian anti-Soviet and counterrevolutionary elements into military units that fought against the Red Army and our allies. They fought viciously and frenziedly, expecting no mercy. But under blows from the Soviet forces and the Allied armies these "volunteers" had to flee to the mountain fastnesses. With great losses they slowly made their way to the British lines and, figuring that both the British and the Americans would soon be waging war against the Soviet Union, they offered them their services. But they had guessed wrong. . . . The Soviet Government made a firm *démarche* to our allies in the matter of Krasnov, Shkuro, Sultan-Girei, and other war criminals. The British stalled briefly; but since neither old White Guard generals nor their troops were worth much, they put them into trucks and delivered them to the Soviet authorities. The entire procedure of turning them over consisted merely in the British guards' being replaced by Soviet guards.

And what did these old "fossils" look like to the Soviet soldiers? The elder Krasnov was a fragile old man (he was born in 1869) with inflamed eyes behind an old-fashioned pince-nez, wearing a German uniform with the epaulets of the tsarist Army. (After all, he had retained the nuance, so to speak.) His manner of speaking was elegant: During his sojourn abroad, Krasnov had fancied himself an author, and had managed to publish several violently anti-Soviet novels—which, for that matter, had no great success with the "White" public. Together with him, the British delivered his nephew, S. N. Krasnov, a major general in the German Army, formerly a colonel in the forces of the Royal Household and a White Guardist. This man, who was not yet old, had collaborated heart and soul with the Nazis, as his uncle had.

Short, generally haggard-looking, and exuding spite, General Shkuro sported a dirty circassian coat. Until the very last moment of his life, Shkuro evinced his violent hatred of the Soviet regime. Prince Sultan-Girei was thin and rather deaf. The black circassian coat he wore concealed the body of a sick man. His former temper showed only in outbreaks of wrath against everything around him—especially Soviet personnel. . . .

All the generals in this foul-smelling "bouquet" were tried by a Soviet court and sentenced to death.

IN LIEU
OF A CONCLUSION

The flags of seven fraternal nations—the People's Republic of Bulgaria, the Hungarian People's Republic, the German Democratic Republic, the Polish People's Republic, the Socialist Republic of Rumania, the Union of Soviet Socialist Republics, and the Czechoslovak Socialist Republic—hang in the lobby of the building housing the Joint Command and the Staff of the Joint Armed Forces of the Warsaw Pact Nations. And next to the flags, on the wall, are the words of Lenin: "You have had the great honor of defending sacred ideas, weapon in hand . . . and of realizing the international brotherhood of nations." Each time I see that quote, my thoughts go back to the past—to that month of victory: May 1945.

Our victory is still a very lively and stimulating topic. Our historiography, art, literature, cinema, and television regularly deal with those heroic days, mentioning the lessons of the war and reminding us to be vigilant.

When the Nazis launched their aggression, the instigators of the last war did not suppose that they were headed straight for the gallows; and they didn't believe it until the very last day. It was only when the Soviet forces had closed their ring around the Reichstag and the Reichskanzlei that Hitler said to the chief of his personal bodyguard: "Rattenhuber, if it hadn't been for the Russians, this horrible moment wouldn't ever have come, and I'd

421

never had talked to you about my death! Just remember where my troops were!"

Even on the threshold of prison the Nazis at Nuremberg could not understand that it had been hopeless even to try to overthrow the most advanced social system. I have before me the rough draft of a note that Von Ribbentrop addressed to Doenitz. Hitler's Minister of Foreign Affairs apparently began to draw up that document in mid-April 1945. Let's see what he wrote:

> Russia and its war industry, distributed over a vast territory, are virtually inaccessible and unshakable. . . . As the war has shown, Russia's 200 million people are biologically strong. The birth rate is high. . . . Russia has all the kinds of raw material needed. . . . The Russian, previously illiterate, is now highly modernized and equipped.

That's the tune the Nazis were singing at the end of the war! And Von Ribbentrop also tried to "explain" what animated the Russian people: "These 200 million people are united by the fanatical, aggressive *Weltanschauung* of Communism, whose political aim coincides with expansionist Pan-Slavism. . . ."

On this basis, the war criminal sketched pictures of the future, each one more frightening than the other, scaring the whole world with the victory (as he said) of Stalin. "Nations, insofar as they are not loyal in the Soviet sense, will be annihilated or exiled, and their property and work places will pass to the Red Army men." Nor did he spare words to describe the prospect of a vast resettlement of people, allegedly in accordance with the plans of the Soviet conquerors: first the complete take-over of Europe, then of East Asia, and finally of the whole world. In this connection England and America were to be weakened by burrowing from within.

Even on the edge of the grave this ringleader of fascist Germany was trying to sow suspicion and undermine the mutual trust of the nations in the anti-Nazi coalition; to bring England, America, and fascist Germany together on a basis of anti-Sovietism! The lesson of history must not be forgotten: The enemy will fight to the end, will look for any way he can take, and will not shun any means to avoid defeat and liability.

Today all of progressive mankind recognizes that the roots of our victory lay in the superiority of the political structure, ideology, and economics of socialism over the political system, ideology, and economics of fascist Germany. The Soviet Armed Forces were stronger than Hitler's Army, which regarded itself as invincible. The genuinely heroic feat of the Soviet people, at the front and in the rear area, has gone down in history as an example of great steadfastness, an unbreakable spirit, and loyalty to their country.

In this connection I must not neglect to emphasize that the objective possibilities to be found in the nature of the Soviet state were successfully utilized to win a victory over the enemy. The chief role in this was played by the Communist Party. It was the party that worked out the general political line, saw to it that the nation was put on a military footing, guided all internal and extra-political factors toward the achievement of victory, and discovered forms of work making it possible to implement the adumbrated program rapidly and with a maximum of effectiveness.

One summer day in 1949, the question of strengthening the country's AA defense was to be discussed at Near House. The Minister of Defense, Vasilevsky, was on vacation. So Marshal Sokolovsky pinch-hit for him, and went along to the session with the present writer. (I was chief of the General Staff at the time.)

When we arrived, Stalin and the members of the Politburo were on the veranda discussing the construction of new plants for heavy industry in the Urals, Siberia, and the Far East, and the manpower problem in that connection.

In the course of the discussion, Stalin suddenly asked me: "And what does the young chief of the General Staff have to say as to why we beat fascist Germany and forced it to surrender?"

I had made ready to give my report on our AA defenses, and my thoughts were centered on that question. Also, it wasn't entirely clear what direction the talk had been taking before our arrival. So that when I had stood up I was rather hesitant about answering.

Stalin, too, stood up. Puffing on his pipe, he came up to me and said, "We're listening."

After I had recovered from the surprise, I decided the best thing would be to play back to Stalin one of his own speeches—the one he had given on the eve of the elections to the Supreme Soviet on February 9, 1946. Also fresh in my memory were pre-election speeches by other members of the Politburo that all of us at the General Staff had studied closely.

Feeling everyone's eyes on me, I put forth the thesis that the war had demonstrated the viability of the USSR's social and state structure and its great stability. Our social system was strong because it was a genuinely popular system that had sprung from within the people and enjoyed their mighty support.

No one interrupted me; but I must admit I felt rather awkward: I seemed to be uttering truisms, and merely taking up time. But everyone remained serious, apparently thinking over the question that had been posed to me. So I went on more confidently, telling how the people had rallied around the Communist Party; telling, too, of its leadership, and how the Soviet foundation of the society had strengthened the ties of friendship among the peoples of the multinational Soviet Union. Then I spoke of the industrial base created during the five-year-plan periods, of the collective farm system, and of how socialism had created the requisite material possibilities for resisting a strong enemy. In conclusion I spoke of the Army and the great art of Soviet military leaders and commanders.

Stalin listened patiently until I had finished. Then he observed, "Everything you just said is true and important, but you didn't cover the whole subject. How many people were in our armed forces when they were at their fullest strength during the war?"

"A little more than 11 million."

"And what percentage of the population is that?"

Quickly recalling the prewar population of 194 million, I replied, "About six per cent."

"Correct. But that still isn't all. We have to take our troop losses into account, since those who were killed or died of wounds also figured in the numerical strength of the armed forces."

So that, too, was taken into account.

"And now," Stalin went on, "let's calculate how things stood with Hitler, who—counting his losses—had more than 13 million in his armed forces, as against a population of 80 million."

We made the calculation, and came up with a figure of more than 16 per cent.

"Such a high percentage of mobilization," Stalin concluded, "represents either adventurism or an ignorance of the objective laws of warfare. More likely it's the former. History and the general laws of warfare teach that no state can hold up under such great stresses: There is nobody to work at the plants and factories, to grow grain, to supply prime necessities to the people and the army. Hitler's generals, raised on Clausewitz and Moltke, either couldn't or didn't want to understand that. The result was that the Nazis overtaxed their country. And that despite the fact that hundreds of thousands of people brought in from other countries were working in Germany.

"The German rulers twice plunged Germany into war," Stalin continued, pacing along the veranda, "and both times they were defeated. One of the causes of their collapse was that they undermind Germany's vital capacity in the two world wars. . . . Incidentally, do you happen to recall what percentage of the population the Kaiser called up in the First World War?"

Everyone kept still. Stalin went into another room, and a few minutes later returned with a book. He flipped through the pages, found the place he wanted, and said, "Here it is: 19.5 per cent of the population, which in 1918 amounted to 67,800,000."

He slammed shut the book, and again addressing himself to me, he said roughly the following: "The second thing you were rather one-sided about was the matter of our remarkable cadres of leaders. You should have said that we had such leaders not only at the front but also in the rear areas. It must not be forgotten that objective possibilities make up only the prerequisites of victory. They're very important; but in themselves they can't assure the defeat of the enemy. They have to be realized and utilized in an organized manner. The role of organizer and leader belongs to the party, and only to the party. War is a harsh test. It brings the strong, bold, and talented people to the fore. In war a gifted man can prove his worth in a few months—something that takes years in peacetime. In our forces, some remarkable commanders showed their worth in the first few months of the war—people who had acquired experience in the crucible of war and become real military leaders."

And he began to list from memory the names of front and army commanders and partisan leaders.

"And in the rear area? Do you suppose other leaders could have done what the Bolsheviks did? To spirit entire plants and factories away from under the nose of the enemy and move them to barren areas along the Volga, beyond the Urals, and in Siberia; and there, under incredibly hard conditions, to get production started and give the front everything it needed in a short time! Yes, we developed our marshals and generals of petroleum, metallurgy, transportation, machine-building, and agriculture. And finally, there are the captains of science. They, too, must be mentioned."

Unhurriedly and smoothly, he began to list the names of scientists and men prominent in industry and agriculture. Then, after a pause, he said, "Hitler had working for him hundreds of thousands of people brought into Germany and made into slaves, essentially. And yet they could not completely supply his army. But our people did the impossible, and performed a great feat. This was the result of the Communists' work in building the Soviet state and developing the new man. . . . And there you have one more cause of our victory!"

Each one of us—from private soldier to marshal—is proud of the high evaluation Stalin gave our Armed Forces. We were all touched by the heartfelt words about our combat troops: those who spared neither their strength nor life itself in defending the honor, freedom, and independence of the motherland.

It is to those glorious combat troops—living and dead—that I dedicate this book.

INDEX

Akimenko, A. Z., 219–20
Albania, 161, 202, 224, 228, 229, 234
Aleksandrov, Rear Admiral, 366
Alekseyev, I. S., 10
Alexander, Albert, 22–24, 385
Anders, W., 44–50, 57, 107
Andrianov, M. A., 222
Anikushkin, F. T., 305, 311
Anoshin, I. S., 178, 180, 190, 193, 223
Anti-Dühring (Engels), 3–4
Antonescu, Ion, 116–18, 131–44
Antonescu, Michael, 142
Antonov, A. I., 8–9, 16, 29, 34, 41, 157,
    257, 352, 362, 388
  Austria, liberation of, 322, 326, 338
  Bulgaria, liberation of,166, 168, 175,
    179, 180, 182, 187–88, 193
  conference at Stavka, 72–76
  Czechoslovaki (Slovakia), liberation
    of, 286–90, 299–303, 399
  defeat of Germany, 406, 409–10, 411
  on Finland, 349, 359, 365
  Hungary, liberation of, 235, 250–51,
    258–61, 266, 283
  Poland, liberation of, 63, 102, 103
  Stalin and, 67, 89, 97, 102, 155–56,
    188
  on Stavka representatives at the front,
    31–32
  Yugoslavia, liberation of, 201, 211,
    215, 258–59
Arkhipov, F. M., 10
Arpad Line, 290, 293, 297
Atanasov, Shteryu, 196, 197
Austria

communism, 324, 325, 335, 337
crude oil, 330
Germany and, 320–39, 394, 403, 416
liberation of, 120, 225, 226, 267,
    277–80, 284, 320–39, 386, 392,
    394, 404, 416
  Vienna, 226, 267, 277–80, 284,
    321–38
resistance movement, 328–33
Social Democratic Party, 324–26, 335,
    337
Avramescu, G., 158, 238, 257

Bagramyan, Ivan Khristoforovich,
    155–57
Bagrianov, Ivan, 164, 166, 167
Baklykov, Peter Stepanovich, 31
Balfour, Counselor, 366
Balkans, the, 72–75, 79, 115, 161, 178,
    189, 203, 219, 244, 256, 258, 416
  Churchill and, 29, 119–20, 186, 258
  See also names of countries
Ballo, T., 376
Baranov, V. K., 68–69, 305, 307, 308
Batov, P. I., 64, 70, 92, 110
Battle of the Bulge, 383
Beaverbrook, Lord, 24
Beckerle, Ambassador, 181
Belgrade, liberation of, 172, 201, 215–24
Belorussian Front, 59–67, 72–76, 87, 89,
    92, 93, 99–101, 105, 108–11, 278,
    357, 387–88, 393, 395
Beneš, Eduard, 286–88, 295, 296, 314
Berenshtein, L. E., 294
Berlin, fall of, 278, 333, 387–93, 406–12

427

Index

S

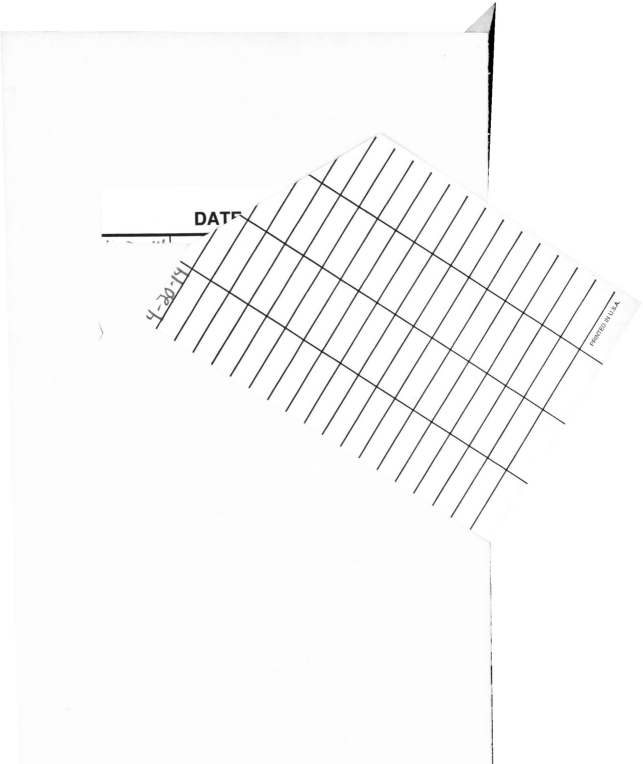

DATE

4-20-19

PRINTED IN U.S.A.